British business history, 1720–1994

'A major work of synthesis which makes a great deal of recent research on Britain's business history accessible to non-specialists and students.'
Professor Geoffrey Jones, University of Reading and President of the Association of Business Historians

This is the first textbook that comprehensively covers the three centuries of British business history from 1720 to the present day. Focusing on the manufacturing sector, John Wilson explains the development of British industry and its decline in the twentieth century.

Wilson argues that company culture has been the most important component in the evolution of business organisations and management practices. The influence of business culture on firms' structure, sources of finance, and the background and training of senior managers are investigated to show its pivotal importance in determining business performance.

The book also examines how British business adapted to changing economic, institutional and socio-cultural environments yet failed to develop the kind of managerial hierarchies typified by American and German corporations. Wilson uses an extensive number of case studies to support his conclusions.

The book covers the subject chronologically with an extra chapter comparing Britain's experience with the USA, Germany and Japan. In addition to a full bibliography, a student's guide to further reading is provided.

John F. Wilson is Lecturer in Economic History at the University of Manchester.

This book is dedicated with love and
thanks to Barbara and Anthony

British business history, 1720–1994

John F. Wilson

Manchester University Press
Manchester and New York
distributed exclusively in the USA by Palgrave

Copyright © John F. Wilson 1995

Published by Manchester University Press
Oxford Road, Manchester M13 9NR, UK
and Room 400, 175 Fifth Avenue, New York, NY 10010, USA
www.manchesteruniversitypress.co.uk

Distributed exclusively in the USA by
Palgrave, 175 Fifth Avenue, New York, NY 10010, USA

Distributed exclusively in Canada by
UBC Press, University of British Columbia, 2029 West Mall,
Vancouver, BC, Canada V6T 1Z2

British Library Cataloguing-in-Publication Data
A catalogue record for this book is available from the British Library

Library of Congress Cataloging-in-Publication Data
Wilson, John F., 1955–
    British business history, 1720–1994 / John F. Wilson.
        p.   cm.
    Includes bibliographical references (p.   ).
    ISBN 0–7190–4132–5. — ISBN 0–7190–4133–3 (pbk.)
    1. Industrial management—Great Britain—History.   2. Business
enterprises—Great Britain—History.   3. Industrial organization–
–Great Britain—History.   4. Capitalism—Great Britain—History.
I. Title.
HD70.G7W55   1995   94–41739
338.7′0941—dc20   CIP

ISBN 0 7190 4132 5 *hardback*
      0 7190 4133 3 *paperback*

First published 1995

10 09 08 07 06 05 04   10 9 8 7 6 5 4

Contents

Contents

Tables and figures

Tables

Figures

Preface and acknowledgements

Even though there are some useful (if chronologically limited) analyses of British business history (Pollard, 1965: Hannah, 1983), and the vigorous efforts of successive *Business History* editors and their many collaborators and contributors have done much to bring the fruits of research in this field to a wider audience, there has been a dearth of general works covering what is a vital subject. I am well aware of the difficulties involved in filling this gap, having taught a course on British business history for over a decade, and the reluctance of more eminent academics to embark on such a venture creates an acute sense of foreboding. On the other hand, if students are to gain a general insight into this fascinating story, a study which can outline the main trends is required. A more detailed explanation of this book's rationale will be given in section 1.1, but it is important to emphasise that my main aim is to provide an assessment of British business evolution over the period 1720–1994. This task will entail a detailed analysis of such key factors as organisational dynamics, business culture, market opportunities, relationships between industry and finance, and shopfloor practices. Insights into developments abroad (especially in the USA, Germany and Japan) will also be provided as a source of contrast, but above all the major focus of each chapter will be British-owned business and the environment in which it has operated. Chandler (1990) in particular has been extremely critical of British businessmen, and especially their failure to adopt strategies and structures similar to those of the major American corporations. As we shall see in section 1.2, he regards the adherence to personal capitalism as the most important obstacle to improved business performance in Britain, and this thesis will provide an interesting benchmark against which we can evaluate different eras.

It is my contention that Chandler is correct in pointing to personal capitalism as the major cultural characteristic of British businessmen at least until the 1970s, but in explaining why they allegedly failed to imitate their American counterparts one must look at a much wider range of factors, and especially the broad environment in which firms operated. This environment consists of the market-cum-technological, financial, socio-cultural and legal scenes, and it is vital to understand exactly how each factor affected strategy and structure in different business communities. If British businessmen were guilty of 'failing' to imitate American firms, then one must demonstrate that the environment encouraged the use of such practices, and as I shall argue this is extremely difficult when examining the period up to the 1940s. The most important era is 1950–1973, when the broad environment stimulated the adoption of American-style business practices, but by that time the culture of personal capitalism was so well-embedded that businessmen experienced great difficulty in making the necessary organisational changes.

The major exceptions to this bleak scenario were those firms which had developed a multinational dimension to their activities, and as we shall see in section 6.5 these were some of the most advanced organisations in the world. In general, though, until the 1970s most domestically-based enterprises were wedded to the traditions of the past, and this proved highly damaging as the levels of competition intensified. It is a story of forceful continuity, begging the question whether British businessmen in general were capable of coping with the challenges posed by foreign competition, even when the environment stimulated the kind of strategies and structures pursued in other economies. Section 6.5 will also illustrate how after the major economic crises of the 1970s and 1980s, some British businessmen started to adopt more effective attitudes towards organisation and recruitment, and by the 1990s such had been the devastation wreaked on industry especially that many sectors had sought refuge in international partnerships. Here again we will see how overseas connections became a crucial component in the drive for competitiveness, and from the 1970s British firms were developing this strategy extensively, providing an optimistic end to our story.

The story we shall relate in this book consequently follows a chronological pattern, but it is important to emphasise firstly how in chapter 1 some crucial points have been made which are central to the whole story. In particular, section 1.2 has been devoted to a review of the key issues in business history, and especially the work of A. D. Chandler, while in section 1.3 some simple thoughts on the nature of management and organisational evolution have been offered. Second, I have devoted chapter 3 and section 5.1 to an analysis of business history in the USA, Germany and Japan, in order to contextualise the history of British business, and readers should be aware of the themes developed there when studying the emergence and organisation of large-scale business. The British story starts in chapter 2, with a review of the classic era of personal capitalism from 1720 to 1870. Chapter 4 then analyses the crucial years from 1870 to 1914, when new challenges appeared on the scene, while chapter 5 examines the inter-war years, and chapter 6 the last fifty years. It is important to note that while a series of consistent themes are developed throughout the book (see section 1.1), each section can be regarded as an attempt at addressing the main debates which are covered in the pertinent sources on that topic. Subheadings have also been used to identify specific subjects, and each section has a conclusion which draws together the main themes, providing a mini essay on the expanding literature.

The main sources for this history have been the articles and monographs published by business historians and industrial economists across the world, and my first debt must be acknowledged to those authors quoted in the text and listed in the Bibliography. I am aware of the many gaps which exist in my coverage, especially with regard to conference and seminar papers, but care has been taken to access the main *published* sources which readers can acquire without too much difficulty. Useful comments on earlier versions of certain chapters were kindly given by Bob Millward, while those long-suffering students who took my course on British business history have no doubt helped me clarify some of the following thoughts. The sections on Japanese business were much improved after a spell as Visiting Professor at Osaka University in 1994, for which I must thank that institution, and my many conversations especially with Takeshi Abe proved extremely valuable. Of course, these people are by no means responsible for anything other than the good bits in this book, but I am deeply indebted to them for their patience and knowledge. Likewise, thanks go to Francis Brooke for asking me to write this book, and for giving me the time to indulge myself.

Finally, my family have once again been outstanding in allowing me time to disappear under a mountain of books and paper, and without Barbara's encouragement especially it would have taken much longer to finish. 'Marvellous!'. I can do no more than dedicate this book to them in return for everything they do for me.

J. F. W., September 1994.

1

Business history:
an introduction

Business history as an academic discipline has evolved from the straightforward study of individual entrepreneurs or firms into a multifaceted subject which now impinges on a wide range of areas, from economic theory and industrial economics to sociology and business studies. It might well have emerged as a sub-discipline of economic history, but a dedicated group has created a groundswell of opinion which demands the right to self-determination. Progress has undoubtedly been faster in the USA than in Britain, but whatever the geographical source of this inspiration, many now agree with Supple's (1977; 1) claim that 'systematic studies of business behaviour, structures and policies, and of their consequences for the economy as a whole, not only comprise a proper activity in themselves, but are also of considerable relevance to a broader understanding of economic processes'. More will be said in section 1.1 about these views, indicating how the purpose of this chapter is to introduce students to some of the main debates conducted by business historians. In particular, it is vital to define the broad parameters within which we shall be operating, to outline some of the major contributions to the field, and to examine various tools and typologies which might be of use to our work. Constant reference to these ideas will be made in later chapters, and it is important at this stage to establish a basis for analysis by explaining some of the key issues which have emerged over the last thirty years.

1.1 Aims and Definitions

The main aim of business history is to study and explain the behaviour of the firm over long periods of time, and to place the conclusions in a broader framework composed of the markets and institutions in which that behaviour occurs. On a more general level, business history can also provide a dynamic insight into the evolution of capitalism, bringing a comparative element to the field which can draw on material from firms, industries, or national groupings of businessmen. It is a discipline which often uses a case-study approach, in order to provide the foundations on which wider general-isations can be built, but there is here what Coleman (1987; 142) has called an in-built Catch-22 which has limited progress. This Catch-22 relates to the reliance on company records, resulting in a failure 'to write business history in the wider sense'. In addition, with much of the work being commissioned by individual companies, authors can frequently find that any attempts at comparative analysis are snuffed out by the whims and fancies of their employers, resulting in a simple narrative approach towards business development which might preclude a concern with the formulation of broad-er hypotheses.

Bearing in mind the definition of business history just offered, however, it is still not clear how we should approach the subject. Of central importance here is the analysis of Supple (1977; 3–4), who has argued that three inter-related models have influenced the work of most British business historians: firstly, the institutional or individual biography; second, the comparative study of business structures and policies; and third, the analysis of entrepren-eurship and its contribution to general economic performance. Sadly, though, there is widespread agreement with Hannah's (1983a; 166) critical assessment of progress, that: 'Most business historians have clung to a tradi-tion which, at its best, is a triumph of narrative skill, honest to the facts of the individual case, but at its worst is narrow, insular and antiquarian'. This view should not be allowed to hide the significant achievements of many individual business historians and business history units over the last thirty years. On the other hand, there is no doubt considerable scope for a more thorough-going approach towards the subject, and a general feeling has now emerged which demands a concerted effort to develop especially the second approach outlined by Supple. Unfortunately, though, no consensus has yet emerged on the most effective approach to be adopted, but this adds to the fascination of a subject which embraces such a wide range of techniques.

Reflecting the need to develop a more generalised approach to business history, four key themes will provide the focus of this book:

1 *The business culture and socio-cultural pressures*, focussing on the evolu-tion of business organisation, managerial recruitment and training, and the attitudes of society towards business (with a strong comparative ele-ment, bringing in the American, German and Japanese scenes).
2 *The recruitment and control of labour*, providing an insight into manage-ment on the shop-floor.
3 *Business and the financial institutions*, analysing the methods used to finance operations, and how the relationship between the two sectors has developed.
4 *Business and the state*, discussing how government policy has affected management strategy.

It is important to note that the first theme will dominate, and in this context we must agree with the point made by Brown and Rose (1993; 1): 'Easily the most important influence on [business] behaviour is shown to be "culture", as reflected in the value systems in society, localities, religious groupings, or firms'. Casson (1993; 40) has called this 'a collective subjectivity – a shared set of values, norms and beliefs', and clearly it has a major impact on management and organisation, on the methods of financing enterprise, on the relationship between capital and labour, and between the state and business. This is why it is so important to understand how and why the British business culture evolved, and to examine whether any ensuing managerial constraints arose which would have inhibited the ability to develop a competitive challenge to the increasingly powerful foreign firms which appeared from the late-nineteenth century. The prominent Harvard scholar, A. D. Chandler (1990; 389), to mention but one authority, has accused British businessmen in the period up to the 1940s of failing to move in what he regards as an appropriate direction, both organisationally and professionally, and to understand that kind of allegation one must be aware of the criteria by which such judgements are reached and the applicability of these standards. As Hannah (1976; 197) has noted, one cannot blindly accept the notion that the Harvard-approved form of organisation is applicable in all circumstances, and throughout this study we shall be testing these wider generalisations against the hard evidence adduced by a growing band of business historians.

1.2   The Harvard school

As an introduction to the subject of business history, one can do no better than review the work of A. D. Chandler, a former member of the pioneering Centre for Entrepreneurial History at Harvard University (Lee, 1990a; 163–7), and more recently of the Harvard Business School. Indeed, Chandler is one of the foremost innovators in his field, having formulated a series of systematic frameworks to describe business evolution, and especially the rise of big business. In his first major publication, Chandler (1962; 1–7) was particularly anxious to develop a comparative approach to business history, as a means of understanding how large-scale enterprises evolved and operated. His basic premise revolves around the notion that, instead of looking at how a single firm operates, greater benefit can be derived from comparing the way in which different businesses carry out the same activity. The most obvious activity to identify as the common denominator linking all firms, Chandler argues, is administration, emphasising how he is most interested in explaining why firms evolve organisationally, and in particular how firms replace the 'invisible hand' of market forces with the 'visible hand' of corporate planning by pursuing the strategy of vertical integration. It should be noted that the book is built around a study of four corporations – Du Pont, General Motors, Standard Oil (New Jersey) and Sears, Roebuck – and how they developed from integrated, multidepartmental organisations into multi-divisional enterprises during the inter-war years. However, a preliminary survey of the fifty largest American industrial companies expands the base upon which Chandler generalises, leading to a model which is both simple and incisive.

Strategy and Structure

The core thesis of *Strategy and Structure* claims that 'different organisational forms result from different types of growth', with the strategy of a company determining its structure (Chandler, 1962; 13–5). In this model, *strategy* is defined as 'the determination of the basic long-term goals and objectives of an enterprise, and the adoption of courses of action and the allocation of resources necessary for carrying out these goals'. *Structure*, on the other hand, is 'the design of organisation through which the enterprise is adminis-tered'. Chandler (1962; 15) is careful to explain that 'changes in strategy which called for changes in structure appear to have been in response to the opportunities and needs created by changing population and changing national income and by technological innovation' – in other words, what has passed into the business history vocabulary as '*the market-cum-technologi-cal environment*'. However, this external perspective on business evolution only serves to emphasise the importance of entrepreneurial vigour at the head of an organisation as the key to survival and expansion. This clearly places administrators in a crucial position, and while the adaptation process is by no means automatic, the way these people 'co-ordinate, appraise and plan' becomes a vital factor in ensuring 'present health and future growth', as long as structure is adapted to cope with the organisational consequences of strategy (Chandler, 1962; 8).

This simple model of organisational change was regarded at the time as a major step forward in the methodology of business history, and while much of the substantiating empirical work still needed to be done Chandler was satisfied that a firm basis had been established for his research. Inevitably, though, not all business historians have accepted his ideas, and a range of explanations have been offered as alternatives. One of the more obvious grounds for attacking the Chandler model, according to Parker (1973; 404), was his failure to provide 'explicit standards of judgement' when examining how administrators fashion appropriate structures, a point to which we shall return later. Alford (1977; 117) has also convincingly argued that the pre-occupaton with management at the highest levels has led Chandler to ignore the extensive amount of 'diffused entrepreneurship' which exists, particular-ly in large-scale companies where the division of functions between top exec-utives and managers is not as clear cut as in smaller enterprises. This point has more recently been given greater substance by Kay's (1993; 154–5) thorough analysis of the relationship between strategy and structure, demonstrating how, in large-scale firms, devising the former is devolved well down the organisational ladder. Such insights present a warning to business historians about the pitfalls inherent in believing that hierarchical line diagrams (see Figures 1.1–1.4) reflect the reality of decision-making in a firm.

Policies, in fact, are derived from an accumulation of information provided from within an organisation, and top executives are obliged to rely on colleagues lower down the hierarchy for advice on new market and technological trends which might be beyond their own fields of competence. This can then lead to divisions or functional departments having a much greater influence on decision-making than Chandler's model allows. Similarly, when entrepreneurship is so diffused, one might then expect structure to have a major impact on strategy, because vested interests within certain parts of a business might well influence policies and prevent the kind of organisational adaptation required.

Not only has Chandler been attacked for oversimplifying organisational evolution, he has also been accused of underplaying the strength of external factors when the consideration of strategy and structure is undertaken. As we noted earlier, Chandler does discuss the role played by market-cum-technological opportunities, albeit only as a means of emphasising the importance of administrators, but Alford (1977; 129) claims that there are many other external factors which can have a major influence on strategy, not least the role of government and the socio-cultural environment. Chandler would no doubt reply, however, that it is the responsibility of senior management to deal with such forces, and adapt strategy and structure accordingly. Indeed, entrpreneurship is at the very core of his model, as it is in business history as a whole, and Chandler (1962; 15–17) was trying to demonstrate the crucial role of diversity in both the range and quality of business practices as an essential determinant of successful growth. In other words, as we noted earlier, business evolution is in his view primarily concerned with the replacement of market forces by the 'visible hand' of corporate planning, emphasising how in reducing the transaction costs (see section 1.4) associated with using market mechanisms, firms pursued vertical integration strategies as a means of improving their efficiency. Nevertheless, even though he was primarily interested in administration, there seems to be general agreement that external factors deserve greater attention when considering business evolution, a point clarified in many parts of this book.

Visible Hand and *Scale and Scope*

The main response Chandler made to his critics came in the form of *The Visible Hand* (1977), a detailed history of American business from the mid-nineteenth century. In this book, he emphasised how the *invisible* hand of market forces was replaced by 'the visible hand of management', with a salaried managerial class becoming 'the most influential group of economic decision makers' in the American economy by the early twentieth century. Chandler (1977; 1, 6) consequently demonstrated that effective administrative co-ordination could control external factors and permit 'greater productivity, lower costs, and higher profits than co-ordination by market mechanisms'. In other words, by arguing that *the visible hand* of large-scale business was more effective than 'the invisible hand' of market forces in co-ordinating the distribution of resources, he was challenging the arguments of those who criticised his earlier work. An enormous range of primary and secondary sources was culled to substantiate this theme, expanding massively on his earlier work in *Strategy and Structure* and providing what to many seemed to be the definitive work on this subject. Yet, this was to be followed by a third monograph, *Scale and Scope* (1990), which was to extend the comparative approach from the United States to Britain and Germany.

Based on a study of the leading 200 industrial companies in the USA, Britain and Germany over the period 1880–1950, *Scale and Scope* provides yet another refinement to Chandler's model for explaining why large-scale businesses evolves in certain ways. The basic approach is to establish the American path of *competitive managerial capitalism* outlined in *The Visible Hand* as the ideal to which all industrial economies ought to aspire, and then assess how the other two economies compared. To Chandler (1990; 8), the key to success was making a 'three-pronged investment':

> The first was an investment in production facilities large enough to exploit a technology's economies of scale and scope. The second was an investment in a national and international marketing and distributive network, so that the volume of sales might keep pace with the new volume of production. Finally, to benefit fully from these two kinds of investment the entrepreneurs also had to invest in management: they had to recruit and train managers not only to administer the enlarged facilities and increased personnel in both production and distribution, but also to monitor and co-ordinate those two basic functional activities and to plan and allocate resources for future production and distribution.

Once again, it is the vital role fulfilled by senior administrators which is central to the whole process, with their ability to see the need for, and then make, this 'three-pronged investment' as the key to understanding what Chandler (1992; 37) later calls 'the logic of industrial growth'. In effect, he is attempting to explain the underlying dynamics of modern industrial capitalism, given the central importance of the enterprises reviewed, expanding significantly on the themes first enunciated in *Strategy and Structure*. As with his earlier works, though, *Scale and Scope* is not free from criticism, and a more detailed review of the thesis is necessary before we can accept its applicability.

In the case of Germany (see section 3.2), Chandler was in little doubt that its form of *co-operative managerial capitalism* came close to the American ideal, in spite of a tendency towards cartelisation and collusion which in certain contexts is regarded as inefficient. As far as Britain's system of *personal capitalism* was concerned, however, he argues that on many counts failure was the distinguishing characteristic. Indeed, not only was there a 'failure to make the three-pronged investment in production, distribution and management essential to exploit economies of scale and scope' (1990; 237), but those sectors most amenable to this kind of investment – principally, industries of the Second Industrial Revolution (synthetic chemicals, motor vehicles, electrical engineering and light machinery) and the manufacture of food and consumer goods – were by the First World War dominated by American and German enterprises. Chandler does accept that 'the window of opportunity' in which these industries developed was very small, lasting only from the 1880s to the First World War, but British failure led to foreign (especially American and German) 'first movers' taking over world markets. In effect, it is a familiar attack on the quality of British enterprise in the late nineteenth century, with the main thrust of his thesis aimed at the weaknesses inherent in a culture of personal capitalism.

As Hannah (1991; 301–303) has noted, however, while Chandler provides abundant evidence of the alleged British failure to develop managerial hierarchies which would compare with those of American or German industrial companies, his explanation of the reasons behind this 'failure' lack consistency. In the first place, reflecting a criticism of his earlier works (Parker, 1973; 404), little quantitative evidence is produced to demonstrate that the behavioural differences between British and American firms 'can explain more than a small fraction of the efficiency and growth differences between national economies'. After all, as we shall see in chapter 3, the German and Japanese economies have experienced significant growth without slavishly copying the American model of business organisation, and Chandler simply does not accommodate this kind of contrast in his thesis. Similarly, linking the tendency towards personal capitalism in manufacturing with cultural factors fails to take into consideration the substantial organisational progress made by British utilities and retailers, not to mention the highly successful multinational manufacturers which flourished in the twentieth century.

One must also question his claim that the internalisation of transaction costs (see section 1.4) was a viable solution in all trading environments, because as we shall see in later sections (2.6 and 4.1 especially), British businessmen were faced with a very different market-cum-technological environment to that prevailing in the USA. As Scranton (1991; 1103) also commented: 'The usual Chandler bracketings apply. Labour, culture, state policies, and all industrial activity outside the top 200 are set aside as secondary or irrelevant'.

It is important to remember, of course, that Chandler's (1990; 13) brief was to provide 'an internal history of the central institution in managerial capitalism, rather than attempt to analyse that institution's impact on the polity or society in which it appeared'. However, one cannot divorce the two elements so easily. Indeed, as Supple (1991; 510) argues, surely Chandler is trying 'to explain the impact of business on the mechanisms and performance of modern industrial economies', and to do that any work must entail an analysis of:

> The nature of markets and culture, the pattern of population movements and state intervention, the economic geography of the two societies, the vigour of small-scale firms or firms in the service sector, the structural balance of activity in general. . . .

Quite simply, by concentrating unduly on the internal history of industrial enterprise, and looking at other countries through 'American-tinted glasses', one must inevitably produce a distorting picture which could well provide an unrealistic explanation of the underlying trends in British business history. It is, in effect, what Scranton (1991; 1104) describes as 'organisational determinism' which is constraining the perception of industrial change, rather than broadening the analysis. American management techniques might have been regarded as the most advanced in this period, but they were not necessarily *appropriate* in environments with different economic, legal and cultural trends and traditions, and this perspective is vital to remember when analysing British business history.

Lazonick

By reviewing some of the weaknesses in Chandler's work, it is easy to ignore his enormous achievements in providing a series of conceptual frameworks for business historians, from the elaboration of a relationship between strategy and structure to explaining how large-scale corporations might exploit the market-cum-technological opportunities available by usurping the traditional role of the market. He has undoubtedly influenced a whole generation of academics, provoking widespread debates in the field which have led to a much more detailed understanding of the dynamics of business evolution in the major industrial economies. One of Chandler's most notable disciples is a Harvard colleague, W. Lazonick, whose earlier study (1983; 230–6) of the British cotton industry's failure to evolve from a highly specialised and competitive structure was later converted (with the help of Elbaum) into a concerted onslaught on the 'atomistic economic organisation' which typified business in this country until the 1950s (Elbaum & Lazonick, 1986; 1–17). This thesis is an attempt at explaining Britain's relatively poor economic performance in terms of the failure by British business to reform a nineteenth-century legacy of 'institutional rigidities' which extended right across the economic, legal and cultural spectra, inhibiting competitiveness in the period 1850–1950, and possibly beyond.

Taking this theme further, Lazonick (1991; 25–7) has more recently developed his own three-stage model to describe the evolution of industrial capitalism, with 'proprietary', 'managerial' and 'collective' being the labels he applies along this path. The most important aspect of this typology as far as we are concerned is his argument that each form is only appropriate in certain circumstances, and because British business clung to the first 'proprietorial' stage so long it lost its way when faced with the more advanced 'managerial' and 'collective' forms of capitalism adopted, respectively, in the USA and Japan. As we shall see in chapter 3, however, it would be dangerous to argue that 'proprietary capitalism' died any more quickly in Germany and Japan, for example, than it did in Britain, and it is clear from Church's (1993; 17–29) analysis of this problem that family firms continued to play a dominant role in many economies. Indeed, it is apparent that the family firm per se is not the problem; what most concerns us as objective business historians is the market-cum-technological, financial, legal and socio-cultural contexts in which businessmen are obliged to operate. These points will be developed further in chapters 3 and 4, but it is important to remember that while personal capitalism does appear to have remained prevalent in Britain up to the 1940s, one might well argue that this was appropriate to *British* circumstances.

The allusion to 'institutional rigidites' and atomistic business organisation, and the discussion of 'proprietary capitalism', are yet further useful reference points for business historians. On the other hand, as with Chandler's work, one must still be aware of the American benchmark against which Elbaum and Lazonick measure British developments. Kirby (1992; 638–56) also points out how they have ignored demand-side explanations for these 'institutional rigidities', and in section 3.2 especially we shall examine some of the key factors inhibiting the introduction of mass-production innovations into British industry which go some way to moderating the criticisms of allegedly conservative business strategy. This is not to deny the existence of what Olson (1982) has described as 'institutional sclerosis' in the British economic system, and Kirby (1992; 656) certainly feels that this would help to explain Britain's relative industrial decline since the late nineteenth century. However, factors other than business organisation clearly played a major role in the process. Elbaum and Lazonick (1986; 1–15) are simply firm believers in the economic benefits to be derived from 'The American Way', and, like Chandler, by imposing a schema on countries with entirely different economic, legal and cultural environments they are distorting views of business evolution.

Porter

While Chandler is more concerned with an internalised approach towards business history, another Harvard academic, Michael Porter (1990; 786), has produced innovative work which places much greater emphasis on 'the environment surrounding firms, and how this influences the creation of strategy, skills, organisational arrangements, and success in particular fields'. In particular, building on his earlier investigations into competitive strategy (1980), Porter is interested in the reasons why some economies gain a competitive advantage over their rivals. Like Chandler, he also provides a microeconomic explanation for a macro-economic phenomenon, stressing the vital role of corporate strategy and structure. To Porter, five competitive forces determine a firm's ability to expand: the impact of new competition; the threat of a substitute product; the bargaining power of consumers; the bargaining power of suppliers; and rivalry among existing firms. Firms which aspire to acquiring a competitive advantage and improved performance are then faced with three options – cost leadership, product differentiation, or focus on niche markets – and it is very much the responsibility of management to make the correct decision. This is similar to the approach pursued by Chandler, but Porter is more aware of the external influences on business development, and for this reason his insights provide a more balanced approach towards our subject.

 Throughout our study of British business history we shall be discussing the significance of the Harvard School models and tools, and especially those of Chandler. As we have already noted, little agreement has yet been reached on the most acceptable methodological approach, but these models are extremely useful in providing guidelines for business historians engaged in pursuing the generalist ideal to which many aspire. The key point would appear to be judging why particular organisational forms persisted in Britain, and in drawing any conclusions it is vitally important to examine the broad environmental influences on both strategy and structure. As we noted at the head of section 1.1, business history can provide an explanation of firm behaviour, but objective criteria must be employed when comparing different systems, and this is why the Harvard School's deliberations must be handled with great care.

1.3 Modelling business evolution

If we are to develop a more generalised approach towards our subject, the first task will be to build a simple model outlining the various stages through which enterprises might pass. It is important to remember that, as Urwick (1960; 11) stated in the 1920s: 'Organisation is a process. It consists of subdividing all the activities necessary to any purpose and arranging them in groups which may be assigned to individuals'. He went on to describe twelve stages of evolution, from the simplest form of one-man business through to complete functional control by specialist professionals, with the crucial changes taking place when the owner-manager is forced to delegate responsibility for an increasing number of tasks as the type and range of 'activities' expands over time. The key to understanding this evolutionary process is consequently the relationship between control and ownership, because as a business grows the degree to which a single individual, or small group, can be responsible for both aspects will decline, leading to a considerable divorce between the two.

Urwick's twelve stage model, while providing some useful insights into the process of organisational evolution, is too cumbersome for our purposes, and it is more convenient to think in terms of the three labels *personal, entrepreneurial* and *managerial* proposed by Chandler and Daems (1974; 11). It is important to note that these stages do not represent a legal definition of business evolution; rather, they amount to an empirical generalisation relating to the sequence of stages through which the economy as a whole passes, indicating what type of business organisation dominates at any one particular point in time. This naturally poses problems of timing the transition, but as we shall see later this model not only provides a useful basis for comparing different economies, it also helps to explain much about the prevailing attitudes towards business organisation. The essential feature of each stage is the extent to which responsibility has been delegated to professional executives, and ownership passed to professional investors. In simple terms, owner-managers feature predominantly in the first, some degree of delegation to professional managers appears in the second, and a complete divorce between control and ownership characterises the third. This model was by no means novel, Urwick (1960) and Florence (1961) having earlier worked along similar lines, yet the proposal has an elegant simplicity which can be applied to British business history.

A simple model

Before going on to describe these three stages in greater detail, it is first of all necessary to discuss the different types and levels of management. A generally acceptable definition of management which was devised by the pioneering thinker on this subject, Henri Fayol, is that it is primarily concerned with planning, co-ordination, implementation and evaluation (Allen, 1958; 13). However, as Figure 1.1 reveals, these functions can be broken down into a series of specialisms performed at three levels of management, the *strategic*, the *functional* and the *operational*. Of course, considerable overlapping of levels would be a feature of the personal and entrepreneurial forms, but over time each becomes the special preserve of identifiable groups. Strategic management is essentially concerned with determining long-term goals and allo-

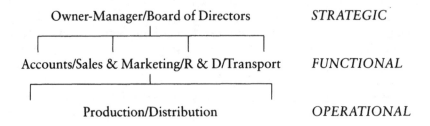

Figure 1.1   *A diagrammatic representation of management levels within modern businesses*

cating resources. This would be distinct from the role performed by the functional manager, whose task it is to implement the decisions passed down from strategic management, while operational managers are responsible for supervising production or distribution. In essence, the strategic managers plan and evaluate, while co-ordination and implementation are the preserve of functional and operational staff working lower down the hierarchy.

The three stages

If these basic guidelines are accepted as a useful means of differentiating between the main levels of management, it is now possible to examine in greater detail the three-stage model. We must clearly start with the personal form of management, where a single individual is often said to perform most of the functions depicted in Figure 1.1. Habbakuk (1968; 3) describes this as the 'traditional form of capitalism', best illustrated in late eighteenth-century Britain, when the first generation of industrialists were struggling with the challenges associated with industrial capitalism. Indeed, as Mantoux (1928; 386) argues, these pioneers performed a wide range of functions, from capitalist and works manager to merchant and salesman. Figure 1.2 depicts a typical enterprise of this kind, although, as we shall see in the next chapter, the degree to which the owner-manager performed strategic, functional and operational management does not come out clearly in such diagrams. On the whole, though, management functions are not yet dispersed, and an individual or small group of partners controlled much of the business personally.

As we shall see in chapters 2 and 3, the personal form of organisation contains many in-built constraints, while external factors may well also inhibit growth, and in order to expand the owner-managers must recognise these problems and derive appropriate solutions. We can save the analysis of these internal and external constraints until later, but the solutions are obviously relevant, particularly when they relate to organisational change. In essence, when a firm converts from a personal to an entrepreneurial (see Figure 1.3) form of organisation, the owner-manager is beginning to delegate

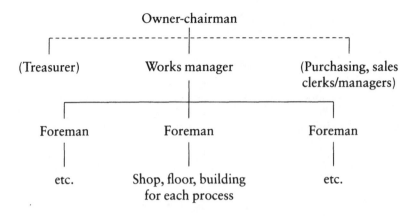

Figure 1.2   *The 'personal' form of organisation*
Source: Schmitz (1993; 38).

responsibility to professional managers, as well as bringing in outside capital from sources unconnected with the family or religious grouping. This means that a growing divorce between ownership and control is beginning to emerge in the entrepreneurial business, emphasising the increasing importance of functional management and the role of outside agencies like stock exchanges. Various constraints of a socio-cultural, institutional or legal nature might well still hinder the degree to which delegation progresses, while timing the transition could also pose a big problem. Nevertheless, this stage is an essential bridging point in the evolution of *managerial capitalism*, and as we shall see in chapters 3 and 4 it was one which dominated in Britain at least until the 1940s.

Ultimately, in the managerial stage (see Fig 1.4) there will be a complete divorce between control and ownership, whereby strategic, functional and operational management is undertaken entirely by professionals, while the bulk of the equity is held by investors who take no role in running the business. This form of organisation can have many different manifestations, from the increasingly dominant multidivisional (M-Form) to the highly centralised, functionally-departmentalised structure (U-Form), but this will be dependent upon a wide variety of factors which we shall discuss later (Schmitz, 1993; 37–46). On the other hand, as Chandler (1990; 239) argues, even in companies no longer dominated by family dynasties, 'personal management' remains a prevalant feature of the organisational style in Britain up to the 1940s. This reveals the crucial importance of placing business history firmly into the socio-cultural context of any one particular society before accepting the general applicability of the term managerial. Indeed, the socio-cultural environment is a key determinant of attitudes within and towards business organisation and management styles, and throughout this study

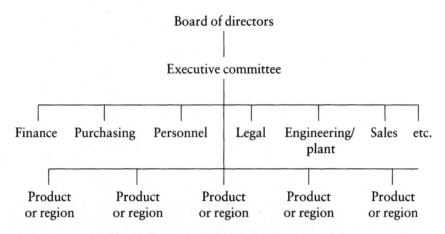

Figure 1.3 *The 'entrepreneurial' form of organisation*
Source: Schmitz (1993; 39).

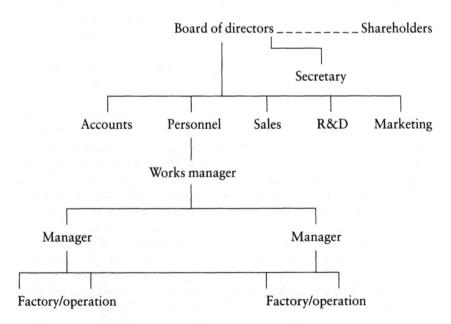

Figure 1.4 *The 'managerial' form of organisation*
Source: Schmitz (1993; 40)

constant allusion will be made to the relationship between these factors when attempting to understand why the British story has such distinctive characteristics.

1.4 Business history and economic theory

The three-stage model which sees businesses pass from the personal to the entrepreneurial and finally to the managerial forms of organisation, evidently has its limitations, yet as a means of explaining the process of business evolution it also has considerable merit in providing a series of easily-discernible steps through which many enterprises have moved. Obviously, where it does pose severe problems is in explaining *why* firms made, or failed to make, the move from one stage to another, and in order to extend the model we need to add a more systematic causative framework as a means of honing our analytical tools. In this context, one can turn to the models presented by Chandler, which (see section 1.2) provide an interesting means of examining the dynamics of industrial capitalism. Alternatively, economic theory might help us explain why, for example, firms grow or operate in certain ways, and as business history in Britain has slowly been moving towards a more generalist approach it has been strongly argued that more use of these concepts would radically improve its academic rigour.

Certainly, there has been no shortage of entreaties which have demanded the greater application of economic theory to the subject. Lee (1990; 176) in particular has argued that business history should equate to applied economics, not only in helping to refine and modify theory by 'testing . . . models against the experience of the real world', but equally by analysing business performance using the techniques familiar to economists. On the other hand, reflecting a more popular feeling amongst business historians, we might be better advised to heed the words of Supple (1962; 85), who warned that economic theory should not be regarded as 'a key marked Truth', but as 'an assortment of logical and conceptual devices some of which can be effectively employed to suggest ways of approaching historical material'. Hyde (1962; 9) was also careful to warn against regarding theory as 'a universal standard of measurement which can be used indiscriminately by the historian', and in a later article (1977; 19–21) emphasised how historians are better equipped to deal with awkward facts like personal characteristics than economists tied to a particular theory. This is a point taken up by Coleman (1987; 151), who noted that there is general scepticism about the value of orthodox British economic theory, because it is 'built up from the Marshallian neo-classical synthesis and then from Keynesian and post-Keynesian macro-economics, [which] is simply of very little use to business historians'.

Transaction cost models

One might well conclude that economics is simply there to be used as 'a cutting edge' to historical analysis, but equally one must be extremely wary of such views, particularly because in Coleman's case he ignores the extensive twentieth-century development of both micro-economics and industrial economics. These disciplines have much to offer business historians, particularly in the discussion of the theory of the firm, which since the pioneering work of R. H. Coase (1937; 386–405) has cast off its unrealistic attachment to the perfect competition model and developed a range of explanations of business behaviour. By the inter-war era, as we shall see in chapter 4, recognising both the enormously increased scale of business activities and the growing divorce between control and ownership, economists had become dissatisfied with a theory of perfect competition which 'assumed that the market was composed of a large number of small firms each of which followed a single-minded, and rational, policy of profit maximisation' (Lee, 1990; 17–27). This consequently led to much more elaborate work on what Coase (1937; 386–405) described as the transaction costs associated with, for example, acquiring raw materials or selling goods. As a result, he dramatically revised the theory of the firm by rejecting the neoclassical premise of perfect markets, providing an insight into why firms use their competitive advantage, rather than sell internal knowledge on the open market (Hutchinson & Nicholas, 1987; 51). Williamson (1985) in particular has developed Coase's work on transaction costs, and utilised Chandlerian concepts in stressing the importance of different 'governance structures' as means of both overcoming market problems and exploiting transaction cost economies. Unfortunately, though, as Lazonick (1991; 193-8) points out, Williamson has misinterpreted Chandler's work, by overstating the 'marvels of the market' while at the same time discussing the internalisation of functions. This reveals how a marriage between the two disciplines might well be difficult to forge, but one can see how transaction cost theory could well help to explain why firms pursue particular strategies.

Arising from the discussions surrounding the theory of the firm, some economists have taken issue with Coase's belief that firms can reach an optimum size, leading to the creation of a new theory of the growth of the firm which has deviated considerably from the basic tenets of its progenitor (Devine, 1976; 176–96). In effect, the traditional theory of the firm is concerned with firms operating in specific and static product markets, with management as a given factor which can only change in the long-run. On the other hand, industrial economists like Penrose (1959) and Marris (1964) in particular have changed the emphasis by claiming that the concept of optimum size has little relevance in the real world, arguing that it is simply sufficient to define the constraints to growth. This refocussed the debate away from the concern of traditional theories with the determination of prices or the level of output, towards an understanding of the way in which management utilises the talents and resources at its disposal, providing a more dynamic model with which business historians might associate. Penrose's (1959; 24–6) view of the firm as a pool of productive resources organised within an administrative framework is especially helpful, and links directly into the kind of ideas proposed by Chandler when discussing the relationship between strategy and structure. Each firm in the Penrose model is regarded as a unique collection of talents, and it is the responsibility of management to exploit the opportunities available, or overcome any obstacles to growth, by utilising those skills effectively. In this sense, the managerial constraint is the key determinant of a firm's rate of growth, a concept with which many business historians would find it easy to deal on both general and case-study levels.

While the Penrose model has much to offer, it is important to stress that she has been criticised for a failure to take account of important external factors like financial and market constraints. Downie (1958; 1–3), in developing a broad analysis of the whole competitive process, has argued that the interaction of financial and demand constraints is actually the key determinant of a firm's rate of growth, rather than management's ability to deal with these forces. This is close to the views propounded by Marris (1964; 45–8), who argues that in the modern corporate world, with firms competing for capital on the financial markets, it is how the stock market perceives the opportunities for investment in each business which is the main determinant. He has actually developed a more theoretical approach (see section 6.1) to the subject than either Penrose or Downie, but it is clear that a knowledge of this work can add a further dimension to business history. Another key point to remember about the theory of the growth of the firm is that it has been derived from industrial economics, a discipline which bases its methodology on inductive empiricism, rather than the deductive reasoning of traditional economics. For this reason alone, the theory has a greater affinity with historical research, and a large literature has been generated through the application of these techniques in the analysis of key business trends like diversification, takeovers and mergers, as well as the relationship between growth and profitability (Devine, 1976; 196–235). This clearly demonstrates the potential for cross-fertilisation between business history and economic theory, and while all of the work to date has been produced by economists it is surely time that historians exploited the techniques which are now available.

This is not the place for an extensive review of the theory of the firm, because later chapters will explain the main developments when appropriate to the history of British business. It is important to note, however, that business historians can clearly benefit enormously from extending their awareness of industrial economics by reading the work of academics like Hutchinson and Nicholas (1987; 46–62) or Lee (1990; 20–4). This is particularly the case when it comes to analysing strategies like vertical integration or diversification, because they have been so crucial to business evolution over the last 200 years. To date, transaction cost models have rarely been used by historians, but if any consistency is to develop in the way business evolution is analysed then utilising such concepts will be invaluable (Hutchinson & Nicholas, 1987; 62). Of course, it is important to be intellectually honest, in that simple reference to theories without a complete evaluation are of little use, and few business historians are actually trained economists. It would consequently be dangerous to use theory simply for the sake of acquiring a dubious kind of academic credibility. Most crucially, because economics is based on rationality, and businessmen are often noted for taking what might be regarded as irrational decisions, it is unclear where any combination of the disciplines would lead. Of course, the behaviouralist school of thought has attempted to accommodate deviant actions, but there is considerable disagreement concerning the motives behind these actions (Devine, 1976; 113-126), and business historians must approach the subject with great care.

Schumpeter and the entrepreneur

Another vital point concerning the relationship between economics and business history is to note that until recently the central figure of much business history, the entrepreneur, had largely been ignored by those working on the theory of the firm (Lee, 1990; 27–29). Economists are more concerned with rational choices concerning the production and distribution of goods and services, rather than attempting to explain the many dimensions of individual personality (Chapman, 1992; 11). There is also considerable disagreement about exactly what constitutes an 'entrepreneur', a debate which was stimulated significantly by the path-breaking work of Schumpeter (1934; 132), who gave this figure a central role in economic development. To Schumpeter, the entrepreneur's prime function is

> to reform or revolutionise the pattern of production by exploiting an invention or, more generally, an untried technological possibility for producing a new commodity or producing an old one in a new way, by opening up a new source of supply of materials or a new outlet for products, by reorganising an industry and so on.

This dynamic kind of innovatory activity would have a disequilibrating impact on the economic system which affects cost and pricing policies and decision-making in many firms. In particular, it was the emphasis on innovation (or commercialisation of an idea), rather than invention (the idea itself), which set his theories apart from the traditional approach towards economic development.

Schumpeter's thesis has, of course, not gone unchallenged (Lee, 1990;

28–29: Ricketts, 1987; 49–73). Kirzner (1979), for example, argues that the entrepreneur's key role is the restoration of equilibrium, rather than its destabilisation. On the other hand, Casson (1987; 31) has claimed that the entrepreneur can be regarded as 'someone who specialises in taking judgemental decisions about the co-ordination of scarce resources', directing attention away from centre-stage to the more mundane level of the individual firm. Of course, innovation remains central to the Casson interpretation, but this process would not necessarily result in dramatic changes to the general scene, emphasising the role played by individual businessmen in maintaining competitiveness. Corley (1993; 11) might argue that 'as yet there is no consensus among business and economic historians on how to treat the entreprenuer', but as we shall see in the next chapter it is surely more realistic to accept Casson's definition, given the role played by a large number of innovators and imitators in establishing the first industrial economy.

This debate about the role and function of the entrepreneur has done much to help clarify the significance of this figure's contribution to economic development. In particular, it provides a methodological basis when following Supple's third approach outlined earlier, which links business history into the analysis of an economy's performance. Schumpeter (1934; 86) argued that 'innovation is the outstanding fact in the economic history of capitalist society', and the direct study of both case-studies and the general business scene can be of enormous value in understanding this process and the varying rates of progress in different environments. Of course, this kind of work has been going on for many years, for example in the analysis of Britain's relatively poor economic performance, but there has been little attempt to relate reality to theory, and vice versa. Lee (1990; 177) is hopeful: 'According to the theory, merger is supposed to make possible increases in productivity through economies of scale, so a little academic vertical integration should be greatly welcomed'. On the other hand, although there is undoubtedly an argument in favour of using what Casson (1987; 87) calls 'a matrix of case-studies' to meet this ambition, there is still little agreement on such issues as 'how many case studies are required to make a case' (Hertner & Jones, 1986; 13), and whether the unrepresentative nature of single firm histories can be overcome.

1.5 Conclusion

Although problems remain with regard to elaborating a business history methodology, one can nevertheless conclude from what we have seen in this chapter that the discipline has clearly made enormous strides over the last thirty years. In the very first article published in *Business History*, T. S. Ashton (1959; 7) claimed that the subject was merely an adjunct to its

'parent study', economic history, providing only an insight into 'the operation of economic forces at first hand'. This view is no longer tenable, and one
can now say with some confidence that an independent discipline exists,
broadly based on the definition provided at the beginning of section 1.1.
Unfortunately, though, the discipline in Britain is still dominated by interpretations based on American experiences, and it is the main purpose of the
following chapters to provide a distinctly *British* perspective which will
incorporate a study not only of organisational developments, but also a
detailed insight into the market, institutional and socio-cultural environments which influence management. Relative failure there might have been,
according to certain preconceived standards, but before blame can be
attached the whole picture needs to be presented, and this will take up much
of the space as we follow the history of British business into the late-twentieth century. The story is both fascinating and complicated, and although a
completely comprehensive overview is impossible, largely because many
companies are still awaiting the attentions of a business historian, we can at
least begin to examine the vast range of influences on the evolution of British
business.

2

The emergence of
modern business, 1720–1870

At the time of the Great Exhibition in 1851, by exploiting a competitive advantage gained from being the first industrial nation, British businessmen dominated the world's markets. Contemporaries described Britain as the 'Workshop of the World', and the Great Exhibition emphatically demonstrated this supremacy as hundreds of thousands of people trooped through the great halls of Prince Albert's Crystal Palace. We now know, of course, that not only had the British economy yet to be fully transformed (Berg, 1994; 144–50), 1851 was also the prelude to a new era of intensifying international competition. Change there had been in Britain, but by mid-century it was still confined to a narrow range of industries in particular regions, and agriculture and domestic manufacturing employment still remained extremely important, even in the most industrialised districts (Hudson, 1992; 101–32). Nevertheless, a steady transition from mercantile to industrial capitalism was gripping British business, and the purpose of this chapter is to examine the organisational implications of the process, evaluating a variety of views expressed about the allegedly backward nature of business organisation and finance in the period up to the mid-nineteenth century.

Inevitably, given the role business history has played in illustrating key debates in economic history, much attention has been focussed on strategic management (see Figure 1.1), because the decisions made at that level most directly affect a firm's competitiveness. This reveals the problem of differentiating between entrepreneurship and management, the former being essentially strategic, the latter tactical, and not just at the personal stage, where there is little divorce between control and ownership, but at the entrepreneurial and managerial stages too. In this context, we are not concerned with the kind of entrepreneur described by Schumpeter (1934; 74), who is supposedly a rare phenomenon capable of drastically altering the economic scene (see section 1.4). Instead, we are to examine the more typical type who was imitative and piecemeal in pursuing change (Coleman, 1973;

112). These individuals were part of the great army of industrialists who were 'dependent for their prosperity, even for their survival, on good management rather than innovation' (Payne, 1978; 184). It was their function to take the judgemental decisions relating to the co-ordination of resources which was so vital to firm survival (Casson, 1993; 31).

Our first problem will consequently be to examine how the various managerial functions discussed in the last chapter (see Figure 1.1) were performed as modern industrial capitalism began to emerge in Britain, assessing the willingness to delegate responsibility, and the various obstacles which existed to limit effective organisation-building. We shall then go on to investigate the other problems facing businessmen at this time, in particular with regard to the labour and financial scenes, and in the conclusion some idea of progress in overcoming these constraints will be presented.

The period we are investigating has often been described as the classic era of *personal capitalism*, representing the first of Chandler's three stages which were described in section 1.3. This *personal* stage is generally characterised by a close relationship between control and ownership, with little delegation of responsibility to professional managers allowed by a highly individualistic business culture. However, clearly such a simplistic view has major weaknesses when one considers the growing amount of evidence now available revealing an extensive degree of organisational improvisation and experimentation. The whole of industry might not have moved towards factory methods of production by the 1850s, but in those sectors which did adopt this new approach, businessmen had to create structures capable of effectively controlling the means of production and distribution (Musson, 1978; 142–6), and the pioneering efforts at organisation-building challenge some of the long-held views about management techniques employed at that time.

Of course, one cannot be too optimistic about this pioneering work, and it is necessary to examine why a highly individualistic approach had such an important bearing on the attitudes towards finance and decision-making. This culture created severe in-built constraints which were later to become even more troublesome as the scale of enterprise increased and the levels of domestic and overseas competition intensified from the 1870s. Furthermore, the main industries were characterised by highly competitive market structures and most firms remained essentially small-scale and specialised, eschewing the potential advantages of greater size and vertical integration. Naturally, not all sectors can be included in these generalisations, with the railways and other network utilities pursuing rather different paths. In general, though, the organisation of British business appeared to ossify at a relatively immature level of development, inhibiting progress at a time when other economies were posing new competitive challenges (Payne, 1988; 40–3). This chapter will consequently provide an insight into the inner dynamics of British business at mid-century, but at the same time many of its conclusions will have an important bearing on our analysis of later periods, building a solid foundation for the longer-term view which will unfold as the book progresses.

2.1 Meeting the organisational challenges

During the eighteenth and nineteenth centuries, as most industries made the transition from mercantile to industrial capitalism by concentrating production (Musson, 1978; 61–77), businessmen were faced with unprecedented organisational challenges. Of course, by the 1760s a concentrated form of production in small workshops was already a feature of some industries, from silk-throwing and calico printing to paper-making, coach-building and the Sheffield steel trades (Chapman, 1974; 451–473). There were even outstanding cases like Lombe's silk mill in Derby, which was built in 1721 at a cost of £29,000, leading Chaloner (1963; 8–20) to call it 'the first modern British textile factory'. The increasing number of coal-fired blast furnaces also revealed new tendencies in business concentration in the iron industry from the 1750s, while developments in coal mining prompted more integrated operations with higher levels of direct managerial control (Crouzet, 1985; 20–36). In general, though, for much of the eighteenth century most manufacturing was carried out using the putting-out, or 'domestic', form of organisation, with merchants playing the pivotal role as principal organisers and financiers. Factories started to emerge in greater numbers after the 1770s, but only gradually did businessmen begin to realise that the potential in the market and technological environment would allow a move towards more concentrated methods of production. One must always remember the decisive comment of Clapham (1926; 143), that even by the 1830s 'no single industry had passed through a complete technical revolution'.

From mercantile to industrial capitalism

While the domestic system was based largely on the avoidance of direct management, modern industrial capitalism involved a much greater commitment of resources and expertise, with three principal characteristics featuring most prominently. In the first place, industrialists were obliged to provide greater levels of fixed investment for buildings and machinery; they would also have to recruit a labour force to work in their premises; and finally, direct supervision of the whole operation would be required. Quite simply, this was the first generation of industrial organisation-builders, and they were faced with the tasks of devising an administrative routine for controlling this complex organism which would, for example, provide a regular flow of raw materials, account for the flow of funds, and control a workforce. These were new tasks for many businessmen, and as this was still very much the personal stage of industrial capitalism (see Figure 1.2) it has been said that they often 'fulfilled in one person the function of the capitalist, financier, works manager, merchant and salesman' (Wilson, 1957; 111). Another distinguished authority, Alfred Marshall (1919; 319), also noted of this form of organisation that: 'The master's eye is everywhere; there is no shirking by his foremen, no divided responsibility, no sending half-understood messages backwards and forwards from one department to another'. However, there is a strong degree of characterisation in these descriptions of the personal stage, and as both Pollard (1965; 308) and Payne (1988; 18) have noted the multi-layered partnership was of increasing importance as a solution to the organisational challenges of the era. Indeed, as we shall see, industrialists increasingly divested themselves of many managerial functions, and although the typical firm remained a single-unit concern there were some interesting organisational innovations which deserve some investigation.

Individualism and self-help

Of importance to this discussion is the highly individualistic culture which prevailed for much of the period. Philosophers and political economists like John Stuart Mill and Thomas Malthus, as well as the later well-known populists like Samuel Smiles, promulgated a philosophy of self-dependence as the key to improved economic and social betterment (Crouzet, 1985; 37–49). They believed that people ought to be measured by a common standard, regardless of means, and that those who succeeded in life did so because of their hard work, thrift and ingenuity, while the poor suffered as a result of personal fecklessness (Smiles, 1859; 47). In simple terms, it was the individual's responsibility to pull him/herself up 'by the bootstraps' and exploit the opportunities available, rather than rely on others, or the state, for succour. Self-help was the key, encouraging those without adequate resources to believe that they could emulate outstanding individuals like Richard Arkwright, the twelfth son of a barber who by the time he died in 1792 owned large landed estates and had been knighted for his services to industry after a career as a successful industrial innovator (Fitton, 1989; 203–19).

Naturally, one must treat much of this proselytising about the benefits of self-help with great caution, because while it is true to say that 'the myth of the self-made man and the ideology of self-help were deep-rooted in British public opinion', Crouzet (1985; 48, 126–43) demonstrates comprehensively that there were actually very few recorded cases of working class entrepreneurs in this period. It is important to stress the contribution made by the lower middle classes to the growth of an industrialist class at this time, because having started off with relatively modest capital resources most of these men were probably 'architects of their own fortunes'. Honeyman (1982; 81) has also conducted a similar analysis of the 'myth of the self-made man', concluding that 'most of the early cotton spinners were men of modest or moderate capital'. Nevertheless, self-made men like Arkwright were extremely rare, revealing a much less mobile society than people like Samuel Smiles would have us believe when creating the illusion of 'working-class-man-made-good'.

The 'high-trust culture'

Having demystified the origins of this new class of industrialists, it is also important to stress that their belief in self-help was further compromised by economic reality. We shall also see later how extensive local networks for the mobilisation of finance, talent or information were utilised as an essential aid to management. These networks were primarily based on what Casson (1993; 42) has described as a 'high-trust culture' which sustained the atomistic industrial structure prevailing at that time, and within the regional context especially, elite groups of businessmen collaborated extensively to reduce the transaction costs arising from the high levels of uncertainty existing at that time. This concept of a high-trust culture and its concomitant networks qualifies the general impression created by contemporary philosophers and populists who insisted on the all-pervading influence of self-help. Religious groupings were especially successful in building up networks, one example being how Quakers in the north-east of England utilised their common bonds to build a mutually-supportive infrastructure which was 'conducive to the formation and subsequent growth of the firm' (Prior & Kirby, 1993; 107–8). Religion, however, was by no means the only bonding agent at work from the mid-eighteenth century, because, as Hudson (1992; 101–8) has argued, the region took on a crucial importance as an integrated unit which provided not only the key factors of production and vital technical and commercial information, but also forged a community of interests. This regional dynamic was to become the abiding characteristic of Britain's first phase of industrialisation, and for businessmen struggling with market uncertainties and deficient knowledge it provided a 'high-trust culture' which would minimise transaction costs (see section 1.4) external to the firm.

Business historians are consequently faced with a confusing picture when attempting to unravel the mysteries of a business culture which, on the one hand, was characterised by a popular belief in self-help, while at the same time encouraged the development of a mutually supportive network system. The key to understanding this situation is the degree to which contemporary businessmen would allow outsiders to influence internal activities within the firm, because while they relied enormously on external networks for certain factors of production, few would initially envisage any interference with management. In this context, the self-help philosophy undoubtedly had an important influence on business development at this time, largely because it placed so much emphasis on the individual as the key to success, leading potentially to a managerial constraint on business growth.

Attitudes towards professional managers

The most obvious manifestation of this introverted philosophy at work was the attitude of businessmen towards professional managers. It is generally accepted that nepotism was the traditional route into management through-out the eighteenth and nineteenth centuries, although some key personnel were recruited through the networks based on religious affiliations or from within the local business community (Pollard, 1965; 20). Unfortunately, though, these traditional sources were not always sufficient to maintain a steady supply of talent in firms which were expanding to sizes beyond the purview of a single individual, and increasingly new avenues were being tried in order to provide strategic management with greater freedom to direct the business effectively. However, this would not only compromise the desire to retain control within the family, it also challenged Adam Smith's view, that managers 'cannot well be expected that they should watch over [other people's money] with the same anxious vigilance with which the partners in a private copartnery frequently watch over their own'. Pollard (1965; 21) has also noted that in the eighteenth century there were many 'examples of dis-honest, absconding or alcoholic managers who did much damage to their firms', posing a major problem for those who required such expertise.

Detailed evidence on the means used to overcome such difficulties is often hard to find, and frequently historians are left with the inadequate tool of quoting individual case-studies. One such example is Ambrose Crowley, an early eighteenth century London iron merchant who devised his own rule book to control the activities of his blast furnaces located in the north east of England (Flinn, 1962; 77–98). Other businessman would not appear to have imitated the Crowley system, however, even though many would have been faced with similar problems as the scale and scope of industrial and commer-cial activity was extended from the late eighteenth century onwards. Pollard (1965; 127) has rightly noted that 'the typical entrepreneur was his own man-ager' at this time, but the growth in size of businesses in some parts of the tex-tile, coal, iron and engineering industries prompted an increasing need to delegate some responsibility in what we described in section 1.3 (see Figure 1.1) as the *functional* and *operational* areas of management. This would naturally pose a problem of supply, and while nepotism might have provided one important source of managerial talent, other means of satisfying the growing demand needed to be found. In this context, Pollard (1965; 127–47) has traced an 'extensive and varied' range of educational and training schemes which emerged at this time, but concludes that the vast majority of managers were actually 'trained by practical work in the firms', where actual business problems could be encountered at first-hand. Boulton & Watt, at their famous Soho foundry, trained Josiah Wedgwood's son, and in the iron and older tex-tile trades 'the amount of deliberate training given in the larger and more pro-gressive firms should not be underrated' (Pollard, 1965; 147–8).

Managers were clearly in great demand from the 1790s, as owner-managers struggled with the challenges associated with modern industrial capitalism, and in spite of the supposedly individualistic business culture an increasing use of professional functionaries characterised many sectors of the economy. A clear indication of the extent to which managers were contributing more extensively to industrial development is the significant rise in their salaries: by the period 1790–1830 top managers could command between £500 and £2,000, compared to between £200–500 prior to 1790. Although what Pollard (1965; 165–73) calls 'typical managers' would only have earned £100–250 by 1830, this again was a significant improvement on the £30–60 they were paid prior to 1760. Clearly, by the early nineteenth century businessmen had accepted the need to compromise their individualism, and although nepotism continued to be a major feature of managerial recruitment for many decades thereafter, professional managers were increasingly regarded as essential features of the business scene. Indeed, Pollard (1965; 174, 185) argues that from the 1790s the 'replacement of nepotism by merit became one of the more significant aspects of the growing rationalisation of industry'. This would help to overcome the widespread aversion to professional managers and provide society with a new means of encouraging the development of much-needed talents. Industrial managers consequently 'formed one of the most dynamic social groups of their age, responsible for initiating many of its decisive changes'. Their training was invariably of a highly practical, on-the-job nature, largely because most were recruited from the ranks of either skilled workers or office clerks, and only slowly did a common body of knowledge evolve as a basis for operations, usually at the industry level. Nevertheless, there is a growing amount of evidence which demonstrates the crucial importance of these managing partners as an effective solution to the organisational challenges associated with the advent of modern industrial capitalism (Crouzet, 1985; 15–18).

The emergence of managing partners

One of the more enduring solutions devised in relation to this need for a compromise between individualism and economic reality was a system of recruiting managing partners. As one prominent cotton manufacturer, Robert Peel, argued: 'It is impossible for a mill at any distance to be managed, unless it is under the direction of a partner or superintendent who has an interest in the success of the business' (Chapman, 1969; 87–8). Peel was faced with the task of running an expanding industrial empire which by the 1790s numbered twenty-three mills and eight printing works spread around Lancashire and Cheshire. In fact, he only had five sons and outside appointments in the form of managing partners had to be made, often on the condition that either they bought a small share of the business, or their remuneration was based on profits. It was what Chapman (1969; 89) has described as 'the empirical discovery of a solution to the problem of organisation and control of the dispersed manufacturing sector', and in this way the early industrialists acquired the necessary skills for their businesses, helping them to overcome many of the organisational problems faced in that pioneering phase.

The partnership system was being rapidly and widely extended from the mid-eighteenth century, taking on what Payne (1978; 192) describes as a 'kaleidoscopic nature' which became the organisational building-block of British business. We shall see in section 2.4 that the partnership system also had its uses as a means of securing access to adequate fixed capital for expanding businesses, but in an organisational sense it allowed owner-managers the opportunity to supplement family sources of expertise.

The rise of the managing partner was indeed a major economic and social breakthrough for the time, and certainly talented individuals could exploit managerial opportunities as apprenticeships for entering business in their own right. Pollard (1965; 163-188) provides abundant evidence to substantiate this theme, particularly from the cotton textile industry, referring to classic cases like Robert Owen and George Lee who were initially managing partners for other Manchester cotton manufacturers, but eventually became successful in their own right as a result of experience gained on the job. James McConnell and John Kennedy also started their careers in the cotton industry as managing partners for a firm of machinery makers and mule spinners, and after this business had been dissolved in 1795 they established a business which by 1810 was Manchester's second largest cotton business (Lee, 1972; 10–12, 167). Similarly, when John Horrocks began to build his cotton firm in Preston during the 1790s, expanding from one mill in 1792 to six by 1801, he promoted several of his staff to the post of mill manager, and in turn at least three of them (Thomas German, George Jacson and William Taylor) established their own businesses in the locality (Whittle, 1837; 226). This firm also devised a suitable 'succession strategy', providing for continuity in management by recruiting a line of managing partners which ensured its survival as one of the leading spinning and weaving concerns throughout the nineteenth century (Rose, 1993; 137–41).

This system of using managing partners was clearly gaining widespread acceptance in many industries between 1790 and 1830, and it complemented the parallel trend of hiring professional managers to perform the functional and operational tasks for which owner-managers had neither the time nor the expertise. Indeed, as Pollard (1965; 186) notes, 'the line between the manager, the managing partner and the moneyed partner was increasingly difficult to draw, as mobility between these categories remained high', demonstrating how a fluid social structure had evolved as a result of industrial capitalism. Just as nepotism featured among the ranks of owner-managers, so also 'dynasties' of managers can be found as the profession expanded its horizons, providing a means of training new generations who aspired to this occupation. On the other hand, this internalised process of training, combined with its practical, on-the-job nature, prevented cross-fertilisaton of skills and personnel, and while common standards evolved in individual industries, they were highly dedicated. In conclusion, one can agree with Pollard (1965; 188), who states that by 1830 'well-defined groups of managers in many industries' had appeared, but as yet this hardly amounted to the creation of a managerial profession.

Cost accountancy

Business organisation in Britain was consequently undergoing a subtle process of transformation, with a significant degree of specialisation emerging in response to the economic realities of industrial capitalism. It is still unclear, however, just exactly how well firms were managed, and the absence of an extensive management literature, the preference for in-house training methods, the dedicated nature of managerial skills, and the persistence of nepotism might well lead us to believe that progress in the development of a 'management science' was slow. With regard to cost accountancy, for example, it has generally been accepted that the 'practice of using accounts as direct aids to management was not one of the achievements of the British industrial revolution' (Pollard, 1965; 288). On the other hand, a more thorough analysis of contemporary evidence has produced some interesting new insights, demonstrating how modern tools of management accounting were in extensive use by 1850 (Edwards & Newell, 1991; 35–57). While diminishing the general level of progress, even Pollard (1965; 288) was willing to concede that some prominent manufacturers developed 'quite advanced and fairly accurate techniques', and it has been known for many years that the leading steam engine manufacturers, Boulton & Watt, had devised quite sophisticated cost accounting techniques in the 1790s (Roll, 1930; 244–52). More recent research has also revealed that 'cost accounting . . . developed to serve management in an increasingly complex and constantly changing social and economic environment' during the eighteenth and nineteenth centuries (Edwards, 1989; 315).

There is clearly an imperative need to re-evaluate views on the subject of cost accountancy, and especially to examine its influence on management decision making. One must first of all distinguish this practice from that of financial reporting, a discipline which was developed in the sixteenth century as an aid to merchants (Garner, 1954; 1–26). It is important to note how, because fixed investments were usually small in mercantile businesses, traditional financial accounting (often double-entry bookkeeping) did not accomodate overheads when calculating a product's cost (Chatfield, 1977; 99–101). Industrialists were consequently obliged to experiment with new techniques which would accommodate their substantial investment in fixed assets, as well as provide accurate data for price-setting. This resulted in such substantial iron producers as the Carron Co., the Crawshays at Cyfarthfa, Darby at Coalbrookdale, and the Guests at Dowlais, devising 'purposeful cost accounting' which resulted in 'a rich tapestry of practices' in that industry (Fleischman & Parker, 1992; 141).

Given that the minimum investment in plant for efficient iron production had risen to approximately £50,000 by the early nineteenth century, at a time when capital and credit markets were still in a rudimentary state, and frequently the owning families had appointed managers to run the production facilites, this had sharpened their costing instincts. Other factors like the need to control factors of production, and the increasing 'sophistication of marketing strategies, operating processes and technical innovations' also forced them to gauge real costs more accurately, resulting in a cost accountancy system which has been called a 'significant precursor of the scientific management movement' (Fleischman & Parker, 1992; 142–150).

We shall be looking at the whole issue of 'scientific management' in section 5.2, but it is already clear that the views of Pollard and of Chatfield do not appear to tally with the new evidence produced by an expanding group of accounting historians. Indeed, costing became a vital aid to planning, and even though its development might well have been of a pragmatic nature, significant progress had been achieved by the early nineteenth century (Fleischman & Tyson, 1993; 503–17). For the small businessman cost accountancy was perhaps an unnecessary addition to his managerial burden, but for those firms committed to substantial fixed investment this tool was absolutely essential as a means of aiding the decision-making process. This is well borne out by the leading pottery manufacturer, Josiah Wedgwood, who developed a range of cost accounting techniques to control his large Staffordshire pottery works at Etruria which guided decision making at crucial times in the business's development (McKendrick, 1970; 63–5).

Cost (or management) accountacy was clearly making significant progress in British business at this time. While it might be correct to argue that cost accountancy results remained a closely guarded secret, because of the valuable information on production which they contained, the techniques were being widely disseminated among large-scale industrialists in a range of industries through the extensive informational networks which existed. Books like those produced by Babbage (*On the Economy of Machinery and Manufacture*, 1834) facilitated this process of dissemination (Chatfield, 1977; 102–3), but it was at the level of the firm that significant progress was made in devising appropriate cost accounting conventions which suited the needs of each individual business.

One can, of course, overstate the extent to which cost accountancy impinged on decision making, because Chatfield (1977; 104–5) is undoubtedly correct in pointing out that 'administrative ability tended to be equated with technical competence' at this time, and this hindered the complete integration of the new tool into management. Certainly, more research into a wider range of industries is required before a complete picture of cost accountancy can be painted. Similarly, one must not imply from this description of the rise of the managing partner and the emergence of a breed of industrial managers equipped with new management tools that British business was making the move from a personal to the entrepreneurial stages of capitalism. Strategic and functional control still rested very firmly in the hands of owner-managers (see Figures 1.1 and 1.2), and only in the exceptionally large firms was some functional and operational management being delegated to professionals. One must always remember that the vast majority of enterprises were small-scale operations, and in those concerns 'industrialists closely supervised everything which went on in their factories: the daily tour of the various departments was part of their life' (Crouzet, 1985; 17).

Conclusion

This was still very much the era of 'personal capitalism', when a highly individualistic approach remained at the core of Britain's business culture and a strong aversion to professional training became an embedded feature of the general approach towards recruitment. One can actually detect the emergence of a structure which was to dominate British business operations for many decades, a structure which was characterised by what Coleman (1973; 92–116) describes as a strong division between 'gentlemen and players'. We shall be examining this thesis in greater detail in chapter 4, but in simple terms it claims that a two-tier structure came to dominate British business, with strategic management retained by the 'gentlemen' of the owning family, while functional and operational management was undertaken by 'players' recruited either from local contacts or existing employees. Strong lines of demarcation existed which prevented the vast majority of 'players' rising into the elite ranks, unless they went into business for themselves, while formal training for any level of management remained anathema to the whole system. We noted earlier that most managers (and businessmen as a whole) still learnt their jobs through practical training, or were brought into the firm because of their family or religious connections, and this tradition became a distinguishing characteristic of British business for much of the nineteenth century. Pollard (1965; 127–147) might well have found evidence of some educational innovations at this time, particularly in the fields of technical training, and clearly some businessmen were willing to try new ideas. On the other hand, as J. A. Bowie (1930; 89) was later to argue, 'the soil of crass individualism is never friendly to standards and ethical ideas', and the distinction between 'gentlemen and players' continued to act as a powerful force fashioning attitudes in this area for many generations.

2.2   Operational management: labour recruitment and control

While the recruitment of managing partners to perform routine functional tasks might have been the response of some large-scale industrialists to the challenge of running their expanding businesses, it has often been argued that labour recruitment and control (or operational management, as we called it earlier in Figure 1.1) was an even greater area for concern (Chapman, 1967; 156: Pollard, 1965; 189). The higher levels of fixed investment in buildings and machinery evidently forced the industrialist to work assets as hard as possible in order to maximise returns, creating a tremendous tension between capital and labour, particularly as the workforce was not attuned to the levels of speed, regularity and direct supervision now imposed on them (Bendix, 1956; 53–4). Those used to domestic manufacturing employment regarded the factory system as alien to their traditional lifestyles, and the industrialist was faced with the task of imposing a new system of time-discipline on a workforce more used to 'maximising subsistence' and operating in tune with the rhythms of nature, rather than the hours of the clock (Rule, 1986; 130–8: Thompson, 1967; 133–65). On the other hand, however, one must not overstate the direct relationship between capital and labour in the new units, because a system of internal subcontracting developed which provided industrialists with an opportunity to delegate responsibility for recruiting and controlling the workforce. It is also important to stress that until the 1890s this form of internal subcontracting prevailed in most industries where high levels of expertise were called for as an essential part of the production process, while only by the 1970s was traditional workshop autonomy being dismantled by management.

The recruitment challenge

Before this system of internal subcontracting could take shape, however, it was first of all necessary to persuade workers to move from domestic or agricultural to factory employment, at a time when 'there was nothing like a single national labour market' (Pollard, 1978; 103). In this context, as well as the many local wakes and feast days peppering the calendar, industrialists were faced with the challenge of overcoming such well-established traditions as 'St Monday', which was regarded as a natural right to the extension of the weekend, and was observed almost universally among manufacturing workers and miners (Rule, 1986; 130–1). Ultimately, of course, over the period 1770–1840 the industrialist was placed in a more powerful position, largely as a result of the impact of technological innovation on domestic manufacturing and agriculture, combined with the pressures imposed by a demographic explosion which created an expanding pool of underemployed workers. In the meantime, new virtues had to be instilled into a working class more used to dictating their own working patterns. Pollard (1965;

189–205) has described these problems in great detail, remarking that: 'There was more to overcome than the change of employment or the new rhythm of work: there was a whole new culture to be absorbed and an old one to be traduced and spurned'. In the first place, as Redford (1964; 18) commented: 'Labourers from agricultural or domestic industry do not at first take kindly to the monotony of factory life; and the pioneering employer not infrequently finds great difficulty in building up a stable supply of efficient and willing labour'. It was a matter of reorientating the working day around the hours of the clock, rather than the rhythms of nature, of converting the task-orientation typical of pre-industrial society into a more systematic approach towards work, and, not surprisingly, workers were often reluctant to buckle under meekly (Rule, 1986; 130–8).

The three essential characteristics of factory life – speed, regularity and supervision – were anathema to preindustrial working patterns, and only slowly over the era 1770–1840 did industrialists manage to impose their system of time-discipline on a recalcitrant labour force. It is, above all, wrong to assume that the working classes sought continuity of work at this time (Ashton, 1955; 203), and traditional work practices were extremely difficult to overcome. An added problem for the industrialist was the reliance on water power for much of this period, forcing him to locate production facilities in the countryside where labour was even more difficult to acquire in adequate numbers around the year.

One solution to these problems which only compounded the aversion to factory employment was the hiring of institutionalised labour like prisoners, orphans and paupers. This tradition was especially strong in the textile mills, and while it might well have provided a docile, captive workforce, to the local population such practices would only have added a social stigma to what was already an unpopular means of earning a living. In any case, non-free labour would not have accounted for more than a third of the total workforce in any one factory, and by and large this was usually child labour in the form of 'pauper apprentices' purchased from agents who specialised in supplying such human commodities. In fact, the 'apprentice' label was little more than window-dressing, and these children rarely received any kind of formal training, other than as the most menial type of labourer for the skilled men employed in the mills. Nevertheless, 'apprentices' were a vital source of labour for the new factories, even though they proved to be almost as expensive as other employees (Pollard, 1965; 194–203).

Although one must remember that industrialists were merely perpetuating a widespread acceptance of the practice of child labour, conditions were undoubtedly harsh in the early factories and corporal punishment was very much a feature of early factory life. In fact, industrialists preferred to fine employees for unsatisfactory work, or simply dismiss them from the premises. Josiah Wedgwood developed an extensive system of fines from the 1760s, in association with what is generally regarded as the first attempt at imposing the need to clock-on at the beginning of the day. He would also tour the workshops regularly, and apart from fining workers for drinking or gaming on his premises, Wedgwood would smash sub-standard work, chalking 'This won't do for JW' on pots as a sign of his authority (McKendrick, 1961; 38). This served as a model for other industrialists, and certainly at between 6d. (2.5 pence) and 2s. (twenty pence) the fines were harsh, when few earned more than £1 per week, and most received much less (Pollard, 1965; 219–20).

Industrial paternalism

Having noted the militaristic nature of early factory life, it is also important to emphasise that some of the more prominent industrialists were keen to generate a co-operative attitude among the workers, using industrial paternalism as an effective weapon. McKendrick (1961; 38) has commented on how Wedgwood 'never forgot that a contented workman is a more efficient workman'. Many of his contemporaries would also have agreed with Ashworth's claim that, in view of the need to preach 'the virtues of thrift, order, promptitude, and perseverance' to the workforce, they needed to 'exercise a control of superintendence over them for their moral and social improvement' (Roberts, 1979; 171–3). This attitude reveals an acceptance by industrialists of the traditional concept of authority, by which, through a strong sense of *noblesse oblige*, those in command took responsibility for the well-being of their social inferiors (Bendix, 1956; 53). It was an attitude which led to the emergence of industrial paternalism as a decisive influence on class relationships in nineteenth-century Britain (Joyce, 1980; 134).

Industrial paternalism was a vital means by which employers were able to inculcate middle class virtues into their workers. Its physical manifestations were housing for the operatives, churches, schools, shops and even recreational facilities, demonstrating how some of the large-scale industrialists were also community-builders, investing considerable sums in unproductive assets (Jeremy, 1990). Those who provided these services 'reads like a roll-call of the giants of the industrial revolution' (Pollard, 1965; 232–6), and among the most prominent in the cotton industry were Robert Owen at New Lanark and the Gregs at Styal, while in coal mining the Lowthers in West Cumberland, in engineering Boulton & Watt at Soho, in pottery Josiah Wedgwood at Etruria, and in iron production the Crawshay family at Merthyr Tydfil. All provided a range of services for their workers, and although town-based industrialists were less likely to be community-builders, even there prominent businessmen had realised the advantages of such practices by the mid-nineteenth century, helping to create what Joyce (1980; 134) has described as a stable society.

The main purpose behind this supposedly enlightened approach towards employment was, of course, to tie the workforce firmly into the system of industrial capitalism. Misbehaviour of any kind, and in Ashworth's case even keeping an untidy home (Boyson, 1970; 127–32) would be cause enough for dismissal and therefore eviction from the community. This emphasises how 'paternalistic benevolence and ruthless oppression often made use of exactly the same managerial devices' (Roberts, 1979; 173). Greg, for example, was fined twelve times in one year for making his children work illegal hours, while Owen's system of having colour-coded monitors over each machine, which allowed him to indicate either pleasure or disdain at the quality of the work done, left no-one in any doubt as to the degree of supervision being imposed. They were capitalists first and philanthropists second, and it seems likely that industrial paternalism facilitated the process of worker-indoctrination which had been going on since the mid-eighteenth century.

Internal subcontracting

Industrial paternalism was consequently a natural extension of the traditional form of authority in British society, but by itself this does not adequately explain the exact relationship between capital and labour. The key figure in this context was the skilled artisan and his role, the most valuable recruit into early factories and workshops who was offered the inducement of higher and more regular wages as a reward for participating in the system of internal subcontracting. Once employed as industrial (as opposed to domestic manufacturing) workers, the skilled artisans were actually given extensive powers over the rest of the labour-force, because they would act as internal subcontractors who were paid by the employer to recruit and control their own co-workers (Littler, 1982; 64–9). In the cotton industry, as Robert Peel attested, 'the hours of work were regulated by the interests of the overseer, whose remuneration depended on the quality of the work done' (Pollard, 1965; 312). This reveals how the internal subcontractor acted as the main agent of control as industrial capitalism evolved. In essence, by paying the most skilled workers to recruit their own labourers and leaving them free to determine key issues like rates of pay, the speed of work and manning issues, the industrialist was relieved of the responsibility for performing these extremely arduous and time-consuming tasks.

The internal subcontractor was, in effect, what many have described as the 'labour aristocrat' of the workforce, and while much controversy surrounds this epithet (Pollard, 1978; 120), there seems little doubt that a privileged elite existed which was accorded both status and higher wages. One should also note that these skilled workers constituted the bulk of the early trade unionists, combining together as much for the ability to limit entry into their trade as to negotiate wage levels with employers (Hobsbawm, 1964; 272–90). This is not the place for a history of early trade unionism (Rule, 1986; 255–81), but it is important to stress how these groups were often little more than combinations of internal subcontractors who controlled labour recruitment and shopfloor operations. Marxists have described it as a system of 'co-exploitation', and while the skilled workers retained their independence from the capitalist classes by joining trade unions, it is possible to see how the whole system of industrial capitalism expanded 'not so much by directly subordinating large bodies of workers to employers, but by subcontracting exploitation and management' (Hobsbawm, 1964; 297).

The key point about subcontracting, from a business historian's perspective, is that it allowed industrialists the opportunity to delay the development of techniques like personnel and quality control, wage payment and, most importantly, operational (see Figure 1.1) management. The extensive system of fines, the threats of dismissal, and the tendency to use corporal punishment were all disciplines imposed by internal subcontractors (Pollard, 1965; 218–225), reducing the need for owner-managers to involve themselves directly in operational management. It was a system which worked because in those pioneering days overhead costs could be minimised, by reducing the need for a large office staff, while the risks attendant on industrial production were also spread between the capitalist and skilled workers (Bendix, 1956; 53–54). Conversely, for the subcontractors it provided status and better remuneration, and indeed many managing partners emerged from these ranks, after artisans had accumulated sufficient capital to buy into a business (Crouzet, 1972b; 165–7). One might also add that because the artisans often hired from among their own families (Anderson, 1971; 112–23), internal subcontracting was an important agent of stabilisation as industrial capitalism evolved over this early period, reinforcing the pressures imposed by technological innovation in facilitating the ongoing process of change which was affecting an increasing proportion of the workforce. This heavily qualifies any belief in a direct relationship between capital and labour, and again one must remember that such was the value of this system to both industrialists and skilled workers that it would survive in most industries until at least the last decades of the nineteenth century (Gospel, 1983; 6–7).

Conclusion

In conclusion, because of its unsophisticated nature, it would be misleading to describe internal subcontracting as an embryonic form of personnel management, but alongside the parallel emergence of industrial paternalism it does reveal the ways in which early generations of industrialists dealt with the problems of recruiting and controlling their workforces. The rise of managing partners and the ubiquity of internal subcontracting are two excellent examples of how businessmen were responding to the organisational challenges of their era, especially where increasing scale severely tested the abilities of a single individual and prompted the delegation of responsibility to those with the skills required to perform a widening range of management roles. Figure 1.2, then, is no mere abstraction of the business historian's mind as far as the early nineteenth century is concerned, because even though little divorce between control and ownership at the strategic level of management had taken place, functional and operational managers were beginning to appear in greater numbers, albeit in a very embryonic form as far as the latter were concerned. Indeed, it is clear that the label personal capitalism had many subtle features which are often ignored in some descriptions of this period of business evolution, although one can firmly state that British business in general remained at the personal stage until the late nineteenth century.

2.3   The utilities and professional management

Railway management

The discussion so far has focussed principally on manufacturing industry because a modern form of business organisation first emerged in that sector. This preoccupaton, however, ignores interesting developments in other parts of the economy which were to bring forward new attitudes towards the functional division of management and the training required for those tasks. Of greatest significance here were the large railway companies created from the 1830s, because not only did these ventures significantly affect Britain's financial systems and institutions, they also 'led the way in developing relatively advanced techniques in business management, making progress in the fields of accounting, costing, pricing, marketing and statistics' (Gourvish, 1973; 290). A full analysis of the widespread economic impact of railway construction and operation is not necessary here, but when one considers the £650 million raised by operating companies between 1830 and 1875, dwarfing the fixed investment in industries like cotton, iron and engineering, it is apparent that we are dealing with a new scale of enterprise which was to have a significant impact on both transportation and financial practices (Gourvish, 1980; 126–140). Railways were still the largest businesses in Britain by the First World War, constituting in 1904–5 the top ten companies measured by market value (Wardley, 1991; 278). They were also, by their very nature, geographically dispersed organisations, stretching the lines of communication at a time when the telegraph and telephone were only just beginning to appear. Furthermore, many had diversified into engineering, adding another dimension to their portfolio of activities. However, whether or not the wholesale re-evaluation of standard management practices by railway companies really amounted to a substantial breakthrough must remain questionable; their approach might appear to have been decidedly innovative, but it is important to assess whether they were able to surmount the obstacles presented by the prevailing business culture.

It is apparent that in the early years railway executives responded poorly to the challenges imposed by the scale and range of their new types of business. The precedents provided by coach and canal travel were at first used extensively, such was the shortage of techniques and appropriately equipped staff, while wildly optimistic traffic projections, combined with badly underestimated construction costs, ensured that 'no traffic manager could produce satisfactory profits, however gifted he was' (Gourvish, 1980; 139). Financial reporting conventions were also still dominated by the needs of merchants, as we noted earlier, and as railways represented unprecedented levels of fixed investment in track and equipment new accounting systems to provide for deterioration and obsolescence had to be devised, along with appropriate cost accounting conventions.

Industrial management at that time was still essentially rooted in the practical problems faced by each sector, as we saw earlier, and while some progress had been made in developing techniques appropriate to individual industries, no generalised ideas had yet emerged which might be suitable to the railways. This left railway companies with the enormous challenge of pioneering their own solutions. There was also a spate of mergers during the mid-1840s, resulting in the creation of much larger railway companies like the Midland and the London & North Western at a time when other pressures were impinging on performance.

The two factors most responsible for a dramatic series of organisational innovations were the intensifying competition for passenger and freight traffic after the second great construction boom in the mid-1840s, and the imposition of much tighter regulations by the Board of Trade on such matters as prices, dividends and the quality of service (Gourvish, 1972; 103–4). When allied with the problems just outlined, these new pressures forced railway managers to readdress the situation, and by the early-1850s significant changes had been introduced which were to have long-term implications for the industry. The leading innovator in this respect was undoubtedly Captain Mark Huish, the general manager of the London & North Western Railway Co. between 1846 and 1858. His main contributions to railway management were the development of adequate depreciation provision for rails and rolling stock, the introduction of internal controls on costing and pricing, and the extensive delegation of responsibility to divisional managers who would report regularly to senior staff at executive conferences. In essence, at a time when professional managers were rarely given much authority, Huish 'helped to promote the growth in stature of the salaried official within the large-scale company' by building a structure which relied to a significant extent on the role they played in running businesses (Gourvish, 1972; 260–7).

A crucial point to remember about railway management from the 1840s is that not only were professional managers placed in such important positions, there was also an extensive divorce between control and ownership within these businesses, giving the salaried officials unprecendented influence over all levels of management. In this context, one can discern an obvious contrast with the partnership system common among manufacturing concerns, because railway operations were all joint stock companies, and this would inevitably have precipitated a divorce between control and ownership. The rise of the joint stock company will be examined in section 2.4, but as far as the railways were concerned it resulted in salaried chief executives soon taking charge of strategic management, a divisional structure operating on the line-and-staff principle for functional tasks, and geographically dispersed managers performing the operational role. This created 'an executive elite, the first group of "corporation executives" to appear in British industry' (Gourvish, 1973; 290). On the other hand, it is important to note how the boards of directors were populated by members of the social elite, because shareholders regarded the aristocracy and prominent capitalists as reliable trustees of their proprietorial rights. This perpetuated what we described earlier as the 'gentlemen and players' structure which was typical of British business generally (Coleman, 1973), and it is clear that railway management was not always as advanced as some would have us believe. Even Huish experienced difficulties in overcoming the reluctance of directors to delegate responsibility down the line to functional managers (Gourvish, 1972; 167–82), illustrating how the so-called 'pioneers of modern corporate management' suffered from the traditional social distinctions within British managerial hierarchies.

Problems with railway management

There are certainly strong grounds for believing that the pioneering role of British railway management must be severely qualified. Hawke (1970; 360) has also demonstrated how they failed to increase efficiency from the 1850s, insisting on regional, as opposed to national, traffic strategies. This brings into question the ability of these new hierarchical structures to perform any better than their predecessors, and while in Huish's case he was no doubt responsible for significant innovations, these did not provide the organisational basis for commercial success. Chandler (1990; 253) has also argued that 'British railroad managers were less challenged to pioneer new methods of organisation and of internal control' than their American counterparts. On the other hand, one might question the specious nature of a comparison with American railway companies which had an average mileage ten times that of the British operations. Furthermore, Chandler (1990; 253) also admits that railway companies 'in Britain [created] the first managerial hierarchies with lower, middle, and top levels of management', revealing a contradictory element in his analysis. Most importantly, though, railway companies were clearly just as prone to the socio-cultural pressures affecting manufacturing firms, and there seems little doubt that as a consequence they were not as advanced as their American counterparts.

Another criticism levelled at this new breed of railway executives was their lack of mobility and consequent alleged resistance to further innovation, the vast majority having received only internal training (Hawke, 1970; 384). This immobility is certainly borne out by Gourvish (1973; 297–316), although he does show that a small number had diverse business backgrounds before entering the industry. More significantly, he also discovers that most chief executives were recruited from the upper middle classes and concludes that this bureaucratic elite was an extension of the existing social structure which dominated Britain, and British business as a whole, for much of this era. Scott (1984; 38–45) reinforces this view, emphasising how railway executives and directors were very much at the core of Britain's corporate and financial system on the eve of the First World War, as we shall see in chapter 4, and given the size of these businesses and their status this is not surprising. Indeed, their elite position isolated them from the rest of British industry, with only rare cases like J. S. Forbes and Felix Pole venturing extensively into other sectors.

By the 1890s, the larger railway companies were beginning to recognise some of the limitations of this highly introverted approach towards recruitment and training for senior management. In this context, the pioneer was George Gibb of the North Eastern Railway Co. (later to become the London & North Eastern Railway Co., in 1923), who introduced a scheme which contradicted many of the firmly-held assumptions within British academia (Gourvish, 1973; 295). Internal management training through apprenticeships had developed extensively among railway companies since the 1840s, but during the 1890s some executives realised the need to tap other sources for their talent, and Gibbs was the first to establish a formal link with an university, the London School of Economics (LSE). The British educational system was still dominated by an attitude which denied any role for vocational training, as we shall see in section 4.4, but the railway companies were able to use their considerable financial resources to convince academics that traditional biases ought to be replaced by a more utilitarian approach. Other companies soon copied this example, and by 1904 a Railway Department had been formed at the LSE (with railway money) while the Faculty of Commerce and Administration at Manchester University had also instituted lecture programmes for the same purpose (Keeble, 1992; 98, 104).

One must not overstate the significance of this venture into management education, in that it would only have reinforced the elitist nature of recruitment practices, rather than extend the social ambit within which they operated. Similarly, the impact on other sectors was extremely limited for many decades, and although the railway companies were pioneering a new approach towards management training few in British business accepted its relevance (Wilson, 1992; 1–15).

Other pioneers

The railways had consequently played an interesting role in the development of business organisation and management training during the nineteenth century, but it is important to note that the progress achieved was severely limited by various institutional features of the business scene. Likewise, one must remember that they were not alone in attempting to deal innovatively with the managerial challenges associated with this new era of industrial capitalism. Pollard (1965; 157) has claimed that 'the genius and experience of civil engineers were responsible for some of the most interesting developments in the genesis of modern management practice' up to the 1830s. He describes how they created their own Society in 1818 as a means of standardising practices within the industry and acquiring a more professional status. Admittedly, subcontracting featured prominently in this field, and the Society of Civil Engineers was principally concerned with technical matters, but these professionals would also perform many managerial duties like recruiting skilled workers, co-ordinating the supply of raw materials, completing accounts, and supervising the actual construction. Indeed, the term 'engineer' was often synonymous with 'manager' in some industries, most notably in the other network utilities emerging at that time, continuing a tradition started by the civil engineers in the eighteenth century which survived well into the twentieth.

An excellent example of this system at work was the provincial gas supply industry, during its first phase of development between 1812 and 1880 (Wilson, 1991; 3–12, 150–9). Gas undertakings were usually formed and financed by local businessmen who were keen to acquire a viable supply of the new, cheaper lighting medium for their premises, and in the early stages of an undertaking's existence the key decisions affecting prices and investment strategy would have been taken by a board of directors representing the main shareholders. At the same time, because these men were also often involved in other business activities, they had relatively little time to devote to the gas company after the initial stages of development, leaving management in the hands of an engineer, or managing engineer (Wilson, 1991; 121–41). Gas engineers were in fact responsible not only for technical operations, but also assembling the accounts, co-ordinating the supply of raw materials, and negotiating with the local authority over main-laying rights, and the board grew increasingly reliant on their advice. In fact, a similar management structure to that prevailing in the railway companies started to evolve in the larger supply operations, and professional gas engineers were clearly influencing decision-making at the functional, operational and strategic levels. This provides a good example of what Alford (1976; 25) calls 'diffused entrepreneurship', because while the company hierarchy might well indicate that the board of directors formulated strategy, in practice it was the engineer who was the real power in most network undertakings. By 1863, following the example of the civil engineers, a British Association of Gas Managers had been formed by the leading engineers in the industry, in an attempt to standardise routines and spread the benefits of work done in the more advanced undertakings. The industry relied largely on internal training for its technical skills, nepotism playing a key role in this field (Wilson, 1991; 156), but the emergence of a professional association (later to become the Institution of Gas Engineers, in 1883) demonstrated the status of these managers in a rapidly-expanding industry.

Conclusion

This brief study of the utility sector has demonstrated that the organisation of railway and gas companies looked very different from their counterparts in the manufacturing sector. One must remember the substantial social gulf which existed in all types of business separating the 'gentlemen' in the board of directors and the 'players' performing managerial tasks, and this clearly limited the extent to which the latter could streamline the organisation and introduce effective procedures. Nevertheless, significant innovations had been introduced by the utlities, and the railway companies especially were very much a part of the financial establishment. We must now go on to examine both the legal forms adopted by business and the methods of financing operations, because it is not yet clear why industry preferred partnerships, while utilities invariably used the joint stock company form. Size was obviously a key factor in this choice, while the legal environment was also influential, but in the next section it will become apparent how once again the business culture often played a determining role in this situation. This confirms further some of the arguments developed in section 2.1 with regard to the central importance of business culture, and in this context it is important to ask whether this created an in-built constraint on business expansion.

2.4   Business and long-term finance

In discussing the subject of business finance, it is vital first of all to differentiate between fixed and working capital: the former represents investment in buildings, machinery and other fixed assets, the latter a business's liquid resources required for keeping it running on a day-to-day basis (Mathias, 1979; 88–109). We shall be considering working capital in the next section, but it is important to note that the means of acquiring these two types of capital were often also distinct, and over this period a variety of institutions evolved to cater for them, often with a highly specialist bent which persisted for many decades. Indeed, perhaps the most interesting business development of the era was the emergence of a more formalised capital market, characterised by banks, stock exchanges, professional intermediaries, legal innovations, and a growing demand for securities from an investing class. On the other hand, one must not forget that an informal capital market, dominated by attorneys working in coffee houses and taverns, remained just as important for providing significant amounts of finance for a wide range of industries, indicating a lack of conformity within the business community as far as long-term business finance was concerned. Clearly, the financial scene was extremely varied, and the primary concern will be to establish whether or not all these changes were sufficient to prevent the emergence of a financial constraint on business expansion up to the mid-nineteenth century. Britain was the wealthiest economy in the world at that time, but this does not necessarily mean that either an adequate transfer mechanism existed which would distribute resources to those areas which required additional capital for their business operations, or that the attitudes towards finance provided an opportunity to exploit the innovations. Opinions vary on this subject, but it is apparent that the traditions and attitudes established by the mid-nineteenth century were to have a lasting impact on British business, and a full analysis is essential if we are to gain a clearer insight into this crucial aspect of business history.

Attitudes towards joint stock status

It has already been established that the partnership was the basic organising principle in British manufacturing industry up to the mid-nineteenth century, but it is not yet clear why the joint stock company was used so sparingly, nor whether this could have acted as a constraint on business expansion. After all, the joint stock company provides the significant advantage of limiting the owners' liability for any losses to the amount actually invested in the business. On the other hand, a partnership provides no such immunity, and each member is in danger of losing all his assets if the firm is bankrupted. The former can also spread the risks involved in business creation among a large number of shareholders, and as it is a legal entity it has the power to sue debtors in the courts, illustrating how much more security is granted to these bodies when compared with the legally precarious partnership.

Some improvisation with a hybrid form of company was attempted by businessmen towards the end of the eighteenth century, but not until the 1860s were many industrialists willing to exploit these advantages, after a series of changes in the law. Even then, though, (see section 4.5) a peculiar form of joint stock company emerged in Britain which owed much to the prevailing attitudes towards ownership and control, emphasising the importance of linking what we said earlier about the business culture with the general pattern of business finance.

The concept of limited liability first gained widespread support simultaneously in France and England during the late-seventeenth century, arousing interest among investors as they searched for means of exploiting the expanding commercial opportunities of that era. By the 1690s, the joint stock company was widely utilised as a vehicle for the bouts of speculation which rocked London and Paris over the following thirty years. It is important to emphasise, though, how investment affairs were conducted on an informal basis at this time, with the coffee-houses of Exchange Alley and its environs in the City of London acting as the geographical centre of this activity (Morgan and Thomas, 1962; 35). In addition, many of the schemes floated there were of a highly dubious character, including companies for importing broomsticks from Germany and even extracting silver from lead, but none excited the coffee-house regulars more than the South Sea Trading Co. and the whole series of speculative 'bubbles' it inspired (Carswell, 1960; 7).

The South Sea Bubble and the 1720 Act

Investors were generally captivated by the illusion of riches which the South Sea trade generated, and considerable interest was expressed when in 1711 a scheme was hatched to incorporate all those holding the estimated £9 million worth of government debts into a company which would exploit that region. In fact, this was a brilliant political manoevre by the Lord High Treasurer, Robert Harley, who was especially concerned with the government's mushrooming debts, but 'as a business proposition [the company] was from the first a sham', and not a single director had any experience of trade with South America (Carswell, 1960; 47–9). The whole episode smacks of dubious political and financial machinations at the highest levels of government, but to speculators the South Sea Co. represented an opportunity to float more 'bubble' schemes, and in 1719–20 a total of £220 million was raised for 190 equally questionable ventures. When this mania finally subsided, and stock prices fell to fifteen per cent of their peak levels (Hasson, 1932; 131), a secret parliamentary committee was appointed to unravel the complex web of intrigue, and after discovering serious accounting irregularities in the South Sea Co.'s books, not to mention political corruption, strong action was recommended to prevent such events recurring (Hunt, 1936; 6–9). This resulted in the introduction of what is now known as the 1720 Bubble Act, severely limiting access to the joint stock company form for the next century.

It is important to stress that the 1720 Bubble Act was passed 'to protect the South Sea's rise, and not in consequence of its fall', mindful as were its influential political supporters of both the huge amounts of money they had invested in the venture, and the need to prevent the emergence of competition (Carswell, 1960; 114–5). The Act was specifically designed to make joint stock company formation as difficult and as expensive as possible, stipulating that, unless firms were incorporated by Royal Charter or private Act of Parliament, they had no right either to transfer their shares or have more than six partners. Large firms could clearly have afforded the legal costs of such a process, but because parliament now had total control over company creation the South Sea Co. was assured of survival, and indeed it struggled on until 1854. On the other hand, for all other businessmen limited liability was from 1720 a luxury acquired at a considerable cost. The Bubble Act was a panic measure, but because it remained on the statute books for the next 105 years, attitudes towards investment were undoubtedly fashioned by those legal restrictions, forcing the vast majority of enterprises to rely on the partnership form.

In fact, the actual impact of this legislation has been hotly disputed. Pressnell (1956; 19) argues that, because personal relationships were at the basis of most investment decisions in the eighteenth century, limited liability would not have been popular. Ashton (1955; 102) has also claimed that the Bubble Act was largely irrelevant, in that large-scale industry did develop after the 1770s, regardless of any limitations on company formation. Du Bois (1938; 16) feels that an 'opportunity to experiment' with other forms of organisation had been presented to businessmen, leading ultimately to the reliance on partnerships. On the other hand, one might well argue that not only did the Bubble Act 'exercise a deterrent psychological effect upon company promotion' (Hunt, 1936; 9), it also *forced* the average businessmen to try alternative methods of financing their ventures. After 1720 it would cost at least £600 in legal expenses to form a joint stock company (Wilson, 1991; 65, 102), and (even in the early-nineteenth century) as average fixed investment in industry would probably not have exceeded a few thousand pounds few were willing to pay so much for the privilege of incorporation. However, the key factor in this context would have been the extent to which socio-cultural attitudes allowed businessmen to exploit this legal device, because as the eighteenth century progressed (see section 2.1) a highly individualistic philosophy pervaded the middle classes, and this would have severely limited the horizons of investment attitudes. There were clearly a growing number of firms in the iron, textile and brewing industries which had capital assets in excess of £20,000 (Crouzet, 1972; 199), yet they were just as likely to be partnerships as their smaller counterparts. In effect, Pressnell is correct when he emphasises the strength of personal relationships in this respect, and one must conclude that the 1720 Bubble Act was simply one of the factors which prevented the emergence of limited liability over the next 150 years, the individualistic business culture being by far the most significant constraint on this trend.

The City and industry

Another important consideration in this debate is the relationship between financial institutions located in the City of London and British industry, because it is not entirely clear whether either had any interest in working with the other. The speculative mania of 1719–1920 was largely a London affair, and over the next 150 years the stockjobbers (or stockbrokers, as we now know them) and major financial institutions located in the capital were primarily interested in dealing in fixed-interest securities associated with either state funding or the mortgage market. The dealing in coffee houses and taverns located around Exchange Alley was beginning to produce standard conventions well before a stock exchange was built in 1773 on the site of one of the most important coffee houses, Old Jonathan's. This, however, did nothing to extend the range of interests pursued by London financiers (Morgan & Thomas, 1962; 42), and indeed stockjobbers generally enjoyed a very poor reputation at this time, because of their alleged role in fuelling several speculative crises, especially in the 1770s (Bowen, 1992; 38–53). Later (see section 2.5), the large banks and merchanting firms which featured prominently in the City of London were to play a major role in the development of an extensive trade credit system for both internal and external trade. This slowly allowed a greater degree of integration between business and finance as the eighteenth century progressed (Buchinsky and Polak, 1993; 1–18), but providing long-term capital for industry was definitely not within the City's brief at this time, establishing a gulf which persisted well into the nineteenth century, and possibly beyond (Kennedy, 1987; 148).

Self-finance

The isolationist approach of the City should not, of course, be regarded as the only reason why industry did not receive much financial support from those quarters, because when it came to fixed investment, bearing in mind the individualistic culture so popular in the eighteenth and nineteenth centuries, most businessmen preferred to rely on either their own resources or those provided by people they knew well. This tendency would have precluded any formal relationship with financiers based in London, and right up to the First World War raising fixed investment for manufacturing industry was predominantly characterised by its personal, local and informal nature. In the first place, most businesses were established with money accumulated from previous occupations, a trend facilitated by the heavy middle class preponderance among the ranks of the early industrialists, the bulk of whom already had access to sufficient capital (Crouzet, 1985; 126). One should also note that, with the possible exception of the iron industry, the threshold to entry into industrial production was generally low up to the 1830s, 'especially in the textile industry, where even the largest production units were small, the plant rudimentary and inexpensive' (Crouzet, 1972; 164). Of course, this should not blind us to the high levels of risk involved in making this transition, and Hoppitt (1987; 176) demonstrates that: 'Bankruptcy was an eighteenth century growth industry'. The reasons for this high level of insecurity will be examined later, but it emphasises an important feature of the business scene which reinforced the general unwillingness to rely too heavily on outsiders. When it came to expanding capacity or renewing machinery, the owner-managers were also generally averse to diluting their control by selling parts of the business to outsiders, indicating again how internal resources were utilised to the full. This is well described by Crouzet (1972; 188), who illustrates with a wide range of case-studies the 'overwhelming predominance of self-finance, [with firms] ploughing back immediately, regularly and almost automatically the greater part, or even the whole of their profits'.

Self-reliance was clearly a key feature of the business psyche at this time, affecting attitudes towards investment and management. One might argue that this would only serve to create a dilemma, because entrepreneurs could be faced with a difficult decision about future development if profits proved insufficient, but as we saw earlier with regard to organisational challenges the contemporary solution was to recruit partners for the resources they might have to offer. Invariably, though, these partners would come from a network of contacts built up through either kinship and religious affiliations, or through mercantile connections in the immediate community (Crouzet, 1972; 168–75, 191). In the case of certain religious groupings, for example the Quakers, Prior & Kirby (1993; 2) have pointed out how their 'family-based networks' provided both an 'internalised source of commercial support and advice', and a supply of capital. This re-emphasises how the highly localised and personal nature of relationships was the bedrock of eighteenth and nineteenth century business organisation and finance, highlighting once again the central importance of what Casson (1993; 42) has called the 'high-trust culture' which would appear to have been a key reason why the small and highly specialised firms of that era were able to survive. Of course, a major concern for businessmen using this system was the latent danger of a partner withdrawing funds for either consumption or investment elsewhere. This certainly occurred in the West Riding worsted industry, where significant use of partnerships was made (Hudson, 1986; 249–55), but such dangers would appear to have been a risk worth taking for most owner-managers with a preference for personal negotiations.

Attorneys

In this context, it is vital to emphasise the role played in local networks by 'the familiar and trusted figure of their local attorney' who frequently acted as the intermediary in the mobilisation of investment funds (Hudson, 1986; 212–7). Anderson (1969; 83) has even described the typical early-nineteenth century Lancashire attorney's office as 'in all important respects, a capital market', such was the profession's significance in this field, and their knowledge of both the law and the local community was ideally suited to serving a general requirement for additional funds. They would have operated where many businessmen spent much of their spare time, in a town's coffee houses and taverns, rather than in their own offices, but this highly informal *modus operandi* clearly served them well until the late-nineteenth century. In the establishment of provincial gas supply companies, for example, attorneys exploited their extensive local networks of contacts to raise finance (Wilson, 1991; 69–73), and in major manufacturing industries they were equally important, demonstrating in graphic form just how crucial these intermediaries proved to be in the development of British business at that time.

These personal, localised and informal characteristics of industrial capital formation were, of course, entirely rational in the context of a society still hampered by poor communications and a highly regional economic structure. Fixed capital requirements were, in any case, still relatively low up to the 1830s, allowing the perpetuation of this system, and with the 1720 Bubble Act severely curtailing access to the joint stock company form, partnerships acted as the most effective means of bringing in additional resources. Only from the 1860s do we see any decisive changes in industrial fixed investment practices, a development which owed much to a series of significant changes to both the formal capital market and company law. Most authorities attribute these innovations to the activity associated with the creation of railway companies and joint stock banks from the 1830s (Thomas, 1973; 8), but in fact they were the culmination of a much longer process of experimentation which can be traced back to the canal-building of the late-eighteenth century and the establishment of other utility ventures after 1810. By 1800, over 100 canal Acts had been passed, and as most of these undertakings used the joint stock company form as a means of raising large amounts of capital, this familiarised large numbers of businessmen with such practices (Hunt, 1936; 10). One must emphasise that the process of canal company formation and financing was an essentially local affair, with prominent attorneys frequently acting as the subscription agent and much of the capital coming from businessmen who would have lived close to the venture. Ward (1974; 97) has consequently claimed that this activity did 'not occupy an important place in the development of a formally organised market for capital'. At the same time, the growing popularity among the middle classes of investing in joint stock companies created a climate which facilitated the reform of company law and established a growing market for securities.

The reform of company law

One of the key innovations arising out of this surge in company creation was the growing use of an unincorporated form of organisation, by which subscribers would sign a deed of settlement as a means of securing all the advantages of joint stock status. This instrument contravened the regulations laid down in the 1720 Bubble Act, which insisted on the acquisition of an Act of

Parliament or Royal Charter before joint stock company status could be bestowed, and consequently it remained 'in a "grey" area of the law' (Cottrell, 1980; 39). Several unincorporated ventures were actually deemed illegal by the courts between 1807 and 1825, but because of its growing use among industrial and utility ventures the unincorporated form 'was one of the main lines of advance towards freedom of incorporation' (Hunt, 1936; 29). Certainly, many of the provincial gas supply companies created after 1815 demonstrated the significant advantages attached to this form of organisation (Wilson, 1991; 73–7), adding to the groundswell of opinion which culminated in the 1825 repeal of the 1720 Bubble Act.

In spite of all these innovations in the process of company formation, a well-organised market for securities with a mature legal and banking framework had yet to emerge. Even the 1825 reform of company law was actually only a nominal breakthrough in extending the availability of joint stock company status, because firms still required an Act of Parliament before limited liability could be granted. This particular regulation was not dropped until 1856, in spite of further changes to company law in 1834 and 1838, and again in 1844 (Cottrell, 1979; 39–54). The 1844 Companies Act was important in introducing the concept of registering with the Board of Trade's newly-created Registrar of Companies, but only the 1856 Act finally removed the last major hurdle to the widespread use of what was increasingly recognised as an effective form of security for both investors and businessmen. Notwithstanding these reforms, there is little evidence that up to 1860 industrialists in general rushed to exploit the company form, and (see section 4.5) its use remained the preserve of large banking and utility operations which had been principally responsible for stimulating the changes in company law (Cottrell, 1980; 39–45).

Although classical economists advocating complete freedom from legal restrictions on trade had played their part in the debates leading up to the 1856 reform of company law, in the main parliament had been responding to the economic and industrial realities of an expansionary era in opening up access to limited liability. Of particular importance were the 'railway manias' of the mid-1830s and mid-1840s, because, more than any other investment trend of that era, railway company creation and financing had a considerable impact on investment practices. Joint stock banking, made possible by an Act of 1826, and the extensive use of the company form among insurance and trading ventures, undoubtedly contributed to the movement, but it was 'railway mania' which resulted in the emergence of a national market for securities (Hunt, 1936; 105–7). We have already seen how railways pioneered the modern form of corporate management, but their contribution to investment practices was just as significant in prompting the establishment of both provincial stock exchanges and a specialised press, and finally forging a national market in company securities. Total railway share capital amounted to £126 million by 1847, dwarfing the levels of investment in cotton and iron, and while much of the activity was initially concentrated in the provinces, by the mid-1840s the London Stock Exchange was beginning to take a greater interest. This coincided with the emergence of a national financial press (transported by the speedier trains) which linked activities in London and the provincial stock exchanges, providing the increased number of people willing to invest in such activities with more information on share prices (Reed, 1969; 179–83).

Conclusion

The reform of company law between 1825 and 1856, the creation of stock exchanges in major provincial centres like Manchester (1836), Liverpool (1836), Glasgow (1844), Edinburgh (1844), Leeds (1845), Bristol (1845), Birmingham (1845) and Leicester (1845), and the evolution of a national market in company securities, illustrates how in the first half of the nineteenth century investment practices were substantially revised. One might also mention in this context the existence of almost 540 provincial stock-broking firms by 1847, compared to just seven in 1830 (Killick & Thomas, 1970; 96), demonstrating the growing level of sophistication in the capital market, compared to the highly informal systems which had dominated up to the 1830s. Nevertheless, until much later in the century, much of the finance raised for British industry continued to come from traditional sources, and especially from internal funds. Jefferys (1938; 138) has claimed that the 'day when a Watt had to find his Boulton had gone', but while in theory this was correct, in practice most businessmen clung to the practices which had been prevalent throughout the eighteenth century. The banking and utility sectors might well have completely overhauled the methods of company formation and financing, but even in the 1860s partnerships and ploughed-back capital provided the bulk of industrial finance, emphasising the continued strength of individualism in British business. This demonstrates the dangers inherent in generalising about trends, because organisationally and financially very different practices were pursued in the various sectors of the economy, and the dichotomy in practice persisted well into the twentieth century.

2.5 Liquidity and the financial environment

The discussion of how British businessmen financed their long-term requirements has revealed an enormous variety of practices which evolved as responses to the various legal, institutional and practical problems of the era. What is not yet clear, though, is the degree to which these techniques were capable of providing sufficient capital. Crouzet (1972; 204–17) has described in great detail how the process of capital formation was discontinuous by nature, with major surges depending on such factors as wars, interest rate levels, demand for particular products, and new technological innovations. These exogenous factors would clearly have had a crucial bearing on investment, but the ability to raise enough capital to exploit opportunities would have been equally important, calling into question the efficiency with which finance could be mobilised. Evidence on business survival rates would appear to indicate that 'longevity was the exception rather than the rule' at this time (Cottrell, 1980; 35), largely because profits were difficult to make in the early stages, and as competition was often extremely intense among the large number of small, specialised firms, a high turnover usually characterised business populations (Hoppit, 1987; 176–8). This consequently changes the emphasis of any discussion concerning business finance away from fixed investment towards the need to maintain short-term liquidity, because a firm could conceivably survive without the former, but it would inevitably collapse if the latter proved impossible to find.

The importance of securing adequate short-term funding is now recognised as the key ingredient ensuring business survival. Hoppit (1987; 178) concluded his study of eighteenth century bankruptcy by noting that: 'Changing patterns of liquidity were crucial and businessmen were always preoccupied with what might be called the "problem of credit"'. We noted earlier that the threshold of entry into most industries remained low up to the early-nineteenth century, but because this claim only related to fixed capital requirements it ignored the considerable demand for working capital which remained a key ingredient in business finance. Indeed, Edwards (1967; 213–4) has estimated that in the cotton textile industry the ratio between working and fixed capital would typically have been 3:1. In the Yorkshire worsted industry rarely did fixed capital account for more than forty-five per cent of a business's total capital, and often it was as low as twenty-five per cent (Hudson, 1986; 48–52). This reveals the tremendous pressures imposed on businessmen by their asset structure, and it is clear that, while few looked outside their firm for fixed investment purposes, they willingly relied on several external sources for working capital.

Liquidity and the 'web of credit'

Access to adequate credit was clearly the key feature of business finance in this period of industrialisation, as entrepreneurs struggled to fund the substantial increase in inventories and wage bills. Again, the difficulties would be at their most acute in a firm's early years, given that credit was granted largely on the basis of trust and personal knowledge, while once established, businessmen would find it necessary to extend credit in order to fuel continued growth in the trade. This is best demonstrated by Hudson (1986; 182–207), who shows in great detail how crucial this 'credit matrix' was in the development of a highly competitive West Yorkshire woollen industry up to 1850, with commission agents, merchants, putting-out manufacturers and factory-owners all participating in the system. There might have been severe short-term fluctuations in the availability of credit, creating a degree of instability which materially affected the smaller ventures in particular, but eventually a stronger system evolved out of these difficulties, reflecting what was happening at the national level.

It is clear that what Pollard (1972; 154) has described as the 'web of credit' became a permanent and vital feature of the business scene from the mid-eighteenth century, and at the centre of this 'web' was the 'high-trust culture' which has already been stressed as a key ingredient in the business scene (Casson, 1993; 42). One cannot claim that this 'web' extended nationally during the eighteenth century, and Neal (1994; 173–81) overstates the case for an integrated system. Nevertheless, at the level of the region there developed markets for both fixed and working capital which bolstered family-based partnerships at crucial times in their life-cycle. These networks used the bill of exchange (now more commonly referred to as the commercial bill) as the main instrument of credit, and during the eighteenth century this became a widespread form of tender at both local and national levels. The bill of exchange was, in effect, a credit note which could be discounted after a given period, varying between two and six months, and it developed in popularity because of the acute shortage of legal exchange media at that time. In the Manchester cotton industry, these terms were extended to as long as eight months, largely because a 'mutual credit club . . . permeated the industry and the region', and while credit contracted in periods of crisis, for example after the 1793 banking crash, it was soon revived as a central plank of industrialists' operations (Cottrell, 1980; 22). Most importantly, this system would allow businessmen the opportunity to reinvest any profits into the business, instead of tieing up scarce resources in stocks, facilitating the process of self-generated fixed investment.

The emergence of country banking and national links

While merchants and commodity brokers were clearly essential cogs in this credit mechanism, the whole system revolved around one of the major financial innovations of the age, country banking. The Charter of the Bank of England, passed in 1697, had granted this institution a monopoly of joint stock banking in England and Wales, limiting its rivals to a maximum of six partners and severely restricting the emergence of an embryonic banking system. By 1750, there were only twelve banks outside London, and those in the City were highly specialised businesses which dealt mainly in credit and mortgages. However, the increased use of bills of exchange, combined with the acute shortage of legal tender, could not be sustained without adequate institutional backing, and this stimulated the establishment of almost 700 country banks by 1825. Pressnell (1956; 14–17, 23–6) has described this movement in considerable detail, illustrating how industrialists themselves were among the main groups responsible for opening what were often small, highly localised banking operations which served specific requirements associated with liquidity and credit formation. The north west of England was perhaps the least well served by the new movement up to 1800, but this region had already developed an extensive market in trade credit, and in any case most towns there did have their own banks by the 1820s.

Apart from the crucial role played by country banks in discounting bills of exchange and providing credit to local businessmen, another important concomitant of their creation was the link forged with London discount houses, the specialist institutions which dealt in credit. Indeed, from the early-nineteenth century country banks became increasingly dependent upon the more ample resources of their London connections, given the inherent instability of a provincial credit network which relied mainly on local resources. This resulted in the emergence of a national credit market which by the 1830s allowed the transfer of funds from agricultural to industrial regions with relative ease, reinforcing a system which had already become the financial foundation-stone of British business (Cottrell, 1980; 16). Furthermore, a growing amount of evidence is now available to demonstrate that local banks not only funded the trade credit system, they also provided longer-term loans which were used for fixed investment. The latter sometimes took the form of rolled-over credits which were continually renewed for periods of up to thirty years (Crouzet, 1972; 193). In regions like South Wales (John, 1950; 43–9), West Yorkshire (Hudson, 1986; 218–23), and Lancashire (Pressnell, 1956; 291), long-term lending was standard practice (Cottrell, 1980; 14–5). One cannot quantify the exact importance of bank loans to industrial finance, because of the paucity of evidence now available, but we are left with the clear impression of a symbiotic relationship between the two sectors. As Hudson (1986; 223) has concluded from her study of the West Yorkshire woollen industry: 'By discounting bills and granting overdrafts and short-term loans, banks financed the movement of goods and production of commodities'. On the whole, country banks were 'credit banks', and they performed a capital-servicing (rather than a capital-creating) function which was vital for the development of British business (Collins, 1991; 25–9).

We noted earlier that, while much of the long-term capital going into British industry came from internal sources, any market for this form of finance which existed was essentially informal and localised. On the other hand, as far as working capital was concerned, London financiers and provincial businessmen had developed a closer relationship through the country banking and credit system, and as working capital was far more important than fixed at this time then clearly tremendous benefits were being derived from such contacts. This substantially refutes the claims of those

(Gerschenkron, 1966; 15) who have argued that the main financial institutions 'failed' British industry, because the banking system was part of a national capital market which provided the type of finance required by its main customers. Dickson (1967) has claimed that a 'financial revolution' occurred in early eighteenth century England, based on three pillars – state funding, the mortgage market and overseas trade credit. This resulted in the development of a complex structure of services, without which the trade credit system just described could never have prospered as extensively as it did. As we have already noted, Neal (1994; 173–81) overstates the central role of the London institutions, because regional differences still existed well into the nineteenth century. Similarly, the overwhelming predominance of government funding, particularly in times of war, could have led to some 'crowding out' of other activities, for example in the 1790s (Buchinsky & Polak, 1993; 18), further undermining the centrality of trade credit.

Joint stock banks

In 1826 the authorities attempted to strengthen the system further by extending to all banks the privilege of joint stock status foremerly preserved only for the Bank of England. This reform was a response to the financial crisis of 1825–6, when over ninety banks in England and Wales were obliged to suspend payments after a sudden and large withdrawal of funds by depositors. Previously, country banks had only been allowed to have a maximum of six partners, but access to joint stock status encouraged local businessmen to build more ambitious banking enterprises, and while the reform did not prevent liquidity crises it would appear that the British banking system was much stronger thereafter (Hunt, 1936; 50, 71). One must emphasise, however, that most of the joint stock banks, like their earlier counterparts, were essentially localised affairs which were closely tied in to the prosperity of their local business community (Collins, 1991; 24). Indeed, as Jones (1978; 165–83) demonstrates, the substantial expansion of Manchester's cotton industry in the second quarter of the nineteenth century was responsible for the creation of eight joint stock banks in that town between 1828 and 1836, and these institutions helped finance a 250 per cent increase in raw cotton imports.

The joint stock banks were clearly an important refinement to the earlier country banking system, but it is important to remember that the latter were by no means extinguished after 1826, because even by 1875 there were still 236 of them, compared to 122 of the former (Collins, 1991; 28). In fact, the 1844 Bank Charter Act severely limited the number of joint stock bank promotions, by stipulating that new enterprises should have a minimum capital of £100,000 divided into shares of at least £100. This was a further attempt to strengthen the system, and while in the mid-1850s two joint stock banks formed under the auspices of the 1844 Act actually collapsed, banking was steadily becoming a more dependable service (Cottrell, 1980; 33–4). The 122 joint stock banks of 1875 had by then opened 1,364 branches, compared to the 595 of the 236 country banks, illustrating how a more extensive network was beginning to emerge. This further facilitated the flow of credit around a business world which relied on this form of finance as its very lifeblood. Again, one must re-emphasise their role as predominantly 'credit banks'. Some were willing to lend long-term, but it is important to remember that only a small demand for fixed capital had emerged by the mid-nineteenth century, limiting the bankers' role to capital-servicing.

The acceptance houses

A further excellent illustration of this system at work was the manner in which the new 'acceptance' houses, largely operating out of London, stepped in to provide credit for the overseas trading activities of British industrialists (Chapman, 1984; 1–38). London had become the premier centre of international trade in the eighteenth century, ousting its European rivals like Amsterdam and Hamburg, and the leading commission merchants who controlled this activity were by the 1820s being converted into commission bankers. This transformation occurred principally as a result of the growing reliance of industrialists on the willingness of these merchants to 'accept' bills of exchange – hence the name 'acceptance' house – providing exporters with the credit to trade in overseas markets. Some of the more prominent industrialists had been encroaching on mercantile functions from the 1780s, in their search for export markets, but they soon realised how expensive this could be, especially in the more difficult trading conditions of the Napoleonic Wars. They also recognised the advantages of gaining credit from the international merchants who were coming to dominate overseas trade, resulting in a greater degree of specialisation by both parties. Principally of emigre origin, firms like the Rothschilds, Barings, Brown, Shipley & Co., Kleinworts, and Peabodys were elevated to powerful positions in the trade credit network (Chapman, 1984; 10–12), particularly as exporting was then a risky and expensive venture. To receive full payment for goods exported to North America, for example, could take up to two years, indicating just how vital was the credit provided by these increasingly influential houses. This resulted in a growing reliance on specialist merchants, and they provided not only credit, but also a wide range of contacts through the teams of commission agents they employed in overseas markets. The implications of this system for British overseas marketing will be examined in section 4.1, but clearly for industrialists who were anxious to minimise both overhead costs and the risks associated with exporting, acceptance houses provided an attractive service.

Conclusion

These acceptance houses are now better known as the merchant banks which dominate the City of London, but they had grown to prominence by taking the financial risks associated with exporting (Roberts, 1993; 22–5). Hudson (1986; 173–4) demonstrates that it was only from the 1830s that these changes occurred in the West Yorkshire woollen industry, but regardless of timing one can claim that acceptance houses became another vital component in the 'web of credit' which had evolved during this initial period of industrialisation. It is too easy to exaggerate the degree of stability in the credit and banking system, and the high incidence of bankruptcy and business failure throughout this period reminds us that what Hoppitt (1987; 178) called 'the problem of credit' remained a constant threat. The term 'slaughterhouse' also came into common use during the 1830s to describe the ruthlessness with which some commission merchants and banks dealt with their clients in difficult trading periods (Chapman, 1979; 65: Hudson, 1986; 177), and recurrent financial crises frequently rocked the money markets. Nevertheless, it was a system which provided the much-needed credit for British businessmen, and this allowed them the opportunity to sink internally-generated capital into fixed assets, revealing the mutually-supportive nature of the continually-evolving financial networks.

2.6   British business by mid-century

It is clear from what we have seen in the last two sections that the financial traditions and institutions which evolved between the early-eighteenth and mid-nineteenth centuries encouraged and facilitated the survival of a highly individualistic business culture. In the first place, company law restricted access to the joint stock company form between 1720 and 1856, by making it prohibitively expensive to exploit its advantages, forcing entrepreneurs to rely primarily on partnerships as the abiding principle of business organisation. The poorly-developed state of the early-eighteenth century capital markets also made it more advisable to rely on internal resources for fixed investment requirements, although informal and localised networks were created by local attorneys in response to the need for additional finance. Much of the capital required over this period was, however, in the form of working capital, prompting the creation of an extensive 'web of credit' which involved networks of industrialists, merchants, banks and acceptance houses, and access to these funds reinforced the tendency among businessmen to reinvest most of their profits. The main financial institutions might well have been capital-servicers, rather than capital-creators, but in an individualistic business culture this proved most appropriate. Self-reliant businessmen in the 1850s were consequently allowed to continue the practices which had been prevalent 150 years earlier, but having noted this one must question why such a high failure rate characterised the business community at that time. What was the attitude of contemporaries towards expansion, and how did they deal with a trading environment which, while being free of extensive foreign competition, was undoubtedly harsh and uncertain? Answers to these questions are essential if we are to understand fully both the businessmen of this era and the traditions and values which they took into the late-nineteenth century.

Business attitudes

A popular view of this early period of industrialisation has been that businessmen were inherently entrepreneurial and expansionist, and that continued technological innovation would result in a process of concentration. These views were understandable, given that the use of steam power was increasing, new machines and processes were being introduced, and firms employing in excess of 1,000 workers had appeared by the 1810s and 1820s. On the other hand, Gatrell (1977; 97) has shown that in the Lancashire cotton industry 'a familiar pyramidical hierarchy' characterised by a few large firms and a much larger number of small and medium-sized ventures was just as much a feature of the 1840s as thirty years earlier. This is surprising, because that period had seen both the construction of large steam-powered mills and the introduction of self-acting mule-spinning machinery and power-loom weaving, all of which were claimed to have produced substantial economies of scale for cotton producers. Nevertheless, Gatrell (1977; 106) noticed 'a curious reticence about the advantages of expansion' among cotton manufacturers, revealing a much more cautious attitude towards investment and innovation than previously acknowledged. A symbiotic relationship between small and larger producers consequently emerged out of this insecurity, with the latter relying on the former as an alternative to adding new production facilities, thereby reducing the financial risks attendant on expansion.

Although some revision of Gatrell's thesis has produced a rather different picture of the cotton industry's pyrammidical hierarchy, his research has significantly revised our understanding of business conventions during this period. In fact, as Lloyd-Jones & Le Roux (1980; 72–81) have demonstrated, Gatrell ignored the substantial difference between factories and firms, leading to some misunderstandings about the exact rate of progress in the pyramidical hierarchy. Focusing only on the Manchester cotton industry, they show how, of the ninety firms examined, sixty shared part of a factory in 1815, while by 1825 there were only eleven operating in this fashion. It is also apparent that size was no guarantee of longevity, with one-third of the top twenty-two firms disappearing between 1833 and 1848. However, it is the increase in minimum efficient size which most interests Lloyd-Jones & Le

Roux, and their evidence shows that the optimum size clearly rose from fifty employees to 150. This converts Gatrell's pyramid into more of a diamond shape (with a flattened bottom and an extended midriff), emphasising the crucial importance of switching business historians' attentions away from the large-scale firms towards those in the medium size range, where the significant changes were occurring.

Another feature of Gatrell's (1977; 100–3) work was his claim that the ratio between working and fixed capital was moving away from the generally accepted 3:1 relationship towards a closer parity, but Chapman (1979; 49–69) has successfully refuted this by reaffirming the conventional view. Indeed, the expansion of credit facilities through the creation of joint stock banks after 1826 and the emergence of acceptance houses in London for the supply of overseas credit were direct responses to the high level of demand for this form of finance. On the other hand, Chapman does concede that, as one prominent Manchester banker (Lewis Loyd) noted at the time: 'Moderate capital and cautious habits do best'. Once again, it was the access to sufficient credit which was the most prominent factor dictating such a stance, and especially for those manufacturers entering the highly precarious export trade. As Chapman (1979; 66) concludes:

> A small firm might grow within the connexions of an established concern, but to grow beyond this size meant breaking into the intensely competitive domestic market, or into the speculative overseas market, and most lacked the means or connexions to do so.

The 'curious reticence about the advantages of expansion' noticed by Gatrell (1977; 106) was consequently forced on to cotton-masters by the vagaries characteristic of the early nineteenth century commodity and financial markets, and the penalty for ignoring conventional wisdom concerning these facts of business life was bankruptcy. Caution and a reluctance to rely excessively on outsiders were the by-words of these Lancashire cotton manufacturers, and it is clear that in many other industries exactly the same conditions and attitudes prevailed (Payne, 1988; 29–33).

Constraints on expansion

This discussion allows us to draw some conclusions concerning the constraints imposed on business development up to the mid-nineteenth century, because one is left with the clear impression of an embryonic system which was struggling to adapt to the demands of industrial capitalism. Access to adequate finance was evidently a major factor, and the 'web of credit' and all its institutional manifestations was one of the most outstanding developments arising out of the need for liquidity, while cost accounting also appeared once industrialists realised the importance of accuracy in calculating prices. Above all, though, an intense individualism pervaded the business scene, and this introverted philosophy, while often born of necessity, dictated that each firm would be an entity in itself, with outside interference in management or ownership regarded as unwelcome. This created an in-built constraint on growth, and while at this stage British businessmen were competing mainly with similar types and sizes of firms, later in the century large-scale foreign enterprises would highlight in stark form the weaknesses inherent in this approach to control and finance.

Undoubtedly, the business culture was what Elbaum and Lazonick (1986; 1–15) have categorised as one of the principal 'institutional rigidities' which hindered British industrial competitiveness in the long term. It was a culture which was responsible for the atomistic structure which characterised most British markets, with large numbers of highly specialised firms competing extensively across a wide range of products. In this context businessmen were simply pursuing one of the three strategies identified by Porter (1990; 33–7) – cost leadership, product differentiation, or market segmentation – as a means of coping with the vagaries of an insecure trading environment. This increasing specialisation allowed a firm to secure a foothold in the market-place, but at the same time, as Payne (1988; 40–3) argues, owner-managers were also taking a conscious decision to 'restrain the growth of the firm within the limits of existing managerial resources'. It was a system which reinforced the already strong beliefs in individualism, and this perpetuated a managerial constraint on the rate of growth of the firm which is inevitable in family firms reliant entirely on internal managerial and financial resources.

Marketing and distribution

One obvious consequence of the small-firm mentality pervading British business up to the mid-nineteenth century was the failure to develop dedicated and extensive marketing and sales networks. This is an important theme of Chapman's works (1979; 66: 1984; 9–15: 1992; 129–66) on mercantile activity, which stresses how in response to the enormous risks associated with exporting, manufacturers soon came to rely on merchants for their overseas trading and credit. This relationship resulted in the emergence of powerful acceptance houses which dominated Britain's export trade, not simply because of the credit they granted to firms, but also because of the commission agents they employed in overseas markets as intermediaries between supplier and customer. The full implication of this indirect method of selling abroad will be examined in section 4.1, but while for cash-starved industrialists it was a system which had undoubted advantages, one can discern here a dangerous tendency to subcontract the vital function of marketing, reducing the ability of individual firms to detect and follow customer requirements. On the other hand, one must understand that the pressure to integrate forwards into marketing and distribution were minimal at this time, leading to a highly specialised system which became one of the hall-marks of British industrial capitalism.

It is generally true to claim that by the mid-nineteenth century much British selling and marketing was conducted at a distance through specialist intermediaries like brokers, merchants and agents (Chapman, 1992; 54–5). Outstanding examples of innovative businessmen like Josiah Wedgwood are difficult to find, because few of his counterparts introduced the kind of direct selling techniques that he pioneered in selling high quality pottery (McKendrick, 1960). Wedgwood was the first to utilise the services of for-eign agents directly tied in to his enterprise, while in the domestic market he opened salesrooms and appointed travelling salesmen to overcome any diffi-culties his aristocratic customers might have experienced in securing goods from the Etruria pottery in Staffordshire. Rarely, however, did contempo-raries imitate him, and although Boulton & Watt appear to have used agents to open up new export markets for their steam engine (Tann & Aitken, 1992; 202–5) few recognised the advantages inherent in such techniques. Payne (1988; 40–3) has also noted how specialisation severely limited the ability of firms to adapt when circumstances changed later in the century, because established mercantile practices proved extremely difficult to alter, and while in the trading conditions prevailing up to the 1860s such a strategy may have been entirely rational, the legacy proved highly damaging (Chapman, 1992; 61–72). In simple terms, the transaction costs involved in internalising vital marketing and distribution functions were too great for the typically small-scale British industrialist, preventing the pursuit of vertical integration strategies which in other contexts would have improved overall efficiency.

Conclusion

This debate about the viability of the family firm will be continued in chapter four, when we shall make an assessment of British business's response to the new forms of industrial capitalism emerging in the later industrialisers like the USA and Germany. As Rose (1993; 128) has noted, however, it is clear that: 'Small, localised and often specialised markets, combined with the need for personal contacts and trust in an age of unlimited liability, rendered the family firm a perfect organisational form'. One might well substitute 'appro-priate' for 'perfect', providing a link with the work of Lazonick (1991; 25–7), but the conclusion has much validity in summarising the state of busi-ness evolution by the mid-nineteenth century. On the other hand, one must also stress how severe constraints on expansion were imposed by a culture which treasured above all the desire for independence, and the strength with which this persisted throughout the nineteenth century will be a major issue when assessing how British business responded to new competitive chal-lenges after 1870. We have certainly seen some evidence of a willingness to adapt, and an embryonic distinction between strategic, functional and operational management (see Figure 1.1) was beginning to appear in those firms with managing partners and large numbers of internal subcontractors. Nevertheless, owners retained complete control over strategic management, and the caution with which businessmen approached investment and marketing strategy was clearly born of an acute awareness of their own managerial and financial shortcomings.

British business by the mid-nineteenth century was still at the personal stage of development, and while railway companies and other network utilities were making great strides forward in the elaboration of corporate management techniques and structures, even they were constrained from developing this system fully by the prevailing business culture. Of course, the prevalance of a highly personalised form of management is perhaps not surprising when one considers the stage of industrialisation reached in Britain by the 1860s, because many sectors were still dominated by traditional methods of production and the large-scale business was a rarity (Musson, 1978; 129–33). Even in the classic factory industry of the era, cotton, the medium-sized firm employing between 150 and 500 was far more typical than businesses like McConnel & Kennedy which had over 1,500 'hands'. Nevertheless, from the 1860s expansion characterised British industry generally, and the factory came to dominate modes of production, and in chapter 4 we will address the crucial issue of whether this prompted a move towards an entrepreneurial, or even a managerial, form of organisation. Firstly, though, a crucial dimension must be added to the analysis, because before we can gauge the degree of progress in British business it is necessary to describe how our main rivals were coping with the challenges of industrial capitalism, providing some benchmarks against which we can measure performance.

3

The rise of big business
abroad up to 1914

It is a common assumption of much business history that in economies like
the USA, Germany and Japan managerial techniques and systems have
generally been much more advanced than those employed in Britain, in spite,
or maybe because, of the latter's earlier start as an industrial nation. We shall
dispute the subjective nature of such judgements in chapter 4, but before we
continue with the description of British business evolution it is interesting to
examine how organisational structures were adapting elsewhere as industrial capitalism started to spread its influence in the nineteenth century. The
most important aspect of this analysis will be an attempt to identify the principal factors stimulating the development of big business in the USA,
Germany and Japan, focusing especially on: firstly, why did big business
appear to have emerged much earlier in those economies than in Britain; and
second, how did management adapt structure to strategy? It is an exercise
which will necessarily involve a detailed study of the market-cum-technological, financial, legal and socio-cultural environments which prevailed at the
time when key innovations occurred, providing benchmarks against which
we can measure British performance in later chapters. It will be above all
apparent that, while the family firm continues to feature prominently in all of
the cases, this institution is adapted to economic and social circumstances.
Even when the multidivisional (or M-form) form of organisation first made
its appearance, an issue we shall examine further in section 5.1, it is interesting to see how family firms were among the leading pioneers in the adoption of this highly sophisticated structure. This emphasises how difficult it
must be to generalise about the relative rates of progress in such contrasting
economies, and one must always be aware of the subtle differences in
approach which are dictated by the varying environments.

In tracing the rise of big business, it is necessary first of all to know exactly
what we are looking for, because such characteristics as a multi-million
pound capital base or a workforce of several thousand do not by themselves
provide much of an insight into its complexity. One must be especially aware

of the two criteria applied by Chandler (1990; 14) in his description of 'the modern *business* enterprise': 'it contains a number of distinct operating units, and it is managed by a hierarchy of full-time salaried managers'. Of course, Chandler was principally concerned with tracing the rise of 'modern *industrial* enterprise', and as we noted in section 1.2 he insisted on the notion that businessmen in this kind of organisation needed to make the three-pronged, interrelated investments in production, distribution, and management if they are going to exploit the opportunities available. The latter was of prime importance, because Chandler (1990; 31–2) placed great emphasis on the role played by managers in adapting structure to strategy, and in developing adequate control and co-ordination procedures. Obviously, however, much depends on the (economic, social and legal) environment in which businessmen were to operate, and before accepting this thesis one must contextualise the rate of progress achieved in each individual economy, providing a more objective benchmark against which to measure performance.

3.1   American managerial capitalism

The Chandler thesis was based on an extensive analysis of American business developments up to the 1940s, and in following this story one can see how what he sees as the vital three-pronged investment in manufacturing, marketing and management became so important in exploiting the tremendous potential in that market, particularly in the high-growth sectors associated with 'the Second Industrial Revolution'. Indeed, he is careful to emphasise that: 'It was the development of new technologies and the opening up of new markets, which resulted in economies of scale and scope and in reduced transaction costs, that made the large multiunit industrial enterprise come when it did, where it did, and in the way it did' (1990; 18). This highlights the importance of external factors in stimulating the rise of big business, and certainly American businessmen were blessed with the significant advantages of a home market which was both geographically much larger and had a population (97.2 million in 1913) over twice the size of that in Great Britain (45.7 million). Furthermore, the growth of this market since the 1870s was accompanied by a 140 per cent increase in GDP per capita, creating the largest, most affluent market in the world at a time when significant technological innovations were beginning to have a major impact in the fields of communication and production (Chandler, 1990; 52).

Marketing and distribution

American businessmen were consequently faced with a highly conducive environment in the late-nineteenth century, but it is important to note that not only was the market geographically dispersed, the existing mercantile and distribution facilities also proved woefullly inadequate, prompting the establishment of such facilities by corporations as an essential basis for operations. Chandler (1990; 140–5) identified three main groups of industries which exploited this situation in different ways. The first group (furniture, leather, shoes and textiles) did not invest substantially in new production and distribution facilities, preferring to rely on existing methods which had been developed over the previous century. Those in the second group, however, including consumer foodstuffs like meat, canned goods, as well as soap and cigarettes, and light machinery producers in the agricultural and business machine sectors, integrated forward into mass distribution and backwards into purchasing networks. And in the third group (petroleum, nonferrous metals, chemicals, rubber, and electrical machinery) corporations were highly capital-intensive in terms of both production and distribution, integrating the two functions so extensively that they were soon converted into highly advanced forms of business enterprise. This integration process allowed producers the opportunity to impose more standardised goods on consumers, while at the same time a much more astute ability to gauge market trends was possible with dedicated sales and marketing teams. Mass retailers, wholesalers and mail-order houses also sprang up from the 1860s, extending distribution networks considerably and linking directly with suppliers and manufacturers to create a much more efficient mechanism. In addition, the railway networks, totalling over 240,000 miles of track, combined with an even larger telegraph system, integrated the various regions into a more cohesive unit, facilitating the development of national sales strategies (Chandler, 1990; 53–62).

These were significant market-cum-technological opportunities for the late-nineteenth century American entrepreneur, but once again it is important to stress how Chandler (1992; 47–8) claims that only those making the three-pronged investment in production, distribution and management were equipped to exploit the openings. Indeed, the three-pronged investment was mutually inter-linked, because without an extensive marketing and distribution system mass production facilities were a risky investment, and *vice versa*, while without a management structure capable of scheduling the flow of goods and information the whole strategy could collapse. Chandler (1990; 34–5) was also at pains to emphasise that those making the initial three-pronged investments – the 'first-movers' – were able to acquire a powerful competitive advantage over their rivals, putting them 'well down the learning curve in each of the industry's functional activities before challengers went into full operation'. Among such first-movers were some of the most famous names in business history, including Duke (cigarettes), Heinz and Campbell (canned foods), Pillsbury (grain-processing), Proctor & Gamble (consumer chemicals), Swift and Armour (meat-packing), Remington (business machinery), Singer (sewing machines), Eastman Kodak (photographic film), General Electric and Westinghouse (electrical engineering), du Pont (gunpowder and chemicals), and Carnegie (steel). Their activities are well described by Chandler (1977; 287–314: 1990; 62–71), illustrating how first-movers were able to dominate markets, nationally and internationally, exploiting a competitive advantage to such good effect that their control survived for many decades.

Mergers

Although these first-movers were able to gain their competitive advantage by exploiting internal economies of scale, most of the industrial giants which rose to prominence at that time did so as a result of the external economies to be gained from merger and acquisition strategies. Price-fixing agreements had at first been used to control the dual problems of rising costs and intense competition, but the 1890 Sherman Anti-Trust Act effectively prohibited such collusion, forcing businessmen to consider the alternative of formal merger in order to achieve the desired level of market control. One should not, however, exaggerate the impact of anti-trust legislation, because not only did this law fail to prevent the rise of an oligopolistic trading structure within two decades of its enactment, the tremendous opportunities associated with exploiting economies of scale and scope in the American market were probably more important in motivating merger activity (Chandler, 1990; 74–5). In addition, as we shall see, the role played by financial interests was also by no means negligible as an influence on events, illustrating how the legal situation was simply one part of the broad environment in which American businessmen operated.

The process of industrial concentration had actually started in the 1880s, especially among railway, refining and distilling firms, but in the 1890s the pace quickened, culminating in a pronounced peak between 1895 and 1903 when on average over 300 firms were absorbed each year. The record year was 1899, when 979 firms valued at over £400 million ($2064 million) disappeared through merger. Merger activity was particularly rife in sectors which were characterised by high rates of market growth, including petroleum products and extraction, chemicals, primary metals, transportation goods, metal products, food, drink and tobacco, and coal mining. It also resulted in the formation of large, integrated, diversified corporations which came to dominate their particular sectors for many decades (Lamoreaux, 1985; 138–58). This emphasises the importance of merger activity in the development of what became an oligopolistic American business structure. At the peak, firms like United States Steel had a nominal capital value of £264 million ($1,322 million), while General Electric was valued at £35 million ($174 million), illustrating how really big business had already come to dominate key sectors of American industry.

Access to capital

Although much of the finance for industrial investment had been internally-generated up to the 1880s (Chandler, 1977; 373), thereafter a much closer relationship with financiers was forged by American businessmen looking to reduce competition and expand capacity. Davis (1966; 255) has pointed out how American capital markets were in fact much less well-developed than in Britain, and in the 1890s this gave prominent financiers like the Rockefellers, the Morgans, and the Mellons an opportunity to exploit their good connections to concentrate business power. These big private banking houses had already risen to prominence as railway financiers, but by the 1890s they had turned their attentions to industrial ventures, developing an intimate range of contacts with leading corporations (Born, 1983; 92–9). Indeed, Chandler (1990; 80–1) has noted that at this time the financier-industrialist relationship was essentially personal, rather than institutional, with investment bankers, promoters and individual entrepreneurs working closely with corporations in the pursuit of industrial concentration. On the other hand, a close relationship between stock price movements and merger activity can be detected (Nelson, 1959; 89–100), indicating how the two sectors were increasingly intertwined. One can certainly conclude that American business was able to acquire the finance it needed from a large and wealthy coterie of venture capitalists, and especially in the period 1890–1910 these people played a crucial role in the merger waves which swept many industries.

American financiers had, of course, first familiarised themselves with industrial investment during the 1850s railway booms, forging such an intimate relationship with these large businesses that the Wall Street district of New York became a major financial centre. This relationship, however, did not extend to direct management of American railway companies by financial interests, because, as in Britain, professional managerial heirarchies soon evolved as a solution to the need for careful scheduling of operations and the efficient use of a massive capital base. The railways consequently pioneered in the USA both a divorce between control and ownership typical of the modern business enterprise, and the functional departmentalisation of management based on a complex managerial hierarchy which later became a model for large industrial enterprises (Chandler, 1990; 53–8). Similarly, the investment bankers who helped finance industrial mergers from the 1890s also had little interest in playing a significant part in the management of these new large-scale corporations, facilitating and extending the trend towards using professional managers.

The family firm in American business

Owner-management had in fact been just as dominant a feature of American industry as it had in Britain up to the 1850s, and it is important to stress how in focusing on the leading industrial corporations, Chandler ignores a significant part of the American economy which, as Scranton (1983; 414–20) emphasises, was based on 'proprietary capitalism'. One must also stress how even at the time of the First World War, as Chandler (1990; 48) himself admits, family ownership was still common among the large industrial corporations which had evolved over the previous generation. This might sound paradoxical, given the large amounts of outside capital raised by American corporations, from the 1890s onwards, but as Berle and Means (1932; 115) demonstrate minority groups were able to retain control of senior management with as little as fifteen or twenty per cent of the equity, while salaried managers were hired in large numbers to perform more routine tasks. Bendix (1956; 235) has also revealed how, in a sample of approximately 1,000 businessmen, original entrepreneurs and their heirs remained in the majority of chief executives well into the twentieth century. This calls into question Chandler's (1990; 47–9) claim that American business can be labelled competitive managerial capitalism, because dynasties like the Carnegies, Dukes, Mellons, Morgans, du Ponts, Dorrances and Swifts were still capable of exerting considerable influence in economic and political spheres well into the twentieth century. Most importantly, though, these entrepreneurs had been organisation-builders, and the large-scale corporations for which they had been responsible were developing into centralised, functionally-departmentalised structures with large teams of salaried managers recruited to perform the wide range of functions required to ensure that the organisation operated effectively. To Chandler (1990; 84–9), this was the climax of a process of organisational metamorphosis which had been occurring since the 1880s, but at the same time the system was much closer to the entrepreneurial stage described in section 1.3, bearing in mind the continued dominance of owner-managers at the senior levels of American business.

Business schools

We shall return to a more detailed analysis of control and ownership in twentieth century business in sections 6.2–6.4, because there are many subtle aspects to this debate which cannot be covered here. However, it is clear that a complete divorce between control and ownership had not happened in American business by the First World War. On the other hand, the acceptance of managers as an intrinsic feature of American business operations was clearly the main reason why Chandler (1990; 47) uses the term competitve managerial capitalism. When we combine this with American society's receptive approach towards industrial capitalism, it is not surprising that business careers were widely regarded as socially acceptable among the elite. Engineering graduates from middle and upper class backgrounds had been entering American corporations in increasing numbers since the 1860s, and although there was initially little interest in formal business education, by the turn of the century a large demand for business graduates had emerged from the concerns formed as a result of merger activity. The first business school, the Wharton School of Commerce and Finance, had been created at the University of Pennsylvania in 1881, and although only another three appeared before 1900, by 1914 thirty institutions were producing around 10,000 graduates per annum (Keeble, 1992; 24–6). This precipitated an extensive conversion of the educational system to vocational training, and American business was able to recruit the talent it required from these institutions, reinforcing the trend towards managerial capitalism which had been developing its own momentum from the activities of large-scale corporations.

One must be wary of exaggerating the sophistication of these early business schools, and as Locke (1984; 114) argues it took until the 1940s before they made the decisive breakthrough to what he calls the 'new paradigm', or 'the application of science to the solution of managerial problems'. Nevertheless, these educational institutions were playing an increasingly important role in training managers in the skills appropriate to the more rational world of big business from the 1890s. This reveals how socio-cultural forces in American society conspired to create a system which not only accorded business careers a high status, but also encouraged a degree of co-operation between the academic and vocational spheres which proved to have substantial mutual benefits. Corporations were consequently able to recruit the large number of professional managers required to staff the functionally-departmentalised organisations that had appeared by the 1890s, and while in-house training remained important in all firms the business schools were increasingly accepted as a key source of talent (Keeble, 1992; 27–8).

Scientific management

One area of management in which academic influence remained minimal at this time was in the control of production, because it was as a result of empirical work on the shopfloor that American business first experimented with what has since come to be known as 'scientific management'. The most famous innovator in this field was F. W. Taylor, a metallurgist at Midvale Steel who also developed alloyed steels for use in high-speed machine tools. We shall be examining 'scientific management' in greater detail when the British response to this innovatory method of scientifically determining work-rates and de-skilling production is assessed in section 5.3. However, it is important to emphasise how most now agree with Nelson's (1975; 72) assertion that all firms introducing Taylorite concepts were obliged to adapt the system to their own individual circumstances. On the other hand, American manufacturers were keen to introduce techniques which would allow them an opportunity to reduce production costs and improve efficiency. The most outstanding example was, perhaps, Henry Ford, who in building his Highland Park plant in Detroit to mass-produce the Model T car (in black, of course) demonstrated the tremendous potential in what then came to be known as 'Fordism' (Lewchuk, 1987; 39–56).

The system of entrepreurial capitalism which had evolved in the United States by 1914 can be regarded as the most advanced form of business organisation in existence at that time. The large-scale, vertically-integrated, functionally-departmentalised corporations controlling oligopolistic market structures became the foundation-stones of American economic success over the following seventy years, and as we shall see in section 5.1 they continued to introduce important organisational innovations which others later copied. It is equally important to note, though, that this system arose out of a combination of factors which, while not unique, were undoubtedly significant. Chandler (1990; 89) gives only three reasons why this system had taken such deep roots in the USA: an enormous and growing domestic market which was relatively more affluent than its counterparts in Europe; the availability of new production technologies for the mass production of goods; and the prevention of price-fixing organisations by federal law. Clearly, these were extremely significant, but they do not cover the wider spectrum of influences which also contributed to the state reached by American business in 1914. In particular, there is no mention of the need to integrate both forwards into distribution and marketing, and backwards into the provision of essential raw materials, as a means of reducing the high transaction costs created by the failure of adequate external services to evolve. This must be a crucial factor in explaining the particular strategies and structures adopted by American business from the 1880s, and as we shall see in section 4.1, this contrasted sharply with the stimulii experienced by British business. Similarly, the relationship between business and finance must be noted, especially as during the intense merger wave of 1895–1904 this at least facilitated, if not precipitated, the rise of big business. In addition, socio-cultural influences were of importance in encouraging the acceptance of business as a worthwhile career, prompting the education system to respond positively to the expanding demand for professional managers. And finally, the state participated in this process, not only in prohibiting cartelisation, but also in protecting the domestic economy from excessive import-penetration, providing American corporations with the most promising market in the world.

Conclusion

There was clearly a wide range of factors which influenced the development of American business up to 1914, from the market-cum-technological through to the institutional and socio-cultural, and it would be misleading to attempt a mono-causal interpretation as a means of contrasting this experience with that in other countries. It is above all evident, however, that a rapid transition from the personal through to at least the entrepreneurial form of organisation had been effected by the First World War. The label 'competitive managerial capitalism' does not appear to carry much weight when describing American business up to the First World War, because family control remained a major influence at the most senior levels of decision-making, but considerable responsibility had already been delegated down the line to professional managers. These well-organised businesses were consequently capable of exploiting their competitive advantage further by extending distribution, and later production, operations into overseas markets, and it is fair to say that the dominance American corporations achieved in the high growth sectors – light and electrical machinery, chemicals, transportation goods, petroleum products, and steel – came as a direct consequence of the strategies and structures adopted from the 1880s in their home market. Many European competitors found great difficulty in withstanding the new challenges, and as we shall see in sections 4.1 and 4.2 British business in particular struggled to cope with this threat.

3.2 The German case: 'Co-operative managerial capitalism'?

The one European economy which proved to be capable of dealing with growing American industrial strength was Germany. In Chandler's (1990; 393) view, success was achieved because business organisation in this country approximated more closely to the American case than any other up to the 1940s, leading him to devise the term 'co-operative managerial capitalism' to describe the German system. As this label implies, however, there are significant differences between American and German business organisations, not least in the degree to which co-operation and collusion impinged on many aspects of the latter's activities. This co-operative spirit is regarded by Porter (1990; 356–69) as one of the main reasons why Germany has achieved considerable success as an industrial power, particularly with regard to the clustering of firms, banks and training institutions as a means of forcing up standards across the whole sector. A particular characteristic of the early phase of industrialisation was the operation of 'Kartelles' (or trade associations, and hereafter referred to as cartels), but it also featured prominently in the relationship between industry on the one hand and both the state and the financial institutions on the other. Notwithstanding these points, German business showed a tendency towards large-scale and vertical integration, and extensive use of professional managers was made. As Carter commented (1913; 7–8), 'Germany seems to be . . . the home of industrial combination, as far as Europe is concerned', substantiating Tilly's (1974; 145) claim that: 'Large-scale business has played an important role in the economic development of Germany'.

Family firms in German business

Notwithstanding these developments, one must also emphasise how up to the 1930s family firms continued to feature prominently in Germany, just as they did in Britain (Church, 1993; 28–9), while Tilly (1974; 155–6) also emphasises how small groups of either entrepreneurs or even professional managers continued to control firms well into the twentieth century. Indeed, as Hampden-Turner and Trompenaars (1993; 230) have noted, even up to the present day: 'An unusual feature of German business culture is the very large number of small and medium-sized private companies, still run by founders and their families and with an extraordinary record of sophistication and export orientation'. As we shall see in section 5.1, this concentrated form of control could well have been a major obstacle to the more extensive adoption of a mulitidivisional form, but in analysing these trends one must always remember the distinctive nature of German business culture.

The rise of big business

Large-scale business had emerged in Germany, as it had in Britain and the USA, with the railway companies formed in the 1840s, and their growth had a substantial impact on heavy industry and the capital market. This stimulus took the form of both a major boost to investment in new plant and a closer relationship between industry and financial institutions, encouraging the wider use of joint stock company status in the large steel, engineering and coal businesses which emerged from a merger wave in the 1850s. These corporations were 'fusions of entrepreneurial-technical talent', initiating a close relationship between industry and finance which became common in German business, especially after the liberalisation of company law in 1870 (Tilly, 1974; 147–54). The unification of the disparate states into a single country in 1871, in conjunction with the completion of an integrated railway network, also encouraged a more aggressive approach towards production and distribution, and by making what Chandler (1990; 393–5, 502) calls the three-pronged investments so essential to the emergence of modern industrial enterprise German corporations were able to exploit first-mover advantages in the burgeoning European markets, especially for producer goods, chemicals, steel and coal. As a relatively undeveloped economy, of course, Germany did not possess an extensive marketing and distribution network, prompting corporations to integrate forwards into these areas at an early stage. This facilitated the adoption of mass-production and mass-distribution methods as an essential feature of industrial strategy, but one should remember that the German market was not as affluent as in the USA, and consequently the packaged consumer goods sector was slower to expand.

The cartels

While German corporations were moving along similar lines to those adopted by their American counterparts, it is important to emphasise the role
played by cartels. By 1905, over 350 cartels had been created, and although
they only accounted for twenty-five per cent of total industrial output their
influence was all-pervasive in those industries – coal, chemicals, and steel –
where the greatest competitive advantages had been secured (Kocka, 1980;
88–9). They had first emerged as a response to the depression in prices lasting between 1873 and 1896, but soon developed a range of functions, from
regulating the level of output to arranging joint marketing organisations,
impinging directly on management strategy in an attempt to create a more
secure trading environment. In the depression of 1901–3, cartelisation was
developed even further in German industry, reinforcing what had evidently
become a prominent characteristic of their approach towards economic
progress. This collusive activity was also supported by the state, not only in
granting cartels a specific legal status in 1897, but also by protecting the
economy from extensive import penetration, indicating how in Germany
industrial interests were given a high priority. Protectionism, of course, had
been a prominent feature of American economic policy in the late-nineteenth
century, but the 1890 Sherman Anti-Trust Act had placed substantial legal
barriers in the way of price-fixing and market co-operation, contrasting
sharply with the German approach.

It is a moot point whether cartelisation can act as a spur to greater efficiency in an industrial economy, and in section 4.2 we shall examine how this
system affected strategy and structure in Britain. In the case of Germany up
to 1914, however, it clearly did not appear to place any substantial barriers
in the way of either relatively rapid growth or the exploitation of first-mover
advantages in a range of industries. Indeed, cartelisation is seen as a positive
asset to German economic development, particularly as a means of creating
greater trading stability, in conjunction with the protective umbrella of
import duties, and the encouragement it gave to marketing through the distribution syndicates which emerged from the 1890s (Carter, 1913; 46:
MacGregor, 1906; 191–216).

Cartelisation did, however, inhibit horizontal merger activity as a means
of concentrating production, largely because the security afforded by cartels
provided little incentive to acquire competitors. On the other hand, mergers
associated with vertical integration and diversification were common,
reflecting the desire of German managers to exploit economies of scope in
the development of their role as leading European progenitors of the modern
industrial enterprise. Kocka (1980; 79–88) demonstrates how by 1907 only
five of the leading 100 German industrial corporations remained undiversi-
fied, while eighty-eight had indulged in some form of vertical integration
(forward into sales and distribution, or backward into securing supplies of

raw materials), and clearly merger activity had contributed significantly in fashioning this integrated structure.

Industrial banks

One of the key reasons why management had been able to pursue strategies of integration and diversification, and one which continues to play a central role in the economy's success in the late-twentieth century (Porter, 1990; 356–69), was the influence exercised over German economic development at this time by the banking sector. As in many other economies, the German financial system had developed rapidly as a result of railway construction, in this case during the 1840s and 1850s, but once an extensive network had been completed, and the state then nationalised most of the mileage, attention turned to the expanding industrial sector. The dominating feature of German financial activities was the banking system (Born, 1983; 82–92), and from an early stage these powerful institutions performed two key roles: they provided long-term loans to corporate customers, and acted as the vital medium of communication between investors and capital-hungry firms by organising industrial capital issues on the stock exchanges. Banking was also highly concentrated, with seven large joint stock banks dominating the Berlin Stock Exchange, and because of their extensive contribution to business financing they soon began to extend their influence directly into industrial management, featuring prominently at the highest levels of decision-making (Kocka, 1980; 89–91).

It is important to understand that the reform of German company law introduced in 1870 stipulated that two boards of directors should be established in each corporation. At the top was a supervisory board (*aufsichtsrat*), elected by shareholders and primarily responsible for strategic decisions on investment and product range, while below was an executive board (*vorstand*) which performed the more mundane tasks associated with functional and operational management (see Figure 1.1). As the representatives of shareholders, the banks were consequently able to populate the supervisory board (Born, 1983; 89–91), and because they supported the trends towards concentration, integration and diversification, finance was provided for such strategies as a means of minimising the impact of market forces on prices and profits. One must be careful not to give the bankers a leading role in this movement, because industrialists were largely responsible for initiating strategy, but 'the banks reflected and strengthened existing trends' (Kocka, 1980; 91–2). The increasing scale of German corporations also resulted in a greater reliance on self-finance by the early-twentieth century, reducing the dependence on outside investors until the crises of the 1930s. Nevertheless, the provision of venture capital by the large banks had been a crucial factor behind German industrial success until then, reinforcing the move towards large-scale enterprise which had been a predominant characteristic of business strategy since the mid-nineteenth century (Chandler, 1990; 416–9).

The role of unternehmer

Having noted the role played by bank finance in the development of German business, one should not forget the continued importance of family enterprise on supervisory boards. In fact, as Kocka (1978; 569) reveals, owner-managers reasserted themslves in the 1890s, displacing bankers as the principal influences on business strategy, and it is apparent that up to the First World War large-scale German business was dominated by the entrepreneurial form of organisation. Church (1993; 28–9) has also demonstrated that possibly up to the 1930s family firms were just as prevalent in Germany as they were in Britain, with ownership still concentrated in the hands of a few members of the supervisory board, where strategic decisions were made, while functional and operational management had been extensively delegated to salaried managers. Powerful industrial dynasties like Siemens, Thyssens and Krupps were regarded as *unternehmer*, a separate social elite whose authority was accepted as being totally dominant, reinforcing the authoritarian nature of German society and its commitment to a clear bureaucratic order which had become part of the national heritage (Dyas & Thanheiser, 1976; 103–8). Indeed, firms copied the bureaucratic procedures followed in public administration, and flexibility at the middle- and junior-management levels was highly proscribed. On the other hand, *unternehmer* were allowed greater freedom to operate within a loose senior management structure, in order to encourage creativity, emphasising how the German corporate structure was both autocratic and flexible. However, the high degree of centralisation at the level of strategic management could well have acted as a major obstacle holding up the introduction of the multi-divisional form of organisation, a subject we shall discuss in section 5.1, but Kocka (1971; 152–5) has noted that the major electrical engineering firm of Siemens had already developed such a refinement to its structure as early as 1905.

The key point to note here at this stage is that Chandler's use of the term 'co-operative managerial capitalism' to describe German business is misleading. Collusion was undoubtedly a prominent characteristic of the system, but the continued dominance of family dynasties undermines any claim that the managerial stage had been reached by 1914. Chandler (1990; 500–1) himself recognises as much by noting that 'German firms differed from the American in that the family often continued to have a powerful, even decisive, say in management'. Of course, there is no doubt that German business employed large numbers of professional managers in a multi-level hierarchy, from the supervisory board down to departmental level, and in this context superficially they would look little different from American corporations. On the other hand, one must remember how *unternehmer* continued to dominate strategic decision-making for many decades, and clearly 'co-operative *entrepreneurial* capitalism' would be a more appropriate label for the German business system.

Managerial training and recruitment

Large-scale business in Germany was clearly more family-based than Chandler's label indicates, but in another important respect the recruitment of professional managers came to take on a similar pattern to that in the USA, particularly with regard to the increasingly intimate relationship developed between industry and academia. The state invested massively in education from the 1870s, and although the German educational ethos, as Locke relates (1984; 71–3), had been heavily based on *wissenschaft*, or an essentially academic approach, the new commitment to modernisation and industrialisation changed the emphasis to *technik*, or a combination of scientific knowledge and practical craftsmanship. This ensured that a significant proportion of the population was trained for some kind of job, but equally one must remember that 'training for business is relentlessly practical' (Hampden-Turner & Trompenaars, 1993; 231), with firms taking responsibility for developing further the skills of all employees. As in America, science and engineering graduates were the first to be hired on any significant scale, to staff the workshops and research departments which became the hallmarks of German industrial strategy, and by the 1890s recruits from the commercial schools were brought in to staff the expanding bureaucracies armed with the lessons taught by 'business economics' and other applied disciplines (Keeble, 1992; 17–23).

Conclusion

The German education system has certainly made a significant and lasting impact on business in that country, providing the trained personnel who were to make such a valuable contribution, technically and managerially, to industrial progress. It had been boosted by the state's recognition of a need for such skills, indicating how Germany's status as a late-industrialiser prompted the complete re-evaluation of priorities as the country's leaders came to terms with the requirements of keeping pace with countries like Great Britain. Kocka (1980; 108–10) places great emphasis on this status as a major reason why large-scale, vertically-integrated and diversified firms appeared very early in the country's economic development, principally as a response to the uncertain and volatile nature of the domestic market. The banks facilitated the implementation of these aggressive strategies, and with extensive protective duties sheltering key industries against the ravages of import penetration the cartels were able to reinforce this tendency towards stability through extensive collusion on prices and marketing. German corporations were consequently obliged to develop sophisticated management structures which, while still dominated by family dynasties in 1914, exhibited all the advantages of functional departmentalisation so common in their American counterparts. It was this environment which allowed the first-movers in a wide range of industries (steel, chemicals and electrical engineering especially) to exploit their competitive advantage domestically and internationally. This could lead us to conclude that they had arrived at the same destination as American corporations, but it is important to remember that the route taken had undoubtedly been different.

3.3 Japanese business and the collective ideal

Another late-industrialiser was Japan, and although Chandler has excluded this vibrant economy from his general analyses there is extensive evidence that prior to 1914 large-scale business started to emerge on an extensive scale, providing a fascinating insight into the subject of organisational improvisation. Lazonick (1991; 25–7) has emphasised how, in attempting to explain why world economic leadership has recently shifted from the USA and its 'managerial' form of business organisation, a so-called 'collective' form of industrial capitalism has emerged in Japan which proved more appropriate to the changing circumstances of the last three decades. This is part of his broader attack on the inappropriateness of Britain's style of 'proprietorial' (or personal) capitalism, implying that family firms played no role in Japanese progress. Church (1993; 26–8), on the other hand, reveals that the family firm ethos remained a vital source of strength in Japanese business, even among the massive *zaibatsu* which came to dominate the industrial, financial and commercial scenes until their dissolution by the Allies after 1945. He fails to note that there were substantial diferences in the nature of the family firm both within and between economies, but it is nevertheless important to emphasise the role this institution played as a major feature of the business scene. This reopens the same kind of arguments we were developing in the last section, and it will be helpful to understand why the family firm proved to be such a decisive advantage in Japan, while in Britain it allegedly proved to be an obstacle to more rapid economic progress (Lazonick, 1991; 25: Chandler, 1990; 378).

Japanese values

Of central importance to our analysis of Japanese business must be the role played by socio-cultural influences in fashioning a business system which Fruin (1992; 47) claims is based on co-operation and dedicated commitment to national goals. Japanese traditions and social relationships are often difficult to comprehend through Occidental eyes, because of the strong degree of individualism inherent in American and West European value systems, but above all it is essential to emphasise how Japanese citizens subsume their own aspirations under the collective belief in loyalty to the country, or in pre-1945 Japan, the Emperor. This can be illustrated by examining the Meiji Restoration in 1868, when a new ruling family ascended the throne and instituted a series of fundamental changes to the political, religious and economic spheres which dramatically altered the country's destiny. Miyamoto (1986; 291–309) has emphasised how Japan was by no means backward in the period (Tokugawa) leading up to 1868, and a market economy revolving around Edo (Tokyo), Osaka and Kyoto had already emerged which undoubtedly influenced the Meiji Era. Nevertheless, a policy of modernisation was pursued rigorously after 1868 and because an individual's loyalty to the Emperor was paramount, society was unified around this new goal (Hirschmeier & Yui, 1975; 70–5).

A strict delineation of ranks remains a characteristic of Japanese society, and each individual accepts that deference is due to superiors (Yamamura, 19 ; 159–63), but the most important characteristics are the organic ordering of command structures and the collectivisation of aims, or the belief in 'the group first' (Hampden-Turner & Trompenaars, 1993; 96–7, 167). Translated down to firm level, this value system means that loyalty to the employer, or 'organisation-orientedness' as Kono (1984; 9) describes it, is paramount, because working hard for the company is the most obvious way in which an individual can contribute to the country's economic well-being. In other words, loyalty to the *Ie* (house) is a manifestation of patriotism, and along with group identification, a strong belief in the need for harmony, and an acceptance of rank differentials, this ensured complete commitment to company strategy by workers at all levels (Yamamura, 1978; 263).

The early entrepreneurs

Clearly, the greatest initial challenge facing the Meiji family was convincing the more influential elements in Japan that modernisation was a viable national priority, and in economic terms it was essential that entrepreneurs could be persuaded to participate in the construction of a modern industrial system. The state actually instituted the policy of *yunyuboatsu* (import-substitution), establishing pilot plants to demonstrate to private entrepreneurs the advantages of Western technology in areas like cotton spinning, shipbuilding, mining and engineering, and often hiring foreign technicians as consultants on the projects. Railways were also constructed, and after three important Acts (1872, 1876 and 1882) a banking system emerged along American lines, with the (private) Bank of Japan acting as central bank to an increasing number of joint stock banks (Hirschmeier & Yui, 1975; 86–91). However, in describing Japan's drive towards modernisation after 1868, it is important not to overstate the government's role in this respect, and many business historians in particular are at pains to emphasise the 'bottom-up' nature of industrial development, as opposed to a top-down process.

Japanese economic history has for long been dominated by a Marxist interpretation which stresses the belief in a corporate economy dominated by monopoly capital, but over the last thirty years business historians like Yui, Nakagawa and Morikawa have revolted against this view by stressing other factors like the dynamism of individual firms. In the first place, Miyamoto (1986; 308–9) has noted how the old order was beginning to break down during the nineteenth century, because the previously inferior merchants were beginning to ascend the social ladder and match the *samurai* for status and wealth in the new market economy. This provided the latter with economic and social incentives to participate in the modernisation process, especially those of a highly marginal nature who had purchased their titles, and we shall see how some of the largest Japanese businesses were to be run by such people. Nakagawa (1974; 197–9) has also argued that the state 'channelled its investment not into industrial production but into the framing of a favourable social setting for the development of private industrial enterprise', providing simply the foundations for what amounted eventually to an 'industrial revolution' implemented by private entrepreneurs.

The zaibatsu

By far the most important of these early entrepreneurs were the *zaibatsu* (Morikawa, 1992), alternatively defined as 'trading families' or 'money cliques' because of their dual involvement in distribution and some form of finance provision (Yasuoka, 1975; 81–2). They came from two main sources, the *samurai* (Mitsubishi and Yasuda) and a class of merchant-financiers (Mitsui and Sumitomo). Yamamura (1978; 221–5) explains how some confusion has arisen over the *samurai* origins of some entrepreneurs: on the one hand 'Meiji entrepreneurs were seen as possessors of the samurai spirit [and] comprised the major part of Meiji business leaders'; on the other, one should remember that most were 'at best marginal samurai' and the merchant-financiers were often of much greater standing. Indeed, prior to 1868 merchants had been the dominant economic power in Japan (Miyamoto, 1986; 308–9), and one should not overstate the importance of *samurai* (Yamamura, 1968; 153–4). Nevertheless, by 1914 the *zaibatsu* controlled the Japanese economy after exploiting their influential position as *seisho* (merchants by the grace of political connections), and using their resources and contacts they contributed extensively to the modernisation policy. By attaining *seisho* status, they were also allowed to purchase the government's pilot plants (Nakagawa, 1974; 197–207), as well as establishing their own banking operations – Mitsui founded its bank in 1876, Mitsubishi in 1895, Yasuda in 1880, and Sumitomo in 1895. It is important to note that while these financial institutions were essential to the modernisation plans, they did not hold large amounts of industrial equities, preferring instead to provide long-term loans to concerns which were closely related to the parent *zaibatsu* (Yamamura (1978; 241–3).

A useful way of illustrating the *zaibatsu* story is to examine the case of Mitsui (Yamamura, 1978; 164–8). This firm was owned by eleven families, but because extensive authority was delegated to professional managers it became the largest and most successful *zaibatsu* after exploiting its position as the most favoured trading house in Meiji Japan. The first move had been to establish Mitsui Bussan as the trading arm, and it was the profits from this expanding business which were used to venture into banking and coal mining, the latter having been one of the government's pilot plants. After 1890, an even more ambitious strategy was pursued, as Mitsui acquired businesses as varied as cotton spinning (Kanegafuchi), silk reeling (Shinmachi), paper production (Oji) and engineering (Shibaura, later Toshiba). An industrial division was formed to control these new ventures, but the reform of company law in 1893 obliged Mitsui to differentiate between wholly-owned subsidiaries and partnerships, leading to a federal structure. When the policy of acquiring more industrial businesses was extended after 1910, Mitsui pioneered the holding company form, a structure many other *zaibatsu* imitated thereafter (Morikawa, 1975; 47–9: Hirschmeier & Yui, 1975; 133–8). This was certainly the case at Mitsubishi (Morikawa, 1975; 55–60), and Suzuki (1991; 33–6) concludes from his survey of the period 1920–1940 that holding company patterns dominated, along with an extensive devolution of many managerial functions. Furthermore, Fruin (1992; 96) claims that by the 1920s over 200 firms came under the Mitsui banner, reflecting the high levels of concentration apparent in the Japanese economy. This is also demonstrated by examining the top fifty Japanese industrial enterprises, because in 1896 independent textile firms dominated, but by 1919 *zaibatsu* subsidiaries and affiliates in a wide range of industries controlled the scene (Nakagawa, 1975; 13–7).

By the First World War, *zaibatsu* had already become highly integrated and diversified conglomerates with interests in many unconnected industrial sectors. They had also ventured abroad, establishing many subsidiaries in Asia especially, and creating the basis for what became in the late-twentieth century a flood of Japanese multinational investments (Wilkins, 1986; 228–9). It is important to emphasise, though, that as Yui (1988; 62–6) argues, while the trading and banking arms of these organisations were central features of both strategy and structure, the industrial operations were managed along highly functional and sophisticated lines. Merger activity featured prominently in this process of concentration, leading to a high level of co-operation and collusion among Japanese firms, but the dynamism came from the individual firms, rather than the central bureaucracy. One must remember that 'in terms of strategy, [firms] were not oriented towards mass production and mass marketing but were instead positively pursuing a strategy of extending their product lines in order to meet the requirement of fine-tuned markets' (Yui, 1988; 63–4). Similarly, marketing and distribution was also controlled by the *zaibatsu* trading houses, known as *soga shosha*, and these powerful firms dominated much of Japan's import-export transactions. Nevertheless, by the 1910s a high level of co-ordination and integration had been achieved within *zaibatsu*, and Japanese business was already beginning to take on the characteristics which have proved so successful in the late-twentieth century.

Management structures

In principle, this system meant that the operating divisions were usually granted independent status, and even though the *zaibatsu* were very much of an entrepreneurial type, because family control and ownership continued at the senior levels of management, Morikawa (1992; 244) and Yui (1988; 62–72) have emphasised how the whole structure was only loosely co-ordinated from the centre. One should not be misled, however, into believing that the divisions acted independently of their parent company, because while *zaibatsu* might well resemble a federation of companies all using the parent name or owned by a single family, the importance of group identity and loyalty provided a greater degree of cohesiveness than would be normal in Western holding companies. Much was made of the federal structure as a means of encouraging entrepreneurship among the professional managers, but the Japanese value systems and lines of authority, based heavily on the Confucian ethics which stressed 'dedication to duty and selfless devotion to the established order and authority', ensured that professional managers would operate in the interests of the *Ie* (Yamamura, 1978; 218). Above all, it is vital to remember that family ownership was a central feature of Japanese business, and in the Japanese socio-cultural context one must emphasise how this would appear to have been a source of strength, underpinning the national drive towards modernisation and improved competitiveness.

The *zaibatsu* were consequently of great significance to the Japanese industrial drive after 1868, and apart from the four largest (Mitsui, Mitsubishi, Sumitomo, Yasuda) other names like Kawasaki, Okura, Fujita and Kuhara also emerged as family-dominated conglomerates. One must not gain the false impression that the only form of enterprise in Japan was the *zaibatsu*, because Meiji Japan witnessed the emergence of many independent firms which did not owe their success to interdependent networks (Yamamura, 1968; 169). This can be borne out by examining the largest industrial sector up to the 1940s, cotton textiles, because here many small-scale firms originated in the mill-building booms of the period 1870–1890. However, by the inter-war years intensive merger activity had created an oligopolistic structure, resulting in at least forty per cent of capacity coming under the control of three large firms, Kanegafuchi, Toyo and Dai Nippon (Farnie & Yonekawa, 1988; 194–7). We shall also see in section 5.1 how a variety of other independent firms emerged after World War I which made a significant impact in their own fields, illustrating the success with which Japanese industrialisation gathered momentum from the late-nineteenth century.

Managerial recruitment and training

Another key feature of the Japanese scene which deserves special mention is the pattern of management recruitment, because while merchant-financiers and 'marginal *samurai*' were willing to establish conglomerate-style operations, the families would have been hard pressed to find enough talent to staff the increasing number of divisions formed from the 1890s. In this context, one must stress the deep respect for learning which had always pervaded the Confucian-based Japanese society, and the large firms were keen to recruit personnel for all levels of management from the educated classes (Yamamura, 1978; 235). On the other hand, while three commercial colleges established in the 1890s (at Osaka, Kobe and Hitotsubashi) had become commerce universities by the 1920s, formal management education was rarely used in Japan because companies made a 'heavy financial commitment to thoroughly educating . . . employees' (Locke, 1984; 282). The much-augmented college and university system was exploited extensively from the 1880s to improve the quality of management, and by 1920 forty-six per cent of Japanese business leaders were graduates, compared to forty per cent in the USA (1925) and nineteen per cent in the UK (1919). At the same time, Japanese companies preferred in-house training as a more secure means of developing the required skills (Nishizawa, 1994; 1–25). Clearly, though, one cannot generalise too much about education and training as an influence on business development, because Japan was very different from the USA or Germany, where vocational education had emerged in those countries as a response to the growing demand for certain types of skill (Keeble, 1992; 17–35). In Britain, on the other hand (see sections 2.1 and 4.4), a preference for internalised management training had already been established by the 1870s, but very different claims have been made about its relative levels of organisational efficiency when compared to Japan.

Conclusion

The organisational precision evident in *zaibatsu* would become a hallmark of twentieth century Japanese business (Yui, 1988; 66), and in many ways this is the distinguishing characteristic of this economy's evolution over the last 120 years. Morikawa (1975; 58) has even claimed that by 1908 Mitsubishi 'can be considered the beginning of the modern decentralised, product-defined, divisional structure', an issue we shall return to in section 5.1, and the extensive degree of co-operation and collusion between firms and their subsidiaries provided the basis for a successful industrial economy. On the other hand, there are other significant features of the Japanese business scene which need to be emphasised. For example, Japanese market structures and consumer tastes prevented entrepreneurs from making the three-pronged investments in manufacturing, distribution and management which had characterised much of American business. In the first place, just as in Britain (see section 4.1), distribution was tightly controlled by myriad levels of *sogo shosha*, and 'it was often more efficient for large industrial enterprises to use this external sales network than to employ a large in-house sales force' (Yui, 1988; 78). On the other hand, of course, the merchant-financiers involved in creating *zaibatsu* were intimately connected into the distribution system, many having originated as merchants, and this provided a degree of vertical integration at a very early stage. Second, though, it was some time before Japanese consumers moved away from their allegiance to traditional tastes in consumer goods, preventing the emergence of mass-production industries for many decades (Nakagawa, 1974; 200).

These factors would clearly play a major role in the development of large-scale business in Japan, but the distinctive nature of the socio-cultural traditions which characterise both Japan as a whole and its enterprise system are the key features of this country's business history over the last 120 years. Indeed, continuity dominates the whole story, in that while corporations have learnt how to adapt strategy and structure according to economic circumstances (Fruin, 1992; 40–7), they have also demonstrated a faith in traditional values and relationships based on family ties and interdependent loyalties. By the 1920s, a devolved form of organisation had become the norm among the leading businesses, with family control and ownership prevalent in a structure which delegated extensive responsibility to the professional managers working in distant operating divisions. At the same time, the extensive networks of interfirm contacts among family-controlled businesses strengthened the system, providing a means by which Japan was able to overcome the disadvantages of industrialising so late (Fruin, 1992; 47–9). The superficial similarities with Britain's system of personal capitalism are striking, as we shall see in the next chapters, but one can only understand the Japanese business scene by remembering how group loyalties and the collective ideal determine all aspects of an individual's life. This reinforces a point made earlier, that the environment in which firms evolve determines their characteristic pattern of evolution, and sweeping generalisations about 'ideal' tracks must be heavily qualified by objective assessments of prevailing circumstances.

3.4   A typology for large-scale business

There is little doubt that by the early-twentieth century big business was beginning to develop a substantial presence in the American, German and Japanese economies. Realising that the transaction costs associated with concentrating and integrating production and distribution were much lower than those in traditional forms of industrial capitalism, entrepreneurs in these countries rushed to build large-scale firms which exploited the available economies of scale and scope. These ambitious and aggressive strategies had also resulted in the formation of extensive multilevel managerial hierarchies which were staffed by large numbers of specially trained professional managers. It is clear from the previous sections that both the circumstances (economic, social and legal) for, and pattern of, business evolution differ markedly across each economy. Nevertheless, the managerial pressures associated with running large-scale, geographically-dispersed, vertically-integrated and diversified enterprises would have been similar, and it is interesting to examine in greater detail the differing responses to such a situation. Schmitz (1993; 41) is clearly accurate when he writes about the 'organisational heterogeneity' evident in an international study of business history up to 1939, but it is also vital to stress how the market-cum-technological and institutional environments in each country were primarily responsible for fashioning the strategies and structures of indigenous firms. It would consequently be interesting to examine whether any typologies of business development can be derived from our study of business evolution in the USA, Germany and Japan, because this would be enormously helpful as a basis for the next chapter's discussions. In particular, when analysing the debate surrounding British business's alleged failure to imitate its more successful rivals, we need to know whether there are any specific factors which are especially important in explaining the rise of large-scale business.

One of the common denominators linking all three countries examined in this chapter is their status as late-industrialisers, and in the German context Kocka (1980; 110) argues that this would help to explain the drive towards large-scale, diversified enterprise. This status might also help to explalian why a tendency towards collusion would appear to have been popular in Germany and Japan, and the way in which, respectively, cartels and *zaibatsu* came to dominate certain key sectors. The comparison should also be extended to an examination of the state's role in encouraging such tactics, not only through the legal system, but also by protecting industries from the extensive import-penetration which might have hindered modernisation. However, emphasising one of the difficulties in generalising about the reasons why modern industrial enterprise emerged at this time, American law from 1890 prevented the establishment or operation of price-fixing arrangements between firms. As we have already seen, though, Chandler (1990; 18) stresses above all the role of what he calls the market-cum-technological environment in explaining why 'the large multiunit industrial enterprise came when it did, where it did, and in the way it did'. However, while this might well be the vital clue in analysing American firms, and especially in explaining why they made the three-pronged investments in production, distribution and management, circumstances were very different in the other economies.

Creating a suitable typology to explain the rise of large-scale business is consequently very difficult when examining different economies. One could point to common factors like the willingness to employ large teams of professional managers in functionally-departmentalised structures which controlled vertically-integrated and diversified businesses, but this still ignores many features of each scene. For example, both in Germany and Japan large-scale business was initially faced with limited prospects for mass-producing consumer goods for the home market, and they relied on marketing specialists, respectively, cartels and *sogo shosha*, rather than making their own investments. In America, on the other hand, dedicated teams of salesmen and marketing staff were built up as part of managerial hierarchies because the existing systems offered only limited services which simply increased transaction costs. This emphasises once again how very different market-cum-technological stimulii can prompt the development of large-scale business, and ultimately it is the response of businessmen which would appear to be the crucial factor explaining strategy and structure in particular circumstances. The only common bond is the prevalance of family firms in all the economies studied, and while Chandler claims that a system of managerial capitalism had evolved in the USA and Germany by 1914, this just cannot be sustained by the evidence presented earlier. Similarly, in Japan the entrepreneurial (see section 1.3) form was very common, indicating how the family firm was not necessarily an obstacle to the rise of large-scale business where the other ingredients were present in sufficient force, a point to which we must return in the next chapter.

Conclusion

Irrespective of the obstacles just outlined, we might nevertheless attempt to create a simple typology by pointing to five principal considerations which contributed in some way to creating large-scale businesses. In the first place, one must examine the role of market-cum-technological factors as a stimulus to substantial investment in production and distribution facilities, whether directly through sales teams or indirectly through cartels or trading houses. Second, it is important to look at business strategy, and especially the possible shift away from specialisation towards integration and diversification, where the transaction costs are favourable. Third, organisational adaptation is crucial, resulting in the recruitment of large numbers of salaried managers to staff the expanding structures. Fourth, there must be financial institutions to support business in its pursuit of new openings, particularly in the provision of venture capital. And fifth, the place of business must have an acceptable status in the broad socio-cultural environment, leading to educational innovation and a sympathetic legal system. Naturally, not all of these factors need to be in place at exactly the same time, and clearly there are many variations around the themes, but in examining the British scene they provide a basis for analysing the constantly recurring allegations of 'failure' and managerial ineptitude.

4

British industrial capitalism under pressure, 1870–1914

Having examined in some detail the rise of big business abroad and suggested the five key factors to be analysed, it is now necessary to return to our study of the British scene. One must remember from chapter 2 that, although some cotton and iron concerns had reached a significant size by the 1820s, and of course the leading railway companies were massive by contemporary standards, the British business scene at mid-century was characterised by an atomistic and specialised industrial structure which had evolved out of the market, institutional and socio-cultural environments prevailing in the previous 150 years. From the 1870s, however, significant pressures were beginning to affect a wider range of industries, firstly because new technology facilitated either the adoption of factory methods of production or an extension of capacity, leading to the rise of much larger businesses in various sectors of the economy (Musson, 1978; 149–70). In addition, after 1870 the emergence of extensive foreign competition became a major feature of international trade, and as this new challenge eventually took the form of vertically integrated firms with much larger production runs there was an urgent need to continue the process of change. These dual pressures prompted what Payne (1967; 519) has described as an 'appreciable increase' in the scale of enterprise, and especially in the manufacturing sector. On the other hand, he also noted that American business was making more positive strides towards an oligopolistic market structure (see section 3.1), resulting in significant organisational innovations which were well in advance of those adopted in Britain. Business historians have since debated extensively the reasons behind these differences, and in this chapter we shall be assessing the various interpretations of the alleged 'failure' of British business to convert from the personal form of organisation which dominated up to the 1860s to the entrepreneurial or managerial forms which foreign rivals appeared to adopt extensively in the late nineteenth century.

Of course, by focusing on this comparative study of business development, one can easily ignore the signs of positive progress in Britain, emphasising the need to consider objectively the reasons for any differences which emerged. Above all, though, as we noted in section 1.2, one must remember how some Harvard academics view business history through 'American-tinted glasses', and it is vital that we contrast British conditions with those prevailing in our main rivals as an objective test of these theses. This approach will help to explain the considerable degree of 'organisational heterogeneity' (Schmitz, 1993; 41) which we noted in the last chapter, illustrating how contrasting market-cum-technological, legal, financial and socio-cultural conditions stimulated a wide variety of business forms. We shall be careful, in this context, to avoid entering the more general debate over Britain's relatively poor economic performance between 1870 and 1914, but inevitably as some of the blame for falling rates of investment and productivity have been attributed to inept entrepreneurship (Pollard, 1994; 62–89), then some reference to these issues will have to be made. We shall leave the analysis of labour management until chapter 5, focussing our attention principally at this stage on the reasons why the rise of large-scale business in Britain differed so drastically from the approach of our principal overseas rivals. Elbaum and Lazonick (1986; 1–15) claim that 'institutional rigidities' in the British business scene help to explain these issues, but this fails to provide the context in which such characteristics persisted. More importantly, it also ignores the many changes to British business which must be analysed before the 'failure' tag can be accepted as an adequate interpretation of events in the period leading up to the First World War.

4.1   The market-cum-technological environment

When testing Chandler's (1990; 235) claim that 'British entrepreneurs failed to make the essential three-pronged investment in manufacturing, marketing, and management in a number of capital-intensive industries of the Second Industrial Revolution', it is essential first of all to examine the trading environment in which they were obliged to operate. After all, as we noted in section 3.1, market stimuli provided the main incentives for American industrialists to build large-scale, integrated corporations capable of exploiting the rapid growth in demand for mass produced goods. One ought to add that while Chandler was more interested in what he calls the 'industries of the Second Industrial Revolution', namely those which emerged in the late-nineteenth century – for example, cars, electrical engineering, new chemicals and consumer goods, and light machinery – his analysis of British business ranges across the spectrum, from textiles, steel, heavy engineering and coal to food, tobacco and other consumer goods industries which expanded rapidly after the 1880s. In effect, he is talking about *general* British 'failure' to exploit first-mover competitive advantages, and the principal reason given is 'the continuing commitment to personal management' (1990; 235–7), rather than the range of external constraints which persisted throughout this era.

It will become apparent, however, that such a monocausal explanation for alleged 'failure' to make the three-pronged investments pursued so aggressively by American (and some German) corporations clearly ignores many features of British industrial and commercial life at that time. One cannot minimise the importance of 'personal management', or personal capitalism, and we shall see later that it undoubtedly affected both the propensity to develop managerial hierarchies and industry's relationship with financial institutions. Nevertheless, in any evaluation of organisational evolution up to 1914, one cannot ignore fundamental features of the British business scene like sluggish growth, the existence of a highly-developed distribution and mercantile network for both domestic and overseas trade, rigid customer-producer relationships in the capital-equipment industries, and the continued viability of labour-intensive methods of production. One might argue that, had the quality of entrepreneurship been more impressive, and there are those who are heavily critical of creative ability at this time (Landes, 1969; 326–58), then some of these 'institutional rigidities' would have been removed. On the other hand, it was surely beyond the scope of individual businessmen to change a system which had taken root so emphatically, and in the atomistic industrial structure of that era few possessed sufficient market power to achieve anything other than tinkering changes (Saul, 1970; 142).

The domestic market

The size, affluence, rate of growth, level of competitiveness and organisation of the domestic market must provide the vital context in which businessmen operate, and the degree to which they can control such factors becomes a major determinant of strategy. In the British context, one must also include overseas markets, given that forty-five per cent of total output was exported, and some of the largest industries sent an even greater proportion of their goods abroad (Pollard, 1989; 15). This naturally added further difficulties to the task of business management at a time when protectionist barriers were rising across the industrialising world, emphasising how competitive pressures were a crucial influence on strategy. We noted in section 1.4, though, that the 'Schumpeterian entrepreneur' capable of having a disequilibrating impact on the economic system was an extremely rare phenomenon, and the atomistic and specialised industrial structure which prevailed in the mid-nineteenth century allowed the invisible hand of market forces to dictate prices, wages and profits.

The questions we now need to examine are whether the late-nineteenth century environment encouraged a more aggressive approach towards investment strategy, and to what extent were British businessmen able to imitate their American rivals and exert greater control over market forces. These issues are evidently interlinked, and finding the answers will help to explain the pattern of development followed by British business in the period up to 1914. In particular, we can assess whether the three-pronged investment in production, distribution, and management was a viable proposition in the trading environment of that era, highlighting the main influences on the form of development pursued in Britain and contrasting this with progress made in other economies.

The most obvious starting-point for this discussion is to examine the issue of retardation, because there is general agreement that the rate of economic growth in Britain was slowing from the 1860s. This phenomenon cannot be analysed in great detail here, but it is clear that the British economy was not only experiencing retardation, but economies like the USA and Germany were expanding at a much faster rate (Pollard, 1989; 3–17). While there was no absolute decline in the British economy after the 1860s, either in terms of GDP, exports or industrial production, the abiding impression is one of relatively sluggish growth. Retardation was also accompanied by a severe depression in prices between 1873 and 1896, and while this was a worldwide phenomenon, in the British context it provoked serious debate over the economy's welfare. Furthermore, profitability suffered badly from the 1870s (Saul, 1973; 41–2: Cottrell, 1980; 258–9), and because much of the finance for industry came from this source, as we shall see later, investment rates would appear to have been low, particularly in relation to American and German trends. As the Royal Commission on the Depression in Trade and Industry (1884–6) concluded, 'in consequence of the unremunerative character of the trade of the country [there was] less inducement to the capitalist to embark his capital in productive enterprise' (Musson, 1959; 212). In an age of *laissez faire*, however, when interference with the operation of market forces was widely accepted in Britain as being highly dangerous, the state was reluctant to embark on a more interventionist approach, and consequently free trade was maintained as the essence of British commercial policy. This provides one obvious source of contrast with the approaches taken by governments in the USA, Germany and Japan, because they adopted interventionist and protective policies as part of a cohesive national strategy.

Of course, because this description of Britain's trading environment has incorporated a comparative element, it is easy to forget the many positive trends which, as we shall see later, stimulated a series of innovations in the fields of retailing and distribution (Fraser, 1981; 3–7, 236). Unfortunately, though, while one can point to some significant market developments at this time, it is apparent that they failed to provide the same kind of incentives as those operating in the USA. Another factor to consider is the nature of the domestic market, because apart from being geographically more concentrated than its much larger counterparts, Britain already possessed a highly integrated urban market structure, with fifty per cent of the population living in towns and cities by 1851. This degree of population concentration had actually risen to seventy-seven per cent by 1901, a level not matched in the USA and Germany until later in the twentieth century. The early start as an industrial nation had also stimulated the creation of an extensive distribution system, and when the railway network was completed by the 1870s it simply reinforced the tendency of manufacturers to produce from single sites, making the branch plant system used in the USA unnecessary. As Chandler (1990; 250–1) accepts: 'In other words, given the size and rate of growth of the domestic British market, investments in production and distribution comparable to those made by American firms in the same industries would have led to under-utilisation and higher costs'.

The organisation of distribution

It is clear, then, that the three-pronged investments in production, distribution, and management so extensively exploited in the USA were not a viable proposition in Britain, and in simple terms the system of personal capitalism was perpetuated by the existing market structure. This point is further reinforced by looking at the organisation of distribution up to the First World War, illustrating how, as Payne (1967; 524–5) reveals, producers were rarely able to develop a close relationship with customers. We noted in section 2.5 that by the early-nineteenth century marketing and distribution was controlled by an extensive and highly specialised network of wholesaling factors, commission agents, brokers and merchants, and Chapman (1992; 232) illustrates how these networks continued to exhibit a high degree of sophistication, especially as the telegraph speeded up communications. This system consequently gave manufacturers the opportunity to sub-contract such functions, because external transaction costs were lower than those achievable by internalising marketing and distribution, reinforcing further the tendency to specialise in a narrow range of output. As Porter (1990; 786) argues, product specialisation is an entirely rational strategy in the context of a highly competitive, atomistic market structure, but in order to exploit its full advantages industrialists would have to market their distinctiveness, and in such a system this proved extremely difficult.

A simple illustration of this problem was the extensive use made of commission agents in British industry (Payne, 1988, 41), because while large numbers of these plied their trade, usually within a single region of the country, rarely did they represent a single firm. The agents might well have extensive contacts, but as their income was dependent upon selling profitable lines it was consequently difficult for producers either to push a particular product or introduce new ideas on to the market with so little directly-acquired information on trends in consumer tastes. Overseas trading was also conducted along similar lines, and the commission agents which were connected directly to the acceptance houses (as we saw in section 2.5) acted as the link between manufacturers and foreign consumers. Chapman (1984; 9–15) has described how this relationship had emerged by the 1820s as a result of the highly risky nature of overseas trading, concluding that by the 1850s up to three-quarters of British industrial exports were handled by commission agents who invariably acted for a large number of firms. Some of the largest businesses, like Horrocks in cotton and Wedgwood in pottery, were able to sustain their own overseas marketing operations, but the majority had built up such a reliance on more indirect methods of selling abroad that this restricted their ability to cater for market requirements when competition intensified after 1870. Once again, we can see how transaction costs were heavily skewed in favour of external dealings, providing little incentive for British manufacturers to internalise marketing and distribution at a time when retardation characterised market conditions.

Marketing

This view of marketing has passed into the general literature as a damning indictment of the British approach (Aldcroft, 1964; 113–34), but in terms of transaction-cost considerations clearly businessmen were acting rationally. It is also important to add that more detailed research into distribution techniques has revealed how, firstly, valuable information on market trends could be provided to manufacturers by the intermediaries, and, second, an extensive agency system was grafted on to the network during the late-nineteenth century. This agency system was in fact the vital marketing innovation of the era, according to Nicholas (1984; 489–506). Much of his evidence is derived from agricultural engineering, but many other industries would also appear to have been exploiting the opportunities associated with having overseas representatives who would be responsible for sales and distribution, as well as servicing and maintenance. In fact, the larger agricultural machinery manufacturers had been among the earliest to employ direct methods of selling in the domestic market (Brown, 1993; 219–21), while in export markets firms like Ransome's had also introduced a 'selling mechanism [which] was particularly highly developed' (Saul, 1970a; 153). Similar progress was also being made in electrical engineering, and even medium-sized manufacturers like Ferranti and larger firms like Dick, Kerr & Co. developed domestic and overseas agency networks which covered their main markets (Wilson, 1985; 33–5: 1988; 103–4).

These revisionist views have naturally not gone unchallenged, and after editing a series of case-studies covering firms like Vickers, Rowntree and Nettlefold, Davenport-Hines (1986; 6–13) has concluded that the case for marketing vigour in the late-nineteenth century has been overstated. Indeed, many of the agents used by British manufacturers were not exclusive to a single firm, and when compared to the sales and marketing teams employed by

American and German companies they were a poor substitute. Farnie (1993; 147) has also noted how after 1893 the leading textile machinery maker, Platt Bros of Oldham, 'increased its reliance upon foreign agents in the place of direct sales abroad', undermining its competitivenes as American competition intensified. This reveals how British marketing innovations could be described as a compromise between the dedicated approach pursued in other economies and the old commission agent system which had dominated up to the 1870s. On the other hand, Nicholas (1984; 496–7) points out how more ambitious approaches were actually emerging at this time, because in attempting to economise on transaction costs manufacturers were 'replacing market allocation with cheaper alternative institutional modes such as agents, licensing, or the hierarchical firm in the form of a direct investment in sales subisidiaries and branch production'. Multinational enterprise will be examined further in section 4.3, but clearly this was a strategy which prominent firms like J. & P. Coats, Lever Bros, Dunlop and Vickers were experimenting with in their attempts at extending a domestic market supremacy into other economies (Stopford, 1974; 316–17). Foreign direct investment was indeed the ultimate expression of a manufacturer's desire to reduce the transaction costs associated with selling and distribution overseas (Nicholas, 1983; 504–6), and from the evidence available it is apparent that some of the larger firms were engaged in marketing experiments which were just as ambitious as those pursued by American and German firms.

It would be easy to extend this analysis into a broad generalisation covering British industry as a whole. One must remember, however, that only the major firms with a dominant position in the domestic market possessed the resources for such strategies, and the vast majority had only a limited ability to overcome the major institutional features of British selling and distribution arrangements. This reinforces the earlier argument that the environment severely restricted the ability to invest substantially in Chandler's second prong, mass marketing and distribution. One should also note that this system strengthened the tendency towards specialisation, because, as Payne (1967; 525) describes:

> Specialisation . . . tends to become increasingly irreversible, for there takes place a concomitant growth of special mercantile relationships, highly skilled labour forces and the evolution of particular types of managerial talent that makes any return to an earlier, more flexible, position more expensive and difficult.

In this context, we can return to the mutually-dependent relationship between mass production and mass distribution which was such a feature of American business from the 1880s, emphasising how in the British context businessmen did not have the incentive to mass-produce a standardised range of goods with so little information on market trends and tastes from an essentially indirect system of selling output. Similarly, both the sluggish rate of market growth and the nature of demand for products also inhibited moves towards Chandler's first prong.

Attitudes towards mass production

When it comes to extending this analysis of Chandler's first prong, it is certainly not obvious whether, even if the British trading environment had been more conducive, industrialists would have been well advised to introduce mass production techniques in the late-nineteenth century. Habakkuk (1962; 194–9) has argued that, when compared to the USA, because labour was cheaper than capital in Britain, industrialists were acting rationally by clinging to labour-intensive production techniques at a time when market growth was slow. In contrast, the reverse was the case in the USA, prompting a widespread exploitation of capital-intensive methods in rapidly-expanding markets. He goes on to explain how after 1880 British industrialists continued to be influenced by 'inherited attitudes moulded by the cost-conditions of the past', hinting at some entrepreneurial deficiencies. In addition, the hostility of organised labour to skill dilution (see section 5.3) would appear to have been a problem, but relative factor endowments, in association with sluggish market growth, remain at the centre of his thesis.

This interpretation provides an interesting explanation for the different approaches towards Chandler's first prong, but inevitably it has been challenged on a number of fronts. In the first place, mass-production methods were extensively employed by German firms, even though labour costs were lower there than in Britain. This ignores the Leontieff Paradox – that the cost of labour ought to be measured by its efficiency, as well as by wages – but productivity growth rates were certainly higher in Germany where capital could be raised more easily from the major banks (Pollard, 1989; 5, 50). Secondly, Saul (1970a; 142) has argued that, rather than the pace of market growth, of much greater significance to this debate about the propensity of British manufacturers to invest in capital-intensive technologies was the nature and structure of demand. Focussing his attentions especially on mechanical engineering, Saul has demonstrated that institutional barriers prevented the adoption of mass-production techniques in most sectors, while only in new trades did British firms invest heavily in what was increasingly coming to be known as 'the American system of manufactures'.

Consulting engineers

Of central importance to Saul (1970a; 146–50) was the institutional framework in which capital equipment firms operated, with the standard conventions of each particular market dictating the practices to be followed in the design and manufacture of most products. An excellent example is the locomotive trade, where producers independent of the big railway companies would be instructed by the consulting engineers representing their customers on the design to be followed, where some of the components should be purchased, and the methods of production. Although the engineering standards of locomotive manufacturers like Beyer, Peacock and the Vulcan Foundry were world-renowned, they were unable to exploit substantial economies of scale in production, restricting their ability to compete on price against American mass-producers like Baldwin's. On the other hand, workshops attached to major railway companies standardised production methods much more extensively, given the steady supply of orders for particular types of engine from the parent organisation. This reveals how such an approach was not alien to this sector in the appropriate circumstances, but clearly until both the big railway company mergers of the 1920s, and the achievement of maturity in locomotive design, standardisation was impossible to achieve in general (Kirby, 1988; 287–302). Furthermore, there was also 'the baleful influence' of consulting engineers on production practices (Saul, 1970a; 168), and clearly this institutional feature of the market played a key role in determining manufacturers' attitudes towards mass production.

The consulting engineer was actually a ubiquitous feature of British engineering markets, and in sectors like electrical engineering, by laying down detailed specifications to be fulfilled by contractors with regard to production, installation and testing of every single order, they prevented the standardisation of production which was developing so rapidly in the USA (Wilson, 1988; 71). On the other hand, of equal importance to consulting engineers was the entrenched attitudes of British engineering manufacturers, attitudes which placed a premium on individuality and quality irrespective of the need for standardisation. This was manifested in the general tendency of most firms to have their own workshop, where special machine tools could be made. This limited the opportunities for specialist manufacturers to influence techniques in the way that American machine tool firms were able to introduce new process technologies from the 1860s (Saul, 1968; 36–41). Only when new sectors like bicycle production took off in the late-1890s did a greater demand for standard machine tools emerge. This period was actually crucial in witnessing a surge in the importation of new American production technologies, making a wider range of modern tools available and influencing practices in the big textile machinery and locomotive makers. However, by 1913 there were still only six British machine tool firms employing in excess of 500 workers, indicating how the general level of demand failed to stimulate large-scale production along American lines.

British engineering firms consequently clung to traditional labour-intensive technologies for reasons firmly related to both the economic realities of their trade, and the belief in quality, as opposed to quantity, production. Similar points can be made about the shipbuilding industry (Lorenz & Wlkinson, 1986; 3–9), where the one-off nature of production was standard practice, while in other industries like steel and textiles the manufacturers relied mainly on batches of orders (Habakkuk, 1962; 210–1). The case of the bicycle industry indicates that, when circumstances were appropriate, mass-production technologies could be extensively exploited as a means of satisfying the demand for such novel consumer goods. On the other hand, when motor cars appeared in the late-1890s, manufacturers had to cater for a luxury market which insisted on a high level of individuality. Saul (1962; 22–44) also illustrates how, while such a market limited opportunities for mass production, the predominance of design engineers over production specialists in this industry prevented British firms from copying Henry Ford's ideas on making a standardised product. Of course, the American demand for cars was much greater than in Britain, but the key factor was how manufacturers' attitudes determined the adoption of production techniques.

The market-cum-technological environment

The case of motor cars provides an opportunity to highlight two key points arising from our discussion of the market-cum-technological environment, namely, that the demand for the new consumer goods of the Second Industrial Revolution only emerged very slowly, while institutional constraints reinforced the preference of manufacturers to concentrate on the production of high-quality goods. In the case of electrical engineering, for example, Chandler (1990; 276) is wrong when claiming that a large market existed in Britain which would have stimulated the creation of firms comparable in size to General Electric and Westinghouse in the USA and Siemens and AEG in Germany. As Byatt (1979; 27–8, 177–8) notes, the existence of a powerful gas supply industry and the extensive use of steam power in industry resulted in an extremely slow start for the new energy source, and the market remained difficult because most of the orders for electrical plant were eventually to come from local authorities which insisted on using consulting engineers as intermediaries. We noted earlier that consulting engineers dictated to suppliers a whole range of specifications, and when one combines this practice with the extremely sluggish development of the market for electric lighting and power in Britain it is not surprising that by the 1890s the industry was dominated by American and German first-movers (Wilson, 1988; 70–85).

It is important to remember that, when discussing the new industries emerging at this time, Chandler (1990; 286) emphasises how the time period in which industrialists should have been making the three-pronged investment in production, distribution and management was extremely brief, perhaps lasting only between 1880 and 1910. He also emphasises how 'once closed, that window was difficult to reopen', because the first-movers, of whatever nationality, were then able to exploit their competitive advantage within and across national boundaries. This created an extremely difficult trading environment for those industries which developed late in Britain, and in general terms one must question Chandler's use of the word 'failure' when explaining why British industry did not make the three-pronged investments in production, distribution and management. In most cases, the British strategy would appear to have been an entirely rational response to the market-cum-technological environment which prevailed in the period up to 1914, and Chandler (1990; 272–3, 285, 292) himself recognises as much at various junctures in his study.

Retailing and branded and packaged goods

This discussion of the British scene has only focussed on the capital equipment and staple industries, and before moving on to assess business structure it is vital to broaden our survey and examine other sectors which were affected by different market-cum-technological factors. Of particular importance here is the considerable expansion of sectors like branded and packaged goods, some new capital-intensive industries, and the service sector, because as Chandler (1990; 255–74) illustrates these are areas where we can find a more aggressive response from businessmen anxious to exploit the openings of the era. One must not forget that, although growth was slower than in the USA, domestic demand in Britain expanded considerably between 1860 and 1914, largely as a result of the significant growth in real wages during the price depression of 1873–1896 (Fraser, 1981; 14–26). This trend stimulated a veritable 'Retailing Revolution' (Jefferys, 1954; 6), manifested in 'new techniques of selling, new methods of wholesale and retail organisation, new trades, new types of consumer goods and new forms of retailing units' like the multiple stores and co-operative societies which cast their net across the highly integrated urban network. Of particular importance here is the strategy of backward vertical integration pursued by some mass retailers, because firms like Lipton's, the Co-operative Wholesale Society and Home and Colonial Stores acquired manufacturing operations to ensure a regular supply of goods at the right quality. This integration of production and distribution was also on a much more extensive scale than in American retailing, and although the British companies were more specialised and their managerial hierarchies less well-developed (Chandler, 1990; 255–61), it illustrates how businessmen were capable of making American-style three-pronged investments when the circumstances proved amenable.

In the branded and packaged goods sector, one can also detect signs of ambitious production and distribution strategies as firms making chocolate (Rowntree and Cadbury), biscuits (Huntley & Palmer and Peek Freens), cigarettes (W. D. & H. O. Wills), beer (Guiness and Watneys), soap (Lever Bros) and other consumer goods (J. J. Colman and Crosse & Blackwell) exploited the substantial growth in demand from both working and middle class consumers. This, along with retailing, was the most expansive sector in the British economy at that time (Wilson, 1965; 194–5), providing clear evidence of a willingness to pursue aggressive strategies which utilised all the most advanced techniques for mass-producing their goods, selling them through extensive distribution systems, and integrating backwards into the supply of raw materials. The classic example is William Lever, who from his Port Sunlight factory near Ellesmere Port revolutionised the soap trade by mass-producing soap in tablets, as opposed to selling it by the block. He also marketed his branded products extensively throughout the British and Empire markets, adopting trade names like 'Sunlight' and 'Lux' which were used as advertising slogans in campaigns which became symbols of the new approach to mass-selling (Wilson, 1954; 60–71).

The new industries

The third sector where Chandler (1990; 268–74) is willing to accede to British progress in making the essential three-pronged investments in production, distribution and management was in the new industries which emerged or expanded at this time. Notable among these were rubber (Dunlop), glass (Pilkingtons), dynamite (Nobel), synthetic alkalis (Brunner Mond), and rayon (Courtaulds). It is also noticeable that, as in the consumer goods industries just described, these firms were able to secure a substantial share of their home market, exploiting the competitive advantages associated with first-movers to eliminate competition through their technical superiority. They became so powerful that most of these companies were able to participate in both multinational activity and international cartels (Stopford, 1974; 306–23), carving up the world's markets with American and German corporations in order to eliminate excessive competition among respective first-movers. This demonstrates how British business as a whole was not being left behind in the general move towards large-scale business. Nobel Explosives was perhaps the most outstanding of these firms, building up a highly integrated operation which was staffed by a team of professional managers after allying in 1886 with four German firms to create the Nobel-Dynamite Trust Co., (Reader, 1970; 137–61). This firm was to become the basis of one of Britain's most successful twentieth century businesses, ICI, as we shall see in section 5.2, and its organisation was a model for others to follow.

Conclusion

In all these new sectors, however, Chandler (1990; 273–4) argues that apart from cases like Nobel very few of the firms were capable of developing extensive managerial hierarchies along the lines adopted in the USA and Germany at that time. In many ways, though, he would appear to have been confusing cause and effect, because it is a continuous feature of his analysis of company strategy that either the relatively small scale of the British market or the ability of firms to finance their own expansion contributed extensively to the retention by family groupings of key managerial positions. Naturally, these factors played a major role in determining the pattern of business organisation, just as they did in the USA and Germany, but Chandler prefers to emphasise the continuing commitment to personal capitalism as the key reason why the traditional system prevailed in most industries, irrespective of the market challenges of the era. On the other hand, one might argue that of far greater importance was the concentrated market structure, its sluggish rate of growth, particularly with regard to industries of both the First and Second Industrial Revolutions, and the well-established institutional features of British marketing and distribution which constrained manufacturers' abilities to extend their own networks. The innovatory approach adopted in sectors like retailing, consumer goods and new processing industries reveals the aggressive nature of British business strategy, where the environment proved conducive to the Chandlerian three-pronged investments. In other sectors, though, the incentive to exploit such an expensive strategy remained limited. Moreover, apart from the market-cum-technological scene, different factors would have contributed to this continuing commitment towards personal capitalism, in particular the general business culture and its impact on attitudes towards combination, and we need to include this in our analysis before drawing any general conclusions.

4.2   Attitudes towards combination

The market-cum-technological environment in which British business operated up to 1914 was undoubtedly a significant factor explaining the persistence of family-based management structures. By itself, however, this conclusion only provides a partial insight into the evolutionary process, and in order to understand fully why personal capitalism survived, and the broader implications of its impact on both strategy and structure, much more careful attention must be paid to the responses of businessmen to the various pressures of the era. We were arguing at the end of section 2.6 that by the 1870s the whole business system had ossified at a relatively immature stage of development, and irrespective of the increasingly difficult trading environment, wholesale changes to business practices were rarely envisaged. In effect, this left a specialised, atomistic market structure to struggle on against American and German first-movers. However, the strength of both internal and external competition from the 1870s, not to mention the inner dynamics of industrial capitalism, required some response from family-controlled firms, and in fact Payne (1967; 519) has demonstrated that these circumstances precipitated the stirrings of a more concentrated industrial structure. There were strong elements of compromise in the strategies pursued, and many businessmen jealously guarded against the loss of family control, but it is important to stress that some changes to the system of personal capitalism were being made from the 1880s.

Trade associations

The most obvious response which family firms might make to intensifying competition would be to create a trade association, providing both the stability required and minimal interference with management. This was clearly a well-established custom in British business, because Adam Smith (1776; I, 75) claimed that: 'Masters are always and everywhere in a sort of tacit, but constant and uniform combination'. Carter (1913; 12) also noticed that 'perfectly free competition has never existed', reporting on the price-fixing combinations which had existed since the sixteenth century. The earliest associations were both highly localised and often temporary responses to trading difficulties, but by the 1870s a whole series of national (and later, international) organisations emerged (Clapham, 1951; 213–4). It was the price depression starting in 1873 which was largely responsible for this move towards greater integration of price-fixing activities, and by the 1880s 'the movement fully revealed system, deliberateness, [and a] thorough and consistent development throughout English industry generally' (Carter, 1913; 2–3). It is important to remember that the organisations were known as trade associations, as opposed to trusts (USA) or cartels (Germany), and they were especially popular in the iron and steel, textiles, metal processing and chemical industries. Their specific aims were to fix prices at a mutually profitable level, allocate market quotas and, in some cases, liaise on technical matters, bringing a greater degree of stability at a time of falling prices and intensifying competition (Levy, 1911; 170–203).

The extensive development of trade associations in British industry undermines the theory that it is only in economies protected by import duties that monopolistic organisations emerge. Unfortunately for their creators, though, because these price-fixing bodies existed in a *laissez faire* environment, durability was sorely tested by both extensive foreign competition and indigenous business attitudes towards monopoly (Levy, 1911; 172–8). An excellent example of the difficulties experienced by British trade associations can be found in the electrical industry, where American (British Westinghouse and British Thomson-Houston) and German (Siemens) multinational subsidiaries had exploited their parent companies' competitive advantages as first-movers in the 1880s and 1890s to dominate the smaller British manufacturers (Byatt, 1979; 149). Such was the intensity of competition by the late-1890s that British-owned companies agreed to form the Electrical Plant Manufacturers' Association in 1898, in an attempt to encourage co-operation, but this soon folded after the big foreign-owned firms refused to join. This was followed by the creation of the National Electrical Manufacturers Association in 1902, but not until 1911, when the

British Electrical and Allied Manufacturers' Association was established, did the American and German subsidiaries agree to liaise on pricing policy (Wilson, 1988; 105–7). In the meantime, electrical manufacturers had operated in such a highly competitive market that few had been able to build up adequate resources for ambitious product development strategies, and even the foreign-owned firms suffered from the dual problems of slugggish growth in demand and falling prices (Jones & Marriott, 1970; 47–69).

Individualism and price-fixing

The case of electrical engineering demonstrates the vulnerability of British firms to foreign interference with domestic efforts at price-fixing, and given the lack of any natural monopoly in the supply of key raw materials or exclusive use of a particular technology, clearly most industries would have suffered from similar problems. This might have been sufficient to undermine the British trade association movement, but another factor was probably of much greater importance in reducing the effectiveness of these organisations, namely, the individualistic tendencies in the business culture. The German cartels had been especially effective because manufacturers had been willing to subsume their own independence under the collective banner of tightly-controlled pricing, marketing and production policies, but in general most British businessmen were never willing to accept that degree of intervention. Levy (1911; 172–6) attributes this independent streak to the power of *laissez faire* economic doctrines and their inference that monopoly was a damaging influence on industry, and clearly this socio-cultural environment bestowed great status on individualism. The consequence was that, while businessmen were willing to participate in price-fixing activities and the allocation of market quotas, organisationally the trade associations were never as rigorous as the German cartels. Furthermore, not only did they lack the cohesion which would have secured greater effectiveness, they were also vulnerable to the fresh competition which classical economists argued was an inevitable consequence of monopoly.

While cartelisation might engender greater stability in highly competitive markets, providing a more secure basis for improved profitability, its opponents argued that the impact on both producer and consumer is extremely damaging. In the first place, the latter suffers because prices are held at an artificially high level, while the former is affected because in such a system little incentive exists to pursue more ambitious strategies (Carter, 1913; 1–7). The German cartels were an exception, because they encouraged members to improve performance, while in Britain inefficient firms could shelter behind price-fixing agreements which might undermine the competitiveness of an entire industry. This, however, would provide an opportunity for an individual, or a small group of renegade producers, to set new agendas on pricing and marketing, subverting the trade association's efforts at creating stability.

No better example of such a scenario exists than that of William Lever and the soap trade, because he pursued such an ambitious approach towards production and marketing that the Soap Manufacturers Association (formed as early as 1867, and later renamed the UK Soap Manufacturers Association, or UKSMA) was unable to control prices and market quotas. We noted in the last section that Lever was as aggressive as any of his American counterparts in making the three-pronged investment in production, distribution and management at his Port Sunlight works from the late-1880s. He also realised that membership of the UKSMA would have severely curtailed his freedom to exploit any competitive advantages gained from this strategy, because it insisted that firms should only operate in their own regions, selling at centrally-determined prices (Reader, 1959; 77). Lever, on the other hand, wanted to advertise his branded and packaged goods nationally at competitive prices, and such was the degree of success achieved that by the mid-1890s the UKSMA had been completely undermined. Lever Bros also acquired several soap manufacturers, building up its share of British soap sales to sixty-one per cent by 1914 (Wilson, 1954; 60–71).

William Lever exemplified both the dangers inherent in cosy trade association agreements, and the possibilities provided for ambitious businessmen who were willing to try new approaches. It was this individualistic streak which had been his greatest asset in the competitive struggle of the 1890s, but one must note that by 1906, after achieving a dominant position in the industry, his strategy had changed. Even Alfred Marshall (1919; 583–4), the Professor of Political Economy at Cambridge, had advised contemporary businessmen that, while 'strong individuality' had been such a crucial asset in the past, in the new climate 'it needs increasingly to be supplemented by a readiness to co-operate with others in large affairs'. This policy was implicitly followed by William Lever when in 1906 he attempted to create a 'Soap Trust' which would co-ordinate the purchasing, advertising and pricing policies of the ten largest manufacturers. Public opinion and self-interest, however, combined to prevent Lever from succeeding in this aim. In particular, Lord Harmsworth of the Daily Mail, motivated largely by the potential loss in advertising revenue, was so incensed about the proposed 'Soap Trust' that he organised a major campaign villifying Lever and his monopolistic tendencies, and within three weeks the combine was disbanded (Wilson, 1954; 72–88).

For a variety of economic and social reaons, it was extremely difficult in late-nineteenth century Britain to succeed in creating durable trade associations which would provide the degree of stability achieved by German cartels. The most successful was the Bedstead Makers' Alliance, based in Birmingham, which from 1893 developed a central selling agency linking producers and distributors. Such cases were extremely rare, though, and as Clapham (1951; 305–17) illustrates, in general, trade associations were either unobtrusive in their impact on competition or in some industries they hardly existed at all. At the same time, the trading environment failed to improve much, even after prices started to rise in 1896, and in several industries businessmen experimented with what is a logical alternative to weak associations, the merger. This strategy of external expansion had been used extensively in the USA and Germany from the 1880s, as we saw in the last chapter, contributing significantly to the establishment of an oligopolistic trading structure populated by large, highly integrated or diversified firms which had exploited first-mover advantages in a wide range of industries. British industrialists also pursued similar strategies, but it is apparent that, for much the same reasons which undermined trade associations, mergers were a half-hearted attempt to create the necessary stability.

Mergers

It is first of all important to note that the American and British merger movements ran in parallel during the period 1890–1905, both reaching their peak around the turn of the century. However, the enormous differences in scale are apparent when one notes that 650 firms valued at £42 million were involved in the British merger peak of 1898–1900, while 979 American firms with a value of over £400 million merged in one year alone, 1899 (Hannah, 1983; 21–2). Although an average of sixty-seven firms disappeared in British mergers each year between 1888 and 1914, this evidently did little to create the kind of oligopolistic market structure which prevailed in the USA by the First World War. It is also interesting to note that the British industries most affected by merger activity were the well-established, yet relatively slow-growing, industries like textiles, chemicals, mining, heavy engineering and brewing. In the USA, on the other hand, high-growth sectors like petroleum, transportation equipment, electrical engineering, and food and tobacco dominated. Similarly, while in the USA vertical integration and diversification were common, ninety-eight per cent of all mergers in Britain were horizontal combinations (Hannah, 1974; 1–20), and once again it was the combination of market-cum-technological and socio-cultural factors which help to explain this contrast.

In simple terms, while anti-trust legislation had played a part in the build-up, most American mergers of this period had been *aggressive* in character, stimulated by a highly conducive market-cum-technological environment which resulted in the closer harmonisation of industrial and financial interests. This dynamic process can be contrasted sharply with the essentially *defensive* nature of most British mergers, because in the vast majority of cases market problems prompted businessmen to fall back on a combination of interests as a last-ditch effort to protect their firms.

There were actually some striking mergers at this time, starting with the Salt Union in 1888 (involving sixty-four firms), and altogether Macrosty (1907) mentions twenty-nine multi-firm amalgamations which incorporated

616 firms (Utton, 1972; 52–5). Unfortunately, though, rarely was there any intention of integrating production, distribution or management, and the new organisations often adopted a federal structure which allowed the former owners to continue running their own businesses without too much interference from headquarters. In fact, what happened in some cases was the conversion of a trade association into a joint stock company, and while this reflected the wider acceptance of limited liability from the 1880s, it is apparent that a legal combination of interests was as far as most were willing to go. This indicates that merger activity was a typical British compromise between the need for greater co-operation and a desire to retain managerial control by the people responsible for establishing the constituent members of the new federations.

The textile industries

The industry most heavily involved in the concentration movement was textiles, accounting for 330 of the 895 firms affected by mergers between 1887 and 1900 (Hannah, 1974; 22). It is also apparent from the names of the ensuing companies – Calico Printers' Association, Fine Cotton Spinners' and Doublers' Association, British Cotton & Wool Dyers' Association, Yorkshire Woolcombers' Association, Bradford Dyers' Association, and the Bleachers' Association – that these were not new organisations. All had been previously associated with the unsuccessful attempts at price-fixing, and in order to provide their operations with some legal authority over members they had merged into a single company. This was the sector in which defensive motives were at their most prominent, given the intensity of competition in trades which were experiencing a considerable slowdown in the rate of market growth after a substantial expansion of capacity during the mill-building booms of the 1870s and 1890s (Farnie, 1979; 120). This situation required what the *Engineer* of 1899 described as 'the advent of some Napoleon in organisation', but it will become apparent that the new combines were simply not prepared to accept the need for co-operation, indicating how the textile mergers were a classic missed opportunity (Payne, 1967; 528–30).

To clarify this point, one need only examine the case of the Calico Printers' Association (CPA), a combine created in 1899 to amalgamate fifty-nine firms which accounted for eighty-five per cent of this trade. They had agreed to merge because for two decades calico printing had been struggling with fifty per cent excess capacity, combined with a downturn in exports since the mid-1890s (Farnie, 1992; 5). From the start, however, apart from being over-capitalised (at £9.2 million) the CPA was 'a study in disorganisation', because the board of directors was no less than eighty-four strong, with eight separate managing directors, preventing the establishment of an effective central administration (Macrosty, 1907; xi). This allowed the constituent family firms to survive almost intact and only a minimal integration of capacity or strategy was effected at a time when both profits and prices were falling (Cook, 1958; 151–68). It was a situation which prevailed in almost all of the big textile mergers of this period. For example, Jeremy (1993; 174–6) has described how at the Bleachers' Association 'a very unwieldy structure was devised', with a main board of forty-nine directors representing the main constituent firms in the merger of 1900. Although most of them managed to merge substantial proportions of their sectors – Bradford Dyers' had ninety per cent of that trade, Bleachers' Association sixty per cent, and Fine Spinners and Doublers' forty per cent (Utton, 1974; 56) – they were organisational disasters. One should add that only the Yorkshire Woolcombers' Association actually collapsed, largely because substantial independent operators were excluded from the combine (Clapham, 1951; 229). On the other hand, overcapitalisation and undermanagement prevented the full exploitation of any potential advantages in merger strategy, indicating just how powerful the family ethos remained in one of Britain's major industries. In spite of this merger activity, Lazonick (1983; 236) has also commented on the failure of British cotton manufacturers to create an integrated industry dominated by large-scale firms with corporate management structures, and clearly serious organisational deficiences remained for many decades.

Ironically, the big textile combines had been provided with a role-model to follow in the 1896 merger of four cotton thread firms with J. & P. Coats Ltd. This Paisley-based family firm had been the UK's largest cotton thread producer for many years before its public flotation in 1890, when the capital was increased to what was a massive level for an industrial concern of £5.75 million (Cairncross & Hunter, 1987; 157). It also operated a central thread agency for the whole trade, by-passing middlemen and dealing directly with retailers and other large consumers, while an increasing number of overseas subsidiaries was established to exploit its competitive advantage as one of the most advanced concerns in this sector (Clapham, 1951; 224–5). When the merger occurred in 1896, bringing the nominal capital up to £7.5 million, a complete integration of production, distribution and management was effected, and by 1905 J. & P. Coats was actually Britain's largest manufacturing concern, with a market value of £42.1 million (Wardley, 1991; 278). The Coats family had played an important role in this success story, establishing a sophisticated management system which was based on clear lines of authority and standardised accounting procedures (Payne, 1967; 530). The key executive by the 1890s, however, was a German, O. E. Phillipi, and he was largely responsible for establishing and controlling the national and international sales organisations.

Other sectors

This case-study provides an excellent British example, albeit with substantial German influence, of how it was possible to exploit both the three-pronged investments so crucial to success in American business, and the potential in merger activity. Rarely, though, can we find many comparable textile mergers. Even at the English Sewing Cotton Co., formed in 1897 with a capital of £2.25 million, and closely allied with J. & P. Coats, the new management 'had not hacked away its dead wood', allowing the eleven constituents to retain their old identity (Clapham, 1951; 225–6). It was a story all too familiar for the period, and not simply in textiles, but also in industries like salt, cement, tobacco and whisky (Utton, 1972; 52–3). In these industries, mergers resulted in the creation of large firms – respectively, the Salt Union (with ninety per cent of the trade), Associated Portland Cement (forty-five per cent), Imperial Tobacco (ninety per cent), and Distillers (seventy-five per cent) – which were organised on the federal principle. At Imperial Tobacco, for example, where thirteen firms amalgamated in 1901 in response to the threat posed by American Tobacco's invasion of the home market, competition among the constituent members continued. The firm actually controlled ninety per cent of the British tobacco trade, and although some coordination of advertising budgets and prices was attempted within Imperial Tobacco, and a central purchasing agency was formed, the old family-managed firms continued to run their plants in much the same way as they had done prior to 1901 (Alford, 1973; 309–26).

Conclusion

As one senior exectuive from English Sewing Cotton claimed at the time, 'it was an awful mistake to put into control of the various businesses purchased by the company the men who had got into one groove and could not get out of it' (Macrosty, 1907; 133–4). It is important to remember that only one of the great mergers (Yorkshire Woolcombers) actually collapsed, while in Imperial Tobacco, Distillers, Associated Portland Cement, and most of the textile combines, we have some of Britain's largest and most consistently profitable concerns up to 1914. Chandler (1990; 291) also remarks after reviewing their creation that 'British mergers worked', by stabilising prices and output trends. He ignores the point that prices and output were in any case on an upward path after the problems of the 1890s (Saul, 1969; 27), but this was a general trend unrelated to merger activity, and without the combinations these trades could well have continued to suffer. On the other hand, the failure to integrate production, distribution and management was a hallmark of the resulting organisations, demonstrating how the continuing commitment to personal capitalism prevented these large-scale concerns from exploiting all the advantages which ought to accrue from merger and concentration. As we saw in the last section, the organisation of British domestic and overseas marketing and distribution inhibited innovation in this area, while the nature of demand placed greater emphasis on batch-production methods, but in organisational terms it was the predilections of family owner-managers which ultimately determined business structure.

4.3 A reawakening?

One can consequently be highly critical of the British merger movement, both in terms of its defensive motivations and the federal structures adopted by most of the new horizontal combines. On the other hand, it is important to question whether apart from rare examples like J. & P. Coats and Lever Bros little of an ambitious nature was happening. Indeed, the negative view is undoubtedly far too subjective, often having been based on a comparison with the most imaginative organisation-building of large American and German business. In fact, Payne (1967; 537–8) has shown that 'the early organisation of many of the giant American corporations was but little more sophisticated than that of the British concerns', indicating how these so-called pioneers experienced just as much difficulty matching structure to strategy as their British counterparts. Furthermore, while in the first stages most of the big British combinations resulted in a federal structure which allowed vested interests to survive, by 1914 most of them had undergone a radical reorganisation. This certainly did not go as far as it had done in either the USA or Germany, and therein lies the root problem in any comparative study, but both the structure of British industry and standards of business organisation were changing more radically in the decades leading up to the First World War than commentators like Chandler (1990; 292–4) would have us believe.

Textile reorganisations

This interesting claim is borne out by examining the textile mergers more thoroughly. We were especially critical of the anarchic pattern followed at the CPA, with its board of eighty-four directors, but as a result of the competition posed by those printing firms which had refused to join the combine, in particular F. Steiner & Co. of Accrington and the United Turkey Red Co. of Glasgow, by 1902 an extensive reorganisation had been initiated (Farnie, 1992; 4–6). The first move was to appoint a committee with responsibility for recommending the required changes, and the CPA hired O. E. Philippi of J. & P. Coats to act as chairman (Cook, 1958; 160–77). This resulted in the concentration of power into the hands of six directors, with an executive committe of just three, while by 1904 a central office had been established in Manchester to house an administrative organisation which made increasing use of standardised information-gathering and integrated policy-making. In spite of its well-known dislike of mergers, even the *Economist* was willing to accept that the reorganisation had been successful, and from 1903 the CPA started for the first time to pay a regular dividend on its ordinary shares (Clapham, 1951; 229).

Some British businessmen were clearly being prompted by continuing problems with prices and profits to wake up to the need for both legal combination and real co-operation. The CPA is also far from being the only case of radical change, because at Fine Cotton Spinners & Doublers (FCSD), which started off as a holding company in 1898, allowing its thirty-one constituents to be run independently, by 1909 A. H. Dixon had been appointed sole managing director with power to centralise financial systems, co-ordinate buying and distribution policies, and generally integrate operations (Howe, 1984; 107–10). This company had also integrated backwards into American cotton plantations and forward into an Egyptian exporting concern (Chandler, 1990; 289), while Clapham (1951; 230) also describes how training schemes for central office staff in Manchester were initiated. Similarly, at Bradford Dyers' Association, by 1909 George Douglas had assumed the role of sole managing director, ousting the other two managing directors, and a process of centralising administration, purchasing, distribution and financial reporting across the twenty-two firms was pursued rigorously (Jenkins,1984; 140–1). O. E. Philippi of J. & P. Coats was also responsible for reorganising the English Sewing Cotton Co in 1902 (Clapham, 1952; 231), while in other large cotton firms like Tootal, Broadhurst & Co. greater integration of operations was being introduced as an essential weapon in the fight against intense competition (Dupree, 1984; 452–3).

Heavy engineering

Although one must be careful not to exaggerate the sophistication of these new managerial hierachies, and Chandler (1990; 289) is at pains to emphasise that 'the central offices were much smaller than those of the successful American mergers', at least we can discern some signs of progress. Moreover, it is progress which was by no means unique to textiles, because in several other sectors businessmen were attempting bold changes, especially in the heavy engineering and metal trades. With regard to iron and steel, Payne (1967; 534) might well argue that 'the perpetuation of family control remained a major desideratum', but this did not limit the 'prevailing tendency in [these] industries . . . for large units to acquire control of a complete vertical integration of production over a wide range of processes' (Carter, 1913; 75).

In the Sheffield steel trades, Tweedale (1995) reveals how the clustering of small firms provided a competitive edge to activity, refuting any claims that size was the key to success. Firms like Bolckow Vaughan & Co. of Middlesbrough, Palmer's Shipbuilding Co. of Jarrow, and John Brown & Co. of Sheffield had all acquired ore and coal mines as an essential complement to their core activities, while mergers like that between Cammell and Lairds (1903), Armstrongs and Whitworth (1897), and Dorman, Long & Co. and Bell (1899) further strengthened the industry. The leading firm in this sector, Vickers, was especially ambitious, and in this case 'complete vertical integration has resulted from the definite and deliberate combination – vertically' (Carter, 1913; 85). Another interesting amalgamation in this sector resulted in the formation in 1902 of Guest, Keen & Nettlefolds & Co. This merger saw the integration of the collieries, Spanish ore mines and blast furnaces of Guest, Keen & Co. with the steel and components business of Nettlefolds, creating a firm with a nominal capital of £4 million (Jones, 1987; 361–3).

These examples in heavy engineering and steel refute the general accusation that such sectors failed to exploit the advantages of vertical integration, but once again emphasis must be placed on the sluggish development of an appropriate structure to cater for these moves. For example, after the 1902 amalgamation of two major steel tube manufacturers, Stewarts and Lloyds, co-ordinated central direction remained weak and changes only came slowly (Payne, 1967; 532–5), while at Guest, Keen & Nettlefold a highly decentralised structure was established which allowed the head offices of each constituent company to function as normal (Jones, 1987; 365–9). Even a firm like Bolckow Vaughan continued to experience managerial and organisational difficulties, after largely casting off its family owners when converting into a public company as early as 1862. This reinforces the point that, while British businessmen were able to fashion strategies which proved appropriate to the highly competitive circumstances of the era, organisationally their response was weak.

The unhelpful market-cum-technological environment can be used as a valid reason explaining why British firms did not implement fully the three-pronged investments in production, distribution and management, especially with consulting engineers and merchants playing such a dominant role in dictating customer relations. In the steel industry, for example, Chandler (1990; 283–5) accepts that, when compared to their American and German counterparts, British steel producers were placed at a distinct disadvantage in having access to a much smaller market which did not provide the incentive to invest in new production technologies. Nevertheless, management attitudes and practices would appear to have been relatively outmoded, even after a merger, and progress towards an integrated structure remained painfully slow. Boyce (1992; 42–62) has demonstrated that some steel firms were developing cost accounting techniques comparable to those employed in many American corporations, but in other areas they were still reluctant to change techniques and structures. As Lord Rendel (chairman of Armstrong, Whitworth) commented after his firm's diversification into car production during the Edwardian era: 'It is in the luncheon room [rather than the workshop] that all goes wrong' (Irving, 1975; 165).

Dudley Docker and Dick, Kerr & Co.

In this context, it is essential to introduce Dudley Docker, an individual who had a major impact on British business in the early-twentieth century. This 'great industrialist' featured prominently in the early-twentieth century, and not only was he responsible for one of the most successful mergers of the pre-1914 era, his role in the fields of industrial rationalisation and business politics was also extremely significant (Davenport-Hines, 1984; 13–54). Trained initially for the law, Dudley Docker started his career in 1881 as a Birmingham varnish manufacturer, but exploiting his reputation as a first-class cricketer he soon established a strong position in the rolling stock industry. This industry was at that time struggling to compete, because of underinvestment over the previous decade, and Docker decided to persuade five of the leading Birmingham firms to combine operations and form a single business capable of substantially improving sales and profitability. It is important to emphasise how the prevailing political climate provided a substantial boost to his lobbying, because as a result of the military humiliations of late-1899 and early-1900 a national 'efficiency movement' gathered widespread support during the Boer War. Docker was eventually to become a leading spokesman for this movement, and in persuading the rolling stock manufacturers to integrate their operations such sentiments proved invaluable, leading to the formation in 1902 of the Metropolitan Amalgamated Railway Carriage and Wagon Co. (MARCWC) (Davenport-Hines, 1984; 24–6).

The merger of the trade's five largest firms provided Docker with the opportunity to integrate production, distribution and management, and certainly he did not envisage the kind of loose federation of interests followed initially in the textile industry. In fact, while each constituent company was allowed three representatives on the board, Docker as chairman was concerned to stamp out any thoughts of independence. Unfortunately, though, in spite of developing a centralised management structure which imposed standardised routines on the geographically-dispersed factories, progress in achieving the necessary degree of integration was slow. Davenport-Hines (1984; 31) argues that one of the main reasons for this tardiness was Docker's inexperience as a manager of such an extensive business, but over the following decade he succeeded in creating an integrated combine which made the three-pronged investments in production, distribution and management necessary to achieve his initial goal of rejuvenating the industry. Chandler (1990; 290–1) actually describes the MARCWC as the merger which 'most closely followed the American pattern', and although Docker experienced some difficulty in recruiting sufficient managers of the right calibre he succeeded in creating 'a showpiece of modern, rationalised combination' (Davenport-Hines, 1984; 28).

During the pre-War years Docker was linked with a wide range of other firms, most notably the arms and motor-car firm, Birmingham Small Arms Co. (Davenport-Hines, 1984; 50–3), but it was MARCWC which dominated his work at that time. One of the more successful projects he negotiated was a complex grouping of firms forged specifically with the intention of loosening the stranglehold American and German firms had on British and world markets in the field of electrical engineering. His principal ally was the Kilmarnock engineering and rolling stock firm of Dick, Kerr & Co, whose two leading executives, John Kerr and George Flett, agreed with Docker on the imperative need to rejuvenate British electrical engineering (Wilson, 1985; 26–41). Dick, Kerr and Co. was an integrated firm with interests in rolling stock, electrical engineering and transport utilities. Their two main works in Preston were run by a team of professional managers recruited directly from American competitors, while marketing operations were integrated into a world-wide agency network, and the collaboration with MARCWC provided strong competition in the electric traction market against the major American firms. One should also note that their activities laid a solid foundation for later developments, because (see section 5.2) it is no coincidence that the inter-war merger movement was initiated by firms like English Electric and Metropolitan-Vickers Electrical Co., and the executives responsible for creating these large-scale businesses were mostly from MARCWC and Dick, Kerr & Co. (Wilson, 1985; 38). In 1912, Docker was even making preliminary inquiries into the possibility of organising a trading agreement with the major German electrical firms, and although little came of these negotiations prior to 1914 they were in tune with the recent consensus among British and American-owned subisidiaries which had helped to create a strong electrical trade association in 1911 (Davenport-Hines, 1984; 25–8).

The awakening?

The work of individuals like Dudley Docker illustrates the degree of progress being made in certain sectors of British industry as businessmen began to realise the need for real changes to outmoded organisations and antiquated practices. It is apparent that the awakening had taken a considerable period of time, originating with the 1870s trade association movement, moving on to the merger waves of 1888–1902, and culminating in the reorganisations and new approaches pursued in the years immediately before the First World War. Nevertheless the case-studies of Lever Bros and J. & P. Coats, of the integrated heavy engineering firms and restructured textile combines, and of rationalisation in the electrical and rolling stock industries, reveal new tendencies in British business organisation along lines which were not too dissimilar from those pursued in the USA and Germany. The movement might well have taken longer to gather any momentum than in other countries, but then Britain had a much more entrenched industrial and commercial system than its rivals, and the old methods were slow to die. Across the industrial spectrum, from textiles and heavy engineering to food and other consumer products, progressive thinking was beginning to make an impact on traditional attitudes, cracking the hardened surface of a business culture fashioned in much different conditions.

Multinationals

Another crucial manifestation of this more progressive approach towards business strategy and structure was the growing tendency among leading British firms to become multinationals, defined here as the creation of subsidiaries in overseas markets. We shall be looking at the figures on foreign direct investment in section 4.5 (Corley, 1994; 72–87), but it is important to emphasise how up to 1939 Britain held the largest single share of this increasingly important flow of funds, while after the Second World War only the USA has contributed more (Dunning, 1988; 74). Indeed, in the USA alone Wilkins (1988; 14) has calculated that by 1914 100 British companies operated approximately 255 plants. Stopford and Turner (1985; 46–55) have labelled the pre-1914 period 'The Cosmopolitan Era', because investment was not limited to any particular politico-geographical area. Similarly, both horizontal and vertical investments were made, respectively, either to extend manufacturing operations or to acquire supplies of essential raw materials. This confirms what we noted in section 4.1 as Nicholas's (1984; 496–7) claim that firms were attempting to economise on transaction costs by expanding abroad. However, Jones (1986; 13–20: 1986a; 96–110) has provided a link between commercial viability and managerial shortcomings, highlighting once again the debates prompted by criticism of British organisational weaknesses.

Although comprehensive evidence is not yet available on both the actual number of British companies venturing abroad and their management and control systems, there is an extensive literature on multinationals (Wilkins, 1991) which provides some interesting insights into business evolution. In the first place, it was at this time that firms like Courtaulds, J. & P. Coats, Cadbury, Nobel, Pilkingtons and Vickers ventured abroad to exploit the competitive advantage they had gained at home, while others (Lever Bros, Royal Dutch Shell and Dunlop) were keen to acquire supplies of essential raw materials. Nevertheless, after editing a collection of case-studies on leading multinationals like Dunlop, Vickers, Cadbury, Glaxo and Pilkingtons, Jones (1986; 13–20) concludes that not only were their financial results disappointing, they also had a tendency to establish subsidiaries for defensive reasons in 'safe' Empire markets. Most notably, the main reason given for these alleged failings was an appalling lack of control over overseas operations, supervision often taking an *ad hoc* form which was typified by visits from a director and little discussion of strategy at board level. Jones (1986a;

106–7) also combines this organisational weakness with an attack on marketing deficiencies, and while this ignores the evidence presented by Nicholas (1984; 489–506) on the extensive use of agencies by the 1890s, one is left in no doubt that in terms of managerial innovation British multinationals were little better than their domestic counterparts.

This critique of multinational activity up to the First World War would not be out of place if included in section 4.2, but before accepting these arguments it is important to ask several questions. In the first place, Nicholas (1991; 141) would like to see 'clearly defined parameters for what constitutes failure in terms of profits or returns on assets', because nowhere in the literature is this done. Another vital point made by Stopford and Turner (1985; 54) is that: 'Multinationals reflect to an important degree the conditioning of their home country environment'. This highlights the importance of noting the conclusions of section 4.1, and in particular to remember that Britain's market-cum-technological environment did not stimulate the pursuit of American-style aggressive strategies, leading to sharp contrasts in the size, nature and organisation of firms on either side of the Atlantic. Wilkins (1986a; 483–510) has also remarked on the role of Britain's domestic market in dictating the pattern of multinational management structures, indicating how any accusations of 'failure' must once again be contextualised. Furthermore, even though Jones (1986a; 109–10) is one of the main critics of British multinationals, he notes that they were not alone in failing to exploit market potential abroad, a point well substantiated by the American cases of Westinghouse, Diamond Match and Coca Cola. And finally, many of the firms which added an international dimension to their activities prior to 1914 have survived well into the twentieth century, an issue we shall examine further in section 6.5, indicating how this was not always crucial to their commercial success. It is perhaps sufficient to remember that significant British firms were building extensive overseas dimensions, and as the internationalisation of production became the most dramatic business development of the twentieth century they were able to participate effectively in this movement. Problems did remain, of course, with management structure and market location, but section 6.5 will illustrate how firms like Glaxo, British Petroleum, Shell and Unilever eventually eliminated these difficulties, providing the British economy with some of the world's most powerful enterprises.

Conclusion

This re-evaluation of the evidence on British business evolution up to 1914 should not be regarded as a complete rebuttal of Chandler's claim that the American and German systems were generally more advanced. The main aim has been to provide an objective assessment of progress which ignores the comparative emphasis predominant in most studies, and at the same time reveal the main market-cum-technological constraints preventing a more widespread acceptance of the need to make the three-pronged investments in production, distribution and management. Hannah (1983; 23) might well be correct in arguing that 'many innovations we now associate with the corporate economy were yet to appear', but he was equally accurate in noting that: 'The foundations of the modern corporate economy were already discernible in the large firms that had been created . . .'. This debate about the meaning and origins of a corporate economy will be developed further in chapter five, but it is important to emphasise how substantial progress was being made in the late Victorian and Edwardian eras.

In general, however, we are still faced with the overwhelming impression created by other historians that there was 'failure' in British business, that personal capitalism still prevailed, and in assessing the validity of such interpretations it is essential that we now examine why a preference for family-based management continued right up to 1914. As we noted in section 2.1, a society's value systems and its shared beliefs have a crucial bearing on entrepreneurial behaviour, and while cultural explanations for British economic decline are no longer regarded as sufficiently comprehensive, we shall see in the next section that in terms of business evolution they played a central role in helping to fashion both management structures and financial practices.

4.4   The business culture and its managerial impact

The concept of personal capitalism has so far been accepted as an appropriate label to describe the British business culture, but the organisational implications of such a term remain unexplained, along with the direct relationship between this culture and management training and practices. The issue revolves around the commitment towards the family firm in Britain, not forgetting a key theme of the last chapter, that this institution was prevalent in other countries, and does not necessarily hinder progress towards more elaborate strategies and structures (Church, 1993; 35–9). In this context, one must remember that 'family firms will be taken to be those, whether partnerships or limited companies, where a family or families were overwhelmingly represented amongst partners or boards of directors' (Rose, 1993; 130). This means that families were involved in both strategic management and ownership of the business, and as we saw in chapter 2 such a system was inextricably linked with the emergence of industrial capitalism in Britain.

The 'cultural critique'

Debate surrounding the importance attached to socio-cultural factors in accounting for the failure of Britain's economy to grow and restructure itself as fast as its main rivals has moved on substantially since Wiener (1981; 154) published his all-embracing thesis blaming the problem on the 'cultural absorption of the middle classes into a quasi-aristocratic elite' after 1850. Other historians had similarly pointed an accusing finger at the apparent tendency of British businessmen to become 'gentrified', and Coleman (1973; 95, 105–6) in particular has argued that 'social advancement was one of the most prized possessions to be bought by an English business fortune'. This thesis revealed how industrialists sent sons to the public schools of England in order to learn how to be gentlemen, rather than scientists or engineers or managers. For example, in the steel industry, taking the period when the leading figures were in office, only ten per cent of those figures had been to public school in 1865, while by 1905–25 this had risen to thirty-one per cent (Erickson, 1959; 33–6, 115). On the other hand, Rubinstein (1993; 102–39) has concluded that while attendance at public schools by sons of businessmen was certainly increasing during the nineteenth century, even by the Edwardian era this practice was still rare in most industries. Wiener (1981; 138–9) is confident that the trend was having a damaging impact, because it provided a 'gentlemanly' education based on the classics and liberal arts which was wholly inadequate for prospective industrial managers. However, Rubinstein (1993; 114–5) reveals an interesting paradox in this thesis, demonstrating how financial and commercial interests were the predominant users of public schools, '*yet it was industry which declined* and finance and commerce which continued to prosper'.

Rubinstein (1993; 25–44) has perhaps done more than any other historian to destroy what he calls the 'cultural critique'. In the first place, contrary to what Wiener (1981; 154) has claimed, he notes that British society was no more 'anti-industrial' than any of its rivals, while at the same time arguing that the economy was in fact never predominantly industrial in nature, because it depended more on the financial and commercial sectors for its wealth and continued growth. This debate need not delay us here, while the role of the City will be examined in greater detail in the next section, but clearly such claims considerably undermine any claim that British industry declined because of broad socio-cultural pressures.

Another aspect of the 'gentrification' thesis is the tendency of industrialists to invest their wealth in landed estates, with prominent examples like Sir Richard Arkwright buying up properties in the Cromford area as a means of acquiring status (Fitton, 1989; 182–4). This was used to emphasise how profits were simply seen as a means to the end of acquiring status in a society still dominated by an aristicratic ethos which laid greater store by rural, rather than industrial, lifestyles.

A case-study to which Wiener (1981; 137) attached great importance was that of Marshalls, a Leeds firm of flax spinners which, as a result of the aggressive strategies pursued by its eponymous owners, had become the largest of its type in the world by the 1840s. Three decades later, however, after the second and third generations of Marshalls had taken over the business, it was in terminal decline, principally because the family preferred to live in the Lake District and 'indulge very civilised tastes' as landowners, rather than reinvest profits in new plant (Rimmer, 1960; 291–9). This personified what has since become known as the 'Buddenbrooks syndrome', the thesis which claims that firms run by third generation owners lose their dynamism, and some feel it undermined the durability of family firms (Rose, 1993; 127–9). It is a thesis typical of the gentrification process, with land-ownership and public school educations draining away the entrepreneurial life-blood of Britain's middle classes, while in contrast American and German industrialists were allegedly accorded a high status as of right in their societies (Wiener, 1981; 136–7).

The Marshalls case, though, is very exceptional, and in general Wiener's thesis clearly has many weaknesses, especially with regard to his inability to provide 'much help in determining precisely when the alleged switch from dynamism to decline took place' (Robbins, 1990; 5). Locke (1993; 56–7) has pointed out that an aristocratic ethos extolling the virtues of land-ownership and gentlemanly lifestyles had dominated British society for centuries, and it could not suddenly have been implanted in late-nineteenth century Britain. In any case, industrialisation was accepted and encouraged by the ruling aristocratic class prior to 1850, and as Landes (1969; 8) observed the two value systems coexisted so profitably that this helps to explain why Britain experienced the first Industrial Revolution. This is a point further developed by Payne (1990; 33–4), who emphasises how British aristocratic values were far from anti-industrial, and even if society remained stratified and hierarchical this does not necessarily mean that the middle classes suffered a net loss of talent to landownership. In any case, the German culture remained 'anti-modern, pessimistic, and specifically anti-industrial' for much of the nineteenth century, and a strong family tradition dominated the recruitment patterns into management for much longer in that country (James, 1990, 96–7). Indeed, the 'Buddenbrooks syndrome' noted earlier was actually derived from a German novel written by Thomas Mann which attacks the German, not the British, business classes (Rubinstien, 1993; 54). This indicates how the alleged uniqueness of British attitudes can hardly be used as a valid explanation for decline, while as we saw in section 3.2 German business was well-known for its efficiency.

Secession from industry?

And where is the evidence of a mass secession from industry in Britain? The few industrialists' sons actually educated at public schools were just as likely as any other second generation industrialist to return to the family firm (Rubinstein, 1990; 81–4), where in-house training remained the most popular means of learning the necessary skills and routines. The oft-quoted

Marshall example also blinds historians to a reality which indicates how, as in the case of Lancashire cotton-masters, most 'retained a lifelong interest in their firms' (Howe, 1984; 43–6). This group was actually more concerned with securing social and political power as the local 'cottonocracy', rather than aspiring to enter a different social grouping, and by the mid-nineteenth century they had utilised their economic power to become a distinct industrial elite. On a more general level, Rubinstein (1981; 178) has concluded from his survey of the wealthiest people in nineteenth century Britain by claiming that: 'Most businessmen . . . were simply carried along by their seemingly preordained roles as successors to their fathers and grandfathers . . . [and] had no desire to rise above their family firms and become something greater'. Some may well have acquired or constructed houses in the country, but this was more often a response to deteriorating urban living conditions, while such assets could be employed as collateral against bank loans or other forms of credit. From the 1880s, industrialists were also being elevated to the aristocracy on their own merits, and while only a narrow range of sectors like the railways, armaments, shipping and banking were represented, at least one-third of all new peerages came from this area of society between 1885 and 1914 (Pumphrey, 1959; 1–16).

The business culture

The gentrification concept clearly appears to have little credibility when examined in detail, but in attacking the general critique one might well argue that historians have ignored a crucial dimension of the socio-cultural scene, namely, the business culture. In particular, when discussing the managerial implications of *personal capitalism* one can only conclude that a business culture which placed so much emphasis on family control and ownership would have acted as a constraint on the development of organisational innovations like functional departmentalisation and the professionalisation of management. As Coleman (1973; 103) reveals, British society in general extolled the virtues of gifted amateurs, rather than professionally trained experts, indicating how a distinction between 'gentlemen' and 'players' continued to determine attitudes towards, respectively, those without formal training and those who had acquired specific skills. At the level of business management, as we noted in section 2.6, 'gentlemen' would populate the senior levels, while 'players' were responsible for routine functions, emphasising how this 'cult of the amateur' limited the avenues of recruitment and advancement in British business. This is naturally a generalisation, and more careful analysis of recruitment patterns is required before accepting its applicability, but there is widespread agreement among historians concerning the antipathy expressed in British business towards professional training (Payne, 1990; 43).

The relevance of such a 'cult of the amateur' is well brought out by Locke

116

(1993; 56), who argues that while practical, on-the-job training might well have been suitable during the first industrial revolution, by the late-nineteenth century rapid technological and commercial development revealed serious flaws in the British approach. This was especially the case when a comparison with the USA and Germany was made, and as we saw in the last chapter their education systems responded imaginatively to the demand for a wide range of technical and managerial skills, while in Britain no such demand emerged.

The nineteenth century deficiencies in British technical education have been widely publicised by Sanderson (1972; 17), who reveals how 'the Englishman . . . [had] yet to learn that an extended and systematic education up to and including the methods of original research [was] now a necessary preliminary to the fullest development of industry'. Of course, one should not forget that in the period 1880–1914 industrialists in the Midlands and North had invested in civic universities, and 'the symbiotic relationship of civic university technology departments and industrial firms was closer than ever before or since' (Sanderson, 1988; 99). On the other hand, this relation- ship did not extend to the field of management education, where the belief that 'managers are born, not made' prevented any major breakthrough in changing both recruitment and training patterns. One might qualify this epi- thet by saying that 'directors are born, not made', because some managers had developed specific skills, while the board members were generally dedicated to the concept of 'amateurism'.

Some of the larger railway companies had encouraged certain universities to provide courses in management-related disciplines (see section 2.3), but there is little evidence of any more general move towards the American busi- ness school system. Keeble (1992; 96) has described how the few manage- ment education pioneers who established business-related degree courses (in Birmingham, the LSE, and Manchester) around the turn of the century 'had to walk a tightrope between attracting business interest . . . and finding acceptance for the subject as one suitably "liberal" for a university to offer'. Mutual suspicions consequently characterised the relationships between both academics and businessmen, and not surprisingly few students passed through the first courses. Even as late as 1930, Bowie (1930; 89) was able to claim that 'Britain [was] still at the crowing of the cock', compared to the rapid extension of management education in the USA. This emphasises how in business circles the maxim 'managers [or directors] are born, not made' prevailed for many decades.

Conclusion

Nepotism and practical training within the context of a family-owned and family-managed firm were consequently consistent features of British busi- ness until the early-twentieth century, inhibiting the opportunities to intro- duce new ideas on management which both American and German corporations were developing at that time. When we combine this with what we noted in section 4.1 were weak market-cum-technological pressures on management to develop extensive hierarchies, it is not surprising that *personal capitalism* continued to flourish. This illustrates how the inner dynamics of British business strengthened the characteristics which had already become so predominant by the mid-nineteenth century, restricting the propensity to utilise new procedures or adopt the organisational structures which were increasingly popular in countries like Germany and the USA. The 'gentlemen', or owners, had developed a greater willingness to delegate responsibility to 'players', or managers, but only with regard to functional and operational tasks (see Figure 1.1), leading to the retention of absolute control over strategic management by what might be described as 'amateurs'. One cannot agree with Chandler (1990; 292), who claims that 'growth was not a primary objective' in such enterprises, because, as we have noted in previous sections, most British businessmen acted rationally in the prevailing market-cum-technological conditions (Payne, 1990; 42). Nevertheless, it is possible that the family firm constrained its own prospects by preventing the infusion of new managerial talent. Furthermore, not only were fresh ideas on organisation and procedures kept at a distance by families suspicious of outside interference, succession problems could severely hamper longer-term development of family firms (Rose, 1993; 133–5).

In evaluating the implications of a business culture which was grounded in the belief that family firms were the most viable form of organsation, one must emphasise that any conclusion which equates poor management with this institution ignores what was happening in other economies at this time. After all, the presence of powerful family dynasties was not unique to Britain, because, as we saw in chapter 3, not only were the large *zaibatsu* owned and controlled by families like the Mitsui and Yasuda families, in Germany and the USA exactly the same situation prevailed among large-scale and other types of business (Church, 1993; 17–39). In other words, the family firm by itself was not the major problem; rather, it was the approach family firms took towards such issues as management recruitment and training which determined business evolution. In this context one can refer back to the more progressive movements in British business which appeared from the 1890s, largely arising out of the wave of mergers. It was argued in the last section that, after struggling with the need to impose more rigorous centralisation on the family firms which had come together to form a single entity, these large-scale companies were beginning to introduce new ideas and structures as a response to the organisational chaos prevailing immediately after the merger. Similarly, adventurous businessmen like Dudley Docker were keen to rationalise and integrate newly-merged companies, while at Vickers, for example, the family owners recruited professional accountants as a means of improving financial control within an expanding business (Irving, 1975; 160–5). This reveals how some cracks were beginning to appear in the surface of a business culture which had so far prevented the introduction of such essential features of modern management. On the other hand, one must wonder just how limited was the progress by 1914. Clearly, the British family firm, allied with the prevailing 'cult of the amateur', proved to be an unwelcome host to new management techniques in many firms outside this 'charmed circle' of large-scale enterprises which were faced with unprecedented organisational challenges.

In emphasising the importance of scale one comes closer to the real problems in the British business scene, because while the industrial structure remained atomistic and specialised the pressures to change would be limited. One must also note how the family firm might well possess an in-built financial constraint, and we must now examine business finance before drawing any firm conclusions regarding the full impact of this particular form of culture.

4.5   Business finance up to 1914

A debate concerning the relationship between British financial institutions and the indigenous business community has been raging throughout the twentieth century (Capie & Collins, 1992; 11–12), and as with the study of organisational evolution the picture is confused by a comparison with practices in other economies. This subjective element should once again be handled very carefully, while the manner in which different types of business finance was raised must also be explained. It has been established in section 2.4 that by the mid-nineteenth century, while British firms provided much of the fixed capital for buildings and machinery from either internal resources or through an informal network of contacts built around the partnership system, an adequate supply of working capital was made available by the large number of private and joint stock banks which were linked into a nationally-integrated 'web of credit'. It was a simple matter of demand-supply relationships, and in any discussion of the role played by financial institutions in assisting British industry this rule must always be applied, particularly when making a comparison with the USA or Germany.

The adoption of joint stock status

One of the most important aspects of any discussion relating to late-nineteenth century business finance is the extensive adoption of joint stock status. As we noted in section 2.4, until the 1856 Companies Act freed businessmen from the burden of acquiring an Act of Parliament before forming a limited liability company, partnerships had been the principal organisational form adopted by the vast majority of firms outside the utilities and banking sectors (Cottrell, 1980; 39–75). Although an unincorporated form

119

of company had grown in popularity since the turn of the century, especially among small utility operations, partnerships remained important in manufacturing because of the sheer expense involved in acquiring joint stock status up to 1856. However, once further refinements had been added to the system, and a Consolidating Act was passed in 1862, a veritable flood of applications came from every sector, and over 24,000 companies were registered in the following twenty-five years. Not even the crash of the major banking operation of Overend & Gurney on the 'Black Friday' of 10 May 1866 could diminish more than temporarily the widespread acceptance of limited liability in the eyes of British businessmen seeking a more secure method of withstanding the dangers inherent in a highly volatile trade cycle (Hunt, 1936; 153–5).

The rise of the joint stock company after 1862, in sectors which hitherto had been averse to such legal instruments, was the era's most significant organisational development (Jefferys, 1938; 441). It is vital to remember, though, that a peculiar approach was taken towards this innovation which reveals much about the business culture of the late-nineteenth century. In theory, adoption of joint stock status leads to an extensive divorce between ownership and control, because equity in the company can be sold to professional shareholders who would have little interest in managing the enterprise. This process of dilution, however, was anathema to the families responsible for creating most British businesses, and in practice a 'private' form of joint stock company emerged which meant that limited liability was secured, yet all equity was retained by those who signed the articles of association registered with the Board of Trade. The private company was actually only recognised in law in 1907, and Payne (1967; 520) has described it as 'a typical British compromise', because while businessmen had accepted the utility of limited liability as protection against economic vicissitudes, by retaining all the equity within the family they had prevented outside capital from coming into the company. In fact, seventy-seven per cent of the 63,000 registered companies in existence by 1914 were 'private', indicating that the nature of business organisation had changed very little since the 1860s, because introverted family groupings still dominated most British firms.

Long-term financing

The growing acceptance of limited liability after 1862 was consequently an illusion, and clearly in terms of providing British business with anything other than a more secure legal status the trend simply reinforced a tendency towards family control. Most importantly, it closed off access to sources of equity financing, and in considering the relationship between business and finance in the decades immediately preceding the First World War one must remember that the demand for long-term capital was constrained by a business culture which refused to accept the need for a separation of ownership and control. This is a vital point, because if firms were unwilling to raise risk-bearing equity capital which only makes a return when the company is in profit, then it must either continue to rely on self-generated funds or issue fixed-interest shares on which interest payments were due, regardless of profitability. One must remember that from the 1860s technological progress was pushing industry and commerce into ever-greater fixed investment programmes, but (see section 4.2) as there is some evidence of poor profitability in this period an increased reliance on fixed-interest capital arose, further undermining the viability of many Briitsh businesses.

A classic example of the problems inherent within this system was the electrical engineering business of Sebastian de Ferranti, because after building up an extensive reputation in the 1880s as a pioneering designer of generating and distribution equipment, he refused to accept the need to convert his firm into a public limited liability company (Wilson, 1988; 51–85). His simple repost to all entreaties on this matter – 'it would take all my interest out of the work' – reflects the individualistic approach adopted by many businessmen towards ownership and control, and even when he finally agreed to float S. Z. de Ferranti Ltd in 1890 seventy-five per cent of the equity was retained by the eponymous creator. Electrical engineering was also still suffering the consequences of the 1882 'Brush Bubble', during which approximately £7 million had been raised for a series of dubious ventures aimed at exploiting investors' ignorance of both electric lighting and industrial investment generally (Reader, 1979; 95–7). After much of the £7 million had been written off or lost in promotion costs, this had severely dented the industry's reputation in financial circles, and when combined with the sluggish growth in demand for this new form of energy it is not surprising that even in the 1890s firms struggled to raise large amounts of capital on the open market. Electrical engineering was simply regarded as a poor prospect, and irrespective of the desire to retain control and ownership firms were obliged to rely on fixed-interest borrowing in the form of debentures, preference shares and loans to finance expansion plans (Byatt, 1979; 158–9).

The City and overseas versus domestic investment

This case-study has already revealed several characteristics of the late-nineteenth century capital markets which had an important bearing on business development, in particular the preference for fixed-interest investments and the lack of expertise regarding industrial investments. Kennedy (1976; 174–7: 1987; 144–7) has been especially careful to explain how on the London stock exchange this 'bias . . . towards safe, well-known securities in general, many of which were foreign' distracted attention away from riskier, yet potentially more lucrative, domestic investments. There certainly appears to be little doubt that Britain sustained a high level of overseas investment up to the First World War, and regardless of the differing estimates relating to the scale of this exodus of capital it is widely accepted that the City of London much preferred to pump money abroad. More importantly, as Cain & Hopkins (1993; 116–25) have described, well into the twentieth century the City of London was dominated by financiers who were marked by 'that characteristic mixture of amateurism and efficiency' so typical of the British establishment. It was a system based on what they have called 'gentlemanly capitalism', where industrial interests were shunned as socially inferior to the more prestigious, and more lucrative, business of exporting capital.

Until recently, Paish's 1913 estimate of £3,714.7 million in portfolio overseas investment raised on the London stock exchange was regarded as a reasonably accurate estimate of the total flow of money out of the City by that time (Kennedy, 1987; 152–3). There are many problems with this estimate, however, and Platt (1986; 60), for example, has argued that it ought to be reduced to £2,600 million, because the figures ignore both foreign direct investment by British multinationals (of around £500 million) and the purchase of stock by foreign investors. This revision is disputed by Davis and Huttenback (1986; 35–6, 40–1), who come up with a range of estimates, from a low of £3,165 million to a high of £4,779 million. Corley (1994; 76–87), on the other hand, has totally reworked the numbers and concluded that in total the accumulated net holdings of overseas assets in 1913 stood at £4,165 million, forty-five per cent of which was foreign direct investment by British firms. We saw earlier how several British firms were already developing multinational characteristics, and these figures indicate how 'British entrepreneurs were substituting overseas investment for visible trade', undermining further any criticism of business acumen in this period.

Another of the crucial findings publicised by Paish, however, was the low earning capacity of overseas investments. Indeed, he noted that only 18.5 per cent of these holdings producing in excess of five per cent per annum. This has lead Kennedy (1976; 152–3) to argue that British investors were 'risk-aversionist' by nature, because of their reluctance to support high technology domestic industries which possessed greater earning potential. Edelstein (1982; 131–40) has attacked this view, after a detailed statistical analysis of 'risk-adjusted' realised returns on domestic and overseas investments, revealing that the latter were actually superior. He would consequently argue that British investors were acting rationally in preferring these less-risky securities, but Kennedy (1987; 146–7, 152–3) replied by noting how Edelstein used only high-quality assets in his sample, ignoring the tendency of British capital markets to undervalue most domestic industrial securities. Davis and Huttenback (1986; 107) also calculated that after 1880 domestic investments proved to be more lucrative than their overseas counterparts, arguing that the most substantial gains from imperial investment had been recouped prior to 1880, rather than in the later 'scramble for Africa' when foreign investments proved more popular.

The 'gentlemanly capitalists'

Debate about the role and character of British capital exports will no doubt continue, but it would seem reasonable to conclude that the bias in favour of relatively risk-free overseas investments could have potentially affected the supply of money into domestic business. This reinforces the strength of Cain & Hopkins' (1993; 182–201) claim that the 'gentlemanly capitalists' in the City continued to dominate Britain's capital markets, imposing their preference for cosmopolitan affairs on the whole system. The most influential of these gentlemanly capitalists were the merchant banking houses, whose business portfolio had extended from acceptances (see section 4.5) to issuing substantial amounts of capital, especially for governments or for government-backed ventures. There were some aggressive merchant banks, for example Schroders and Kleinworts, which acquired an increasing share of the acceptance business (Chapman, 1984; 121–5). However, in spite of their relatively small capitals, firms like Rothschilds, Barings, Hambros, Sassoon, Anthony Gibbs and Morgan Grenfell dominated the prestigious issuing market. It would be partners in these firms who sat on the Court of the Bank of England (Cassis, 1985; 309–10), manipulating monetary policy, just as they controlled much of the activity in the City. A classic example of this mutually-supportive relationship was the Baring Crisis of 1890, when the prominent merchant bank of Baring Brothers found itself unable to meet its obligations, having underwritten a disastrous public works programme initiated by the Argentinian government in the late-1880s. The crisis could have precipitated major problems in the market for international credit, but the Bank of England joined forces with the major merchant banks to create a fund of £17 million, preventing Barings' collapse and restoring confidence in the City before any wild panic ensued (Chapman, 1984; 78–81).

The City was consequently run much like 'a gentleman's club', and the 'gentlemanly' approach adopted by the merchant banks and their subordinates ensured a successful assimilation of the aristocratic establishment and its replacement with a similar kind of amateurish spirit (Cain & Hopkins, 1993; 125–31, 153–6). This attitude was particularly well manifested in the pace at which the City worked, because as Cassis (1985; 304) commented it was a sure sign of impending trouble if a person was working hard, such was the leisurely nature of business. Hours at work were often not long, usually from 10am to 4pm (now known as 'gentlemen's hours'), and much of it was spent cultivating contacts, leading to the conclusion that 'leisure was often difficult to distinguish from work' (Cain & Hopkins, 1993; 126). More importantly, the hallmark of their affairs was the way in which leading institutions like the merchant banks were able to manipulate activity within the City to suit their own interests, in particular with regard to the strategy of joint stock banks.

The banks

The provision of trade credit, both for domestic and overseas commerce, had been the most valuable role played by British banks since the mid-eighteenth century, as we saw in section 2.4, but in the decades leading up to the First World War important changes in the banking sector put at risk a relationship which had been the financial bedrock of the previous era. The effectiveness of these connections between banks and industry has been hotly disputed, of course, Kennedy (1987; 120–4) in particular accusing the banks of pursuing a conservative, liquidity-conscious strategy which undermined industrial competitiveness. He focusses especially on the banking crisis of 1878, when the City of Glasgow Bank collapsed, precipitating the worst run on liabilities of the nineteenth century. Collins (1990; 222), on the other hand, attempts to play down the watershed nature of 1878, arguing 'that there was an already well-articulated view of what was considered . . . "unsafe" business to bankers'.

The provincial, and later the joint stock, banks had in fact 'routinely provided some medium and long-term loans' to local businessmen up to 1878, building on the intimate relationship the two sectors had forged since the mid-eighteenth century. They also funded the overdrafts on which most businesses relied, and in this respect performed the vital function of maintaining the liquidity of British business at a time when working capital requirements usually far exceeded those for fixed capital (Collins, 1991; 26–30). However, according to Kennedy (1987; 121–3), after the severe crisis of 1878 the banking community withdrew from the provision of long-term funds, largely because it was widely accepted in those circles that they had overextended their industrial lending activities. In effect: 'A point had been reached where the entire system had either to be reorganised to withstand the greater risks of steadily enlarging industrial requirements or the system had to withdraw from long-term industrial involvement. The system withdrew'.

This cautious approach to banking was the principal reason why no equivalents to the German industrial banks emerged in Britain during the nineteenth and twentieth centuries, a thesis well borne out by the strategies pursued after 1878 (Capie & Collins, 1992; 37–43). It might be correct to play down the climacteric of 1878 and describe the year simply as symbolic of the changing attitudes towards long-term lending among bankers, but clearly the German model was never copied in Britain. The most important trend of this era was actually the extensive degree of concentration experienced as a result of the bank mergers which occurred after 1880. This might be described as the third evolutionary stage through which the sector had passed by 1900, following the emergence of country banking after the 1760s (first stage), and the rise of joint stock banking from the 1820s (second stage), and it undoubtedly resulted in the much greater domination of City of London interests over strategy and structure. Nishimura (1971; 1–3, 77–83) has demonstrated that this third stage was not by itself responsible for the old view that bank mergers were responsible for the declining use of bills of exchange, because substantial improvements in communication were far more important in explaining this trend. Of course, the mergers brought substantial benefits to the system, because by 1900 most of the provincial banks were connected formally to the larger resources of a London house, while the extensive national branch network brought greater cohesion to the provision of funds. On the other hand, it is possible that the end of locally-controlled banking could well have disrupted the traditional relationship with industry at a time when liquidity requirements were increasing.

The Scottish banks were the first to indulge in mergers, resulting in a reduction from eleven to eight houses between 1875 and 1913, but the process was most intense in England and Wales, especially in the peak period of 1888–1894, when sixty-seven occurred. By 1913, there were only twenty-nine private banks and forty-one joint stock banks remaining in England and Wales, compared to 236 and 122, respectively, in 1875. This created a much more concentrated system, with fifty-six per cent of total deposits held by the top ten London-based banks. The branch networks also expanded considerably, and by 1913 the average number of branches per bank had increased to 156, compared to five in 1850, while Barclays had 599, Lloyds 673 and the Midland 846 (Cassis, 1985; 302–5; Cottrell, 1980; 196–7). Collins (1991; 37–41) has argued that such a process of concentration created greater stability, emphasising how the last serious banking crisis was that of 1878. It is also essential to stress how the new bureaucratic structures imposed by London headquarters, coupled with the introduction of 'mechanically-trained branch managers' who had little knowledge or experience of local business affairs, would have undoubtedly strained the traditionally strong relationship with industry. Furthermore, the directors in London were rarely full-time bankers, and they used their seats on the board to ensure that 'the prime function of the joint stock banks was to make possible the financial and commercial activities of the private firms and the overseas activities of their partners by providing the required cash' (Cassis, 1985; 303).

The evidence and interpretation of late-nineteenth century banking developments consequently appears to substantiate the claims of those who are critical of their reluctance to participate in industrial affairs as extensively as the German, American and Japanese institutions (Kennedy, 1987; 123). It is vital to remember, though, that while the big joint stock banks operating out of London were less inclined to provide long-term funds than their foreign counterparts, they still supplied the short-term credit which had always been so essential to business liquidity. Cottrell (1980; 210–36) has also revealed how many provincial banks like Glyns, the Cumberland Union, and the Swansea, for example, 'went as far as [they] possibly could to meet the needs of [their] clients and did make substantial loans of a duration of a year or more, sometimes to finance capital projects'. Such counter-examples, however, would appear to have been exceptional, because with City interests taking a firmer grip of the powerful joint stock banks by the 1890s, bureaucratic procedures, rather than local knowledge and instinct, dictated managers' actions. Only nine per cent of the directors from eleven leading joint stock banks had any connection with British industry, and most of them worked for the Midland, while general strategy took on a much more conservative approach, in line with the traditions of a City of London culture which avoided risk at all costs (Collins, 1991; 38–41).

British banking had clearly lost all the dynamism it had shown in responding to the requirements of British business expansion since the mid-eighteenth century, and in this context it would certainly appear to have been the allegedly baleful influence of the gentlemanly capitalists of the City which had been responsible for this change in structure and strategy (Cain & Hopkins, 1993; 199–201). The preoccupation with safe overseas investments for much of the period, allied with a reluctance to purchase anything other than fixed-interest securities, was preventing the creation of an institutional floor in domestic industrial financing in the City. In addition, it was prohibitively expensive to issue capital on the London money markets for all but the largest enterprises, particularly when new companies were being floated. This constraint was publicised as early as 1909, when Lowenfeld (1909; 172–5) pointed out how advertising and the fees paid to banks, solicitors, brokers and accountants would amount to at least 2.5 per cent of an issue, while underwriting costs would vary between one and six per cent, depending on the reputation of the company being financed. Furthermore, the more prestigious merchant banks proved reluctant to handle small issues (Chapman, 1984; 134–5), creating a situation in which not only would it be extremely costly for the typical British business to raise money, they would also have to deal with institutions which found it difficult to sell such share packages. This would later be referred to as the 'Macmillan Gap' (Thomas, 1978; 116–21), as we shall see in section 6.1, revealing an institutional constraint preventing greater co-operation between small and medium-sized companies on the one hand, and on the other the major British capital market in London. The 'Brush Bubble' of 1882 also indicates the depth of ignorance among British investors concerning industrial affairs (Reader, 1979; 95–7), as did the experiences of other new industries like cycles and cars (Harrison, 1981; 182–3). Indeed, this lack of knowledge in domestic matters further substantiates Kennedy's (1987; 144–7) claims of a capital market bias against riskier domestic investment.

Industry and finance

Of course, much of this debate is predicated on the premise that a large demand for external sources of capital was emerging in the late-nineteenth century, but from what we have seen in the Ferranti case one can infer that any criticism of the supply-side must be tempered by the knowledge that most British businesses continued to rely on traditional sources of fixed investment. Only the largest industrial, utility and financial companies offered shares to the London markets, partly because of the costs involved in such flotations, but principally because of a continued preference for the local dealings which had always characterised capital formation in British business. It is notable that the average nominal capital of all existing companies actually fell between 1885 and 1915, from £54,000 to £40,744, while the proportion of paid-up capital allocated to vendors rose from 43.2 per cent between 1885–1889 to 58.8 per cent in the years 1910–4 (Cottrell, 1980; 163). This reveals how fixed capital requirements remained on the small side, especially when compared with the activities on Wall St in New York or in Berlin, while the 'private' company form prevented the extensive distribution of equity to professional shareholders, whether on a local or a national basis.

As we noted earlier, the liking for fixed-interest securities resulted in preference shares and debentures accounting for almost seventy-one per cent of the aggregate paid-up capital of all companies listed in Burdett by 1915 (Cotrell, 1980; 163–4). Furthermore, up to seventy per cent of industrial capital formation would have been 'carried out by small, segmented groups who were well acquainted with each other through personal or business contacts', with the provincial stock exchanges acting as 'an extension of the closed circle of local associates' (Kennedy, 1987; 124–5).

Provincial stock exchanges

It is clear from a study of late-nineteenth century capital formation that deep divisions existed in the markets. Davis and Huttenback (1987; 211) actually claim that: 'Britain was not one capital market but two'. At the pinnacle was the City elite which continued to operate in much the same way as it had done since the mid-eighteenth century, focussing on overseas investment, acceptances and government funding. Industrialists, on the other hand, exploited the local contacts on which they too had always relied, albeit with greater interest being shown in the provincial stock exchanges established as a result of the 'railway manias' of the 1830s and 1840s and the company promoters who replaced attorneys as agents of financial mobilisation. Indeed, the growing importance of provincial stock exchanges from the 1860s would appear to have been the most visible sign of change in the methods adopted to service the fixed investment requirements of the typical British firm. It was at this level that a more formalised relationship between the worlds of finance and business first began to emerge, especially after the conversion of firms into limited liability companies prompted a need for the professional services these institutions could offer at a much cheaper price than in London (Thomas, 1973; 114–39).

One of the most buoyant periods for domestic capital issues was the mid-1890s, when a significant boom in the economy, associated with cheap capital, precipitated a mania in company promotions associated with new industries like bicycles, motor cars and machine tools. The decade had actually started very badly for financiers, when the 1890 Baring Crisis broke, shaking the City to its foundations. This crisis reduced interest in overseas investment for over a decade, and when the home economy moved into a boom phase after 1895 investors naturally turned their attentions more to domestic activity. Prominent in this movement were company promoters like E. T. Hooley and H. J. Lawson, both of whom were guilty of 'watering' capital – namely, overvaluing companies in order to sell more shares and earn a higher commission – creating substantial problems for the firms once they began trading (Cottrell, 1980; 173–6: Saul, 1962; 22). Armstrong (1990; 128–32) is also highly critical of the company promoter, because they were often 'leaving the individual companies they promoted over-capitalised, under-resourced and unattractive to the investor'. This again highlights the paucity of accurate information on domestic industrial investments which had badly affected relationships between financial and other business interests. As with the 'Brush Bubble' of 1882 which so badly damaged the electrical industry (Wilson, 1988; 14–15), investors were duped into buying shares by dubious claims on which they were unable to pass a rational judgement. Furthermore, as much of the capital for cycle and car companies was raised on the Birmingham stock exchange (Cottrell, 1980; 174–6), the problem was clearly not unique to London, indicating how the whole system exhibited fundamental weaknesses which undermined the competitiveness of key British industries.

Firms in the engineering, iron and steel, and cotton industries were among the first to make this transition from the informalised methods of an earlier era to using the provincial stock exchanges, and prominent local company promoters were used as the vital means of communication between investors and companies (Cottrell, 1980; 112–28). One of the most successful promoters was David Chadwick, of Adamson & Collier, a Manchester accounting firm. He raised over £16 million in the 1860s and 1870s for almost fifty coal, engineering and steel companies – Palmers Shipbuilding, Ebbw Vale Coal, Manchester Carriage, and Vickers, to name but four of the more prominent – by tapping into the extensive number of contacts he had built up as an insurance agent and accountant. Chadwick would also be responsible for providing the management of some newly-floated companies, introducing Manchester businessmen into the boards when required, but in many cases vendors accounted for most of the equity. The shareholdings in these companies had their own unique geographical pattern, indicating how both investment patterns continued to have a highly localised character, and the 'private' company form remained popular. The process of change was evolutionary, rather than dramatically rapid, but the provincial institutions and intermediaries were taking on a position of much greater significance as the scale of industrial investment continued to increase. The difficulties experienced in floating companies on the London stock exchange also meant that there was little competition for this business from the City.

The 'Oldham Limiteds'

Another of the industries which adopted limited liability most extensively was cotton spinning, because 162 companies in that industry appeared between 1856 and 1862, and a further 154 between 1868 and 1896. At the centre of this movement were the 'Oldham Limiteds', a large number of spinning companies spawned by the tremendous success of the Sun Mill Co. Ltd of that town during the 1860s. Previously, cotton manufacturers had remained aloof from 'joint stock schemers', priding themselves on their ability to remain independent, but once Oldham had led the way there were three further booms in cotton company formation, in 1873–1875, 1880–1884 and 1889–92, when over 540 companies were created (Farnie, 1979; 212–20). Many of the Oldham ventures had been formed by specialist mill-building firms which would establish new spinning enterprises at the peak of the trade cycle, raise the capital locally and implant a multi-functional management team capable of running such a venture (Holden, 1992; 243–57). Share dealing at first took place in four local public houses, and not until 1883 was a stock exchange established, but by 1886 almost £7 million in shares and loans had been raised for ninety 'Limiteds', primarily from the local business community.

Conclusion

The conclusion one might draw from this discussion of industrial investment and the rise of limited liability from the 1860s is that some formalisation of the process was occurring. Nevertheless, it was undoubtedly limited by the unwillingness of British businessmen to give up control of their family firms. Thomas (1973; 137–9) has estimated that by the period 1890–1914 on average £4–5 million was raised annually by provincial stock exchanges for British industry, with Manchester probably accounting for the largest share. The bulk of this money was provided by a close circle of local associates collaborating together to raise the capital demanded by local firms. However, as Lavington (1921; 208) noted, this would have amounted to no more than ten per cent of gross domestic capital formation up to 1914. Furthermore, the category 'manufacturing and commerce' only accounted for 7.1 per cent of the total value (£11,262.5 million) of securities quoted on British stock exchanges by 1913, while foreign and domestic governments were responsible for 44.7 per cent (Morgan & Thomas, 1962; 280–1). In fact, self-generated capital was still the most popular means of funding the investment programmes initiated by British industrialists, contributing over seventy per cent of the total. Indeed, the ease with which firms were able to sell fixed-interest securities locally allowed businessmen the luxury of retaining total control of their ventures, revealing yet another institutional reason why personal capitalism could survive and flourish in the late-nineteenth century.

It is clear from a general standpoint that major divisions in the British capital market still existed by 1914: the major houses of the City of London like Rothschilds, Barings, Morgan Grenfell, and Hambros concentrated on large overseas issues, preferrably backed by indigenous governments, while provincial stock exchanges and company promoters satisfied any demand for capital emanating from locally-based industrialists. Company promoters, from Chadwick in the 1860s to Hooley, Lawson and O'Hagan in the 1890s, were able to bring a new dimension to investment activities. Even here, though, the absence of a 'floor' in industrial securities gave them the opportunity to mislead investors into believing that their holdings would prove remunerative. Manias like those of 1882 and 1896–1897 would consequently have reinforced any bias the financial community would have held regarding the risky nature of domestic investments, accentuating the difficulties faced when raising much-needed capital for development purposes. This provides a stark contrast with the attitudes of institutions and investors in the USA, Germany and Japan, where, as we saw in the last chapter, venture capital was much easier to secure and companies often developed an intimate relationship with major domestic finance houses.

Further discussion of the relationship between City financiers and British business will feature prominently in section 6.1, but it is clear that there are two major flaws in the arguments of those who accuse the British financial system of failing to support their indigenous business communities. Firstly, as we have continually emphasised, there was not a significant demand for risk capital from firms which essentially were founded on the principle of family control and ownership. Fixed-interest capital in the form of debentures and preference shares was issued in significant quantities, and both the London and provincial stock exchanges satisfied this demand adequately, especially in the 1890s (Thomas, 1978; 116). Rarely were investors provided with the opportunity to purchase the controlling equity stock in anything other than utility or banking companies. This significantly qualifies any criticism of British capital markets with respect to fixed investment, while as Chapman (1984; 173–4) demonstrates the main merchant banks played the key role in mobilising substantial quantities of money for infrastructure projects which undoubtedly facilitated the development of a more sophisticated world trading economy. Furthermore, and this is the second of the flaws, not only did capital exports provide overseas markets for British goods, credit provided by the acceptance houses and joint stock banks oiled the wheels of international and domestic trade, without which most businesses would have ground to a halt. One cannot consequently be too critical of the fragmented nature of the financial markets and the allegedly 'risk-aversionist' nature of financiers, and even though domestic investment struggled to keep pace with the growth in output over this period many other factors must be considered before attacks of this kind can be accepted (Cottrell, 1980; 262–4).

4.6   British business by 1914

The central conclusion from section 4.5 would appear to be that, while the City did not show much interest in domestic investment prior to 1914, any financial constraints which resulted from this situation were largely self-imposed by a business community which failed to provide much of a demand for the services of the world's largest single source of capital. This provides a fascinating insight into the dynamics of personal capitalism, substantiating what we have argued in earlier sections of this chapter, namely, that the major institutional features of the business scene up to 1914 allowed such a system to survive and flourish. While all the market-cum-technological, financial and cultural factors operating in the USA and Germany encouraged the rise of big business and *corporate* capitalism, the environment in Britain was much more conducive to an individualistic and atomistic approach. Large-scale companies were beginning to appear after the 1890s mergers, and firms like the big railway companies, J. & P. Coats and Imperial Tobacco were comparable in size to some American and German businesses (Schmitz, 1993; 31). Shaw (1983; 48) has also revealed in her study of the largest manufacturing employers in 1907 that 'the multi-plant business was already a feature of the scene', calculating that for the top 104 firms each possessed an average of six plants and a workforce of 6,820. Further discussion of this issue will feature in section 5.3, where we shall see that as a result of the substantial changes affecting workshop practices from the 1880s, firms were developing sophisticated and extensive administrative mechanisms which were more capable of effecting control over crucial aspects of a business, prompting a significant increase in the size of office staffs. However, it is clear that the British market was wholly inappropriate to the creation of a business system comparable to that dominating the USA and Germany by 1914, and pursuing strategies like vertical integration and diversification, or making the three-pronged investments in production, distribution and management, would continue to remain uneconomic in the trading circumstances of the Victorian and Edwardian eras.

It is vital to stress, of course, how this comparative approach to British business history can only provide a subjective analysis of progress from the 1860s, and as we have continually argued throughout this chapter one must not fall into the obvious trap of judging everything from an American or German viewpoint. The achievements of entrepreneurs like Dudley Docker and his associates at Dick, Kerr & Co., for example, the reorganisations forced on major textile companies after their mergers, and vigorous growth in the branded-packaged and service industries, all reveal positive signs of progress by the 1890s and 1900s. It was developments in these sectors which laid the basis for further progress during and after the First World War, because, as we shall now go on to see, the inter-war era reveals more evidence of British businessmen waking up to the unfolding opportunities and challenges of industrial capitalism. One cannot deny that by 1914 American and German corporations had made much more extensive progress towards a system of managerial capitalism, but equally one must question whether such a response would have been entirely appropriate in the British context, given the different conditions and pressures affecting businessmen.

The key point arising from this analysis of the business scene up to 1914 appears to revolve around the assumption that British businessmen ought to have moved in the same direction as their counterparts in the USA, Germany and Japan. Kirby (1992; 641), on the other hand, has concluded that the allusions to 'institutional rigidities' by Elbaum and Lazonick, rather than acting as an insurmountable obstacle, presented a 'retarding influence' on the emergence of corporate capitalism in Britain. British businessmen were making the same moves as their foreign counterparts, albeit at a rather slower pace overall, while in the right circumstances progress was as impressive. Changing the total environment was beyond the powers of individual businessmen, and with a state reluctant to interfere in the workings of a free market it is irrational to have expected the same kinds of changes as those occurring in the more corporatist economies abroad.

Admittedly, personal capitalism remained popular among British businessmen up to 1914, but one cannot say that the family firm *per se* was a problem, because, as chapter 3 revealed, family dynasties continued to play a leading role in German, Japanese and American business well into the twentieth century (Church, 1993, 35–9). Notwithstanding this observation, the reluctance of family owner-managers in Britain to delegate responsibility to professionally-trained managers would help to explain the lack of depth to which Chandler (1990; 291–4) refers when assessing managerial hierarchies in this country. Ultimately, it was the introspective nature of company culture and the firm belief in ideas like 'managers are born, not made' which differentiated the British family firm from its foreign counterparts. Until such powerful influences could be banished from the scene, business organisation would remain grounded in the stultifying traditions of past practices and standards. One can consequently conclude that the British system of *personal capitalism* remained pervasive because it was appropriate to the market-cum-technological, financial, legal and socio-cultural environment prevailing up to 1914, and it would be difficult to argue that businessmen were guilty of 'failing' just because they did not slavishly imitate their American counterparts.

5

Rationalisation and corporatism, 1914–1945

Although one must be wary of periodising history, and consequently ignoring much of the continuity evident in both economic and political spheres, there is little doubt that between 1914 and 1950 the business scene changed markedly from that described in the last chapter. One of the most important features of this period is the increasing concentration of business activity, caused by unprecedented levels of merger activity, indicating how the oligopolistic trading structures of the USA, Germany and Japan (see chapter 3) were at last beginning to feature more prominently in Britain. Running in parallel with this trend was a much enhanced role for the state in economic affairs, and in this context World War One certainly acted as a climacteric. During the 1920s successive governments certainly pursued the same kind of orthodox macro-economic policies as their predecessors. On the other hand, an increasingly intimate relationship between state and business can also be detected, and Hannah (1980; 60) argues that in this period a 'corporate economy' started to emerge. It is a moot point, however, whether these corporatist tendencies precipitated any dramatic managerial innovations, leading Chandler (1990; 389–92) and others (Elbaum & Lazonick, 1986; 1–9) to conclude that by the 1940s British business organisation was inefficient and inappropriate.

There is, indeed, a welter of opinion and evidence which reveals that British businessmen remained firmly attached to the traditions of their predecessors, particularly when we consider such vital issues as business organisation and ownership, management recruitment, and industrial relations. Payne (1984; 196–7) actually regards the inter-war era as of crucial importance in retarding the British development of managerial capitalism, because family-controlled holding companies which emerged out of the intense merger activity of the 1920s and 1930s failed to implement fundamental structural changes. While attaching blame to one time-period might well be dangerous, given the long tradition of personal capitalism in British business, it is important to emphasise the context in which these changes occurred. In particular, the distinct lack of change in terms of market-cum-technological, legal, financial and socio-cultural pressures ought to be noted, indicating how British businessmen were still not being pressured into imitating their counterparts in the USA or Germany.

This discussion of the general environment returns us to the appraisal of family firms, emphasising especially how Church (1993; 35–9) reveals the persistence of family ownership and control in many modern industrial economies. The essence of the problem is once again attempting to understand why corporate management structures developed so impressively in countries like the USA, Germany and Japan, while in Britain relatively little progress was made in this respect. This is why section 5.1 has been devoted to an examination of organisational evolution in other economies, providing an insight into the major twentieth century changes. Of course, as we saw in section 4.3, there was already evidence of a more aggressive and ambitious British approach towards both investment strategy and organisational techniques, particularly from the late-1890s. On the other hand, we also noted how the market-cum-technological and institutional features of the pre-1914 era allowed the system of personal capitalism to survive, and in this chapter we shall see how little changed in this respect over the following thirty years. One cannot deny that some progress was made, and by the 1940s Britain's industries were very different from their Edwardian predecessors (Musson, 1978; 273–96), but great care will be taken to emphasise the continuous features of a business scene which was reluctant to accept 'American' ideas.

5.1 Business abroad and the multidivisional

To understand fully the relative rates of business progress in the major developed economies of the interwar era, it is first of all important to examine once again those countries discussed in chapter 3. We noted there that by 1914 large-scale, vertically-integrated and diversified firms had already come to dominate many sectors in the USA, Germany and Japan, and that appropriate management structures had been devised in order to exploit the potential economies of scale and scope arising from such strategies. This contrasted sharply with developments in Britain, and many authorities argue that the gap failed to narrow for many decades after 1914, especially with regard to progress in adopting the multidivisional form (M-form). However, not only must we ask why it took many large British businesses over forty years to introduce the M-form, it is also vital to examine the German and Japanese responses, especially as rarely can we find examples of this structure in two of the world's most successful economies.

The rise of the M-form in the USA

Although the large-scale American firms which emerged from the 1880s were able to develop increasingly sophisticated organisational structures based on multilevel hierarchies of professional managers (see Figure 1.4), it became apparent that the highly centralised nature of their operations severely restricted administrative efficiency. As Chandler (1980; 32) comments: 'Managerial hierarchies that had been created to co-ordinate, monitor, and allocate resources for one line of products had great difficulty in administering the processing of several sets of products for new and different markets'. This situation was rapidly leading to organisational paralysis, and managers were obliged to consider a much more decentralised structure which might help them differentiate more clearly between functional and strategic management. We shall examine later when and whether American corporations were the first to adopt what is now called the M-form (or multidivisional structure), but according to Chandler (1962; 104–13) the major chemical firm Du Pont pioneered the concept just after the First World War, and then General Motors imitated this innovation. In simple terms, the M-form was coming to be regarded as an appropriate solution to the problems of proliferation experienced by many American corporations in the early-twentieth century. Indeed, by the 1940s most of the larger firms had followed the Du Pont example, institutionalising the strategy of diversification as a crucial feature in the twentieth century expansion of American business (Chandler, 1977; 456–76). Williamson (1975; 382) has claimed that the M-form was 'American capitalism's most important single innovation of the twentieth century', extolling the virtues of what Chandler (1990; 189) regards as an 'increasingly essential' response by such firms to the managerial pressures associated with product proliferation.

The M-form is best described by the first chairman of ICI, Sir Alfred Mond (see section 5.2), when he said that the secret involved in organising highly diversified, large-scale businesses 'consists in effective central control with sufficient elasticity lower down to allow action to be neither arrested nor delayed' (Hannah, 1983; 81). In this structure (see Figure 5.1) autonomous operating divisions are created, each with their own functional levels of management, while a general office acts as the focal point for corporate strategy, allocating resources and supervising performance through an extensive reporting system (Chandler, 1976; 23–5). This means that strategic, functional and operational management are in this kind of organisation devolved down to the divisions, while the general office also performs some strategic role, advising managers on issues central to the corporation as a whole. It is, as Mond implied, a matter of achieving a balance between delegation and centralised control, and above all sophisticated control procedures are required if the necessary degree of coordination is to be achieved.

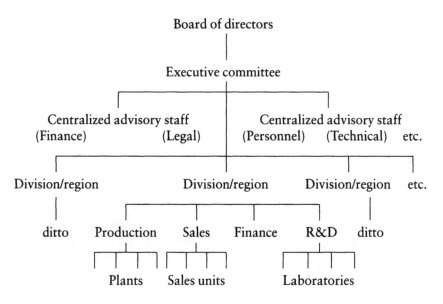

Figure 1.5 *The multidivisional form of organisation*
Source: Schmitz (1993)

The M-form has over the last seventy years come to be regarded by many American and some British authorities as the most effective means of controlling the modern corporation. However, there is some confusion as to its origins, because since 1962 Chandler (1962; 104–13: 1974a; 44: 1980; 32–4) has consistently claimed that it was in the USA that the M-form first appeared, arguing recently that 'Du Pont led the way, inventing the new form in 1920–21' (1990; 181). Kocka (1971; 147–55), on the other hand, has shown that Siemens, a leading German electrical manufacturer, developed the M-form as early as 1910, and curiously Chandler (1990; 471) has accepted that this 'was the forerunner of the multidivisional structure which Du Pont and General Motors began to fashion in the United States shortly after the war'. Further uncertainty is provided by Morikawa (1975; 58), who has noted that before becoming a holding company in 1914 Mitsubishi had been using the M-form for six years (see section 3.3). This provides business historians with a major problem in dating the M-form's origins, but it is above all apparent that, while individual firms in Japan and Germany experimented with this structure, it was in the USA that it made most progress. Indeed, if we focus on the period up to the 1960s, as far as Japanese business was concerned the M-form was 'not so common and not so highly regarded' (Fruin, 1992; 3–4), while in Germany decentralisation remained a rarity (Dyas & Thanheiser, 1976; 102–7).

German business and the M-form

The conclusion that until the 1960s M-form structures were rarely adopted in the highly successful Japanese and German economies undermines the claim that this organisation played a central role in improving business efficiency. Indeed, even where structures analogous to the American M-form can be discerned, at Siemens or at Mitsubishi (for six years), one must never forget the intrinsic features of the management cultures and business systems which have been described in chapter 3. For example, the role played by *unternehmer* in German corporations as central decision makers prevented the necessary degree of decentralisation which is the hallmark of M-form structures. Indeed, only after 1960 did large-scale German firms begin to experiment with the M-form, and even then the tradition of centralised control died slowly (Dyas & Thanhesier, 1976; 102–7, 115–30, 137–8). American practices were certainly infiltrating the business culture, but German managers remained confident of their own traditions and practices, leading to some deviation from the generally-accepted M-form pattern. In simple terms, to paraphrase Hannah's (1976; 197) judgement of British business prior to 1950, it would be too simplistic to look only for the Harvard Business School-approved M-form as a clue to the organisational efficiency of individual business systems; what might work in one context does not always provide a solution to problems experienced elsewhere.

The organisation of Japanese business

Perhaps the most decisive proof of this point comes from Japan, where large-scale, vertically-integrated and diversified concerns had come to dominate by the First World War. As we saw in section 3.3, these *zaibatsu* were characterised by a holding company form dominated by a *soga shosha* (trading company), and as in Germany it was not until the 1960s and 1970s that the M-form was adopted by a significant number of major firms (Suzuki, 1991; 33–6, 101). Yui (1988; 68) has described how by the inter-war period Japan's manufacturers had experienced 'a managerial evolution . . . based on an emphasis on industrial professionalism in top management . . . an increase in the number of technical and clerical employees, and a development of internally complex organisations'. It is easy to fall into the classic Marxist trap, so long influential in both Japan and the USA, of believing that *zaibatsu* groupings like Mitsui, Mitsubishi, Sumitomo and Yasuda dominated the industrial scene, because this ignores the dynamism of individual managers who ran the constituent parts of these conglomerates, as well as the small size of the head office staffs (Yui, 1988; 56–7). The federal structure worked in Japan for so long because it was appropriate to the collective nature of Japanese society (see section 3.3), and the sophisticated control systems typical of an M-form were simply not needed when socio-cultural ties remained strong.

Furthermore, given the nature of *zaibatsu,* 'vertical organisational structures between enterprises, that is to say, such vertical corporate groups, substitute for the "pure" divisional structure of the West' (Yui, 1991; 60). Fruin (1992; 16–36) has also emphasised how interdependence has become a hallmark of the Japanese enterprise system, reflecting a general acceptance of the need for co-operation as an essential tool in the struggle for competitiveness.

Another vital aspect of Japanese business which deserves a rather more detailed analysis is the role of *soga shosha,* because not only were they central to the development of *zaibatsu,* during the twentieth century they also became the main agents of Japanese trade across the world (Young, 1979; 1–9). The most successful was Mitsui Bussan, which had built up a world-wide branch network by the 1920s extending from the Far East to the USA and Europe (Yamazaki, 1989; 167–9). There were actually ten major *soga shosha,* including Nihon Menka, Mitsubishi Shoji and Suzuki Shoten, but none matched Mitsui Bussan in terms of capital and share of Japanese trade, while its employment of university graduates was already well developed by 1914. After 1945, *soga shosha* continued to control Japanese trade, and by the 1970s the annual sales of Mitsui Bussan and Mitsubishi Shoji exceeded $30 million each (Young, 1979; 25). It was also after 1955 that the *soga shosha* linked up with major banks to create new *keiretsu* which, as we shall see later, provided the foundations for Japan's period of rapid economic growth between 1955 and 1973.

Although *soga shosha* and *zaibatsu* were the main features of Japanese business up to 1945, the pre-War history of Japanese business would not be complete without noting how some Japanese firms bucked the system, both in terms of direct marketing and sales, and in employing the M-form. The classic example is Matsushita, whose founder, Konosuke Matsushita, was one of the first to develop trade-names and market his range of electrical appliances independently of the established mercantile networks (Nakaoka, 1992; 1–18). This strategy provided a competitive edge to Matsushita's drive for greater market share, and when combined with the introduction of an M-form structure in 1933 as a means of controlling the expanding business it is clear that this firm was a pioneer in several respects. At the same time, it is vital to stress that there has always been a deeply spiritual and personal side to the Matsushita corporate philosophy, a tradition established by the founder in the early-1930s. This culture is manifested in the practice of every employee reciting a code of values drafted by Konosuke Matsushita and singing the company song at the beginning of every working day (Pascale & Athos, 1982; 28–57; Fruin, 1992; 148–51).

The post-War scene and keiretsu

Matsushita is clearly an unusual Japanese firm, not only in terms of its highly spiritual approach, but also as an example of the M-form structure and the use of direct sales methods. One might add that while it remained independent of *zaibatsu* control, after 1945 Matsushita became part of an extensive network of interfirm sourcing which typified the whole system, revealing how even the untypical enterprises conformed to some Japanese conventions. The *zaibatsu* had actually been dismantled by the Allied Powers immediately after World War Two, in an attempt to establish a competitive market structure which would prove conducive to industrial expansion. By the late-1950s, however, the old groupings like Mitsui, Sumitomo and Mitsubishi were beginning to reform, this time as *keiretsu* (industrial groups), and in the initial phases of Japan's period of rapid economic growth (1955–1973) they proved to be extremely effective in channelling scarce resources into a wide range of highly competitive industries. It was also in this period that the Ministry of International Trade and Industry (MITI, founded in 1949) was influential, acquiring foreign technology for Japanese firms and stimulating innovation in what were perceived to be sectors with the greatest potential, in particular automobiles, electronics, steel and engineering.

The combination of *keiretsu* control and MITI influence has led some American observers to coin phrases like 'Japan Incorporated', hinting at a highly intergrated and corporate structure which controls every aspect of the economy (Johnston, 1982). Fruin (1992; 18–20) has also described the system as a highly interconnected network of firms which is based on 'an evolving, hierarchical, functionally differentiated, structure of economic activities existing at discrete levels of organisation'. These networks have also been studied by Ueda (1986; 248–52), who reveals how by the 1980s 1,082 corporations were linked by multiple directorships in an intercorporate network which is unrivalled. He also talks about an 'inner circle' which is controlled by a series of Presidents' Clubs attended by the senior managers of the *keiretsu*, which in turn meet at the *Keidanren* (Japan Foundation of Economic Organisations) to discuss more general business issues. In simple terms, these sources argue that the economy was based on reciprocity and complementarity, characteristics which are allegedly central to the Japanese way of life (Hampden-Turner & Trompenaars, 1993; 193–6).

While there is some truth in these views, and there is no doubt that the *keiretsu* and MITI were influential during the period 1955–1965, it is dangerous to use such an interpretation of Japanese economic development for the last thirty years. In the first place, Calder (1993; 245–68) has demonstrated how even though MITI draws up elaborate plans it has for many years been incapable of dictating industrial strategy, while in the crucial field of industrial finance it has been the individual firms which identify and develop new ideas. This revisionist view also fits in well with the recent attempts of Japanese business historians to reinterpret the old Marxist line which claims that the economy was dominated by monopoly capital. It is consequently important to note that there are at least three different types of *keiretsu*: the first type are those like Mitsui which is composed of companies in different trades linked financially and through a *soga shosha*; second, there are large-scale companies like Matsushita and their many of subsidiaries; and third, Toyota Motor Co. has an extensive network of subcontractors. This reveals the danger in generalising about a system with so many dimensions.

In spite of these points, Yui (1991; 59–62) is still willing to accept the term 'enterprise system' as a description of post-war Japanese business, because *keiretsu* are characterised by vertical groupings which exploit economies of scale and scope and reduce transaction costs by employing a complex network of subcontractors. At the same time, he is keen to emphasise how the long-term relationships with suppliers must not be mistaken for firm ties, because in theory all companies are free agents. This is a point Wada (1991; 46–7) substantiates by analysing the Toyota Motor Co., demonstrating how the several thousand suppliers linked to this substantial firm work in a tiered interfirm structure which is highly flexible. In effect, Japanese firms co-operate because it reduces both the risks and costs involved in either acquiring raw materials or developing new products, and care must be taken not to mistake this for a system based on monopoly capital. As Yui (1991; 63) concludes, 'transactions between enterprises within these giant corporate complexes, while of a long-term character, are subject to fierce competition within and between groups'. This also reveals some of the reasons why Japanese business has pioneered innovatory approaches towards productive efficiency like 'just-in-time', a technique which allows firms to keep stock costs to a minimum yet depends on a high level of co-operation from suppliers.

Conclusion

This brief review of the Japanese enterprise system has further substantiated our claim that by taking American yardsticks to measure business evolution historians create inordinate methodological problems. Most importantly, though, when considering organisational effectiveness one can conclude that adopting the M-form was by no means essential. Both Japanese and German business have reputations as highly effective and efficient operators, and only in the 1960s did the M-form begin to feature in these economies, often in an adapted form. We must now go on to examine the British response to the American style of M-form, and in judging the relative rates of progress an objective standpoint must be taken before accepting any claims of 'failure' or 'backwardness'.

5.2 'Rationalisation', mergers and the business culture

Our review of the British scene starts with the First World War, because to many forward-looking businessmen this dramatic event provided an opportunity not only to extinguish German competition, but also to build on the ideas relating to organisational efficiency which they had been advocating at least since the 1890s. Leading industrialists like Dudley Docker, Sir Vincent Caillard and Sir Alfred Mond shared the views of A. W. Tait, who argued that, while traditional British 'individualism' had been an asset in the past, it had recently become a 'curse' which was preventing the introduction of more rational business practices (Davenport-Hines, 1986a; 431). Many of these leading figures also wanted greater state involvement in industrial and commercial affairs, and as we shall see later they especially requested protectionist policies. It is important to emphasise how protectionism was becoming a majority view among British industrialists by the First World War (Marrison, 1995), and when in 1915 the Ministry of Munitions was created it was expected that the tentacles of government interference would extend far beyond the limited pre-War levels. Most importantly, though, they were anxious to improve business efficiency, and several worked energetically for this end.

The 'Rationalisation movement'

The all-pervasive role played by the state between 1915 and 1918 was certainly regarded by many as the dawn of a new era in its relationship with businessmen and their trade associations, and we shall see in section 5.4 how this influenced the development of a more corporatist outlook in the inter-war era. Another issue we shall examine in section 5.3 will be the impact on attitudes towards new mass-production techniques, a trend which markedly affected the relationship between capital and labour after 1914, laying the basis for greater experimentation with what was widely known as 'scientific management'. Of much greater relevance to our discussion here is the growing influence of what was called the 'Rationalisation movement', because this came to symbolise the hopes and expectations of many prominent industrialists, bankers and trade unionists as they strove to enhance the British economy's competitiveness. There is some disagreement, however, as to just how much this movement influenced the real world of industry and commerce, because while Hannah (1983; 39) might well be able to argue in favour of 'an enthusiastic espousal of the doctrines of rationalisation', by quoting from the speeches and pamphlets produced by various prominent individuals, it is not exactly clear whether such abstract notions actually motivated much of the activity in British business after 1918.

One of the major problems facing historians when assessing the influence of this movement is the wide range of meanings applied by contemporaries to the word Rationalisation. It is consequently important to emphasise that we shall always refer to Rationalisation, rather than rationalisation, because in the inter-war period the latter had a literal meaning often associated with closures and unemployment, especially in the older industries, while the former ought to be seen as a specific concept. One must also stress that the Rationalisation movement originated in Germany, where a Board of National Efficiency was established in 1918 as a means of introducing such concepts into much-disrupted indigenous industries (Urwick, 1929; 13–14). To this Ministry, Rationalisation 'consist[ed] in understanding and applying every means of improving the general economic situation through technical and systematic organisation'. This demonstrates how a relationship between an improved standard of living and the greater co-ordination of economic effort was often regarded as an essential feature of the movement, and prominent British businessmen like Docker and Mond were certainly talking in these terms towards the end of the War (Davenport-Hines, 1984; 84–6, 105–32). Although nobody used the term Rationalisation movement until the late-1920s (Barley, 1932; 31: Thomas, 1931; 48–53), one could reasonably argue that similar concepts and arguments were being advocated much earlier.

During the 1920s, once businessmen and management thinkers in other countries latched on to what they were attempting in Germany, much greater thought was given to a more detailed definition of Rationalisation. The term was examined in great depth at the World Economic Conference of 1927, and its industry sub-committee decided that:

> Rationalisation, by which we understand the methods of technique and of organisation designed to secure the minimum waste of effort or material. They include the scientific organisation of labour, standardisation of both materials and products, simplification of processes, and improvements in the system of transport and marketing.

Urwick (1929; 20–7) is careful to point out that, because no French word for 'management' exists, the phrase 'scientific organisation of labour' should have been translated from the original passage into 'scientific management'. He also stressed that the work of this Conference 'indicated a revolution in world economic thinking', emphasising especially how the ideal towards which businessmen should work ought to be 'the application of the methods of science to all problems arising in the organisation and conduct of production, distribution, and consumption'. Other advocates stressed the need to link a scientific reorganisation of industry with the British economy's problems (Barley, 1932; 15–7), indicating how a strict definition of the term ought to be applied to any examination of the movement's impact.

Rationalisation and British business

It is not exactly clear, however, whether anything more than a handful of leading management thinkers and businessmen either understood this definition or were interested in applying it to actual practices. One might actually argue that the history of Rationalisation in the inter-war period passed through three distinct stages: in the heady reconstruction period up to 1920, even though few used the term it was associated with dreams of a new future; once economic activity dipped alarmingly after 1921, contemporaries saw it as a cover for factory closures, unemployment and defensive mergers; while after 1931 state-assisted Rationalisation overlapped with continued depression in many of the older industrial regions. Even to such distinguished industrialists as Sir Alfred Mond (later Lord Melchett, the first chairman of ICI) Rationalisation simply involved the elimination of inefficient firms through a process of horizontal amalgamation (Mond, 1927; 210–21). This view was strongly endorsed by other prominent contemporaries like D. H. MacGregor, when observing the intense levels of merger activity after 1918 (Hannah, 1982; 30). Another leading member of this movement, Henry Clay, Professor of Social Economics at the University of Manchester, argued that Rationalisation involved 'the reorganisation of an industry in the light of a rational criticism of the fitness of the existing organisation to meet the technical and commercial problems of an industry' (Grieves, 1989; 156). This lack of any consensus is indicative of a widespread disinterest among businessmen in abstract notions associated with 'the application of the methods of science', emphasising how what we saw in the last chapter as a traditional British business aversion to professional training for management continued to predominate (Urwick, 1929; 146–7). Furthermore, as we shall see in the next section, Child (1969; 86–7) reveals how industrial psychologists of the inter-war era were highly critical of the behavioural effects of 'scientific management' on capital-labour relations, undermining further the arguments proposed by Urwick and his fellow-Rationalisers.

Although there is much evidence to support this negative view of the Rationalisation movement's impact on actual business practices, it is not shared by Hannah (1983; 36–40). This authority has argued that, apart from the impressive range of contemporary publications and speeches on this issue, certain strategies were prompting a significant response to these new ideas. In particular, he claims that Rationalisation 'was able to induce investment in innovating techniques of intra-firm organisation, and thus motivated the cheapening of management within the firm relative to transactions in the market'. Businessmen with German or American backgrounds might well have been to the fore in this movement, while foreign competition continued to act as a spur to combination, but he feels that 'from more circumstantial evidence . . . the rationalisation movement was likely to exercise a strong influence on the managerial strategies of a significant number of important companies'. Of course, Hannah also provides more substantial grounds for making this claim, referring especially to merger activity and other key business developments in the inter-war period as manifestations of Rationalisation, and concluding that these were 'an integral part of the rationalisation movement as well as a condition of its success' (1983; 89). It is important to note, though, that this view of the movement's influence during the interwar years has largely been unchallenged by business historians, and it is necesary to examine the contemporary evidence before accepting such claims. For example, if Rationalisation was so influential then one might expect to see a widespread review of management practices in Britain, contradicting Chandler's (1990; 391–2) claim that conventional ideas associated with personal capitalism remained an overriding force.

Mergers

Of central importance to Hannah's case is the extensive range of merger activity affecting much of British industry after 1917, and as Table 5.1 reveals one can certainly agree that businessmen were concentrating activity on an unprecedented level. There had, of course, been a considerable number of mergers during the period 1888–1914 (see section 4.2), but from 1918 the annual average number of firms disappearing through merger increased considerably, peaking impressively in the 1920s when almost 1,900 companies were involved. Hannah (1983; 74–5, 90–122) has analysed this movement in some detail, and it is interesting to discover that no less than twenty-two of the leading 100 companies of 1970 were formed as a result of inter-war merger activity. This indicates how the giants created at that time became 'enduring features of the British corporate economy'. In this context, one might mention firms like ICI, Unilever, Turner & Newall, BICC, Reckitt & Coleman, and Cadbury-Fry, while several older companies (GEC, J. & P. Coats, and some large brewing concerns) continued to expand by pursuing a careful acquisition policy. Moreover, as we shall see in section 5.4, because concentration ratios rose substantially in all the fifteen major industry groups (see Table 5.3), by 1930 the top 100 companies accounted for twenty-six per cent of net manufacturing output, compared to fifteen per cent in 1907 and seventeen per cent in 1919 (see Figure 5.1). This reveals how an oligopilistic trading structure would appear to have been emerging in Britain along the lines earlier pursued in the USA, Japan and Germany. Although one can question just how extensively this movement affected business organisation, a task we shall undertake later, it is fair to conclude that mergers enhanced the ability of businessmen to moderate the free play of market forces by imposing the 'visible hand' of corporate influence on economic activity.

The first stirrings of this merger movement could well be said to have originated with the formation of Metropolitan-Vickers Electrical Co.

Table 5.1 *Merger activity in UK manufacturing industry, 1880–1950*

	No of firms Disappearing	Values (at current prices) £M	Values (at 1961 prices) £M	Merger value as % of TIE[i] %
1880–9	207	10	136	–
1890–9	769	42	401	–
1900–9	659	55	483	–
1910–9	750	161–173[ii]	998–1060[ii]	–
1920–9	1884	360–411[ii]	1654–1886[ii]	32
1930–9	1414	184–218[ii]	759–907	21[iii]
1940–9	778	–	–	–

Key:
[i] TIE – total investment expenditure
[ii] There was a major break in the series at these dates, leading Hannah to offer a range of estimates.
[iii] For 1930–1938 only.
Source: Hannah (1983; 178).

(Metrovic's) in 1917, a firm which combined the American-owned British Westinghouse with the electrical division of Vickers and Dudley Docker's Metropolitan Co. Although Docker undoubtedly made a substantial personal profit on this deal, out-manoevring even the Americans on the repayment terms for British Westinghouse (Davenport-Hines, 1984; 156–8), the merger was regarded as a major step in the right direction for British business. To Docker, Metrovics was 'executed in the spirit of a trade war', heralding his intention to eliminate both foreign competition and the antiquated business methods inherent within the British scene. One must remember that he had been working along these lines well before the First World War (see section 4.3), and it is important to see Metrovic's as simply an extension of his beliefs, rather than a new beginning. Nevertheless, the merger stimulated an impressive consolidation of firms within the electrical industry (Jones & Marriott, 1970; 144–54), because by 1930 Metrovic's had been absorbed into a new conglomerate, AEI, and the three largest firms (English Electric, GEC and AEI) controlled sixty per cent of the heavy plant side and thirty-five per cent of all output in this sector (Hannah, 1983; 111).

Metrovic's was not only important for its role in stimulating concentration among electrical manufacturers, it also reflected a growing interest in the strategies of integration and diversification as businessmen began to realise the advantages inherent in either reducing transaction costs by combining vertically or using the profits accumulated from wartime defence contracts to venture into new markets. For example, when Dick, Kerr & Co. created a new group of companies in 1919 much of the £5 million capital for the newly-formed English Electric Co. came from the heavy engineering firms of John Brown, Cammell Lairds and Fairfields (Jones & Marriott, 1970; 144). Similarly, while horizontal combination remained a popular means of exerting greater control over traditional markets, other firms in the engineering, steel and chemical sectors were committed to adventurous strategies which necessarily involved mergers and acquisitions as a means of securing greater competitiveness in a wider range of markets (Hannah, 1983; 107–8). Inevitably, though, merger and acquisition policies placed an increasing burden on existing management practices, and in this context, if the Rationalisation movement was to have some influence at this time, one might look to these companies for illustrations of how the new ideas were applied in practice.

The 'management movement'

It would certainly appear that from the First World War a plethora of literature on management became available. Child (1969; 44–105) describes the emergence of what he calls a 'management movement', which was dominated by increasingly influential individuals like Lyndall Urwick, John Lee and E. T. Elbourne, as well as prominent industrialists like Seebohm Rowntree and Hans Renold. Lee in particular attempted to popularise what he called 'the science of industrial administration', while Urwick (1929) was similarly active in extolling the virtues of Rationalisation. Their activity was reinforced by the establishment of new research organisations like the Industrial Welfare Society (1918) and the National Institute of Industrial Psychology (1921), while later in 1926 a Management Research Group evolved out of a series of Oxford conferences initiated by Seebohm Rowntree. The universities which had started degree courses in commerce and administration prior to 1914 (Manchester, Birmingham and the LSE) also expanded their offerings, and in Manchester's case they were able to raise some of the necessary finance from local businessmen (Keeble, 1992; 93–124). This effort was matched by the formation of professional associations like the Institute of Industrial Administration (1920) and the Institute of Cost and Works Accountants (1919) as a means of harmonising practices and disseminating new ideas. Clearly, managers were beginning to aspire not only to greater professionalism, but also independence from their employers, whose organisations were more attuned to political and industrial relations issues (Child, 1969; 15–6).

'Sequential acquisition'

But did the mergers stimulate a wider acceptance of the need to introduce new ideas into British business? One of the most startling features of pre-war

Table 5.2:   *Multi-firm mergers in UK manufacturing industry, 1880–1939*

	Mergers of 20+ firms	Mergers of 5+ firms	Average No. firms in Col.A & Col.B	Firms in Multifirm mergers as % of Total[i] %
1880–9	1	5	19.6	57
1890–9	6	28	14.6	64
1900–9	4	20	14.6	53
1910–9	2	24	10.4	36
1920–9	1	40	9.1	20
1930–9	0	18	6.9	9

[i] See Table 5.1 for the total number of firms involved in mergers over this period.
Source: Hannah (1983; 75).

merger activity had been a series of multifirm consolidations, especially in textiles, drinks and chemicals. After 1918, however, Hannah (1983; 74–6) describes how the process of 'sequential acquisition' was more prominent, and few mergers involved more than a doubling in size for the parent firm. Indeed, Table 5.2 reveals that while the number of mergers involving five or more firms certainly increased during the 1920s, only twenty per cent of the firms were involved in multi-firm consolidations, compared to well over fifty per cent in the pre-war era. Furthermore, illustrating how the process was more piecemeal than in the earlier decades, there was also a decline in the number of mergers absorbing more than twenty firms, and by the 1930s the average number of firms in large mergers had fallen to just 6.9. Even the one large-scale merger of the 1920s arose out of exceptional circumstances involving the Bank of England, and as we shall see later the resulting Lancashire Cotton Corporation was forced on a reluctant industry (Hannah, 1976; 197–8). In general, it was much more a matter of 'core' firms acquiring identified targets as part of a planned strategy of growth, obviating the kind of organisational strains imposed by absorbing several new businesses which had been apparent in many of the pre-war multifirm mergers (see section 4.2).

The process of sequential acquisition would certainly appear to have been a common feature of inter-war mergers, but in claiming that businessmen of the inter-war period pursued this strategy because of the unfortunate experiences of the large pre-war mergers Hannah (1983; 74–6) has ignored the extensive reorganisations implemented by most of the newly-created companies in the 1900s and 1910s. As we saw in section 4.3, while initially there had been grave limitations to the structures adopted by most of the big firms created as a result of multifirm mergers, by 1914 many were much more integrated and streamlined. This provided some objective lessons in how to deal with the organisational consequences of merger, and one might ask why, in pursuing a more conservative acquisition strategy, inter-war businessmen would appear to have ignored them. Similarly, one ought to question Hannah's claim (quoted earlier) that the ideas of the Rationalisation movement were 'able to induce investment in innovating techniques of intra-firm organisation, and thus motivated the cheapening of management within the firm relative to transactions in the market'. Had such concepts been so influential, then one would have expected a more aggressive approach towards organisation-building. Instead, though, reflecting some problems in the translation of theory into practice, we can only record a conservative approach which might be regarded as a manifestation of what Hannah (1983; 73) himself later describes as a 'managerial limit to the rate of growth (rather than the size) of the firm'. Indeed, the very process of sequential acquisition could well be regarded as a reflection of management's inability to cope with the organisational consequences of large-scale change, and with this in mind one can hardly support any claims that Rationalisation influenced much of British business.

There is, of course, an increasing amount of evidence to suggest that during the inter-war period British business was undergoing a significant process of change, and both Wardley (1991; 278–9) and Hannah (1983; 101–3, 120–1) demonstrate how, when compared to 1914, large-scale, vertically-integrated firms were much more a feature of the scene by the 1930s. Contemporaries were also increasingly impressed by the scale of British firms, and J. A. Bowie (1930; 8) noted that business was by the 1920s so transformed that it was 'demanding of its personnel a wider knowledge, a keener specialisation, and . . . a more intensive training'. It was also during the 1930s that a significant revision of the theory of the firm was published by R. H. Coase (1937; 388–95), introducing the concept of transaction cost theorems in explaining how the market and price mechanisms operate (see section 1.4). Sadly, though, such an incisive interpretation of business trends was completely ignored for the next thirty years, by both economists and businessmen, indicating how innovative ideas produced in an abstract fashion were not at that time affecting the real world (Schmitz, 1993; 67–8).

Business and the M-form

The key point arising from this discussion of the changes in the scale of business operations is the organisational response to the strategies of horizontal or vertical combination. As we have already seen in the last section, in 1921 corporations like Du Pont and General Motors were pioneering the use of what has now passed into the vocabulary as the M-form, and many of their American counterparts were copying this example and introducing a much more sophisticated means of controlling integrated, diversified or dispersed operations (Chandler, 1962; 362–78: 1976; 27). In Britain, however, in spite of the widespread publicity associated with this innovation, and its use by such giants as ICI (Reader, 1975; 140–3) and Unilever (Wilson, 1968; 27–44), by the 1940s M-forms were still scarce features of the business scene (Channon, 1973; 44). Hannah (1976; 184–200) himself has also argued that in several key industries (cars, electrical engineering, rubber, and metal fabrication) management responded inadequately to the organisational challenges they faced as a result of pursuing ambitious new strategies. In other words, one can conclude that Rationalisation could not have influenced developments in anything other than a limited number of companies.

This clear evidence of a general reluctance to introduce the M-form of organisation must inevitably be placed in an appropriate context, because by taking such a standard one can ignore other developments which might have been significant. It is especially important to note that, while not faithfully imitating American multidivisionals, companies like Dunlop recruited distinguished accountants as a means of radically overhauling their financial controls, after having expanded and diversified into a range of new markets (Hannah, 1976; 190–1). Dunlop is actually an excellent example of how some firms were adapting structure to the organisational demands imposed by ambitious strategies, because a divisional operation emerged once Sir Eric Geddes became chief executive in 1922 (Grieves, 1989; 108–33). The company had previously suffered from severe difficulties arising from the poor management of the du Cros family, and Geddes was brought in to provide some much-needed changes to both financial practices and business direction. Geddes was principally responsible for a strategy of acquiring competitors like the Macintosh Rubber Co., of diversifying the product range, of integrating backwards into rubber plantations, and of superimposing a divisional structure on the company to allow for more careful co-ordination of activity within the different parts of the business. He also recruited the professor of accounting at the LSE, F. R. M. de Paula, as financial controller at Dunlop, and a sophisticated network of controls was consequently developed to provide management with accurate data on the performance of each of the divisions.

Argument by case-study, as we have noted before, is a dangerously inadequate means of proving a point, but one can see from Dunlop that a divisional structure was emerging in Britain by the 1920s, while highly trained professionals were also being recruited to implement key changes in both strategy and structure. Turner & Newall, the leading asbestos producer, pursued a similar policy of divisionalising production, after having initially operated as a loose federation in the years following the merger of four major concerns in 1920. In fact, it was only once they had acquired more asbestos manufacturers, and integrated backwards into mining, that in 1929 greater co-ordination through a divisional structure was achieved (Hannah, 1976; 189). As with Dunlop, though, Chandler (1990; 304–16) claims that 'a full-fledged [sic] multidivisional was not articulated' at Turner & Newall, revealing how British reorganisations in this and associated cases would not appear to have been as extensive as those in the USA. Hannah (1983; 80–1) describes how other influential accountants featured in the changes implemented by some of the leading companies at this time, for example Josiah Stamp at Nobel Industries and F. D'Arcy Cooper at Lever Brothers (Wilson, 1954; 269–312). On the other hand, one must emphasise that these instances were highly exceptional, substantiating the impression that only a small number of companies were benefitting extensively from the new ideas available. Had there been more examples, then perhaps the managerial constraint on the inter-war rate of growth of firms noticed by the same source (1983; 73) would perhaps have been less imposing than it apparently became.

Vested interests and organisational change

The divisional form of organisation emerging in some sectors of British business could be regarded as yet another compromise by owner-managers who were faced with the growing organisational strains arising from their ambitious strategies. One must remember that adopting a full-blown M-form structure inevitably resulted in considerable delegation of authority to divisional managers, because the very essence of this organisation was the autonomous nature of activities which in a centralised firm would have been much more proscribed. Inevitably, though, in a business culture which presented major obstacles to the dilution of ownership and control, passing such authority down the line from the 'gentlemen' at the head of the organisation to the 'players' in functional and operational posts would have been anathema to current conventions. Hannah (1974a; 65–9) has described the inter-war era as 'the golden age of directorial power', illustrating how 'gentlemen' continued to dominate policy-making in much of British business. Even at ICI, until what Reader (1975; 245) describes as 'the barons' revolt' in 1937, Sir Harry McGowan completely dominated the organisation, undermining the ratonale behind the M-form of organisation adopted earlier. The steps taken by the directors (or 'barons') in 1937 to force McGowan to delegate greater responsibility were also unsuccessful, demonstrating how even in the best British example of managerial capitalism personalised control was still treasured as one of the enduring characteristics of its company culture.

The divisional structure would consequently provide owner-managers with an appropriate structure which perpetuated traditional patterns of decision making, while at the same time refining the organisation to cope with the firm's strategic direction. However, in most large-scale businesses relatively little organisational innovation was attempted, largely because, as Chandler (1990; 366) comments after studying the ICI case: 'Very few Briitsh companies could have had "a revolt of the barons", because hardly any of them had enough barons to revolt'. This reveals how, as far as the control and ownership of British business was concerned, what Florence (1961; 195) described as 'leadership by inheritance' persisted at least into the 1940s. Furthermore, most authorities (Church, 1993; 31–9: Payne, 1978; 201–18: Gourvish, 1987; 26–34) agree that such a pattern of control and ownership acted as a retarding influence on organisational innovation, even where ambitious strategies of vertical integration or horizontal concentration were pursued. In the case of Vickers during the 1920s, the eponymous owning family did not even go as far as adopting a divisional structure, even though it was one of the country's most diversified and vertically-integrated businesses (Hannah, 1976; 191–4). Progressive directors like Dudley Docker and Sir Vincent Caillard sat on the board, but 'Vickers became a rather formless aggregation [and] systematic reform of management and marketing strategy was too long delayed' (Davenport-Hines, 1984; 186). The 1930 merger with its major rival, Armstrong-Whitworth, which resulted in the creation of Vickers-Armstrong, was also a defensive move, and little integration was effected during the 1930s after a holding company structure was imposed (Scott, 1962; 144–89). Furthermore, their multinational ventures proved disastrous, largely because the political beliefs of many directors dictated strategy, rather pure commercial considerations, and many of the investments were eventually sold off at much depreciated prices (Davenport-Hines, 1989; 123–31).

Vickers and Vickers-Armstrong demonstrate the power of vested interests in determining a degree of structural inertia which proved extremely damaging to the ability of firms to compete in a range of markets. Similarly, at Courtaulds the firm was still in the 1930s 'run in the manner of an autocratic family business', even though some graduate recruitment had been initiated and accountants were reaching senior levels of management (Coleman, 1980; 237). This traditional pattern of control and ownership at the company was also responsible for the abandonment of ambitious plans to acquire all other rayon producers in 1937, because the owning family felt that the existing organisation was incapable of absorbing more plants. It is a case which typifies the British approach right up to the 1940s, substaniating Chandler's (1990; 390) claims of a 'continuing failure [in Britain] . . . to recuit and train the necessary managerial staffs' and build managerial hierarchies which would provide for long-term growth.

As we argued in section 4.6, one can dispute Chandler's 'failure' tag when applied to the period up to 1914, because in most cases British businessmen acted rationally in the prevailing circumstances. Similarly, as Church (1993; 35–9) argues, 'the case against the family firm *per se*, stressing the institutional rigidity which it represented, cannot be proved convincingly by linking a greater persisitence of family firms with a relative decline in Britain's industrial performance'. Notwithstanding these points, there would appear to have been an acute shortage of evidence to indicate that new approaches to management were adopted extensively after the First World War, demonstrating how the persistence of personal capitalism stultified an effective structural response to the challenges of that era.

Multinationals

This critical review of inter-war organisational progress can also be further extended by examining British multinationals, because while Jones (1986; 15–20) has found evidence of some improved structures, for example, at Courtaulds, Cadbury and Dunlop, he remains sceptical of the benefits this strategy brought to the parent company. As we saw in section 4.3, foreign direct investment by British firms was greater than in any other economy by 1914, a position which was retained up to 1938, when Britain accounted for 39.8 per cent of the world's total ($26,350 billion), compared to 27.7 per cent from the USA (Dunning, 1983; 87). It is important to stress how the Empire received most attention during the inter-war period, but as Stopford and Turner (1985; 55–61) explain this trend was directly linked to the cartelisation of world markets during the 1930s. We shall be looking later at cartelisation, but it is important to stress how British firms were obliged to focus on the Empire as a consequence of joining these organisations because the German members insisted on control over Europe, while American firms wanted no interference in their continent (Wurm, 1989; 112–6). Indeed, such was the extensive participation in cartels that by the 1930s multinational activity had stagnated, ossifying their geographical orientation for several decades (Jones, 1984; 148). The obvious conclusion is that the Empire became 'a haven of sanity and security' for British multinationals who were unwilling to compete directly with their overseas rivals (Stopford, 1974; 327). Nicholas (1991; 141–2), on the other hand, concludes from his quantitative analysis of British multinational investment strategy that 'managers were making investment decisions consistent with economic factors', qualifying any criticism of what might be regarded as a highly rational course of action.

The debate about multinational performance will continue, but it is important to note that three crucial points can be made about the position in 1938: firstly, large British firms were still heavily committed to overseas activity; second, the Empire was coming to dominate their geographical horizons; and third, sophisticated management structures had yet to be devised as a means of controlling these dispersed operations. We shall see in chapter 6 how eventually the second and third characteristics were decisively overcome, but this only took place after 1970, re-emphasising the vital importance of the inter-war era in retarding business evolution in Britain. Furthermore, the tendency to join cartels limited incentives to change strategy or structure, and once again we are left with the clear impression of an environment which simply encouraged the survival of personal capitalism.

As we saw in section 4.3, the limited size of their home market had limited the incentive for British multinationals to build sophisticated management structures, and clearly because in the interwar era little changed in this respect their management structures remained inappropriate to such highly dispersed businesses. Of course, firms like Unilever, ICI, and Shell were exceptions to this rule, but in general 'global management structures remained limited' (Jones, 1986; 15), indicating how new ideas on management were yet to make a significant breakthrough even in the largest firms.

The recruitment and training of managers

Of course, as we noted earlier, there was an increasing amount of evidence to suggest that new ideas on management were being extensively publicised, from the voluminous writings of the 'management movement' to the widely-publicised speeches from prominent businessmen. Similarly, professional associations had been emerging from the 1910s and 1920s, while management education was also undergoing something of an expansion as universities increasingly recognised the value of such courses. At the Manchester College of Technology, for example, a department of industrial administration was started in 1919, and its director, J. A. Bowie, was responsible for initiating the first post-graduate course in this subject (Wilson, 1992; 2–3). This was complemented by the establishment of management consultancies by Lyndall Urwick and others, and office practices were allegedly being revolutionised through the extensive introduction of new types of office machinery, from the increasingly ubiquitous telephone to duplicators, typewriters and accounting machinery (Hannah, 1983; 77–8). But just how far did these developments actually percolate down into the general British business *milieu*? Was the vast majority of practising managers really interested in abstract notions and professional training? Could one convincingly argue that the system was undergoing a process of metamorphosis?

One crucial area in which dramatic change might be expected, if all these new ideas were affecting British business, would be the recruitment and training of managers. Unfortunately, though, the census data on this subject is rather equivocal. Certainly, the proportion of manufacturing employees classified as 'administrative, technical and clerical' rose from eight per cent in 1907 to fifteen per cent by 1935. On the other hand, Hannah (1983; 86) claims that this largely 'represented a strenthening of centralised, functionally differentiated management', rather than a significant deepening of managerial hierarchies. Keeble (1992; 45) has also noticed how 'directors and senior managers normally involved themselves in the day-to-day running of the firm, preferring not to delegate and so create more positions with authority'. This is indicative of what we saw in the late-nineteenth century, and in particular of what Coleman (1973; 92–116) has described as the traditional distinction between 'gentlemen' at the head of a business and the 'players' who performed the most mundane managerial and supervisory tasks in British business.

It is clear that during the inter-war era British patterns of managerial recruitment underwent little change at all. Keeble (1992; 45–61) describes how even up to the 1950s two main trends persisted, namely, 'patronage' and 'compartmentalism'. The former must be distinguished from nepotism, because in non-family firms directors regarded the ability to find employment for friends as part of their privileges. In practice, though, British business was dominated by both patronage and nepotism, and the distinguished economist J. M. Keynes was able to claim from first-hand experience that 'hereditary influence in higher business appointments is one of the greatest dangers to efficiency in British business' (Keeble, 1992; 47). What internal training existed also 'compartmentalised' talent in a highly restrictive manner by preparing managers for specific tasks, rather than for the performance of a range of duties. More importantly, firms wanted men with so-called 'leadership qualities', rather than with specific skills, and in particular, as Gourvish (1987; 34) argues, they needed to be able to fit into the 'clubbable' atmosphere of most British boardrooms.

The holding company form

In this context, it is interesting to return briefly to the intense merger activity of this period, because while the M-form structure would appear to have been shunned by the vast majority of British businessmen, another important point to make about some of the big firms appearing at this time is the propensity to adopt a holding company form (Hannah, 1976; 198–9: 1980; 52–6). This ruse was simply a perpetutation of the older style of federation which had characterised the initial history of many pre-war multi-firm mergers, and Payne (1984; 196–7) has argued that it was crucial in preventing a wider acceptance of *corporate managerial* capitalism by allowing family firms to shelter from competitive pressures. Foreman-Peck (1994; 397) has also noted that in these holding companies 'there was no integration of the activites beyond market-rigging', a trend which affected significant sectors of the economy. Indeed, some of the largest firms of the 1930s were still holding companies, from AEI in the electrical industry to Tube Investments and GKN in engineering. Even in firms like English Electric, which were characterised by a considerable dispersion of ownership, a holding company form was adopted until 1929 when it was bought by the American firm, Westinghouse. Thereafter, under George (later Lord) Nelson's industrious guidance, English Electric was organised along divisional lines, but much damage had been done to the business as a result of the previous laxity (Jones & Marriott, 1970; 144–54). This reveals the latent dangers inherent in adopting a holding company structure at a time when large-scale firms were pursuing ambitious strategies which radically altered the scale and scope of British business. In spite of such ambition, management persisted with what can only be regarded as an anachronistic structure, reflecting the strength of traditional approaches to ownership and control well into the twentieth century.

Merger activity clearly resulted in only rare cases of dramatic restructuring, and the widespread propensity to create holding companies should be held up as a clear sign that managers were side-stepping the associated organisational challenges. Above all, as Coleman (1987; 8–9) has noted, it was the 'implicit and unacknowledged obeisance to the god of continuity' which predominated in British business. In simple terms, owner-managers either perpetutated the traditional culture of their firm through the persistence with autocratic, centralised organisations, or they sought the security of a merger as a means of preserving control in a holding company structure. After studying ten leading companies, Gourvish (1987; 33–4) suggested a 'corporate lag' when compared with the USA, because he concluded that British business in the inter-war era still demonstrated 'a preference for internally-recruited directors, and the retention of owners in entrepreneurial positions'. In this context, the process of sequential acquisition facilitated the gradual absorption of new businesses, forestalling the need for any wholesale change to an organisation.

One should also note that 'defensive' motives laid behind most mergers of this period, the creation of ICI in 1926 being a classic example of, as we shall see in section 5.4, British firms responding to the threats posed by exogenous pressures. Indeed, foreign competition remained a major spur to combination, especially when the international economy slumped into a deep depression after the initial phase of post-war euphoria. In this respect, the strategies pursued would appear to have been rational, but the organisational limitations of large-scale business remained a major obstacle to the exploitation of potential economies of scale and scope.

The power of trade associations

Another crucial point to make in this respect is the strong tendency to join trade associations (Fitzgerald, 1927; 1–4), especially when in 1932 British trading policy became overtly protectionist for the first time in over 100 years. This sheltered system provided firms with an excellent opportunity to band together in the interests of guaranteeing minimum prices and market quotas, and such was the success achieved by British trade associations at this time that many entered into world-wide agreements with European and American firms (PEP, 1957; 1–21). By 1944 there were 2,500 trade associations operating in Britain, 1,300 of which covered manufacturing industries, and while one might here be witnessing a wider acceptance among traditionally individualistic British businessmen of the need to co-operate, once again one must question the incentives provided to restructure business in circumstances where prices and market quotas were guaranteed. Fitzgerald (1927; 4–6) describes how the pooling of price and other commercial information created a cosy environment of collusion and compensation, ensuring firms a profit even if they did not achieve their allocated quotas. Even ICI was criticised for 'making comparatively few products extremely well and selling them at prices usually fixed by international agreement' (Reader, 1975; 405–7), emphasising how the most progressive managements were willing to hide behind these systems. As Chandler (1976; 48) has argued:

> Under no legal pressure to consolidate, these combinations of autonomous firms made little attempt to benefit from the economies of speed by rationalising facilities and by employing salaried career managers ... [and this] certainly extended the life of many family and entrepreneurial enterprises in Great Britain.

Conclusion

The effectiveness of trade association activity in the inter-war era is one of the strongest arguments in favour of the case that British businessmen, rather than favouring abstract notions and new approaches, were much more concerned with what one might describe as 'bread-and-butter' issues, and with surviving in a trading climate which in the inter-war era experienced wild vicissitudes (Musson, 1978; 262–6). During and immediately after the First World War, many trade associations advocated ambitious ideas concerning the rationalisation of British industry, but thereafter they succumbed to the inevitable pressures of the market and simply acted as price-fixing agents (Turner, 1988; 193–4). In this context, one must also examine more closely the extent to which the 'management movement' actually influenced business activity, because in large part the major figures were often simply preaching to the converted. Child (1969; 103) has concluded, after reviewing the major inter-war developments in management thought, that 'the new literature, and the activity of the [movement] at the Oxford and similar conferences, continued to remain alien to the great mass of practising managers and employers'. Membership of the Works Management Association, for example, totalled around 900 by 1929, but there were approximately 250,000 works managers in the country at that time. Similarly, the Institute of Industrial Management, formed in 1920 as a key vehicle for spreading the gospel of Rationalisation, was by the end of the decade almost moribund. Recruitment on to the new management courses at Birmingham, the LSE and Manchester also remained frustratingly low, while the early rejection of such forms of education at Oxford and Cambridge ensured that a liberal arts tradition would prevail in the recruitment patterns of those people who had been to these conservative institutions (Keeble, 1992; 120–2). This tradition was perpetuated by the prevalance of Oxbridge or public-school educated types on the boards of large companies, hindering the work of pioneers like

J. A. Bowie in attempting to convince businessmen that a more formal approach to training had a future. In other words, the idea that 'managers are born, not made' still held sway by the 1940s.

There might well have been an 'enthusiastic espousal of the doctrines of rationalisation' during the inter-war years, but it is clear from what we have just seen that both the attitudes to management and its practice do not seem to have changed drastically by the 1940s. As J. A. Bowie (1930; 59) concluded, after reviewing the progress made in persuading British business to accept the need for an expansion of management education: 'The soil of crass individualism is never friendly to standards or ethical ideas'. The Balfour Committee on Industry and Trade also concluded in 1928 that 'a further great modernisation effort was necessary', confirming the views of many contemporaries that in industry especially progressive movements had been unsuccessful (Thomas, 1931; 53). The greater levels of concentration, coupled with the pursuit of strategies of vertical integration and diversification, indicate that more careful thought was being given to industrial structure after the First World War. On the other hand, the widespread allegiance to personal capitalism was preventing a more thorough-going transformation of British business organisation, and one need only remember that even as late as 1950, 110 of the leading 200 firms still had representatives of the owning family sitting on the board of directors (Hannah, 1980; 53). Personal capitalism was still rife in British business by the 1940s, and clearly the market-cum-technological and general institutional features of the British scene had still not forced through a wholesale change in attitudes towards organisation and management. In effect, it was this continuity which acted as the major obstacle to the implementation of Rationalisation and a stronger structural response to the strategies of concentration and integration.

5.2 Scientific management and British workshop practices

One of the major preoccupations of those who advocated concepts like Rationalisation during the inter-war period was undoubtedly the thorny issue of industrial relations, but such was the divergence in both opinion and practice across British industry that here again no generally accepted consensus emerged on the solutions to be adopted. Child (1969; 22–4) has emphasised how the dual focus of British management thought on legitimatory and technical functions was a manifestation of this concern with the crucial issue of managerial authority, and from the late-nineteenth century onwards members of the management movement, as well as some prominent businessmen, spent a considerable amount of time discussing such issues. In essence, although some Quaker employers like Cadbury and Rowntree talked about the need to work more closely with the labour-force, at the root of these debates was the 'right to manage' issue, and how best to extract the maximum amount of effort from workers without creating an antagonistic climate which would disrupt production. One of the major influences in these debates was F. W. Taylor and his ideas on scientific management (see section 3.1), but it will become apparent that few British employers accepted what was widely regarded as a dehumanising influence on workshop practices, leading to much improvisation in the field. Similarly, practices like industrial paternalism, or 'welfarism', as it came to be known, were also adapted to the particular circumstances prevailing in individual firms or industries, emphasising the difficulties of generalising about these developments.

Changing approaches to industrial paternalism up to 1914

It was described in section 2.2 how internal subcontracting and industrial paternalism had been the two most evident features of labour management in Britain up to the 1880s. The former had evolved as a solution to the problems inherent in controlling workshop practices where high levels of skill were involved, while the latter not only provided a solution to the recruitment problems experienced by the first generation of industrialists, it also contributed extensively to the inculcation of capitalist ethics into a workforce by binding each individual's interests inextricably to the firm. From the 1880s, however, the two systems came under increasing pressure to adapt in circumstances which were rapidly changing, leading to substantial changes in management's attitudes towards both industrial relations and workshop practices. Religous influences may well have played some part in this movement, but above all it was a range of exogenous pressures which forced management to readdress their traditional approach towards labour, and over the period 1880–1940 this aspect of business underwent an extensive process of change.

Industrial paternalism had long been recognised as an effective means of instilling supposedly middle class virtues like time-discipline into the workforce, but by the 1880s it was increasingly evident that the system would have to be adapted to the changing environment. In particular, a combination of rising real wages and the improved benefits provided by the so-called 'new model' trade unions allowed skilled workers much greater independence from employers, providing them with the financial strength to acquire their own housing or unemployment and sickness benefits. Of course, the growing influence of trade unionism was seen as a major threat to management from the 1880s, not only because the new model unions were extending their influence among skilled workers, but also because so-called new trade unions were beginning to recruit semi-skilled and manual labour, especially in the trade cycle peaks. Matthews (1988; 306–24) has described how in the London gas industry, after major victories in 1888 by the stokers' union, a profit-sharing (or co-partnership) scheme was devised as 'undoubtedly part of an attempt to smash the . . . union'. He goes on to note how 'profit-sharing had little effect on the quality or quantity of work done', but trade union influence was successfully 'smashed', and until nationalisation in 1949 strike activity was a rarity in those companies adopting such schemes.

Co-partnership was, of course, not unique to the gas industry, because major engineering firms like Whitworth's and the big railway companies had since the 1860s operated similar schemes (Melling, 1983; 62). One must also stress how profit-sharing was but one aspect of a broader management strategy employed in the struggle against growing union strength, because employee welfare schemes were developed as a means of encouraging greater loyalty. As early as the 1790s Boulton & Watt had devised one of the first industrial welfare programmes, while Wegdwood had also experimented with similar ideas (see section 2.2), but by the late-nineteenth century a small group of industrialists was beginning to elaborate more clearly their ideas on this strategy (Melling, 1983; 55–77). Again, the big London gas companies were among the most extensive providers of pensions, sick pay, accident benefits and recreational and sports facilities, while matchmaking and port transport also witnessed similar developments from the late-1880s (Fitzgerald, 1989; 51–62). However, the most striking developments in what has been described as 'welfarism' came in the confectionary trades, in which the major Quaker employers like Cadbury (Rowlinson, 1988; 377–92) and Rowntree extolled what they saw as the virtues of co-operation between management and workforce.

While firms like Lever Bros (Jeremy, 1991; 58–78: Wilson, 1954; 142–58), Renold's and Mather & Platt were among the more prominent advocates of this thorough-going approach towards industrial welfare, the most publicised efforts were those of Cadbury and Rowntree at their plants in, respectively, Bournville (near Birmingham) and York. Bournville is perhaps the classic example of welfarism in action, and by copying some of the techniques from American and European competitors, Edward Cadbury was able to establish clear managerial responsibility for personnel, health and safety issues, as well as providing the usual services listed above (Rowlinson, 1988; 387–8). Seebohm Rowntree was similarly responsible for introducing a more systematic approach towards welfare, becoming in 1890 what must have been the first labour director in British industry. Much of this activity culminated in the formation in 1914 of a new type of organisation, the Welfare Workers' Association, and although only twenty-five firms affiliated initially this was a solid foundation for the much greater interest shown in industrial welfare during and after the First World War (Child, 1969; 36, 79–81).

Inter-war attitudes towards welfarism

It is apparent from Jones's (1983; 61–72) research that 'from the First World War welfare work came to play a more central role in employers' industrial relations strategy', and she illustrates this claim by referring to schemes in the textile, engineering and paper industries. Of course, there was a considerable variety of experience both within industries and across geographical boundaries, but a close look at the Lancashire cotton industry reveals how the larger firms especially provided private occupational welfare services (Jones, 1988; 64–77). One of the main reasons for this extension of welfarism was the increase in size of business as a result of intense merger activity, a trend which exacerbated the problems of communicating with a larger workforce. As Johnman (1986; 229) has demonstrated, in attempting to identify the largest manufacturing employers of 1935, merger activity substantially increased the size of workforces, and the top 100 accounted for 1,243,922, as opposed to 682,084 in 1907. Living standards were also rising for those employed in the expanding industries located in the more prosperous south, where the problems of attracting and retaining scarce skilled labour forced employers to devise new schemes. State intervention, in the form of new factory regulations and direct negotiations between civil servants and employers' organisations, played a part in this movement, but of central importance was the innate pressure on management to control the workforce. An Industrial Welfare Society was created in 1918 as a vehicle for advising on the implementation of new schemes, and although he does not emphasise the work of this organisation Child (1969; 70–103) describes how British management thought was increasingly focussed on improving labour management techniques. There is, indeed, a proliferation of organisations and literature on this subject, some of which was heavily influenced by the work of American thinkers like Mayo and his experiments at the Hawthorne plant of Westinghouse. Child (1969; 94–6) is quick to point out, however, that British management thought had already been moving along Mayoist lines well before his work was published in the 1930s, especially with regard to the need for harmony at workshop level, and this was being achieved by the implementation of welfarist strategies.

Management and the right to manage

It is quite readily apparent that from the 1880s industrial paternalism was evolving into a more systematised means of imposing greater control over the workforce, especially at the level of the large-scale firm (Melling, 1983; 74–7). This must not, however, be seen in isolation from other trends in the field of labour management, because as Fitzgerald (1989; 48) has argued: 'The creation of internal labour markets within firms, founded on schemes of decasualisation, centrally-directed hiring and training, and welfare benefits, could be coupled with the managerial standardisation, measurement and control of work methods'. In other words, following Chandler's (1962; 13–5) simple typology of business development, as a direct result of the strategy aimed at increasing managerial control over the workplace, significant structural adaptation occurred. Here again the growing strength of trade unions, especially of the new model type, was a cause of considerable concern to employers, particularly in the context of increasingly competitive markets at a time when levels of fixed investment were rising. Few now accept Braverman's (1974) neo-Marxist interpretation, which argues that 'monopoly capitalism' resulted in the de-skilling of labour by the imposition of managerial directives on the shopfloor. This thesis oversimplifies the evolutionary process, and especially the acceptance of Taylor's ideas on scientific management (McKinlay & Zeitlin, 1989; 32). There were, nevertheless, some changes taking place in British workshop practices from the 1890s through to the 1940s, providing a challenge to traditional modes of organisation.

Burgess (1975; 29) has concluded that by the 1890s: 'The essence of the employers' struggle was the unitary organisation of production where the authority of the employers and their subordinates runs unchallenged throughout the enterprise'. This insistence on what was known as management's right to manage involved a direct challenge to the traditional system of internal subcontracting (described in section 2.2), in which skilled artisans effectively controlled workshop practices by default. The most important innovation came when from the 1880s, in the engineering industry especially, foremen were introduced as direct agents of management policies on crucial issues like manning, the pace of work and rates of pay. These foremen replaced the internal subcontractor in these respects, becoming what Melling (1980; 77) calls 'non-commissioned officers' in the industrial army. Although often recruited from among the ranks of skilled workers, and frequently they remained union members, foremen acted as the 'shock-absorber' between management and the skilled workers, particularly in implementing the drive for greater efficiency. Foremen were also part of a 'multirole supervisory system', composed of rate-fixers, 'feed-and-speed' men, cost accountants and draughtsmen, substantially overhauling workshop practices in the larger engineering firms of the late-nineteenth century.

Inevitably, the Amalgamated Society of Engineers (ASE) refused to accept this assualt on their former control over workshop practices without putting up a struggle, and in 1897 there occurred a major dispute in the engineering industry. McKinlay & Zeitlin (1989; 32–44) dispute any claims that engineering employers 'pursued a collective strategy designed fundamentally to transform the nature of work', but they were able to combine under the common aim of reducing worker control, and by 1898 the ASE had been forced to accept 'the key principles of managerial prerogative' (Zeitlin, 1983; 34). In spite of this victory, however, it is apparent that engineering employers failed to exploit their hard-won rights, and by 1910 skilled workers had been able to reassert many of their traditional practices. This was also the case in the shipbuilding industry, when after the employers launched 'a co-ordinated assault on craft unionism' between 1902 and 1906 the unions continued to control crucial aspects of production (Lovell, 1992; 39–56). In other words, 'the fragmented ownership of firms, the structure of the market, and the nature of existing plant discouraged major retooling, so that innovation consisted rather in the introduction of new machine tools and work practices within a workshop organisation that remained structurally unchanged' (Zeitlin, 1983; 38). The meant that the de-skilling of work and intense subdivision of labour fundamental to F. W. Taylor's system of scientific management had no place in British engineering, or, indeed, in the rest of industry, given the persistence of traditional modes of production and purchasing. A handful of firms (Willans & Robinson, Renolds, and Dick, Kerr & Co.) introduced variants of scientific management (Urwick, 1938; 30–3, 38–44: Wilson, 1985; 34), but for the majority Taylor's notions seemed abstract in the extreme. It is an attitude typified by the instance in 1910, when he lectured to the Institute of Mechanical Engineers on the virtues of his system, but most were disappointed that he had not come to talk about his more celebrated technical achievements with high-speed steel.

The British variant of scientific management

The antipathetic British approach towards Taylor's ideas on production and management is yet another illustration of how, as we noted in chapter 4, techniques employed in the USA were not necessarily viable in different market environments. Many commentators also poured scorn on the 'scientific' basis of scientific management, while by the inter-war years considerable concern was being expressed about the dehumanising approach which was fundamental to this American system (Lewchuk, 1987; 91–3). During the First World War, much of the engineering industry had been converted to munitions production, and under the auspices of the Ministry of Munitions (established in 1915) mass production techniques were employed extensively in order to satisfy the insatiable demand for the weapons of war. This had a dramatic impact on both the attitudes to, and practices in British workshops, but even though in 1922 the Engineering Employers' Federation once again successfully engaged the engineers' unions in a major conflict over the right to manage issue, the American methods of direct control were flatly rejected as unhelpful and counter-productive. Even in the archetypal mass-production industry, car production, there evolved what Lewchuk (1987; 183–4) has called the 'British system of mass production', based on indirect control of workshop practices. C. S. Myers, director of the National Institute of Industrial Psychology, also noted that workers rejected the 'American' methods because in the context of mass unemployment they were seen as an attack on jobs. On the other hand, it is similarly clear that management was just as reluctant to move in this direction, and Lyndall Urwick accepted that 'the predominantly technical character of those who were responsible for management in this country' ensured that scientific management would never take a firm hold in Britain (Lewchuk, 1987; 92, 107–11).

This brief description of inter-war attitudes reveals the strength of traditional approaches towards labour and production, and the emphasis of management writers and commentators on human relations reinforced such beliefs (Child, 1969; 75–83). The substantial investment in welfare services noted earlier was a further manifestation of this culture, and while major disputes like the 1926 General Strike have created the impression that inter-war industrial relations were difficult, it is important to note that employers regarded such action as highly damaging. The 1926 dispute was also followed by extensive talks between Sir Alfred Mond (chairman of ICI) and Ben Turner (general secretary of the TUC) on how to avoid clashes of this kind (Mond, 1927; 143–6), emphasising how attitudes amongst some major employers (especially in expanding industries like chemicals and electrical engineering) were heavily influenced by the work on human relations. The Institute of Labour Management had, by 1939, 760 members, compared to the twenty-five of its predecessor, the Welfare Workers' Association (Child, 1969; 113), and although one can derive few concrete conclusions from such figures it is evident that greater interest was being shown in the burgeoning literature on this subject.

The Bedaux system

Having noted this trend, it is interesting to examine a peculiar episode in the history of inter-war labour management which further reinforces the view that both management and workers were reluctant to accept new ideas on production. F. W. Taylor actually died in 1915, and his mantle as leading advocate of 'scientific management' was inherited by another American, Charles Bedaux, who had developed the 'Bedaux System' (Littler, 1982; 99–116). The essence of this variant of Taylor's ideas was his use of a 'B-Unit' as a means of measuring units of work, providing a basis for job simplification and the bureaucratisation of shopfloor practices. In retrospect, one might argue that 'B' represented 'bogus', rather than Bedaux, because when applied to real-time situations many firms experienced great difficulty in interpreting its application (Nockolds, 1976; 237–8). Nevertheless, such were Bedaux's skills as a salesman that, after establishing an office in London in 1926, over the next thirteen years he was able to persuade 250 firms to hire the services of his consultant-engineers. This would appear to contradict our earlier claim that most British businessmen were reluctant to accept scientific management as a viable option, but Littler (1982; 99–116) is careful to emphasise how a more detailed analysis of the Bedaux system in operation would simply reinforce the views expressed above. In the first place, Bedaux's techniques were mostly introduced into processes employing unskilled labour, and craft de-skilling was only rarely envisaged. Second, such was the antagonism of workers to the Bedaux system, and especially to its insistence on new work patterns and the posting of performance rates on wallcharts, that management was forced to modify and then drop the practices soon after the Bedaux consultants had left (Wilson, 1996).

Conclusion

One could take up a considerable amount of space examining how the Bedaux system fared in particular locations (Nockolds, 1976; 237–8), and similarly it would have been interesting to discuss further how firms like Lever Bros (Jeremy, 1991; 58–78) and Rowntree implemented their welfarist strategies. It is nevertheless apparent, though, that attitudes towards labour management remained firmly embedded in nineteenth century traditions associated with paternalism and the indirect control of production. As we noted in concluding the last section, only a vociferous minority was willing to push the new ideas on Rationalisation. In the older industries like textiles, coal, iron and steel and heavy engineering, becalmed by international trading difficulties, management was much more interested in what we have described as the 'bread-and-butter' issues of maintaining liquidity and cutting costs. They would no doubt have argued that implementing Rationalisation concepts would have been prohibitively expensive, given their trading difficulties, but even in expanding industries like car production, where Ford's mass-production techniques were extensively employed, Lewchuk (1987; 152–84) has vividly demonstrated how management proved unwilling to substitute direct for indirect control procedures. It was a situation symptomatic of inter-war developments in British business as a whole, indicating how the fundamental characteristics of a business culture steeped in tradition remained unchanged up to the 1940s.

5.3   The rise of a corporate economy

Although the first sections of this chapter have concluded with a highly critical appraisal of the slow pace of change in Britain's business culture, this view should not obscure the developments arising from intense merger activity which affected industrial structure and the increasing scale of operations. Almost 3,700 companies were involved in mergers during the inter-war period, and it is not surprising that levels of concentration increased markedly over this period. Indeed, as the main authority on this issue, Hannah (1980; 60: 1983; 90: Hannah & Kay, 1977; 68–71) is convinced that the inter-war mergers were vital in laying the foundations of a modern corporate economy. In this context, it is important to note that a corporate economy is synonymous with control, whereby industry is highly concentrated and government plays a direct role in influencing business strategy.

There are many problems with the statistical measurement of this trend, and Hart (1979; 211) has been extremely critical of Hannah and Kay's (1977; 64–81) claim that mergers were the main cause of concentration increases. Nevertheless, there is an acute paucity of alternative information from either company balance sheets or government censuses, and from what is available there seems to be ample evidence to reveal that a series of decisive changes in key features of economic activity had occurred by the 1940s.

Rising industrial concentration

In the main, when describing the rise of a corporate economy in Britain, Hannah (1983; 120) is principally concerned with charting industrial concentration. It is also important to note that he does not regard government influence as significant, arguing that as a result of merger activity the large-scale firms created by 1930 'remained the mainstay of Britain's corporate structure', and revealing how thereafter stability was a major feature of the top 100 companies. We have already noted how twenty-two of the top 100 companies of 1970 were formed in the inter-war period, a figure only rivalled by the 1960s, when another great surge in merger activity occurred. Figure 5.2 also demonstrates the steady increase in industrial concentration, from fifteen per cent in 1907 and seventeen per cent in 1919, rising to twenty-six per cent by 1930. Of course, after 1930 the graph dips to twenty-three per cent, and it took another twenty years before concentration started to rise again. However, Hannah (1983; 91–1932) notes that imprecise data could explain this trend, while in addition one might mention other contributors such as the major depression of 1929–32, the reduction in merger activity (see Table 5.1), and preparations for, involvement in, and recovery from, World War II.

We shall return to an analysis of declining levels of concentration in the 1930s and 1940s towards the end of this section, but in the meantime it is essential to explain just how extensively industrial structure changed during the 1920s. Hannah and Kay (1977; 64–71) have conducted the most extensive statistical survey of these changes, using the standard measurement of concentration ratios which is revealed by CRN (where N is the number of firms). It is important to remember that, because of the enormous limitations in data provided by company accounts or the census of production, they were obliged to measure concentration by using only the market valuation of firms as an indication of size, and Hart (1979; 20) has pointed out how major problems exist in the calculations. Regardless of this criticism, they argue that their results are indicative of general trends within the economy as a whole, providing some substance to the general conclusion that concentration levels increased significantly in their sample between 1919 and 1930. The objective measure taken is CR10 (to measure the shares of the ten largest firms in each industry) for eleven major industrial groupings, and in Table

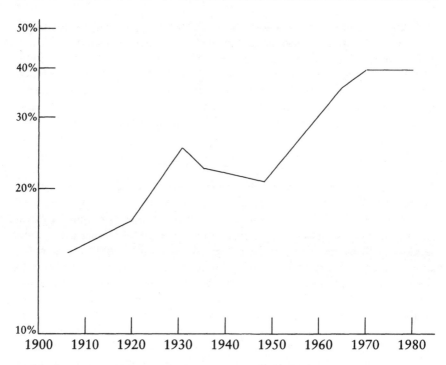

Figure 5.2   *The proportion of net manfacturing output accounted for by the largest 100 companies* (semi-log scale)

5.3 one can see how this grew in every single case. The most striking gains can be found in 'Food', 'Building Mat' and 'Paper, etc' (which includes publishing), while in the miscellaneous categories and 'All Manuf[acturing]' impressive progress towards an oligopolistic trading structure was made. Again, the statistical limitations inherent in this excercise must be considered, but even if there is some margin for error it is nevertheless apparent that concentration levels were rising significantly, and merger activity was primarily responsible for these movements.

There is a clear tendency in Britain over the inter-war period towards the kind of oligopolistic trading structure which had earlier developed in the USA and Germany, while the levels of vertical integration had also increased substantially. In this respect, one might question the claims of Elbaum & Lazonick (1986; 1–14), when they argue that by the 1940s British industry was characterised by an atomistic trading structure. On the other hand, as Hannah (1980; 59–71) is careful to point out, one must be careful not to overstate any similarities with the USA, because the British trend 'showed distinctive national characteristics', particularly in relation to the number of large corporations and a notable absence of modern managerial structures. Nevertheless, it is important to realise that significant progress had been

Table 5.3 *Concentration levels in British industry, 1919–1930 (per cent of total)*

	CR10 in 1919 %	CR10 in 1930 %
Food	52.9	85.1
Drink	35.0	52.6
Tobacco	98.2	100.0
Chemicals	76.7	93.2
Metal Manuf	44.3	65.4
Eng, etc [i]	42.1	48.6
Metal Goods	68.0	87.1
Textiles	60.7	78.2
Building Mat	69.1	94.0
Paper, etc	56.0	88.8
Miscell [ii]	46.0	77.1
All Manuf	43.4	63.7

[i] Engineering, Vehicles and Shipbuilding
[ii] All other industries
Source: Hannah & Kay (1977; 69–70).

made in Britain, bringing industrial structure closer to the American pattern. Clearly, the *visible hand* of business control would appear to have been usurping the pervasive pre-1914 influence of market forces, and there seems to be little doubt that, in statistical terms, a modern corporate economy had emerged in Britain by the 1930s.

The role of the state

We shall return in the next section to analyse the reality behind this increase in concentration, but having noted these tendencies in British business practices it is now important to broaden our view of this trend and ask whether in any other respects corporatism came to characterise aspects of the economy. After all, one cannot discuss this issue without assessing the state's role and its relationship with business (and labour), because extensive government intervention could well have a decisive influence on strategy and (possibly) structure. Middlemass (1979; 14–23), in particular, has argued that a 'corporatist bias' emerged in Britain during the First World War, involving employers' associations, trade unions and government, and he claims that over the following sixty-five years this tripartite alliance played a major role in dictating the policy-making process. However, few have accepted such an interpretation of twentieth century politics (Turner, 1984; 2–3), although there is no doubt that many businessmen wanted to extend the role performed during the First World War into a more thoroughgoing influence on policy and a number of new organisations were created as means of co-ordinating views on key issues. Indeed, while the 'corporatist bias' thesis might well have been overstated, there are still strong grounds for believing that during the interwar era government-industry relations were more intimate than at any time in the previous century, and in important respects this had a crucial bearing on strategy and structure in several industries.

Docker and business politics

After the British economy had been placed firmly on a war footing in 1915, when the Ministry of Munitions was created as a vehicle for extending government influence over key industries like engineering, steel, coal, chemicals and transport, an increasingly influential group of businessmen realised the need to influence such policies. The most active of this group was Dudley Docker, who by this time had become a leading figure in the business world as a result of his achievements at the Metropolitan Co. and other major engineering firms (see section 4.3). He was in fact one of the most vociferous advocates of a group of industrialists known as the 'productioneers', arguing that the War must be seen as an opportunity to halt British industry's relative decline, compared to Germany and the USA. The productioneers wanted protection of British markets and greater unity amongst manufacturers, both in terms of business units and through effective trade associations which would be capable of influencing government policy (Davenport-Hines, 1984; 84–7). In effect, Docker was a corporatist, because he wanted to create a triangular structure composed of government, business and labour which would formulate policies capable of improving Britain's industrial performance, at a time when in other economies (especially in Germany and Japan) such collective approaches had for long been popular. Indeed, Docker was heavily influenced by the corporatist movement on the Continent, and working closely with the British Electrical and Allied Manufacturers' Association he was able to establish the Federation of British Industries (FBI) in July 1916, as a means of co-ordinating business policy.

The principal aim of the FBI was to act as a 'business parliament' which would co-ordinate the views of manufacturers and lobby government in favour of policies which would support and nurture British industry. Initially, just 124 companies and trade associations could be persuaded to join this organisation, but within a year membership had risen to over 400 (Davenport-Hines, 1984; 105–14), while by 1931 the roll stood at 2,480 firms and 157 associations (Foreman-Peck, 1994; 398). This provided Docker with a potentially useful vehicle for spreading his corporatist beliefs. Unfortunately, though, as Marrison (1995) argues, while by this time the industrial constituency had predominantly accepted the need for protectionism, few manufacturers were willing to co-operate with labour on an equal footing, and by 1919 a National Confederation of Employers' Organisations

(NCEO) had been created as a forum for discussing labour issues. The major force behind the NCEO's creation had been Sir Allan Smith of the powerful Engineering Employers' Federation (Rodgers, 1986; 100), and although the FBI was able to help launch the Whitley scheme of joint industrial councils in 1917, this was as far as Docker's brand of corporatism was allowed to progress in business circles. This was a major defeat for Docker and 'extirpated the vestiges of the FBI's involvement in labour relations and crushed Docker's last hope of a business parliament concerned with every aspect of manufacturing policy' (Davenport-Hines, 1984; 116). On the other hand, Marrison (1995) is clear that protectionism remained a major influence in industrial circles, and organisations like the British Manufacturers' Assocation (1914), the London Imperialists (1916) and the British Commonwealth Union (1918) were also formed to persuade politicians that free trade ought to be abandoned. Furthermore, almost forty-one per cent of the Conservative MP's elected in the 1919 general election were active businessmen (compared to just under twenty-five per cent in 1914), leading to that party's growing reputation as the 'bosses party' at a time when Labour was beginning to emerge as the second major political group (Turner, 1984; 14–5).

The crucial issue, though, is whether all this activity materially influenced government policies once the War had ended; whether, as Middlemass (1979; 150–1) argues, after 1918 'a new form of political activity was growing up' involving what he calls 'governing institutions' like the FBI, the NCEO and the TUC working closely with government ministries. In this context, it is important to stress how Davenport-Hines (1984; 117–9) overstates the lack of unity among British industrialists on the crucial issue of protectionism, because while Docker certainly faced considerable opposition to his 'trade warrior' rhetoric from such organisations as the Imperial Association of Commerce, these opponents were mainly merchants who remained firmly wedded to the doctrines of free trade. The main reason why businessmen were unwilling to force the protectionist issue in parliament was the decisive changes occurring in British politics at that time, because after 1922 especially, the only viable opposition to the Conservatives was Labour, and few in the FBI were willing to envisage such a radical alternative with its belief in high tax policies and nationalisation.

Industry-government relations after 1918

In retrospect, there would appear to be very little doubt that by the early-1920s industry-government relations differed only marginally from those prevailing in 1914 (Roberts, 1984; 93), and far from wishing to pursue new ideas the Treasury devoted all its energies to restoring the *status quo ante bellum*. This is not the place for a detailed analysis of inter-war economic policy, but until the *debacle* of 1931 British governments were committed to the three major tenets of neo-classical economics, namely, restoring the pound sterling to the gold standard, balancing the annual budget and pursuing free trade (Pollard, 1992; 105–11). In other words, corporatist influences were swiftly marginalised and organisations like the FBI were unable to convince politicians and civil servants of the need for a radical rethink. Middlemass (1979; 18–20) would consequently appear to have exaggerated the post-war impact of any 'corporatist bias' detectable in the period 1915–1918, and while the FBI and NCEO continued to flourish in the 1920s only in the field of labour relations did they achieve much.

One must also add that the number of active businessmen involved in politics dwindled to thirty-five per cent in the 1924 general election, a level at which it remained throughout the inter-war period. In any case, while in the House of Commons they were politicians first and businessmen second, responding principally to the party whip, rather than to the lobbying of extra-parliamentary organisations like the FBI (Turner, 1984; 15–18). The Parliamentary Industrial Group, composed of coalition MPs with business interests and headed by Sir Allan Smith, might well have lobbied for greater government involvement in the economy (Rodgers, 1986; 100–19), but its failure to influence policy reflected the political realities of an era in which such ideas were treated with little respect.

Most authorities have consequently concluded that little evidence exists to support any claims of a general post-war 'corporate bias', and although Docker and his colleagues continued to lobby aggressively for the policies initially voiced by the productioneers during the First World War, they rarely succeeded in convincing a sceptical public that such a strategy was needed. On the other hand, one cannot help feeling that the preoccupation with trading policy has distracted some historians' attentions away from a series of government interventions which would appear to reflect a growing political interest in industrial affairs. In particular, where special circumstances came into play or strategic interests were affected, governments of the inter-war era adopted an increasingly corporatist stance which reflected the desire of senior politicians and officials to provide some form of assistance. For example, while free trade was regarded as the main theme of British trading policy, in 1921 a Safeguarding of Industries Act was passed which provided protection for several products (aircraft engines, optical glass and fine chemicals) regarded as strategic to Britain's defence. More importantly, in reorganising the railway industry in 1921 (Grieves, 1989; 89–91) and establishing the British Broadcasting Company (1922), Imperial Airways (1924), and the Central Electricity Board (1926), government ministers were responding to obvious weaknesses in the market which had resulted in chaotic disorganisation. We shall also see later how government was directly responsible for prompting mergers which resulted in the formation of ICI, while after 1929 some industries, especially coal, cotton, shipbuilding and steel, were also affected directly by statutory intervention which was to have a considerable impact on business strategy. The shipbuilding industry had been especially badly hit by a combination of falling orders and greater competition from continental rivals, and even though firms like John Browns, of Clydebank, made some investment in new facilities and some old working practices were overhauled difficulties persisted (Slaven, 1977; 215).

'Government by subcontract' and 'industrial diplomacy'

An increasing number of government departments were clearly taking a more interventionist line after 1920, but it is essential to emphasise how as a result of ministerial reluctance to manage these new organisations a system of 'government by subcontract' was adopted. As Turner (1984; 13) has noted:

> The creation of Imperial Airways, like the establishment of the National Grid, of ICI or of the Bank of England's industrial organs, was made possible by a network of businessmen, politicians and civil servants who co-operated to promote, but also control, state intervention in the economy.

Prominent industrialists like Lord Weir, Sir Eric Geddes, Sir Charles Gardner and Sir Harry McGowan were among the most effective influences on this strategy, and it is important to note that most were also leading figures in the FBI. Roberts (1984; 92–104) has argued that the decisive period was 1929–1935, when as a result of what he calls 'industrial diplomacy' government officials negotiated directly with industrialists on key issues like protectionism and rationalisation. Although an Economic Advisory Council was established in 1929 to examine industrial problems and recommend action to the Cabinet, and by 1930 Sir Horace Wilson had been appointed Chief Industrial Advisor to the Board of Trade, much of the consequent action was conducted on an informal, pragmatic basis. Indeed, the assistance given to cotton, coal, shipbuilding and steel during the 1930s arose out of an uncoordinated series of responses to particular problems, demonstrating the 'anxieties felt by officials about the conflicting demands of economic theory and economic reality' (Roberts, 1984; 98).

The extensive emergence of 'industrial diplomacy' was one of the more obvious manifestations of a growing awareness at government level that the invisible hand of market forces was no longer capable of achieving economic equilibrium. It is important to emphasise, though, that this interesting development should not be used to support Middlemass's (1979; 372) claims that employer organisations had achieved the status of 'governing institutions', because far from elevating them into a new source of power 'industrial diplomacy aimed to achieve the very opposite, to attach the increasingly important trade and industry pressure groups to the existing parliamentary process' (Roberts, 1984; 100). The main role of Sir Horace Wilson was to monitor the process of rationalisation in troubled industries like cotton, coal, steel and shipbuilding, intervening on an informal basis and implementing legislation only as a last resort when all other avenues had been exhausted. Hannah (1983; 51) is also quite sure that inter-war governments eschewed the role of 'trust promoter', a strategy which was 'explicable in terms of the ideology and motivations' of the period. One might well point to instances like the 1930 and 1936 Acts enforcing rationalisation in the coal industry (Kirby, 1973; 160–73), or government encroachment on the oil industry after 1914 (Jones, 1984; 146–62). On the other hand, at no time did politicians develop a desire either to fashion a co-ordinated industrial strategy or intervene directly in the field of industrial management.

The creation of ICI

A classic example of this approach can be provided by examining the creation and early history of ICI, because as Reader (1976; 227–9) demonstrates, this was part of a 'conscious design on the part of government to bring the chemical industry up to the standards set by Germans with regard to the application of science to industry'. One must not confuse this claim with a general desire to implement Rationalisation policies, because it is not clear whether government officials accepted the need for the kind of policies advocated by Urwick and the 'management movement'. As with the 1921 Safeguarding of Industries Act, though, politicians were willing to support strategic industries which were essential to Britain's security. In this context, the initial stimulus was neither armaments nor aircraft engines but dyestuffs, the government having discovered the humiliating fact in 1914 that British army uniforms were produced with German dyes. This had led to the enforced merger of most Manchester-based dyestuffs manufacturers in 1916, when British Dyes Ltd was created as a result of government dictat, while in 1919 the British Dyestuffs Corporation (BDC) had evolved out of this initial attempt at strengthening the industry. In spite of receiving limited protection in 1921, however, it is clear that BDC remained vulnerable, not only because a weak holding company structure was adopted, limiting any advantages to be gained from integrating capacity and expertise, but principally because German dyestuffs were still regarded by most British textile manufacturers as superior. The situation deteriorated even further when in 1925 the four leading German chemical manufacturers combined to create I. G. Farbenindustrie (I. G. Farben), following which they made a bid to acquire BDC as a launching pad for further penetration of British and Empire markets. It was this move which precipitated decisive action at the highest levels of government, indicating how senior politicians were willing to respond quickly to situations which seemed to threaten strategic industries.

The response to I. G. Farben's predatory action was, in fact, to come from the Prime Minister himself, because it was Stanley Baldwin (newly-elected in

October 1924) who requested that Sir Reginald McKenna (who also acted as chairman of the Board of Trade's committee responsible for dyestuffs, as well as chairman of the Midland Bank) should discuss the situation with interested parties (Reader, 1970; 445). This reveals how government preferred to work indirectly through agents, and McKenna was used as the intermediary in devising a satisfactory solution to the BDC predicament. As we have just noted, after 1929 businessmen and officials met frequently to discuss industrial matters through a system of what Roberts (1984; 93) describes as 'industrial diplomacy', but in the preceding period negotiations were conducted through conduits like McKenna. It was McKenna who in January 1926 invited to lunch the managing director of Nobel Industries, Sir Harry McGowan, and it was McKenna who reported back to the Prime Minister the inclination of McGowan to merge his firm with three other major chemical manufacturers (including BDC) as a solution to the threat posed by I.G. Farben and its American counterpart, Du Pont. In the meantime, Sir Alfred Mond had travelled to the USA in the hope that he could negotiate an Anglo-American merger involving his company, Brunner Mond, but his proposed partner refused to co-operate, at which time McGowan appeared in New York to persuade him that a British merger was more promising. It was consequently on the voyage home to Southampton that McGowan and Mond draughted out the plans for creating what on 1 January 1927 became Imperial Chemical Industries (ICI).

One might well argue that government involvement in the actual merger of Nobel Industries, Brunner, Mond, the United Alkali Co. and BDC was minimal, but there is no doubt that the Prime Minister's initiative had been crucial in prompting the actions of both McKenna and McGowan. Similarly, in ICI's early development government support would prove equally important, and not only were its headquarters located in Millbank, just a few hundred yards from parliament, directors like Lords Weir, Ashfield and Birkenhead were also appointed to sustain the business-politics relationship. Reader (1976; 227) has argued that ICI always had a 'strong sense of public purpose', and this can be further substantiated by examining the interaction between company and government over the issue of protection for a major investment at Billingham.

The Billingham incident

Since 1919 Brunner Mond had been developing a new process to produce ammonia, and by 1926 a substantial plant had been erected at Billingham (Reader, 1977; 233–7). Unfortunately, however, even though £20 million was pumped into the Billingham venture, it proved to be a commercial disaster, and by 1930 ICI had decided to convert the plant to the hydrogenation process, to produce oil from coal. This was a bold decision, not simply because the technology had yet to be fully developed, even in Germany, but principally because coal-based petrol was more expensive than its natural counterpart imported from the USA, forcing ICI management to seek government support for its new project. Little help was forthcoming from the Labour government in 1930, but by 1932 ICI had been granted adequate protection against imports, after free trade had been abolished by a new coalition government as a rational response to the crisis conditions of that era. Reader (1977; 236) describes the final meeting between ICI executives and government ministers as 'almost like a diplomatic interchange between two soveriegn states', with the former delegation consisting of an ex-Viceroy and an ex-Secretary of State for Air, and the Chancellor of the Exchequer representing the latter. The first protected petrol did not start to flow until 1936, but a year earlier the Prime Minister had officially opened the Billingham hydrogenation plant, reflecting further the intimate relationship which existed between state and company.

Conclusion

There seems little doubt that ICI's initial development owed much to government support, revealing the general acceptance of a pragmatic interventionist policy at official levels for much of the inter-war period. Clearly, after 1929 the 'industrial diplomacy' noted by Roberts (1984; 93) marked a more decisive attempt to develop greater understanding of the problems faced by especially the contracting staple industries of coal, cotton and shipbuilding. The work of the Import Duties Advisory Committee after 1931 was also equally supportive, particularly in encouraging steel producers to merge and rationalise their activities. However, since the 1921 Safeguarding of Industries Act there had run a consistent thread throughout government actions, namely, that where British strategic interests needed to be secured then action must be taken. At no stage was a co-ordinated industrial strategy ever elaborated, even during the most difficult years of the early-1930s, but this should not detract from the extensive impact government actions had on business strategy in a wide range of industries right up to the Second World War. After 1935, of course, a substantial rearmament programme was also implemented, boosting activity in many industries (Wilson, 1996), but one can hardly regard this in the same light as the work of ministers and officials since 1921 in sectors requiring positive assistance as a result of market failings. In effect, by 1939 a tradition had already been established of government involvement, and from the 1940s this was extended so drastically that it was increasingly regarded as one of the most important influences on business strategy. This subject we shall examine further in the next chapter, but it is vital to emphasise the crucial importance of the inter-war era as the period in which the solid foundations of a modern corporate economy were laid, both in terms of industrial concentration and increasing government involvement.

5.4 Business by the 1940s

Although the level of merger activity declined in the 1930s and 1940s, and ambitious strategies like vertical integration and diversification were less popular among British industrialists, one can conclude from the work of Hannah (1980; 44–60) and Wardley (1991; 279–85) that five significant changes had been made to the business system. In the first place, one can see how, when measured in terms of value, the leading companies were by the 1940s much larger than they had been thirty years earlier. Second, reflecting the changes in industrial structure at that time, they were also closer in type and classification to their American equivalents, with high-growth industries like cars, aircraft, electrical engineering, consumer goods and chemicals significantly increasing their representation at the expense of textiles and heavy engineering. Third, reflecting the impact of merger activity, the number of multi-unit enterprises among the top 200 firms increased from fifty-one in 1919 to 153 by 1948, while in sectors like shipbuilding, retailing, brewing and other consumer goods industries (rubber, asbestos, food and drink) extensive levels of vertical integration had been effected. Fourth, as we saw in the last section, concentration levels had increased in all industrial sectors, while as a result of government intervention sectors like railways, electricity supply and aviation were better able to exploit the economies of scale inherent in such large-scale organisations. And fifth, trade associations had established a firm grip on all aspects of industrial pricing policy and market-sharing. The main question remains, however, as to the organisational impact of these trends; whether by the 1940s structure had been adapted to the strategies pursued since the First World War.

In attempting to unravel this debate, it will be immediately apparent that the five main trends just outlined could produce mutually incompatible consequences. On the one hand, the first three might well create substantial centrifugal forces within these much larger, more vertically integrated and geographically-dispersed businesses, putting substantial pressure on the highly centralised and family-dominated management structures which had been typical up to the 1920s. At the same time, given the higher levels of concentration and extensive cartelisation, it is not clear whether any incentive to improve performance existed, especially after 1932, when effective levels of protection were imposed on imported goods (Pollard, 1992; 114–21). One must also challenge the assumption that, as a result of intensive merger activity and cartelisation, traditional business attitudes towards family control and ownership had changed. Prior to 1914, the individualistic business culture had acted as a substantial obstacle to achieving much integration, whether through mergers or trade association activity, and while greater success was achieved in both respects during the inter-war era one can hardly argue that as a consequence the British business psyche had changed. Indeed, the overwhelming predominance of holding company patterns of organisation, characterised by simple federations of family firms, and the retention of owner-management patterns of control, reflect this continuity, emphasising how mergers and trade associations were simply the more visible manifestations of a search for defensive security prevalent amongst most British businessmen. In simple terms, the increased levels of concentration and greater size of British business creates the misleading impression that American patterns of organisation were being imitated, while in practice one can barely discern much change in either habits or form. As we have noted in section 5.2, even in 1948 almost sixty per cent of the top 200 firms still had representatives of the owning families on their boards of directors, while the federations of family firms hardly witnessed any changes in either management structure or senior personnel (Hannah, 1980; 52–5).

One can clearly conclude, then, that continuity was as much a feature of British business evolution between 1914 and the 1940s as it had been in the period 1880–1914, attitudes to and the practice of management having changed very little. Of all the large-scale companies which had emerged as a result of merger activity, only ICI (Reader, 1975; 21–31) and Unilever (Wilson, 1954; 231–7) had adopted the M-form of organisation, and although a divisional form was growing in popularity, having been introduced in firms like English Electric, Dunlop and Turner & Newall, even here extensive centralisation handicapped any more effective exploitation of the advantages inherent in such businesses. Chandler (1990; 389–92) does recognise that in sectors like the production of branded and packaged goods (soap, meatpacking, whisky, beer, cigarettes, chocolate and metal canning) British businessmen were willing to make the three-pronged investments in mass-production, marketing and extensive managerial hierarchies capable of controlling such enterprises, continuing the progress these industries had made prior to 1914 (see section 4.3). However, he is also quick to point out that such industries were virtually free from foreign competition, while the extensive levels of cartelisation of the 1930s further limited the incentive to improve performance in other sectors which had foremerly been dominated by the 'first movers' from the USA and Germany. In effect, he is arguing that 'the capability to compete' was sadly lacking in much of British business, and once again it is the committment to personal capitalism which he regards as the key factor explaining this lethargic approach towards organisational innovation.

The British family firm

As we saw in section 3.4, there are many problems with the simple argument that the preponderance of family firms in a business community can help explain performance levels, because as Church (1993; 35–9) has described such a form of industrial capitalism featured prominently in many economies, and especially in the USA, Japan and Germany. In this respect, one must look for different characteristics, and one obvious source of contrast would be the propensity to hire large numbers of professional managers, to whom significant responsibility would be delegated as a result of the general belief in their value as effective contributors to business success. This characteristic was no doubt present in American, Japanese and German business from at least the late-nineteenth century, but as we saw in section 5.2, in Britain one can hardly discern much change in the classic distinction between 'gentlemen' and 'players'. The failure of the Rationalisation movement to influence more than a handful of firms and business leaders is a reflection of this antipathy towards professional management, British businessmen in general having much greater faith in the concept that 'managers are born, not made'. More crucially, the reluctance to encourage a greater divorce between control and ownership perpetuated outdated management practices, and those functionaries who worked their way up through the business into a position of responsibility would rarely know much about the more general aspects of their jobs as managers.

It is clear that the traditional belief in what we described in section 4.4 as the 'cult of the amateur' survived well into the twentieth century, and along with the dramatic growth of both defensive federations of family firms and the influence of trade associations over much of British business this can help to explain the stagnant level of organisational innovation in British business up to the 1940s. In some respects, there had been some significant changes, especially with regard to the growing absolute scale of firms and the increased levels of concentration, both of which were superficially moving along lines pursued in the USA and Germany a generation earlier. On the other hand, these strategic initiatives were not matched by commensurate organisational innovation, principally because of a reluctance in the business class as a whole to pursue anything other than defensive strategies which were based on the aim of preserving family control and ownership, whatever the costs. When this scenario is combined with the lack of change in many other aspects of the economy, from industrial relations to market organisation, and from educational attitudes to the industry-finance relationship (see section 6.1), it is not surprising that *managerial capitalism* still featured rarely on the British scene. As Elbaum & Lazonick (1986; 15) have concluded from their study of what they describe as the system of 'competitive capitalism' prevailing up to the 1940s: 'Britain was impeded from making a successful transition to mass production and corporate organisation in the twentieth century by an inflexible nineteenth century institutional legacy of atomistic organisation'. One might point out that all industries were characterised by high levels of concentration by the 1940s, undermining their notion of an atomistic trading structure. On the other hand, as we noted earlier, the statistics belie the actual reality of a host of 'family' firms operating within loose federations and strong trade associations, substantiating the claims that, in effect, an atomistic trading structure still prevailed.

Conclusion

Having come to this highly critical conclusion, emphasising how the structure of British business had not been adapted to the rather more expansive strategies of the inter-war era, inevitably one must attempt to provide a balanced overview of the scene. As we noted in section 4.5, the pattern of business organisation in the period up to 1914 would appear to have been entirely appropriate to the market-cum-technological, financial, legal and socio-cultural environments prevailing at that time, and in many ways this could also be said about the next thirty years. Hannah (1976; 197) has noted that although there was no tendency 'to introduce the Harvard Business School-approved diversification strategy and mature multidivisional structure' one cannot classify British business developments up to the 1940s as an absolute sign of failure. For example, the extensive national and international networks of merchants, agents and trading houses provided British firms with few incentives to establish their own marketing and sales operations. This reveals how transaction costs did not necessarily favour wholesale adoption of the Chandlerian model of investment in mass production, marketing and new management techniques. More importantly, though, Britain's high levels of cartelisation, as well as the effective protection afforded after 1932, provided few incentives to managers in the search for greater productivity. Broadberry and Crafts (1992; 534–5), having examined several of these trade associations, criticise Chandler for overstating the impact of organisational lethargy on Britain's sluggish productivity. They argue that he has 'paid insufficient attention to the conduct as opposed to the structure of industry', demonstrating how cartelisation failed to stimulate greater organisational inventiveness. Furthermore, we will see in section 6.1 how continuing problems with the provision of capital by major financial institutions also limited the opportunities in this important respect, reinforcing further the tendency to cling to traditional patterns of ownership and control.

In reviewing this story, one must consequently accept that, as in the pre-1914 era, factors conspired to limit the need to revolutionise British business organisation. Lazonick (1991; 44) has argued that while in some respects traditional modes of organisation might have remained viable, one can question the efficacy of refusing to move towards the system of managerial capitalism, because 'proprietorial' capitalism was no longer appropriate to the levels of competition prevailing in international trade. On the other hand, it is important to repeat the objective conclusions noted earlier, that 'proprietorial' capitalism was provided with a conducive environment in which it could flourish at will, because by the 1930s and 1940s it was immune from these competitive pressures. This means that 'failure' is difficult to prove, given the enormous differences in experiences on either side of the Atlantic, and any evaluation of British business history must take account of this point. As British businessmen discovered after the 1940s, however, when the market-cum-technological, legal and financial environments changed drastically, it was essential to adapt strategy and structure to the new climate, otherwise competitive forces would prove too powerful. This is the period we shall now go on to study, bearing in mind Elbaum and Lazonick's (1986; 14–15) allegation that British business was ill-equipped to deal with the rapidly changing situations of the post-war era.

6

Managerial capitalism:
evolution and impact, 1945–94

In spite of the proselytising by leading advocates of Rationalisation, it is clear from sections 5.2 and 5.4 that up to the 1940s the pace of organisational innovation in British business had been slow. Even though more aggressive strategies would appear to have been pursued, the key influences on business evolution – namely, the market-cum-technological environment and associated 'institutional rigidities' – had yet to force through a more aggressive approach towards structure. Indeed, the cosy security of extensive cartelisation and increased concentration which had been achieved by the 1930s acted as a positive disincentive to businessmen in any search for improved ways of performing basic managerial tasks. As Turner (1969; 432) claims, perhaps exaggerating the period by fifteen years, 'nothing had more disastrous effects on the quality of our industrial life than the decline of competition in the fifty years after 1914'. Hannah (1983; 124) might well be able to notice 'clear lines of continuity between the corporate economy of the 1930s and that which we now know', but many of the inter-war changes had been superficial, lacking the necessary degree of co-ordination which was apparent in the USA, Japan and Germany. One must now assess whether the significant market-cum-technological, legal and financial changes which occurred from the 1940s forced senior management to follow the leads given by American corporations and build organisations capable of exploiting all the advantages of greater scale and integration.

The most interesting trend which we shall be following in this chapter is the rise of managerial capitalism, whereby an extensive divorce between control and ownership occurred in British business and professional managers started to rise to positions of strategic responsibility. As we noted in the Preface, though, while dramatic changes certainly occurred after 1950, the culture of personal capitalism had become so embedded in much of British business over the previous generations that it was difficult for managers to change their approach towards such crucial issues as organisation and management recruitment. One American noted at the height of the late-1960s merger mania that there was in British business 'an in-built hunger for the *status quo*' (Turner, 1969; 431), and we need to understand whether this generalisation applies either to the entire business culture or just to a particular type of firm. In fact, it will become apparent that a significant dichotomy of experience emerged over the period 1950–1994, because while those businesses with an international dimension proved to be extremely durable, those based mostly in the UK experienced severe difficulties in dealing with the rapidly changing environment. The multinational sector actually underwent a dramatic upheaval, especially from the 1960s, prospering from both the rapid expansion of international trade up to 1973 and their own inherent strength thereafter (Cantwell, 1989; 22). In contrast, on the domestic front, while the ethos 'big is beautiful' became the slogan of the era and many of the old constraints on management strategy were removed, it will become clear that by the 1980s the managerial shortcomings of many firms precipitated a massive corporate shake-out. We must consequently try and understand why this dichotomy of experience appeared after 1950, because such an exercise will provide a useful conclusion to our story. A monocausal interpretation is difficult to find, but clearly the broad environment played a substantial role, while the very nature of British managerial capitalism must also have been instrumental in fashioning attitudes.

6.1 'Finance capital' and relations with the city

In charting the rise of managerial capitalism in Britain, our first task will be to examine the changing relationship between business and finance over the period 1918–1980, and in particular to see whether 'finance capital' – the dominance of financial interests over other sectors of the economy – became a major feature of the British business scene. The divorce between control and ownership took some time to materialise, and as we saw in section 5.2 little progress along this path had been made by the 1940s. However, foundations were being laid in this initial period which culminated in dramatic modifications to the dynamics of late-twentieth century business practices. Marris (1964; 45–8) has actually concluded from his theoretical study of the growth of the firm that by the 1950s and 1960s the stock exchange had become the major determinant of business growth, such was the impact of these alterations on traditional patterns of business control and ownership. One might argue that such a claim ignores key features of the financial scene by the 1960s, and we shall return in section 6.3 to a more detailed analysis of Marris's theory. At the same time, whatever the explanation for the growth of the firm, there is no doubt that as a result of the metamorphosis from personal to managerial capitalism City interests were much more influential by the 1970s.

The pre-1914 situation

Up to the First World War, as we saw in section 4.5, apart from the willingness of clearing bankers to provide short-term liquidity, there had been a weak relationship between the big financial institutions operating in the City of London and much of British industry. We do not need to rehearse all the arguments here, but in essence both supply-side and demand-side factors played their parts in creating such a divorce between the two interests. On the one hand, such was the control exercised by what Cain & Hopkins (1993; 199–201) have described as the 'gentlemanly capitalists' running merchant banks that City attitudes and practices demonstrated a significant bias against domestic industrial activity. Instead, they preferred to indulge in large, risk-free governmental or overseas issues which provided secure, yet unspectacular returns. At the same time, given the prevailing individualistic business culture, most industrialists relied predominantly on their own, or localised, sources of fixed capital, and only a few of the largest companies raised either equity capital or fixed-interest securities in the City of London. As a result, as Davis & Huttenback (1987; 211) claim, 'Britain was not one capital market but two', and in 1913 domestic securities (nominally valued at £873 million) accounted for under eight per cent of all those quoted on the London Stock Exchange (Morgan & Thomas, 1962; 281–2). The picture is different when assessing the figures for new issues, because between 1911 and 1913 domestic investments accounted for thirty-four per cent of the total, but once again the preponderance of overseas activity is apparent.

The City and domestic securities after 1918

In the inter-war period, while some progress occurred, one can hardly claim that by 1939 all the barriers between industry and finance had been dismantled. In fact, by the 1930s domestic securities accounted for up to eighty per cent of total London Stock Exchange issues, having averaged over sixty per cent in the period 1919–1933 (Thomas, 1978; 24–7). This emphasises how both the City was showing a much greater interest in this form of investment activity, while British businesses were clearly more willing to raise external capital in the City. Notwithstanding this trend, in 1933 these securities (valued at £1,223.7 million) still only accounted for 9.6 per cent of all those quoted on British stock exchanges. The impact of a much-increased National Debt on inter-war investors was of particular relevance here, and domestic government issues (standing at almost £7,000 million in 1933) accounted for 37.8 per cent of all quoted securities. As Michie (1986; 104–9) has argued, this provided a risk-free alternative to the shortage of overseas issues for investors and institutions which had traditionally been averse to funding unknown and low-status domestic activities. It is also vitally important to stress that, as we shall see shortly, the City was forced to commit more of its time to domestic activity because of the exogenous pressures affecting its traditional markets. Furthermore, one should remember that internal resources continued to act as the major contributor to capital formation, and business savings still accounted for approximately eighty per cent of total industrial investment in the inter-war era (Thomas, 1978; 7–18). Nevertheless, a larger number of companies were raising an increased amount of external capital after 1919, when compared to the pre-1914 era, and financial institutions were developing a wider range of contacts at home, providing the basis for a more decisive move in these directions from the 1940s.

Before going on to examine the mid-twentieth century developments, it is important to stress some of the limitations apparent in the inter-war era, because these would have an important influence on the later story. Above all, one must emphasise how the City's growing interest in domestic investments after 1918 arose not out of choice but out of necessity. The First World War had been a decisive watershed in this respect, because London's position as the world's premier centre for finance had been irretrievably lost to New York by 1918, dramatically affecting demand for its services (Cain & Hopkins, 1993a; 14–20). Not only had the government banned all foreign issues during the War, pushing former customers firmly towards New York's Wall St, from 1918 the Bank of England pressured financial institutions into an unofficial policy of limiting overseas issues. This policy was pursued because the government's main aim was to return to the Gold Standard and restore the pound sterling to its pre-war parity of $4.86, and the Bank of England worked to ensure that British capital exports would not affect international prices unduly. Unfortunately, though, the result was an increase in both the price of British exports and the rate of interest, making the City even less attractive as a lender. Furthermore, when international commodity prices slumped after 1921, the growing reliance of primary producing nations on Wall St also increased because these relatively undeveloped economies were obliged to borrow further to help pay the interest on previous loans (Pollard, 1992; 105–11). Capital exports did continue, averaging £115 million between 1925 and 1929, much of which went to the Empire. However, when one considers the £162 million exported annuallly between 1911 and 1913, and the doubling of prices between 1914 and 1919, it is clear that this business was in decline (Cain & Hopkins, 1993a; 45–6).

The economic crisis of 1931 also forced the government to impose further controls on capital exports, as a means of safeguarding reserves, severely restricting the ability of financiers to work in overseas markets. The legal position was tightened up even further in 1936 when the Capital Issues Committee was established, providing a formal means of vetting both domestic and foreign applications for City funds. In fact, on average only £31 million was exported annually between 1932 and 1936, indicating how the precipitous collapse in overseas business was forcing City financiers to seek alternative sources of business (Ingham, 1984; 195–7).

Rising domestic demand

The City's traditional overseas orientation was consequently severely affected during the inter-war era by factors which were largely beyond its control, and as we have already noted this trend was paralleled by a growing demand for external sources of capital from British business. Thomas (1978; 24–5) has argued that one of the main factors behind the growth in domestic demand was a substantial depletion in the traditional sources of capital, but this claim hardly seems credible when we remember that even in the inter-war era eighty per cent of industrial capital formation came from business savings. A much more likely interpretation would be to link capital issues with both increased merger activity (see section 5.2) and the rapid development of capital-intensive processes in the so-called 'new' industries of car production, electrical engineering and synthetic chemicals. One might also note how the first major boom in share issues during the reconstruction years of 1918–1920 was associated with a disastrous recapitalisation of several older industries, and in particular cotton and shipbuilding (Porter, 1974; 1–10). In simple terms, new trends in business finance were evident in the inter-war period, especially in the two major surges of 1927–29 and 1932–36, and it is vitally important to assess whether the City was capable of dealing with this market more effectively than it had done prior to 1914.

Although he is willing to accept that several imperfections persisted, Thomas (1978; 34) argues that between 1919 and 1939 'the new market [in industrial financing] did accomplish the transition from foreign to domestic service'. This argument would appear to be well supported by the considerable increase in domestic activity on the London Stock Exchange, especially when combined with the appearance of new investment syndicates created specifically with the intention of exploiting this growing demand. On the other hand, one must remember the preference of major merchant banks like Rothschilds, Barings, Hambros and Lazards to participate in only the largest of issues, and as Diaper (1986; 74) argues with regard to Kleinwort Benson these highly influential institutions were 'slow to develop a strategy' for industrial issues. Similarly, as Thomas (1978; 116–21) himself admits, the new specialist finance institutions (for example, Charterhouse Industrial Development Co., Credit for Industry, and Leadenhall Securities Incorporation) failed dismally to live up to their creators' expectations. Indeed, the influential Macmillan Committee of 1931 highlighted a substantial 'gap' in the provision of funds for small and medium-sized enterprises, offering the benchmark of £200,000 as the minimum amount established financial institutions would regard as an acceptable issue (Michie, 1986; 95, 105–6). It was partially as a result of Macmillan's exhortations that the specialist institutions were established in 1934–1935, but their failure is symptomatic of the City's sluggish development, casting doubt on any optimistic interpretation of the transition process.

Company promotion

The lack of progress in City attitudes towards domestic investment is further revealed by examining the continuation of nineteenth century practices associated with company promotion. One of the key problems highlighted in section 4.5 was the City's failure to develop an institutional floor in industrial securities prior to 1914, a situation which resulted in a series of speculative manias characterised by ruthless company promoters exploiting the ignorance and greed of speculators (Armstrong, 1990; 128–32). Such dangerous practices would clearly have to be eradicated if the City was to exploit effectively the growing domestic demand for funds, but there is little evidence to demonstrate that either the supply of information was improved or the tendency to overvalue shares was moderated. As the Macmillan Committee noted, the merchant banks could be reproached for 'being better informed on conditions in Latin America than in Lancashire or Scotland', concluding that 'in some respects the City is more highly organised to provide capital to foreign countries than to British industry' (Cain & Hopkins, 1993a; 19). The reluctance of major merchant banks to develop appropriate sources of information was, indeed, a major problem in the inter-war era, emphasising how 'for the great bulk of industrial issues the market was bereft of financial institutions of any standing with the necessary specialism and expertise to advise and inform the investing public' (Collins, 1991; 84–5). This informational constraint was further compounded by the standard problem of interpreting balance sheets, because company law had failed to progress in line with the growing scale of business at that time, allowing promoters or owners the opportunity to hide the real asset positions of the companies concerned (Hannah, 1974a; 69–71).

The evidence of a closer relationship between the City and industry is, indeed, very thin, and as Reader (1979; 145) has argued, 'the whole weight of tradition . . . on the Stock Exchange and elsewhere, was against widespread investment by private individuals in industrial shares'. One need only examine the consequences of the 1928 share boom, because this resulted in some 'spectacular casualties' and by 1931 the average depreciation in share values was forty-two per cent (Hannah, 1983; 61). It was during this investment mania that one of the most prominent City names, C. C. Hatry, was found to have overextended himself and broken the law, resulting in considerable unease among the leading financiers about industrial activity. A further point of note is made by Michie (1986; 111), showing that in response to the competition from provincial institutions, in 1909 and 1912 the London Stock Exchange had imposed highly restrictive regulations on trading which prevented any improvement in service over the inter-war era. In fact, these regulations – jobbers were prevented from making a market for outside brokers, and the establishment of minimum commission rates – were only abandoned in 1986 (see section 6.5), revealing the highly conservative nature of Britain's premier financial institution.

There are clearly only weak grounds for believing that the City of London responded positively to the inter-war changes in its core issuing business, and it is consequently no surprise that business savings continued to account for the bulk of industrial investment at this time. The 1930s did see some more important developments, particularly with the establishment of new types of finance houses, and this was a harbinger of things to come after 1945. On the other hand, while these institutions had appeared partly because of the Macmillan Committee's revelations, the main reason for their creation was the government's 1931 decision to discourage flows of 'hot money' seeking the highest rates of interest by keeping bank rate at two per cent. This strategy also had the important side-effect of increasing the attractiveness of domestic fixed-interest securities (often offered at rates of between four and seven per cent), a trend which prompted certain City interests to devote more attention to such stocks. Many industrial companies also took advantage of this 'cheap money' policy, which persisted throughout the 1930s and 1940s, to convert stock to lower yields, reducing substantially their debt burden (Thomas, 1978; 33–4). Nevertheless, as we noted earlier, the enormous growth in Britain's National Debt after 1914 still provided investors with a risk-free form of investment, when compared to industrial securities, indicating how traditional attitudes died only very slowly. In effect, the major institutional features of the issuing market in the 1930s – especially the 'Macmillan gap', a preference for risk-free investments, and the reluctance of 'gentlemenly capitalists' to indulge extensively in domestic activity – were those of the pre-1914 era, and they continued to act as major obstacles to the integration of finance capital with the rest of British business.

The banks

Having noted the persistence of all the worst features of late-nineteenth century City practices, it is important to remember that the clearing banks would appear to have continued to provide essential short-term support to business, further strengthening the traditional ties which stretched back to the eighteenth century (see section 2.5). On the other hand, even here one might be critical of the banks' failure to respond effectively to the requirements of some sectors of British industry, particularly the struggling export industries. This emphasises once again the strong desire for continuity within Britain's financial sector.

Banking did actually experience some significant changes in terms of both structure and composition over the inter-war period, most notably in terms of the emergence of what came to be known as 'the big five' (Barclays, Lloyds, Midland, National Provincial and Westminster banks). By 1920, these five banks controlled 65.6 per cent of total deposits, having pursued an aggressive merger strategy which witnessed the absorption of many large provincial banking networks by the big London institutions (Capie & Rodrik-Bali, 1982; 280–92). Nevertheless, in spite of their greater size and geographical spread, Collins (1991; 69–70) concludes that their 'views towards liquidity, towards the desirability of certain forms of lending and investment, remained cautious and conservative . . . In other words, the clearing banks' public position was that it was not their role to supply long-term funds for industry'.

One of the most damning insights into the inter-war activities of British bankers comes from a close examination of their lending practices, because while in evidence given to the Macmillan Committee they declared an aim of advancing between fifty and sixty per cent of their deposits, it is clear that actual practice varied widely both between banks and over the period. The Midland Bank had always been heavily involved in industrial activity, and throughout this period it consistently lent over sixty per cent of its deposits to a wide range of industries (Thomas, 1978; 76–7). On the other hand, Collins (1991; 72–3) reveals how for all London clearing banks advances had declined to just 41.2 per cent of deposits by the mid-1930s, and industry and trade accounted for only 46.3 per cent of these advances. Ross (1990; 52–66) has claimed that most banks were intimately involved in supporting and advising their industrial clients, but even this view must be tempered by the knowledge that after the 1918–1920 boom highly cautious lending strategies were pursued. The most striking development in bank lending after 1920 was, in fact, the growing commitment to public sector debt, revealing how their evidence to the Macmillan Committee was a smoke-screen. There was extensive inter-war banking involvement in the steel industry, but even here, as Tolliday (1987; 170) has emphasised, their strategies were not only 'clumsy and ill-directed', they also reinforced the traditional attitudes which warned against long-term entanglements with industry. Even the Midland Bank was obliged to pursue a highly cautious lending strategy after the early-1930s depression (Holmes & Green, 1987; 190), indicating how those most committed to industry followed conventional banking wisdom.

The Bank of England

In simple terms, clearing banks were primarily concerned with safeguarding their own positions, and even where one can find examples of extensive involvement with industries or companies it was more often the case that institutional inertia inhibited the pursuit of more ambitious, long-term strategies (Collins, 1991; 79–82). A classic example of this conservatism was the Bank of England's adventures into industrial reorganisation, because superficially this might well be interpreted as the dawn of a new era in banking, but when examined in greater detail reveals the standard tendency to preserve the *status quo*. This claim is well born out by the formation in 1929 of the Bankers' Industrial Development Company (BIDC) which was funded by forty-five of the leading City houses (Thomas, 1931; 280). Its main aim was to assist ailing industries, but in fact was an attempt by the Governor, Montagu Norman, to pre-empt government intervention in industrial finance (Tolliday, 1987; 197–210). One of BIDC's first measures was to force through a merger of seventy cotton spinning firms, to create in 1929 the Lancashire Cotton Corporation. This was a reflection of Norman's belief in big business as a more secure means of improving the efficiency of capital, but in fact in the case of Lancashire Cotton his actions were prompted more by grave worries about the future of several banks who were heavily committed to the industry (Porter, 1974; 11–6). In other words, apart from the political motive of forestalling government involvement, BIDC was more concerned with bank liquidity than it was with cotton spinning. Bowden and Collins (1992; 120–1) argue that Norman did have progressive ideas about the relationship between the City and industry, for example in his support of hire purchase schemes after 1929, but once again only limited successes were achieved, substantiating our earlier claims regarding the nature of this sector's relationship with domestic business.

The rise of finance capital after 1945

One must consequently agree with Collins (1991; 92), when he concludes that by the 1940s finance capital had yet to become the major influence on business that it had in economies like the USA, Germany and Japan. In other words, there still remained major institutional obstacles, on both demand- and supply-sides, to a greater integration of leading financial institutions with much of the domestic economy. After 1945, however, we can discern a much more extensive and fundamental switch towards finance capital. It is in the post-1940s era that we can see the rise of wholly new approaches towards both business finance and merger activity, precipitating the emergence of the takeover bid as a major influence on managerial performance. It was also an era when the major financial institutions moved more decisively towards domestic activity, and while problems remained with the attitudes towards investment trends and practices there is little doubt that the City was heavily involved in business finance after the Second World War. Indeed, while in 1913 domestic securities had accounted for only eight per cent of those quoted on the London stock exchange, from the late-1940s their share would consistently amount to over ninety per cent as capital exports continued to remain in the doldrums (Thomas, 1978; 145).

As in the inter-war era, the City did not turn its attentions to the domestic market voluntarily, because similar circumstances prevailed after 1945, most notably effective government control of capital exports. In fact, the Second World War had not only reinforced New York's position as the world's financial capital, it had also witnessed a massive sale of British overseas assets, and up to the late-1950s the Capital Issues Committee continued to limit further activity. The Capital Issues Committee was also charged with the task of vetting domestic issues, and in the period 1945–1950 anything over £50,000 was rigorously examined, while the Bank of England was brought in for any schemes in excess of £100,000. These controls were, however, progressively relaxed after 1950 (Morgan & Thomas, 1962; 210), allowing the City greater freedom to exploit the growing domestic demand for external sources of capital. Even the merchant banks turned their attentions decisively towards the domestic market, and when the Issuing Houses Association was formed in 1945 fifty-two of these institutions instantly joined, providing a means of co-ordinating and monitoring this activity (Thomas, 1978; 177–9). Morgan & Thomas (1962; 210–6 & 231–9) have also emphasised how important changes were introduced into stock exchange practices, especially in the transmission of company information to investors, and while one cannot claim that this eradicated all the old problems, as we shall see in the nect section, clearly the City was responding more effectively than it had in previous years.

New issue activity after 1945

In fact, largely because British industry emerged from the War in an extremely liquid state, new issue activity was slow to revive in the late-1940s, and it was not until 1949 that demand for capital started to rise. This first investment boom, which lasted until 1954, was to be a harbinger of future trends, because not only was there a major surge in domestic share issues, it also witnessed the early stirrings of a phenomenon which was to have a major impact on business, the takeover bid. We shall be examining the origins and impact of the takeover bid in the next section, but it is important to emphasise how from the early-1950s, largely as a result of the changes being made to the methods of business financing, an institutionalised market for corporate control emerged in Britain (Roberts, 1992; 183). Above all, though, one must emphasise at this stage how British business was building a much closer relationship with City institutions. There are some fluctuations in new issue activity, as Thomas (1978; 145–52) describes in great detail, but the long-term trend was for the volume of domestic capital issues to increase significantly, from an average of around £70 million (at current prices) in the late-1940s to over £650 million in the early-1970s. Again, one must emphasise how business savings continued to account for a substantial proportion of total industrial investment over this period, but the key point here is that by the late-1960s external sources of capital for the first time contributed over half, and thereafter the balance consistently favoured the latter.

Although at times British tax laws favoured the issue of fixed-interest capital, and in particular debentures, the bulk of company securities sold on the open market after 1945 were equities, or ordinary shares. Debentures proved especially popular in 1953–1954 and 1964–1967, when, respectively, profits tax and corporation tax allowed companies to write off against tax their debt interest payments. For most of the period after 1945, however, management preferred to raise capital in the form of ordinary shares, and Reader (1979; 160–82) describes this as 'the rise of the cult of the equity'. One must remember that stock exchange regulations insisted on existing shareholders having first call on what were known as rights issues of equity capital, but as the new shares were often sold at a discount to the market value of existing equities this provided an incentive for owners to capitalise on their gains. Thomas (1978; 161–72) demonstrates how issues to shareholders were especially popular up to 1976, at times (1956–1962 and 1974–1976) accounting for most of the new issue activity, but in association with the growing popularity of public issues, tenders and placings with institutions, this simply served to boost substantially the market in corporate ownership.

Growing divorce between control and ownership

The huge increase in share trading on the stock exchange, and in particular the trading in domestic equities, would inevitably have a dramatic impact on the control and ownership of British business. In an exhaustive survey of British industrial companies covering the period 1936–1951, Florence (1961; 185–7) concluded that a divorce between control and ownership had only become apparent among the largest firms, while few interlinking directorships connected boardrooms. However, according to Prais's (1976; 89) estimates of directors' shareholdings in the top 100 non-financial companies of 1972, in only fourteen cases did they amount to over ten per cent of the equity, while in fifty-six companies they held less than 0.5 per cent. This clear evidence of an apparently substantial divorce between control and ownership is further substantiated by Martin & Moores' (1985; 14) work on the leading 250 companies of 1975, because they reveal that in only twenty-two known cases did directors own over fifty per cent of the equity, while in 123 companies they held less than ten per cent.

It is important to note, of course, that much of this evidence is misleading, because when an assessment of control procedures is conducted one might conclude that in effect very little had changed in British business. In the first place, it is well known that executives are able to control a company when holding much less than fifty per cent of the equity, while as a result of the growing importance of institutional investment, and the appointment of financial representatives on to the boards of most publicly-floated companies, one might argue that there had been no substantial divorce between control and ownership. Indeed, as Zeitlin (1974; 1107) has argued with regard to American corporations, the alleged separation of ownership and control could well be described as a 'pseudofact', because all that had happened was a change in controlling interest. Similarly, while terms like managerial capitalism are extensively employed to describe the post-1945 trends in British business, it is important to question whether or not much had changed. Certainly, the long history of family boardroom domination might have ended in all but a few of the large businesses which dominated the industrial landscape by that time. However, ownership interests were still clearly in influential positions at the head of many firms, indicating how finance capital might well be a more appropriate label to describe British business by the 1960s.

Institutional investors

The ending of family control was clearly the most siginficant post-war business trend, and in the next section we shall examine in greater detail what impact this had on the dynamics of British managerial capitalism. It is vitally important to emphasise, though, how this was associated with another change in ownership patterns, because from the 1950s institutional investment grew in importance as pension funds, insurance companies, unit trusts and finance houses started to take an increasing proportion of the shares traded on the stock exchange. This trend had actually been initiated by J. M. Keynes, during his period as fund manager for the Prudential Insurance Co. (Westall, 1992), but progressively over the post-war years these increasingly powerful institutions had built up a substantial portfolio of industrial equities. By 1970, although individuals still held 44.7 per cent of the £38,000 million worth of shares in the 2,765 companies trading on the stock exchange, institutions held forty-three per cent (Moyle, 1971; 7). More importantly, these institutions accounted for the bulk of the new money flowing into the market, and by 1977 they consequently held sixty per cent of all equities, indicating how over the post-war period ownership was being transferred from family groupings to fund managers who represented the interests of large numbers of small investors. Francis (1980; 10–4) has indicated how through minority control (at most ten per cent, but falling down to five per cent of the equity) 110 of the top 227 British firms were run by either an individual, a cohesive group, or a financial institution. Even where a descendent of the original owner-controllers is still in a position of responsibility on the board, such is the power of the institutional investors that they are able to influence key policy decisions, severely constraining management autonomy (Scott; 1987; 52). The formation in 1973 of an Institutional Shareholders Committee, now known as the Investment

Protection Committee (Hilton, 1987; 42), also reflected their belief in co-ordinating actions when handling estimated resources of £44,000 million.

The banks

This discussion of ownership provides us with a vital insight into the changing nature of British business over the post-war period, and in particular it highlights the growing importance of finance capital in the determination of company strategy. This conclusion is further confirmed by a brief study of the relationship between industry and the clearing banks, because while only short-term funding was provided by these increasingly influential institutions it is important to emphasise how by the 1970s they had substantially extended their contacts with the productive sector. The growing importance of clearing banks to industry was, in fact, achieved in spite of certain features of the post-war scene, because one of the major problems affecting bank lending strategy up to 1971 was the pursuit by successive governments of a highly restrictive macro-economic policy which was based on the Treasury belief that aggregate demand could be managed through the use of credit control policy (Pollard, 1992; 354–75). In effect, bank lending was used by the Treasury as a weapon in the battle against the usual post-war British problems of inflation and balance of payments deficits, and at times the clearing banks were obliged to observe strict lending ceilings. One must also emphasise how a clearing bank cartel set fixed rates for all borrowing, further restricting their ability to develop new approaches towards lending. In spite of this, though, influential studies of the financial institutions like the Radcliffe Committee (reporting in 1959) were generally satisfied with the performance of the clearing banks, commenting on how only rarely did companies use more than two-thirds of their overdrafts (Thomas, 1978; 188).

From the 1960s, however, business reliance on the banks increased significantly, the London Clearing Bank committee claiming in evidence given to the Wilson Committee (on Financial Institutions, 1977–1979) that bank borrowing had increased from just over a half of all external funds raised by industrial companies in the early-1960s to an average of sixty-five per cent in the 1970s. In the highly unusual year of 1974, when power cuts and a three-day week created severe illiquidity, this proportion jumped to ninety-four per cent, indicating how the banks had become vital to British business finance (London Clearing Banks, 1978; 81–2). This extension was futher facilitated by the Bank of England's relaxation of some controls in 1971, when it published 'Competition, Credit and Control', opening up new opportunities for a more expansive approach. The overdraft facility remained the most important source of financial aid for business, providing essentially short-term support, but medium-term lending also developed at this time, as well as useful new services like lease-back and factoring. The leasing agreements proved especially helpful to business, because equipment valued at between £5,000 and £100,000 could be acquired by a firm without the incumbrance of raising fixed capital on the open market. By the mid-1970s, banks were the leading providers of leasing facilities, with assets valued at £672 million (London Clearing Banks, 1978; 102–3). Indeed, by that time the only limitation on bank lending practices was the demand for funds, and while we are not necessarily concerned with this indication of investment performance in British business it is worth noting that in the difficult trading conditions of the 1970s rarely did manufacturing companies take up more than fifty per cent of the facilties made available by the banks (London Clearing Banks, 1978; 89). One cannot claim that the banks were free from criticism over this period, particularly in the property boom of 1972–1974 (Cooper, 1984; 335), and they still refused to develop the kind of long-term lending strategies pursued by their American, German or Japanese counterparts. However, once again we can see clear evidence of closer integration between financial institutions and the rest of British business.

This growing reliance on bank borrowing was clearly indicative of the period's general trend towards greater contact between financial institutions and the rest of British business. One can illustrate it further by examining another increasingly important feature of the business scene, because not only was British business raising much greater quantities of external capital, representatives of the financial institutions involved were also beginning to find places on their boards of directors. For example, in a study of the fifty largest manufacturing companies in 1976, Utton (1982; 32) has revealed that thirty-two of their directors represented a clearing bank. Scott (1987; 60–1) has also argued that the extensive number of interlocking directorships occupied by such representatives demonstrates how these financial institutions 'were pivotal points in loose groupings of industrial, trading and financial enterprises . . . act[ing], in effect, as proxies for the wider financial community; they act as the guardians of the interests of the hegemonic financials'. Indeed, Whitley (1973; 622–9) has described how most large financial institutions were interlinked with each other, while Stanworth & Giddens (1975; 22–3) show how the top fifty industrial companies had ninety-four directors with City loyalties.

Conclusion

One is left with the clear impression that the City of London and much of British business had forged an increasingly intimate and mutually-dependent relationship; that, in effect, finance capital had finally appeared in Britain. In a detailed summary of this debate, Scott (1984; 180) has concluded that by 1970 the City provided the nucleus of a new corporate class which dominated British business, and working through a series of interlinking directorships there had developed a 'national intercorporate network, with financial and non-financial enterprise fully-integrated'. This might well have taken much longer to happen, when compared to the German, Japanese and American economies, but the evidence points clearly to a much greater integration of what had been up to 1914 two separate sectors of the British economy. Of course, a comparison with other countries would indicate how qualititative differences remained, particularly with regard to the propensity to operate in the long-term, and we shall focus in the next section on the British inclination in favour of short-term investment horizons. This discussion will be particularly pertinent when analysing the links between financial institutions and the intense merger activity of the period up to the mid-1970s, because while one can conclude that the British corporate network revealed an unprecedented degree of integration, it is a moot point whether the change in ownership patterns provided a positive boost to business performance at a time of substantial increases in the scale and scope of business operations.

6.2 Mergers, takeover bids and managerial capitalism

While from the 1950s finance capital certainly started to feature more prominently in British business, it is vital to emphasise how this growing level of contact between City institutions and company boardrooms was paralleled by substantial growth in both the size of firms and prevailing levels of concentration. The 1920s had evidently witnessed intense merger activity and increased concentration (see section 5.2), but those years were but a pre-lude to the vigorous growth of large-scale business which occurred after 1950. This trend is demonstrated graphically in Figure 5.1, indicating how, after over twenty years of stagnation during the 1930s and 1940s, the share of net manufacturing output taken by the leading 100 firms rose consistently after 1953, reaching forty-one per cent in 1978. When discussing this increasing level of concentration it is equally important to emphasise how, just as in the 1920s, the main reason behind the move towards a modern cor-porate economy was a series of intense merger waves (see Table 6.1) which rocked the British business community to its very foundations. Furthermore, this acquisitive streak was yet another manifestation of the growing degree of integration between City and other business interests, facilitating the replacement at board level of family/personal interests by representatives of the major financial institutions which had provided much of the finance for business over the previous decades. To many, it appeared that nothing in this new climate was sacred, whether it be directorial hegemony or business inde-pendence, and there was certainly a general belief in the maxim 'big is beau-tiful' (Davis, 1970; 32–7). An alternative phrase coined at this time was 'acquire or be acquired', revealing what we shall see later was an inherently defensive reason for the mergers. Whatever the motives, though, there was certainly a general desire to expand business size, and City interests played a leading part in the process of concentration and acquistion.

Table 6.1   *Merger activity in British Business, 1920–1979*

	No. of firm disappearances by merger	Values (at current prices) of firm disappearances (£ million)	Values (at 1961 share prices) of firm disappearances (£ million)
1920–29	1884	360–411[1]	1654–1886[1]
1930–39	1414	184–218[i]	759–907[1]
1940–49	778	–	–
1950–59	1867	797	1507
1960–69	5635	5837	4709
1970–79	3166	5223	2736

Key: – signifies that the data is not available.
   [1] signifies a major break in the series, requiring the provision of two estimates
Source: Hannah (1983; 178).

Post-war merger trends and concentration

Although Hannah (1983; 169–74) is careful to emphasise that there are major difficulties in compiling and comparing merger trends over such long periods, it is fair to conclude from Table 6.1 that this activity intensified after the 1940s. One must remember that the final three rows include for the first time foreign acquisitions by British companies, but this would not alter the general conclusion, that acquisitions were on the increase, especially in the 1960s. While not quite matching the 1920s (in terms of 1961 values), more companies were involved in the 1950s merger wave than any other previous decade, and as Figure 5.1 reveals the level of concentration had consequently increased to thirty-three per cent by 1958. In the 1960s, though, all three indices in Table 6.1 witnessed an even greater leap, and at the peak of this activity between 1967 and 1969 the value of companies disappearing (worth £2,300 million) exceeded the 1950s figure. This 'merger mania' also continued into the early-1970s, as we shall see in section 6.5, and much of the activity denoted in the final row of Table 6.1 occurred in the first four years of that decade. Thereafter, businessmen showed much less interest in acquiring new interests, a point supported by the stagnation in concentration levels depicted in Figure 5.2, but by that time Britain had the most concentrated industrial economy in the world (Hannah & Kay, 1977; 3–4).

While Figure 5.2 is a useful indicator of the increasing levels of concentration, a more detailed insight is provided by the information on thirteen major industries in Table 6.2. One must be careful not to compare this information with Table 5.2, because as Hannah & Kay (1977; 83–97) explain there is little commonality in the two samples, while in any case Table 6.2 examines CR5, rather than CR10. Nevertheless, there is little doubt that, apart from

Table 6.2   *Concentration in industry, 1957–1969: shares of the five largest firms*

	1957 Population (%)	1969 Population (%)	Proportion of the increase due to merger (%)[i]
Food	41.3	52.7	75
Drink	32.7	69.5	98
Tobacco	96.5	100	100
Chemicals	71.0	73.7	130
Metal Manuf	45.7	59.5	132
Non-Elec Eng	29.8	25.3	–
Elec Eng	47.2	68.0	57
Shipbuilding	62.1	74.2	73
Vehicles	50.4	71.0	125
Textiles	44.2	65.1	128
Clothing/Shoes	63.8	78.4	50
Building Mat	53.1	51.1	–
Paper/Publish	47.5	63.2	112
All Manuf	60.1	74.9	103

Key: [i] a merger contribution above 100 means that, but for merger activity, concentration levels would have fallen.
Source: Hannah (1983; 144).

the cases of non-electrical engineering and building materials, the largest five firms increased their share of total output in most industries between 1957 and 1969, creating a highly oligopolistic trading structure in most parts of the economy. Furthermore, the final column also indicates that at least fifty per cent of the rise was due to mergers, while in several cases (where the figure exceeds 100) concentration would have fallen without the mergers. The process continued up to 1973 (Hannah & Kay, 1977; 93–7), but as we have already noted little further increase in concentration was achieved during the 1970s as a whole (see Figure 5.2), indicating how the period 1957–1969 was instrumental in creating the British corporate economy.

The reasons for mergers

Of course, the most vital issue arising out of this description of merger activity and the development of a strongly oligopolistic trading structure is to assess how it all affected British business performance, and in a later section we shall discuss this topic in some detail. Our first task here, though, is to understand the circumstances in which it happened, because this will provide a detailed insight into the attitudes of businessmen at a time of tremendous opportunity and challenge. As we have seen in previous discussions of such trends, both aggressive and defensive reasons can be identified as major influences on acquisition strategy, and in the post-1950 era one can identify a curious combination of pressures which created this unprecedented degree of interest in mergers. This is not the place for a detailed economic history of the period (Feinstein, 1994; 95–122), but one must remember that, on the one hand, rising living standards at home and vigorous growth in international trade provided a highly conducive market-cum-technological environment, encouraging firms to exploit the economies of scale available in large-scale operations. On the other hand, having signed the major international free trading treaties of the era (GATT and EFTA), as well as adopting anti-monopoly policies, successive post-war governments were more interested in encouraging competition among British firms than they had ever been. Notwithstanding this general stance, we shall also see how some governments directly encouraged mergers, especially in sectors which were seen as vital to the future of Britain's economy. At the same time, with City institutions playing an increasingly influential role in business finance, one must always remember that most large firms were much more vulnerable to takeover bids from predators, forcing management to pursue strategies which reduced their liability in this respect.

There are clearly many factors which help to explain why from the early-1950s British business indulged so extensively in merger activity, and in trying to identify the most crucial one must remember that market-cum-technological, legal and financial circumstances conspired to create a climate in which acquisitions were regarded as a safety-valve when dealing with the period's opportunities and challenges. We shall take the healthy trading environment as an essential feature of the period, and although government's pursuit of Keynesian demand-management policies clearly played their part in creating what was known as a 'stop-go' economy, there was up to the mid-1970s steady growth, high levels of employment and a substantial improvement in living standards (Pollard, 1992; 262–80). The major market-cum-technological problem facing British business at home was the establishment of, and renewed investment in existing, American multinational subsidiaries, especially in high growth sectors like automobiles, electrical engineering, electronics, office machinery and capital equipment (Bostock & Jones, 1994; 89–121). More recently, Japanese firms have also started to establish subsidiaries in these areas (Trevor, 1985; 13–25). This competition materially affected commercial prospects in several industries, and when combined with the growing tide of imported goods flooding other markets (domestic appliances, motorbikes and steel, for example) British firms were clearly no longer allowed to dominate their home market in the way they had done since the 1930s.

Government and trade associations

Not only were trading circumstances changing dramatically after the Second World War, increasing the competitive edge in domestic and international markets, the formerly dominant trade associations were also coming under greater pressure. Protectionism since 1931 and a benign government approach had provided trade associations with a powerful position, but once Britain had become one of the founder members of the General Agreement on Tariffs and Trade (GATT) in 1948 this position was rapidly undermined. Furthermore, 1948 also saw the first piece of legislation which destroyed trade association immunity from statutory controls, and although it was another ten years before the new regulations started to bite, thereafter trade associations lost much of their former power and influence. Many economists and politicians had been arguing throughout the 1940s that price-fixing and the allocation of market quotas undermined industrial efficiency, and this lobbying culminated in the 1948 Monopolies and Restrictive Practices Act (Guenault & Jackson, 1974; 1–6). In fact, the Act would not have worried the trade associations unduly, because, as Mennel (1962; 99) concludes of its ineffective powers, there was 'a great deal of inquiry, but precious little control'. The Act actually established a Monopolies and Restrictive Practices Commission, and although this body produced seventeen reports which examined certain industries in great detail, and in 1953 its composition was extended to cover more industries, very little action was taken by its supervising department, the Board of Trade (Swann et al, 1974; 46–54).

The reports produced by this new commission were not completely irrelevant to the situation, however, because as a result of their revelations on price-fixing and other abuses another piece of legislation, the Restrictive Trade Practices Act, was passed in 1956 (Guenault & Jackson, 1974; 85–96). This second Act would actually mark a vital breakthrough in controlling trade associations, because its basic assumption was that restrictive practices were harmful, unless the newly-created Restrictive Practices Court could be persuaded otherwise (Swann et al, 1974; 64–73). Under this legislation, all trade associations were obliged to register their agreements with the Court, posing a considerable challenge to the operations of Britain's 1,300 trade associations (PEP, 1957; 153, 249–50). In fact, in the course of the following ten years 2,550 agreements were registered, and the Court terminated over 2,100, severely limiting the freedom to fix prices and allocate market quotas (Walshe, 1991; 363). Furthermore, resale price maintenance was also outlawed in 1956, preventing firms stopping supplies to wholesalers or retailers who chose to sell at prices which undercut those set by a trade association. Of course, through tacit or informational agreements, firms were still able to by-pass these new regulations, especially where an oligopolistic trading structure existed and multinational subsidiaries dominated a market (Devine, 1976; 436). This informational agreement, however, was later brought within the law, when in 1968 another Restrictive Trade Practices Act was passed, further undermining the ability to fix prices. One must emphasise that the Monopolies Commission created in 1956 remained powerless to prevent the wave of mergers occurring in the late-1950s, even though its ability to investigate what was regarded as a potential monopoly – defined in the 1948 Act as a situation in which a firm controlled one-third of a market – was enhanced by the Act. Nevertheless, the political climate had clearly turned decisively against trade associations after 1945, and it was becoming increasingly difficult to justify restrictive practices (Swann et al, 1974; 80–5).

The legislative assault on trade associations was one of the more significant business moves of the post-war period, but in reviewing this legislation one might also argue that it was self-defeating. As Newbould (1970; 143–8) has emphasised, making restrictive practices illegal dramatically undermined business self-confidence and helped to create the feeling that mergers were a logical alternative to price-fixing. Indeed, the legislation could be regarded as one of the direct causes of merger activity, creating in turn a much more concentrated, oligopolistic trading structure. Of course, it is difficult to prove this claim without investigating the motives of each group of firms, but clearly when faced with the imminent collapse of pricing agreements which had been in existence for at least twenty years management might react by concentrating production in their sector as a viable alternative to the trade association. Even when in 1965 the Monopolies and Mergers Act was passed, giving the Monopolies Commission power to investigate all mergers with a market value in excess of £5 million, merger activity was hardly affected at all (Devine, 1976; 435–6). The 1965 Act allowed the Monopolies Commission either to prohibit or break up (within six months of its creation) a merger, but it is interesting to note that between 1965 and 1973 of the 833 cases which fell within its operating criteria only twenty were investigated, and in just six instances was action taken (Hannah, 1983; 154).

Government encouragement of big business

In effect, there was at least considerable government complicity in the move towards big business, while at times it is also possible to say that ministers openly conspired to encourage the creation of firms which would be more capable of competing with the large American and European corporations dominating many sectors of world trade. A good example of this approach can be provided by examining the aircraft industry, because the 1960 concentration into three principal groups happened because the Ministry of Defence influenced events. A highly provocative defence white paper of 1957 had predicted the need for a considerable rationalisation of aircraft production, indicating how the dual pressures of mounting development costs and intense American competition were forcing the highly dispersed British industry into niche markets (Gardner, 1981; 19–22). There were at that time twenty British aircraft manufacturers, and as a monopsonist in both defence and civil markets government used its influence to goad the industry into a series of mergers which concentrated activity into three main groups, Westland (for helicopters), Hawker-Siddeley, and the British Aircraft Co. (Hayward, 1989; 45–82). The latter would be by far the most important firm, having merged the aircraft activities of English Electric and Vickers with the Bristol Aircraft Co, and in general this strategy created a much stronger industry which was capable of developing the increasingly sophisticated and expensive aircraft which were required by the 1960s (Gardner, 1981; 35–53).

The most outstanding post-war example of government involvement in concentrating production came immediately after the Labour Party won the 1945 general election. It was this government which implemented an extensive programme of nationalising crucial industries like transport (railways, roads and ports), steel and energy supply (coal, electricity and gas). The public sector (Hannah, 1994; 168–94) is not covered in this history, but as Millward (1991; 19) emphasises the government's strategy could well be regarded as an extension of the 1930s attempts at state-assisted rationalisation, forcing through essential changes in industrial structure which market forces had never been able to achieve. The survey by Foreman-Peck & Millward (1994; 115–40) provides substantial material on the management and performance of the nationalised sector, indicating how severe constraints were imposed on management by successive governemnts, and in this sense typifying business evolution at this time. In a different vein, in 1948 and 1959 two pieces of legislation were passed to encourage cotton manufacturers to concentrate production, and although this policy was not as successful as the intervention in aircraft production it was a further manifestation of post-war governments' intentions to intervene when necessary (Singleton, 1991; 154–60). One must remember that this was an era when politicians regarded full employment as a central guiding principle of economic policy, and in order to achieve this goal government intervention was accepted as an essential feature of the business scene (Lee, 1976; 391).

The IRC

A more relevant example of this interventionist tendency came in the late-1960s, when another Labour government developed a range of policies which directly affected trading structure in several key industries. An essential feature of the economic strategy devised by this Labour government (elected in 1964) was the creation of big businesses as a springboard for greater industrial competitiveness, a strategy which resulted in the creation of the Industrial Reorganisation Corporation (IRC). This new institution was charged with the task of building firms capable of competing with multi-national giants which dominated the high-growth sectors of international trade (Devine, 1976; 439–41). There is a paradox here, because the IRC decided that size was the key to success, undermining any attempts at controlling monopolistic tendencies. However, as we noted earlier, while government was keen to dismantle price-fixing agreements, the Monopolies Commission was kept in abeyance throughout this period, emphasising how big business was regarded as the way forward. As the IRC stated in its first report, it was set up 'to promote industrial efficiency and profitability', and that aim would be fulfilled by concentrating production in certain key sectors, choosing what its advisors felt was the best managed firm as a nucleus for the new venture (Hague, 1983; 20–25). It is also important to emphasise how the IRC was run not by politicians or civil servants, but by businessmen seconded to the organisation, giving it an air of political objectivity, and with funds totalling £150 million its first managing director (Frank Kearton, chairman of Courtaulds) set about building a series of industrial giants.

The two most important criteria by which the IRC operated were scale and managerial ability, and in its five years of operations, during which time it was involved in approximately ninety projects (Hague, 1983; 252–306), several companies were created which were the very manifestation of the era's guiding principle, 'big is beautiful'. The most outstanding mergers were British Leyland (in the automobile industry), GEC (electrical engineering), ICL (computers), and Swann-Hunter (shipbuilding), forcing through what the IRC saw as essential changes by a combination of financial manipulation and extensive bullying of unhelpful executives (Devine, 1976; 470–1). One might argue that in the context of an unprecedented wave of mergers, especially between 1967 and 1969, the IRC was not needed. Likewise, some of its successes might well be regarded as Pyrrhic victories, because the mergers, for example in computers (Campbell-Kelly, 1989; 258–63) and electrical engineering, would probably have happened anyway. Alternatively, as we shall see later, in the case of British Leyland one might think that pushing together volume car-producers and truck and bus manufacturers was a foolhardy move. However one views the viability of these mergers, though, and we shall return to examine some of these cases in the next section, the IRC certainly contributed to the late-1960s wave of mergers. Indeed, by dismantling the trade associations and undermining price stability, by returning to a free trade policy, and by participating in some mergers, one might conclude that government had played a leading role in persuading businessmen that size provided a more secure platform for the competitive challenges of the era.

The rise of the takeover bid

This brief review of the broad economic and political environment facing British businessmen from the early-1950s has indicated how a combination of market-cum-technological stimuli and legal reforms could well have been responsible for the contemporary interest in mergers. On the other hand, one might argue that this interest had started to manifest itself well before both the economy had moved on to its post-war growth path and anti-monopoly policies had started to bite, indicating how other factors could have contributed to this scenario. In particular, much greater emphasis should perhaps be paid to the changes taking place in the spheres of business finance, company law and taxation, because these were creating opportunities for a new breed of aggressive businessmen who built up substantial empires by developing what has since come to be known as the takeover bid. Running in parallel with the emergence of this new approach was what we noted in the last section was a growing divorce between control and ownership, and when the term first became popular in 1953 contemporaries were surprised to discover that businessmen were bidding directly to shareholders over the heads of directors. This reveals how City influence was clearly increasing very early in the post-war period, bringing to an end what Hannah (1974a; 65–9) has described as the 'golden age of directorial power'. Here, indeed, was a new era in the British history of both merger activity and business finance, irreversibly affecting much of what was to happen in these areas.

Although the growing divorce between control and ownership was clearly a major influence on events, it is important to emphasise how for certain technical reasons take-over bids emerged in the early-1950s. In the first place, as a result of the 1948 Companies Act, management was thereafter obliged to provide details on the true asset and earning positions of firms when presenting consolidated annual balance sheets. This removed what had amounted to a substantial informational constraint on takeover bids prior to 1948 (Hannah, 1974a; 75), and in particular it revealed to potential predators the highly liquid state of many firms as they emerged from a profitable era. Roberts (1992; 184–6) has also emphasised how company taxation played a role in this scenario, because it had been increased substantially between 1938 and 1952, from thirty-seven per cent of gross trading profits to fifty-six per cent, encouraging management to retain funds, rather than distribute profits to shareholders. Furthermore, not only did post-war governments advise dividend restraint as part of their anti-inflationary strategies, there was also a significant differential in the level of taxation levied on distributed profits, dividends being taxed at thirty per cent while profits retained within the company were only taxed at three per cent. This tax was in 1958 equalised at ten per cent, but in the meantime it had encouraged firms to build up their reserves, rather than reward shareholders, forcing down share prices at a time when many firms traditionally undervalued their assets. Wright (1962; 465–6) has also emphasised how restrictions on bank borrowing and the Capital Issues Committee's work in limiting access to the capital market further encouraged firms to build up their internal reserves, and as share prices were so depressed this made them extremely vulnerable to a takeover. Finally, one must remember that short-term capital gains were not taxed until 1965, giving speculators a huge incentive to acquire these cash-rich firms.

Clore and the empire-builders

In simple terms, circumstances had created a situation which was ripe for exploitation, especially with share ownership now being much more dispersed. Previously, merger negotiations had been the exclusive preserve of directors, but now that more accurate information was available on companies whose equities were held by investors unconnected with management, this left many open to a bid from an outsider (Hannah, 1974a; 75). The pioneer of this new approach was allegedly the highly colourful Charles Clore, and because of his background as the son of a Jewish immigrant East End tailor he was often portrayed as a swashbuckling entrepreneur who took on, and humbled, the City establishment (Davis, 1970; 17–23). Clore's first spectacular success was the acquisition of J. Sears & Co. in 1953, having discovered that this company, following standard contemporary accounting procedures, had underestimated by £10 million the real estate value of its 900 shoe shops (trading under the Freeman, Hardy & Willis name). When the Sears board finally realised that he was bidding directly to the shareholders, they retaliated by tripling the dividend, but this move simply emphasised how poorly the company had been managed, and as Clore had offered a price above the market value of the company's shares disenchanted investors soon sold out. This set the pattern for a series of takeovers in the 1950s (Davis, 1970; 17–31), and although the Conservative government and the Bank of England restricted this activity by warning off the insurance companies and American banks which had been financing the bids (Roberts, 1992; 187–91), the establishment was powerless to prevent the practice becoming a permanent feature of the business scene.

The early-1950s has actually been described as 'the era of the independent tycoon', when without the assistance of merchant bankers, businessmen like Charles Clore, Isaac Wolfson, Jack Cotton and Hugh Fraser built up substantial empires by bidding directly to shareholders for assets which were undervalued and managed by allegedly 'sleepy' boards of directors (Wright, 1962; 461–3). By the late-1950s, such was the growing acceptability of the takeover bid, that the City establishment was even beginning to participate, and after another wave of takeover bids upset the normal workings of the City, the Issuing Houses Association produced the first set of regulations covering such events, in October 1959. Roberts (1992; 196–8) has emphasised how these 'Notes on Amalgamations of British Businesses', while forestalling statutory intervention, were largely ignored until a more precise code was elaborated in 1967. Nevertheless, they represented an acceptance by merchant banks, investment trusts and other financial institutions that the takeover bid was too important to ignore.

Conclusion

Although it is important to remember that most amalgamations in the 1950s did not arise out of a takeover bid, the pioneering work of Clore and his counterparts had clearly established a new *modus operandi* in British merger activity. Most mergers were in fact similar to their inter-war predecessors, resulting from a single company absorbing smaller rivals through personal negotiations between directors. However, by the late-1950s takeovers were beginning to take on a much more prominent role as a major means of acquiring assets, and thereafter they dominated the scene as a psychological influence on decison making (Davis, 1970; 1–16). One must note, though, that while the 1950s take-overs were largely prompted by individuals seeking to make rich pickings from the financial state of many firms, by the late-1950s they were motivated more by a desire either to increase market share or reduce vulnerability to acquisition by other predators. As Wright (1962; 467) explains, by that time 'factors had caused a rise in share prices which had largely closed the gap between market valuation and real value'. This reveals how as the post-war period progressed the market-cum-technological and legal stimulii discussed earlier were starting to overlap with the decisive changes in control and ownership which had accelerated significantly during the 1950s. However, one cannot yet be certain about the actual motives of senior management, because the dynamics of British managerial capitalism could well have been pushing them into takeovers for reasons unconnected with economic rationality. This is the issue we must now go on to address, linking our study of merger activity with the last section's analysis of changing control and ownership patterns.

6.3   The dynamics of British managerial capitalism

It is apparent that over the period 1953–1973 several factors had prompted the growing interest in merger activity, ranging from the availability of rich financial pickings in the early-1950s through to the decisive market-cum-technological, legal and ownership changes affecting business after 1957. No clear answer has yet emerged, however, as to the key questions of motivation and consequences, particulalry in relation to the mergers occurring after Clore and his counterparts had finished building up their personal empires. Neo-classical economics would have us believe that firms are run by entrepreneurs whose only concern is the maximisation of profits, but as Devine (1976; 147–50) emphasises the increasing divorce between control and ownership prompted economists to explain the potential divergence of interest between shareholders and managers. Indeed, substantial changes to the theory of the firm were appearing at the same time that managerial capitalism was emerging in Britain, and some insight into this literature would be helpful to our analysis.

New interpretations of business behaviour

One of the most interesting of these new 'managerial' theories was provided by Marris (1964; 45–7), who argues that while shareholders might well want to maximise the return on their investments, managers could be more interested in maximising growth and personal security. He also extended this insight into a much broader hypothesis, claiming that the major constraint on the growth of the corporate firm was the threat of a takeover, in that managerial independence can be severely constrained by the market's perception of a firm's prospects. In simple terms, this theory postulates that when a firm's 'valuation ratio', namely the ratio of stock market value to book value, falls below what a potential bidder perceives to be its real value, then a takeover struggle will ensue. This forces existing management to maintain a high stock market value, often by increasing dividends, indicating how their principal aims no longer bore much resemblance to the maximisation of profitability. Marris (1964; 63) is also willing to accept as 'working assumptions . . . that in addition to "narrow" economic rewards, such as salary, bonus, stock options . . . and the like, executives desire power, status, opportunity for creative satisfaction, opportunity for group-belonging and security'. This approach has been described by Williamson (1964; 17–19) as the pursuit of 'utility', and clearly many questions can consequently be asked about the propensity of managerial capitalism to encourage long-term planning, given the short-termist pressures imposed by the City.

Linked very closely with the insights provided by Marris's theory is the work of behavioural economists like Cyert and March (1963; 116–25), whose main concern is the understanding of organisational dynamics. They have argued that, because business organisations are composed of groups and individuals, each of which have their own goals and aspirations, decision making is much more concerned with 'satisficing' (defined as the achievement of these goals and aspirations), rather than maximising profitability. Firms might well attempt to reduce uncertainty, but they only respond when problems arise, revealing an essentially short-termist approach in dealing with either the environment or the need for organisational change. On the other hand, while accepting the point that a firm is an administrative organisation composed of different interests, Penrose (1959; 15–6, 43–9) has claimed that the main constraint on a firm's growth is the quality of its management, given that growth needs planning and decisions must be taken based on an assessment of opportunities and challenges. This idea, of course, is related with Coase's (1937) argument that the limits to growth are imposed by the transaction costs imposed by internalising functions foremerly performed through the market. Penrose (1959; 144–5, 153–8), though, is particularly concerned with diversification, rather than vertical integration, as an effective response to problems in a firm's existing markets, and she is at pains to argue that merger activity is an indication of rational economic planning. No theoretical model is constructed to prove the point, but her inductive empiricism has provided another dimension from which to approach the business history of this period.

The work of these industrial economists has certainly opened up many fresh insights into business evolution, and historians are heavily indebted to both their theories and empirical investigations. More detailed analyses of their theses can be found in Devine (1976; 108–233), but it is above all important to emphasise that this work demonstrates how the old neo-classical preoccupation with maximising profits ignores many of the more subtle changes taking place both within businesses and to their scale of operations. One must remember that industrial economists are principally concerned with explaining general business behaviour, rather than simply merger activity, but they have revealed how the combination of an increasing divorce between control and ownership with the greater scale of business completely altered its dynamics. With specific regard to merger activity, though, it is important to ask whether a rational assessment of acquisitions was ever made by management, or whether the financial, legal and economic pressures of the period pressured executives into measures that were ill-planned and illogical.

The takeover bid and managerial discipline

One of the main claims Marris (1964; 45–8) made on behalf of the existence and potential impact of the takeover bid was its influence on managerial discipline, arguing that unless firms maintained their 'valuation ratio' they would be vulnerable to moves from predators. Hannah (1974a; 75–7) has also noted how 'the disciplinary function of the stock market' was reinforced by this means, while Wright (1962; 261–3) felt that the threat of a takeover, or even its implementation, would reinject enterprise into firms which had either been 'sleeping' on their assets or were reluctant to introduce the new ideas which were purportedly sweeping through other economies. Again, one must emphasise how takeovers only accounted for approximately twenty per cent of all mergers up to 1970 (Hannah, 1983; 149), but the key point made by these authorities is that the *latent threat* of a bid to all companies whose equity was widely distributed forced management to pursue new strategies. Of course, this is extremely difficult to substantiate, but by analysing the achievements of British mergers up to the mid-1970s we can gain some understanding of the issues involved.

One of the best examples of a takeover bid instilling greater discipline into management is the case of Courtaulds, Britain's pioneering rayon producer

(Coleman, 1969). When in December 1961 this firm came under siege from ICI, its major competitor in the artificial fibres market, there followed both a significant structural reorganisation and a host of acquisitions aimed at increasing its market strength. The two companies were already partners in a joint venture (British Nylon Spinners) established as long ago as 1940, but Courtaulds relied substantially on ICI for its supplies of basic raw materials, while they also had overlapping interests in the production of paint. During the late-1950s Courtaulds had been rationalising its capacity, as well as acquiring several competitors, but by 1961 profits had slumped by over fifty per cent, compared to five years earlier, and consequently the dividend was cut. Inevitably, this further weakened the company's share price, after several months of stagnation, 'and it seemed to underline the widely-held view that Courtaulds was a stodgy, badly managed company which was very much on the decline, and which had no real thought for its shareholders' (Davis, 1970; 40). ICI had already started exploratory talks on a possible merger by September 1961, and the reduced dividend provided an excellent opportunity for its chairman, Sir Paul Chambers, to announce a formal bid. The offer valued Courtaulds at £200 million, making this the largest bid ever made, but by this time its board, and in particular Frank (later Lord) Kearton was keen to remain independent, resulting in a long battle which lasted until ICI announced in March 1962 that it had only acquired 37.4 per cent of its victim's equity (Davis, 1970; 38–50).

Having successfully repelled ICI, Courtaulds then proceeded over the following ten years to pursue a highly aggresive strategy based on the simple aim of making itself bid-proof. Kearton was made chairman in 1964, and under his leadership Courtaulds built up an even stronger position in the artificial fibres market, while at the same time rationalising the organisation and introducing a variation on the multidivisional structure which was more capable of coping with the demands of a much-expanded business (Channon, 1973; 177–8). Although thwarted by the Monopolies Commission in its attempt to acquire English Calico in 1969, Courtaulds spent £176 million purchasing over sixty garment, hosiery and spinning firms between 1963 and 1974, extending its control of artificial fibre production into other parts of the textile industry (Cowling, 1980; 290–302). Its valuation ratio must clearly have been favourable to a takeover bid in 1962, demonstrating how firms can become vulnerable to predators by giving the impression that they are not making full use of the assets at their disposal. Thereafter, though, Kearton and his team ensured that no repeat of the ICI threat would recurr. However, one might well dispute the typicality of this case-study, because in an examination of the valuation ratios of firms involved in merger activity during the peak years of 1967 and 1968 Newbould (1970; 97–107) has concluded that this concept cannot be applied. Indeed, eighty-eight per cent of the twenty-seven takeover bids studied had valuation ratios in excess of unity, while the figure for seventy-four merger situations was eighty-five per cent. This reveals serious flaws in the Marris theory, because one would have expected the majority to have had valuation ratios which were well under unity, but clearly firms were making bids for firms irrespective of financial considerations.

Mergers and synergy

Of course, one must be wary of drawing firm conclusions from a study of seventy-four mergers which happened in just two years of a period when literally thousands of firms were being acquired. However, even though Kuehn (1975; 71–86) has found some evidence of an inverse correlation between valuation ratios and takeover threats, there seems to be general agreement among economists (Singh, 1971; 145) and historians (Payne, 1978; 225–30) that the motives for and consequences of mergers rarely fulfilled any rational expectations based on improved performance. This brings up the concept of synergy, defined simply as the achievement of '2 + 2 = 5', whereby, through the pursuit of rationalisation and extensive exploitation of economies of scale, the firm resulting from a merger would amount to a greater whole than the sum of its constituent parts (Cooke, 1986; 26–7). The achievement of synergy would evidently require effective planning of a merger, and once the event had been consummated management would have to pursue a ruthless strategy of closing down plant or offices where unnecessary duplication existed, creating a much more efficient business which was integrated and streamlined. This might be regarded as a rigid test of the economic rationale behind acquisitions, but by applying the concept of synergy to the actual experiences of the era one can start to understand why mergers were so popular.

With regard to the first step in achieving synergy, namely, planning a merger, Newbould (1970; 113) concludes from his sample that 'it does not appear that . . . there is a belief in, or a practice of, carefully considering the economies of scale, the balance of costs, the relative profitability of internal and external growth, or other economic rationalities'. Furthermore, in two-thirds of the actual mergers studied no factory or office closures had occurred in an average of seventeen months after the event, executive redundancies were limited to ten per cent in thirty-three out of the thirty-eight cases analysed, while twenty-three firms reported no increase in sales arising from the combination of resources (Newbould, 1970; 162–75). There had, of course, been cases where substantial synergic gains had been made, but the general conclusion is inescapable, that a failure to plan mergers had resulted in missed opportunities. Indeed, after emphasising the difficulties experienced with both truculent managers of acquired firms and integrating other operations, Newbould (1970; 175–80) coins an alternative term to synergy, arguing that 'antagony', or '2 + 2 = 3', could well have been the result in many cases.

British Leyland

Although Newbould (1970; 180) recognises that it would be an exaggeration to say that antagony was a common result of the 1967–1968 mergers, there is plenty of evidence to support the general point that post-war mergers rarely resulted in anything approaching synergy, or any other beneficial consequences. A classic example of this failure to exploit the full advantages of a merger was British Leyland, a company formed in 1968 by combining British Motor Holdings Ltd (BMH) with the Leyland Motor Co., after the Industrial Reorganisaton Corporation (IRC) had stepped in to force through what it regarded as an essential rationalisation of this vital industry (Davis, 1970; 94–109). Leyland was by the mid-1960s run by Sir Donald Stokes, who was regarded by the prime minister (Harold Wilson) as one of the dynamic new breed of managers capable of building businesses which would be capable of competing with the large American multinationals. Stokes was, in fact, a highly successful salesman, rather than a manager, a point to which we shall return later, but as Leyland had been extremely successful as a truck and bus manufacturer the Labour government was willing to back him. It was actually on Harold Wilson's instigation that the IRC supported Leyland's merger with BMH, bullying the latter's reluctant executives and lending the former £25 million to build what was regarded as a 'national champion', British Leyland (Church, 1994; 84–6). It is interesting to see how the IRC code-named BMH 'cress', because it was badly managed, while Leyland was called 'mustard', as a reflection of its supposedly strong organisation. In fact, this was the last in a series of car company amalgamations which stretched back to 1936, when the Nuffield Organisation was formed through the absorption by Morris Motors of Wolseley. The most important of these mergers had been the creation of BMC in 1952, when the two largest car firms (Austin and Nuffield) came together as a major force to compete with the growing power of Ford and Vauxhall in the domestic market.

In spite of all this history of combination, BMC in particular (renamed BMH in 1966, after acquiring the Jaguar Group) had failed to pursue a policy of rigorous integration and rationalisation. The main problem had been the rivalry between the two chief executives, Leonard Lord (Austin) and Lord Nuffield (Morris), and even though the latter retired in 1956 his successor (George Harriman) was also reluctant to initiate a substantial reorganisation. Leyland had also diversified into the car market after buying Standard-Triumph in 1961, and Stokes had ruthlessly reorganised this ailing business, revealing to contemporaries just how synergy could be achieved. On the other hand, when in 1968 he was appointed chief executive of British Leyland he would appear to have lost this ruthless streak. An M-form structure was formally adopted in 1969, and then modified in 1970, but 'the group still remained largely unconsolidated' seven years after the merger, and severe difficulties were experienced in rationalising capacity (Channon,

1973; 106). Furthermore, a large central staff was recruited at the duplicated headquarters, in London and Birmingham, while Stokes refused to delegate responsibility for decisions of both a trivial and major importance, 'perpetuating the personal, hierarchical tradition of the company [Leyland Motors] he had worked for since boyhood' (Church, 1994; 88–9). As Turner (1971; 212) has also concluded, Stokes 'brought together two enterprises, each an amalgamation of companies loaded down with unresolved problems of their own, and tried to unite them with an assemblage of management skills which were utterly inadequate for the job'. British Leyland suffered from many other problems after 1968, especially in the crucial fields of industrial relations and new product development (CPRS, 1975; 82–6), but the organisational failings would appear to have been the most fundamental obstacle which limited its ability to exploit all the potential advantages of a merger.

By 1975, having accounted for forty per cent of new car registrations at the time of the merger, British Leyland's share (thirty-one per cent) had fallen below the import sector's (thirty-three per cent) for the first time, while severe financial difficulties were also threatening its future (Cowling, 1980; 186–90). Such were the difficulties, indeed, that in 1975 another Labour government felt it necessary to nationalise the company and inject £50 million of loan guarantees, and as we shall see in the final section the new business was only capable of surviving with substantial government funds and Japanese technology. This is a damning indictment of the largest merger of this period, and although Stokes later commented that he was faced with the enormous task of controlling 'fifty or sixty different companies all trying to retain their independence even though they had been taken over', it is clear that he failed to cope with this challenge. One might also question the IRC's policy of creating 'national champions' to compete with giant American multinationals, and clearly in giving a salesman like Stokes ultimate responsibility for organising such a business there are grounds for believing that British Leyland was a case of wishful, if not naive, thinking.

We shall return to the subject of managerial qualifications in the next section, but British Leyland can be held up as supporting evidence for Newbould's (1970; 100) claim, and that of several other authorities, that merger activity was rarely successful. Unfortunately, much of this research was conducted using different methodologies and indices of performance, while often varying time periods and sample sizes were also covered. Nevertheless, where accounting data was used to give rates of return (whether on assets or capital employed), a general consensus emerges which reveals that mergers rarely resulted in improved profitability. The most significant of these studies were by Utton (1974), Singh (1971), Meeks (1977) and Newbould (1970), and they are summarised in Cooke (1986; 43–9) and in Walshe (1991; 352–4). Each leave little doubt about the financial failings of most mergers, and even though industrial concentration was increasing at an unprecedented pace, and most of the large firms were heavily involved in merger activity at some time in the post-war era, this does not appear to have resulted in improved profitability. Indeed, Walshe (1991; 354) has concluded that 'in the short to medium-term there is much evidence that mergers have contributed to a deterioration in industrial efficiency', such were the heavy transitional costs associated with this movement and the organisational deficiencies in many companies.

A successful merger: GEC

Having come to this highly critical conclusion, in the interests of balance it is important to discuss some of the firms which proved to be exceptions to the general rule. In particular, one might mention GEC as a company at the opposite end of the efficiency spectrum to British Leyland, because after its acquisition of AEI in 1967 and English Electric in 1968 one can only conclude that its management team succeeded in achieving synergy. Once again, the IRC was heavily involved in events, pursuing its aim of creating 'national champions' in the face of overwhelming American competition in high technology markets, and GEC was supported because its management team was regarded as superior to its British rivals (Jones & Marriott, 1970; 309–67). In fact, GEC had only recently overhauled its organisation, having struggled to improve performance since the 1940s. It was the acquisition of Radio & Allied Ltd in 1960 which brought two talented managers into the firm, Arnold Weinstock and Kenneth Bond, and by 1963 they had risen to senior executive posts at GEC. After 1963 a new financial structure was introduced, while the head office staff was ruthlessly streamlined from 2,000 to 200, and unprofitable factories were closed (Davis, 1970; 69–71). Weinstock, in particular, was regarded alongside Donald Stokes at Leyland as 'a symbol of industrial efficiency' (Jones & Marriott, 1970; 260), and even though this ignores the substantial contribution made by Kenneth Bond to the company's success it is vital to remember that the IRC backed GEC's bids for AEI and English Electric because of its superior management.

The intricate details of the AEI and English Electric acquisitions have been related elsewhere (Jones & Marriott, 1970; 309–67: Davis, 1970; 72–93), but it is important to emphasise that together with the creation of British Leyland this accounted for almost one-half of the total market value of all merger activity in 1967–1968. Similarly, one must also stress how one of Weinstock's first actions after acquiring AEI was to close its telecommunications plant at Woolwich, resulting in the loss of 5,000 jobs. Although this factory was producing outdated equipment, and so would probably have been closed in due course anyway, considerable popular concern was expressed at Weinstock's action because it created 'the impression that mergers and takeover bids invariably mean unemployment' (Davis, 1970; 86). In fact, by 1971 GEC employed approximately 225,000 people, compared to a combined total of 268,000 for the three companies in 1967, and while this ignores the sale of some enterprises in the interim period, clearly Weinstock was willing to take the hard decisions which would result in the achievement of synergy (Jones & Marriot, 1970; 377).

GEC announced that by 1971 complete integration of AEI and English Electric had been achieved, and thereafter the rate of return on capital employed rose to the levels pertaining in the mid-1960s, in spite of the severe economic dowturns of the 1970s. Cowling (1980; 198–212) has also concluded that GEC's performance was much better than the industry average, and as its labour force continued to fall, reaching just 166,000 in 1976, profitability has been impressive. One might question Weinstock's preference for accumulating substantial cash balances, which by the mid-1970s were producing interest of £50 million, rather than investing in the business, but the style of his management was nevertheless held up as the key reason why GEC achieved synergy. By 1970 GEC had adopted the M-form of organisation, but its head office of just 200 staff was much smaller than many of its counterparts, particularly in the USA, and its main function was to impose a rigid system of financial controls on the divisions (Channon, 1973; 136). One must remember that Weinstock believes fundamentally in devolving responsibility down the line to divisional and departmental managers. However, it is his energy and attention to detail which is central to the system's effective operation (Jones & Marriott, 1970; 378), indicating how GEC is a combination of personalised and corporate management.

Who gained?

When assessing the contribution of effective organisers like Arnold Weinstock one can only conclude that a wide performance spectrum can be applied to British business, with GEC at one end and firms like British Leyland at the other. Unfortunately, however, the latter would appear to have been more typical of the general business *milieu*, indicating how synergy was a forelorn hope in the context of British merger activity up to the mid-1970s. Perhaps in many ways this can hardly be regarded as surprising, because the lack of planning and integration noted earlier would have been combined with the heavy transitional costs arising from a merger. At the same time, this still leaves the vexed question of why management persisted with this strategy, and an important part of the answer must be an examination of who actually gained from this activity. Firth (1976; 83) has demonstrated that the shareholders of acquired companies can certainly be included among those who benefitted, but this group was not responsible for initiating any mergers, putting the emphasis back on to the executives who indulged so extensively in the 'mania'. In other words, the pursuit of what we described earlier as 'utility' would appear to have been more popular and common than the so-called rational alternative of synergy. This indicates how managers were much more interested in the enhanced prestige and remuneration large-scale operations would give them personally, and as efficiency gains were so negligible, or even negative (Cowling, 1980; 168), in the vast majority of mergers it was this group who emerged with the greatest benefits from merger activity.

Of course, when assessing this widely-accepted conclusion one must never forget the environment in which management was working, because this would have had a decisive influence on their actions. In the first place, because ownership was from the 1950s so widely dispersed away from the board of directors, and institutional investors were playing an increasingly important role in company financing, a potential takeover bid was always latent. This situation would inevitably pose a threat not only to the independence of most firms, but also to the influence senior executives would be able to exert over policy. Another dimension one must add to this broader perspective of the factors prompting mergers is Newbould's (1970; 143–60) general conclusion that one of the most important motives benind mergers was the general level of 'corporate uncertainty', and although he is only analysing the 1967–1968 mergers one might well agree that this hypothesis has considerable credibility as an explanation of all mergers from the late-1950s. After all, once the restrictive practices legislation had been tightened up in 1956, anti-monopoly policy had successfully undermined the trade associations' ability to fix prices, successive post-War governments had pursued macro-economic policies which created the highly destabilising 'stop-go' cycle, and the intensifying competition from American multinationals and other forms of foreign competition was further undermining confidence among manufacturers who were being squeezed out of many markets. Furthermore, the potential threat of a takeover bid was ever-present in the minds of many managers, forcing them to pursue strategies which would reduce their vulnerability to acquisition. Size was consequently seen as a relatively secure form of defence against these environmental pressures, indicating how defensive motives were a principal reason why from the late-1950s merger activity was so intense.

Conclusion

One might well conclude, then, that a combination of the period's economic and legal changes with the dynamics of British managerial capitalism had precipitated the growing propensity to indulge in mergers and acquisitions. Of course, there were clearly some instances of planned and economically rational combinations, but the evidence (Walshe, 1992; 349–54) demonstrates how such events were exceptional. Another point to make in this context relates to the economic efficiency of managerial capitalism, because when firms made generous dividend payments from profits in order to retain shareholder loyalty they would have little left for investment in new plant.

We noted in section 6.1 how by the 1970s business savings had for the first time become a minority contributor to industrial investment, signifying how managerial, rather than personal, capitalism could well be synonymous with a greater distribution of business earnings. Similarly, size rather than valuation ratio was regarded as a more effective form of security against takeover bids, forcing management to adopt the policy of 'acquire or be acquired', even if the mergers did not necessarily make economic sense. This is a point reinforced by Chandler's (1992; 28, 33–9) analysis of more recent trends in American business, because he has emphasised how by 1960 the 'institutionalised market for corporate control' in the USA, based largely around the investment activity of pension fund and insurance company managers, was also forcing American industrial executives to abandon long-term investment strategies in order to keep their shareholders happy. Roberts (1992; 197–8) concurrs with this view when analysing British developments in the 1950s, arguing that by 'institutionalising the market in corporate control' and imposing only a loose regulatory framework, the authorities were guilty of ignoring the potential implications for long-term growth strategies. Of course, by acquiring competitors and eliminating competition, management was also attempting to create a more secure environment, but because the mergers rarely resulted in improved performance one must conclude that utility prevailed over synergy.

6.4   A managerial revolution?

Although one can draw some strikingly negative conclusions about the nature of British managerial capitalism from this study of post-war merger activity, before criticising businessmen for ignoring the full possibilities it is important to examine in greater detail key issues like business organisation and culture, the training and recruitment of senior executives, and the influence of financial representatives on decision making. There are actually some positive signs of progress from the 1950s, most notably the growing popularity of multidivisional forms of organisation, the establishment of postgraduate business schools (with generous business endowments), and the growing scale of business operations. On the other hand, one can easily be fooled into thinking that a 'revolution' was happening, because a more detailed analysis of business practices reveals the superficiality of these innovations. 'Big is beautiful' might well have been the era's epitaph, and there was undoubtedly greater integration between the worlds of finance and industry, but given the highly defensive nature of many mergers it is clear that there was still a tremendous desire for continuity within the business community.

Table 6.3   *Diversification and multidivisional structure in the largest 100 Firms, 1950–1970*

Product type	1950		1960		1970	
	A	B	A	B	A	B
Single	31	2	18	1	6	1
Dominant	38	4	35	8	34	24
Related	21	6	39	19	54	43
Unrelated	2	0	4	1	6	4
Total	92	12	96	29	100	72

Key: A – Number of firms in this product range.
   B – Number of firms with M-form structure.
Source: Channon (1973; 67).

The changing nature of post-war business

As we noted in section 6.2, one of the most dramatic features of the period up to the early-1970s was a considerable increase in concentration across most industries, creating an oligopolistic trading structure which contrasted sharply with what Elbaum & Lazonick (1986; 15) have described as the atomistic structure prevailing up to the 1940s. In addition to greater scale, British business was also changing in nature, casting off the traditional dependence on limited product ranges. This trend is illustrated in column A of Table 6.3, which is based on Channon's (1973; 50–88) study of British business strategy and structure over the period 1950–1970. An obvious conclusion from this research is that in 1950 only twenty-three of the ninety-two leading companies on which he could find information had diversified or integrated away from their main product line, while by 1970 this figure had risen to sixty of the top 100 firms. Furthermore, not only were an increasing number of firms either more diversified or integrated, they were also highly geographically dispersed, the average number of plants per company among the top 100 firms rising from twenty-seven in 1958 to seventy-two by 1972 (Utton, 1982; 24–5). It is also important to stress that average plant size also fell over this period, from 750 to 430 employees, because many smaller competitors had been acquired, but clearly this expanding empire required more careful management. Indeed, the combination of greater scale, wider product ranges and increased geograhical dispersion was creating powerful centrifugal forces within the firms who were at the centre of 'merger mania', and given Chandler's (1962; 13–7) simple claim that structure ought to adapt to strategy one might consequently expect a wholesale reevaluation of management practices within many British businesses in order to accommodate these significant changes.

The M-form

Up to the 1950s, most large-scale British businesses used either the central-ised, functionally-departmentalised form of organisation or a holding company structure (Alford, 1988; 62). In fact, fifty-two of the former existed in the ninety-two firms listed under the 1950 column of Table 6.3, and there were thirty-eight of the latter (Channon, 1973; 68–75). We noted in section 5.5 that only ICI and Unilever had in the 1930s copied the American-style multidivisional (M-form) form, but according to Table 6.3 there were twelve of this type by 1950. This difference can be explained by Channon's inclusion of eight subsidiaries of American multinationals (Ford, Vauxhall and Massey-Ferguson, for example) among that twelve, while in two other cases (Smiths Instruments and Spillers) only a divisional form had been adopted by 1950. Table 6.3 consequently reiterates a point made in section 5.5, that British management practices remained firmly wedded to much earlier tradi-tions. During the 1950s, however, Table 6.3 reveals that a further thirteen M-forms appeared in the top 100 companies, especially in the 'related prod-uct' category, as management adapted structure to the strategies of increas-ing scale, widening product ranges and geographical dispersion. At the same time, one must remember that the most significant organisational change of the 1950s was a move towards the holding company form by thirty-one firms which had foremerly employed the centralised, functionally-depart-mentalised mode. Here again we can see how executives were able to retain control over their firms by agreeing to a merger which simply resulted in a federation, emphasising a point made earlier about the lack of redundancies in this category after most mergers. It also substantiates the claim that most mergers were defensive combinations of firms seeking refuge from the highly competitive post-war environment, particularly as trade associations were no longer capable of fixing prices effectively.

There would appear to have been only limited organisational progress during the 1950s, but Table 6.3 illustrates how by 1970 seventy-two of the top 100 firms had adopted the M-form, creating the impression that a dramatic turnaround had been effected in British business practices. There might well still have been twenty holding companies in 1970, but forty-three firms had apparently realised that the M-form possessed the requisite degree of sophistication to control their expanding and dispersed industrial empires. One of the main influences on this trend had been the increasing number of American multinational subsidiaries implanted in the UK after 1945 (Bostock & Jones, 1994; 104), demonstrating to the indigenous busi-ness community the advantages of an M-form of organisation. Futhermore, an American management consultancy firm, McKinsey & Co., was responsi-ble for advising on many reorganisations, especially in the chemical, petrole-um, engineering and electronics sectors. Whatever the reason and however the process was implemented, though, seemingly British businessmen had recognised the need for such an innovation, and by 1970 substantial progress had been made in effecting a major transformation in the traditional modes of running large-scale firms. It is also worth noting that, while the M-form had made a belated entrance on to the general business scene, by the early-1970s there were more M-forms operating in Britain than in any other country outside the USA. Certain socio-cultural and economic characteristics might well explain the lack of progress elsewhere (see section 5.1), but American practices had clearly been extensively copied by British firms, providing some evidence of organisational innovation after a century of apparent stagnation.

This conclusion might well come as a welcome relief from the unrelenting criticism of managerial developments which has been a major theme of the previous chapters. Inevitably, though, one must be extremely wary of reading too much into Table 6.3, because as Channon (1973; 239) himself admits after studying a sample of twenty-five firms covered by Table 6.3, 'British general executives had not wholly emulated their American counterparts in adopting certain characteristic mechanisms associated with [the M-form]'. Although American management consultants were frequently employed to advise on the reform, rarely were the duties and functions of a general office enunciated, while the involvement of divisional managers in policy discussions at board or central committee level meant that they were responsible for checking up on their own performance (Channon, 1973; 200–11). Annual budgeting had also only just appeared in many firms, while divisional performance was measured largely by examining the return on investment, and reward systems still relied on simple salary payments, rather than on incentive schemes. The failure to develop what in the USA was regarded as a cadre of central staff general executives was another major source of contrast, although some of the major chemical, pharmaceutical, electrical and electronics firms had implemented control and planning procedures which were as sophisticated as those used by American corporations. In general, though, such practices were only just beginning to percolate down into the British business community, while long-term planning remained a mystery to many.

While one might be able to explain these differences by noting both the relatively smaller scale of British firms, when compared to their American counterparts, and the recent adoption of the M-form in the UK (Chandler, 1976; 25–6), there are still grounds for believing that they were yet a further manifestation of the backward nature of management practices. In any case, given the substantial increases in scale, product range and geographical dispersion, British firms required a more sophisticated form of organisation than the traditional holding company or centralised structure. This begs the crucial question concerning the ability of senior executives to comprehend their radically changing situations, because while on the one hand they were pursuing ambitious strategies, their structural responses would appear to have been inadequate in coping with the organisational challenges of the era. The growing divorce between control and ownership had evidently put professional managers in a much more powerful position, but it is not yet clear whether in the British context this had produced the same type of results as in the USA, Germany or Japan.

Post-war managerial recruitment

In pursuing this critical approach, it is first of all important to examine post-war managerial recruitment, because in assessing the quality of British decision-making it is important to know whether the executives at all levels were better qualified than their predecessors. 'Managers are born, not made' had been the most popular maxim in this respect up to the Second World War, and in section 5.5 we were highly critical of the 'gentlemanly' nature of British boardrooms, to which appointments were based more on personal contacts and social status, rather than on qualifications (Hannah, 1983; 88). In the post-war period, and at least until the 1970s, however, little seems to have changed, and the extensive research of many social scientists has revealed a consistent preference for traditional recruitment patterns at all managerial levels. Coleman (1973; 116) might well have claimed that the distinction between 'gentlemen' and 'players' had disappeared by 1962, largely because the traditional cricket game between amateurs and professionals no longer took place. Rubinstein (1993; 86) has also questioned the 'cultural critique' and its emphasis on blaming public school-educated businessmen for Britain's economic ills. However, as we saw in section 4.3, this ignores such crucial issues as the conservative and 'amateurish' nature of a business culture which is grounded in traditional practices. Stanworth & Giddens (1974; 99), for example, have illustrated from a study of company chairmen over the period 1900–1972 that the vast majority originated from the 'established inner circle' who would have been educated at public school. Copeman (1955; 49–66) also estimated that at least fifty per cent of the 1,000 directors he studied had been to public school, while a survey by *Management Today* in 1970 estimated that the average company director was aged fifty-six, had been to public school, and only nine per cent had any formal qualification for their job (Channon, 1973; 212). At the level of line manager, Clements (1958; 82–96) calculated that approximately thirty per cent had worked their way up from either the shopfloor or an office, but this pales into insignificance when put alongside the Acton Society Trust's (1956; 56) claim that anybody who had been to public school had a tenfold better chance of securing a managerial post than any internal candidates.

Senior British businessmen of the 1970s would consequently bear a very close resemblence to their inter-war predecessors, both in terms of recruitment from the highest social classes and the possession of very few formal qualifications for management. There might well be some evidence of what were pejoritavely known as 'grammar school executives', but as Stanworth & Giddens (1974; 101) have concluded 'the plausibility of such a transformation of the existing economic elite must at the very best be regarded with a certain scepticism; while this may take place at other levels of industrial management, it is likely to stop short, as in previous generations, at the doors of the board-room'. They noted that financial institutions exhibited even greater levels of elitism, a point substantiated further by Whitley (1973; 618–9), who calculated that eighty per cent of all City directors had been to public school, while sixty-six per cent of those in industry were educated in this way. This elitism was also true of the retail sector, where according to Thomas (1978; 310) eighty-eight per cent had a private education.

Another key point to make about senior management is its lack of mobility, emphasising how the provision of non-transferable 'top hat' pensions for these people created an unwillingness to take risks with either career or firm (Channon, 1973; 46). This helps to explain why firms adopting the M-form structure between 1950 and 1970 failed to incorporate many of its key features, because senior management was reluctant to accept a complete change in organisation. The most important conclusion arising from this analysis of the British business elite, however, is the reluctance among the main policy-makers to acquire formal qualifications for the posts to which they were appointed. Coming into industry or finance with an arts-based education from the leading public schools, where vocational education was scorned as second-rate, they worked their way through the management hierarchy picking up particular skills, rather than an understanding of general management principles. This helps to explain why, as Channon (1973; 240–2) observes, British businessmen clearly lacked the expertise to employ the highly sophisticated control and planning procedures required in an M-form organisation, while coming from such a background one might argue that they were also reluctant to change the system too drastically for fear of disturbing the *status quo*.

Management education and the business schools

In retrospect, it is clear that one of the major challenges facing British business up to the 1970s was the need to change traditional patterns of management recruitment and training. This was certainly the view expressed by a dedicated group of businessmen and executives who worked energetically for the establishment in Britain of university business schools along the lines pursued in the USA since the 1880s. Among the most influential of this group were the three founders of the Foundation for Management Education (FME), John Bolton, Sir Keith Joseph MP and J. W. Platt, while in the academic world Teddy Chester, Tom Lupton, Grigor McClelland and Douglas Hague were establishing a range of new management courses and research programmes which helped to reinforce the idea that university business schools would have an important role to play in reinvigorating British business performance

(Wilson, 1992; 3–10). There had also been other innovations in this field since the late-1940s, including the Administrative Staff College at Henley in 1947, which was established to provide twelve week general management courses, while the British Institute of Management (BIM) was also formed in 1947 and immediately started a diploma in management studies for practising and potential managers. The diploma scheme was never very successful, having been taken by just 1,450 students by 1962. On the other hand, by that time the FME and their supporters had convinced the government of the need to found university business schools, and many were anticipating the creation of a more progressive system.

It was just at the time that both the University Grants Council and the National Economic Development Council had incorporated the FME's case into influential reports that the 'Savoy Group' was established as a means of advocating rather more traditional approaches towards management training. This new lobbying organisation was headed by leading industrialists from GKN and English Electric, and it was directly as a result of its work that Lord Franks was invited to adjudicate on the two contrasting views proposed by the FME and the Savoy Group. Franks would eventually come down firmly in favour of the FME, recommending the establishment of business schools attached to the univerisities of London and Manchester. Nevertheless, as a result of what he perceived to be a 'mutual uneasiness' in relations between business and universities the report also insisted that the new institutions' start-up capital and running costs should be met in equal parts by the two sides. It was this compromise which would hamper the progress of academic management education over at least the following ten years (Wilson, 1992; 11–5). In fact, to many people's surprise over £5 million was raised for this cause in 1964 from a public appeal addressed at British business, exceeding the target by over twenty per cent. However, one must not read too much into the appeal, given the failure of most firms to provide much support (Whitley, 1981; 47). The acid test, of course, would be the willingness of British business either to recruit the postgraduates who passed through the Master of Business Administration (MBA) courses or send their own managers on post-experience programmes.

Business school strategy

Although after opening its doors in 1965 London Business School was able to recruit large numbers of students on to the MBA and post-experience courses, it is important to emphasise the role played by overseas sources in maintaining intake at respectable levels (Barnes, 1989; 147–8). Manchester Business School (MBS), on the other hand, experienced severe financial problems until the late-1970s, principally because recruitment consistently failed to hit the targets set by Franks, and as they were obliged to raise half of their funds from non-governmental sources this precipitated an acute liquidity crisis. In fact, a cumulative deficit of over £110,000 had appeared in the accounts by 1974, and in 1975 MBS was only able to pay its wages because of a loan of £50,000 from the FME (Wilson, 1992; 36–9). One solution which MBS devised as a means of generating more income from the post-experience side was to pioneer a range of courses which involved client firms in the design process, and once the banking sector had been persuaded to use these programmes considerable surpluses started to appear in the accounts (Wilson, 1992; 68–75). On the other hand, by accomodating the traditional British business preference for in-house training into their post-experience courses, it is important to emphasise how in pursuing this strategy MBS had simply bowed to market pressures, indicating how they had failed to change attitudes in this crucial area.

The successful 1964 business school appeal had clearly created a false impression, and although by the early-1970s thirty-three universities had initiated courses in this field there is little evidence of a wholesale conversion of attitudes towards management education. A series of reports commissioned by the BIM also emphasised how British firms were generally unhappy about the new MBA's appearing in the job market (Wilson, 1992; 52–3, 69), describing them as abrasive, prone to move from firm to firm, and lacking in skills relevant to actual business practices. This scepticism about the postgraduate courses was also mirrored in the reviews of post-experience provision, because many were demanding programmes which would deal with the specific needs of managers at all levels. Furthermore, not only was there excess capacity in the post-experience field, another 1972 report produced for the NEDC also concluded that in the context of increasingly difficult trading conditions 'management training is unlikely to come very high in the determination of priorities at a time of great competition for very scarce resources'. British firms quite simply preferred to train their own managers, and Keeble (1992; 154) demonstrates how by 1970 over 150 had developed management development schemes which were widely regarded as more effective than the business school alternative. Even as late as 1987, Constable and McCormick (1987; 85) were able to claim that in only twenty-nine per cent of the 206 large public and private businesses surveyed was there any belief in the value of formal qualifications for the crucial role of management.

The 'cult of the amateur'

While Wheatcroft (1970) might well have been able to write about a *Revolution in British Management Education*, one will look in vain for positive signs of progress in the fields of management recruitment and training. Indeed, a second business school appeal in 1970 fell £1.25 million short of its £7.5 million target. As Handy (1988; 164) later argued, 'in Britain management education and training is *too little, too late for too few*', because by the time business schools had appeared attitudes had become so well entrenched that it is difficult to see how they could have made an immediate impact. Turner (1969; 92) has also concluded that: 'Business schools are about as British as drum majorettes: in fields where they believe success depends primarily on experience and instinct, the British only turn to teaching as a last resort'. This might well indicate that in copying the American concept of business schools, or what Handy (1988; 169) calls going down the *academic* track, Britain had failed to reinforce the attempts made by firms to develop the *corporate* approach. After all, since the 1940s both West Germany and Japan have managed to improve industrial competitiveness without imitating American training methods, preferring instead to recruit well-educated people and train them internally in highly advanced regimes which produce competent managers (Wilson, 1995). Aaronson (1992; 172–3) has also observed that by the 1980s American business schools were being heavily criticised for their failure to develop courses capable of preparing potential managers for the challenges from Japanese and European firms. It is impossible to predict whether more investment in the *corporate* track would have improved the organisational performance and competitiveness of British business, but the business schools had made little impact by 1980, and internal training continued to be regarded as the 'Cinderella' within most overhead structures.

Conclusion

One might conclude from this brief survey of attitudes towards recruitment and training that in Britain professional managers were those who held little equity in the company for which they worked, rather than a cadre of people with identifiable standards and qualifications. In other words, the 'cult of the amateur' was still extremely popular, leading to what PEP (1966; 13) described as 'almost complete indifference to modern managerial practice in the widepsread strata of British industry'. These are allegations repeated by Channon (1973; 43–6, 240–2), who emphasises how the prevalance of 'amateurism' across industry was the main reason why firms which moved towards the M-form up to 1970 were incapable of adopting all its detailed requirements. Furthermore, it is clear from the earlier study of merger activity that most senior British executives were quite simply afraid of taking risks which might affect their vested interests, because acquisitions were rarely followed by a wholesale reassessment of capacity, resulting in federations of firms within a holding company structure. One must also remember that as the major financial institutions were by the 1960s interlinked with the major companies which had emerged out of this merger activity (Stanworth & Giddens, 1975, 5–25), there is a tremendous degree of commonality within the British business community, reinforcing this belief in a preservation of vested interests.

It is consequently clear from this analysis of managerial capitalism in Britain up to the 1970s that continuity was a principal theme of the way in which businessmen pursued both strategy and structure. Much of the merger activity was highly defensive in nature, protecting both firms against the dual pressures of intensifying competition and vulnerability to takeover bids, and managers from losing their jobs. Indeed, such was the desire for utility, rather than synergy, that many of the potential advantages associated with industrial concentration were lost. Even when an M-form structure was adopted, often on the advice of American consultants, senior executives were able to resist wholesale changes to their established positions, resulting in many of the worst features of a holding company structure – the lack of co-ordination, poor planning and control procedures, and antiquated reward systems – remaining in place (Channon, 1973; 213). At the same time, given the changing pattern of control and ownership, management decision making was more attuned to the dynamics of a stock market dominated by powerful financial institutions, further reinforcing the need to pursue short-term strategies which increased share values, rather than the chances of long-term growth. As the banks and financial institutions 'moved more and more into the centre of the [corporate] networks', then the process of concentration gathered a kind of natural momentum (Stanworth & Giddens, 1975; 24). This also created a market for corporate control which Chandler (1992; 35–9) claims is so heavily biased towards short-term gains that 'the logic of industrial growth' becomes neglected. In other words, concluding on a damning note, British (and American) business by the 1970s was more interested in short-term financial gain and enhanced executive status than investing in long-term growth strategies which exploit the potential advantages of large-scale operations. Hampden-Turner and Trompenaars (1993; 60) regard this as typical of the highly individualist approach pursued in Western society, whereby managerial capitalism creates a situation in which the business organisation simply becomes a vehicle for personal aspirations. It is a sad indictment of the performance of these economies over the last forty years, but from what we have seen in this chapter one can only agree that the rise of a market for corporate control has acted as a disincentive to pursue risky, long-term strategies.

6.5 Business into the 1990s: a changing culture?

The British experiment with big business which had lasted from the early-1950s through to the mid-1970s produced some remarkable developments, not least the unprecedented levels of merger activity, increased industrial concentration, and a vibrant market for corporate control. Sadly, though, little had changed in terms of culture and organisational sophistication among many of those firms which sought size as a defensive strategy, and for this reason business structure remained essentially inappropriate to the size and diveristy of British firms by the 1970s. Thereafter, however, as we shall see later, in the last generation economic necessity has prompted a dramatic change in attitudes among those firms which survived the severe depressions of the period. In particular, we shall see how by the 1990s British business was much stronger and more capable of coping with international competition than in previous generations, especially in those sectors where multinational activity featured prominently. The downside to this movement was a significant decline in the 'Britishness' of many industries, but with production moving inexorably towards a much more international level this was perhaps inevitable. Notwithstanding this comment, firms like ICI, BP, Shell, RTZ and Glaxo had developed world-wide reputations by the 1990s, and there is evidence that they were dealing very successfully with American and Far Eastern competition (Guterl, 1989; 63–6). One must be careful not to exaggerate the degree to which a revolution had occurred by the 1980s and 1990s, but careful optimism can be expressed at the new movements affecting many large-scale British firms.

The 1970s lull in merger activity and MBO's

After the huge surge in merger activity lasting from the late-1950s through to the early-1970s, it was perhaps not surprising that therafter British businessmen showed much less interest in external expansion. The last major 'merger mania' of that era occurred in 1972–3, when over 2,400 companies (currently valued in excess of £3,800 million) were acquired, but as Table 6.4 illustrates there is a significant lull over the following decade. It is important to note that, because the information in Table 6.4 is derived from a source which benefitted from access to recent government statistics, the figures differ markedly from those used by Hannah (1983; 177). Both sources are in agreement, though, on the significant downturn in merger activity after 1973, when all three indices in Table 6.4 fall markedly, and authorities like Newbould and Jackson (1972) were writing about *The Receding Ideal*. To illustrate this point further, it has been estimated that between 1967 and 1973 expenditure on mergers as a proportion of gross domestic fixed capital formation averaged almost forty-three per cent, but over the following ten years it rarely rose above ten per cent (George, Joll and Lynk, 1991; 84–8).

In trying to explain the significant reduction in acquisitions after 1973, it is important to remember how at that time the international economy was beginning to experience the full impact of the collapse of the Bretton Woods system of fixed exchange rates which had provided so much stability since 1945. It was also in 1973 that oil prices trebled, bringing the continuous post-war growth of international trade to a grinding halt and further exacerbating Britain's balance of payments difficulties. Again, the details of this worsening economic environment can be left to other sources (Pollard, 1992:

Table 6.4   Merger activity in British business, 1970–1989

	No. of firms disappearing through merger	Merger expenditure (at current prices) (£ million)	Merger expenditure (at 1987 prices) (£ million)
1970	793	1,123	8,951
1971	884	911	6,144
1972	1,210	2,532	13,409
1973	1,205	1,304	7,982
1974	504	508	5,296
1975	315	291	2,423
1976	353	448	3,118
1977	481	824	4,472
1978	567	1,140	5,489
1979	534	1,656	7,025
1980	469	1,475	5,855
1981	452	1,144	4,024
1982	463	2,206	6,712
1983	447	2,343	5,636
1984	568	5,474	11,069
1985	474	7,090	11,614
1986	696	14,935	19,718
1987	1,125	15,363	15,363
1988	1,224	22,123	24,592
1989	1,039	26,104	24,220

Source: George, Joll & Lynk (1992; 84).

289–300), but it was no doubt important in determining investment plans. Even those mergers which did occurr in the 1970s were also no more success-ful than their predecessors, and Luffman and Reed (1984; 44–60) conclude that although the economy experienced some deep vicissitudes few compa-nies managed to exploit their acquisition strategy effectively.

Although trading circumstances clearly affected prospects in the mid-1970s, another interpretation of falling merger activity is 'disillusion with the exaggerated hopes of earlier merger strategies' (Hannah, 1983; 153), and evidently the disappointing results associated with earlier combinations would have persuaded senior executives in favour of greater moderation. One might also add that the major firms had evidently reached such a scale by the early-1970s that directors no longer felt as threatened by potential takeover bids, reducing the level of uncertainty which had been a major influence on the earlier merger waves. Indeed, Hannah (1983; 155) has explained how an important feature of merger activity after 1970 was the propensity of firms to sell off subsidiaries, creating 'an active and fluid market' which allowed 'some unwise conglomerate diversifications to be unscrambled, and generally enabled more rational (and perhaps more anti-competitive) horizontal matches to be made'. This re-emphasises the vital importance of horizontal combination to British businessmen, and it is interesting to note how subsidiary sales were particularly buoyant after periods of depression (for example in 1970–1971, 1975–1976 and 1982–1983), when they accounted for approximately thirty per cent of all mergers (George, Joll & Lynk, 1991; 85–7),

The decline in merger activity combined with a growing propensity to sell off troublesome subsidiaries is indicative of the weak organisational response made by British businessmen to their expansive strategies. 'Big is beautiful' was certainly a popular belief from the early-1950s, and this encouraged the creation of large-scale firms which were more integrated, more diversified and more geographically dispersed than their predecessors. Nevertheless, organisational innovation proved to be woefully inadequate in dealing with this new type of firm, and interestingly many of the 1970s and 1980s subsidiary sales were to local management teams, sparking the emergence of a new phenomenon in British business, the 'management buy-out' (MBO). The MBO was pioneered in the USA, where it is known as a 'leveraged buy-out', and brought to the UK by Investors in Industry (3i), a venture capital firm concerned with financing small and medium-sized businesses (Carter, 1988; 126). Approximately sixty MBO's were effected in the 1970s, but during the 1980s there were almost 200 each year, and by 1985 their value had exceeded £1,000 million. More importantly, MBO's would appear to have produced better results than other types of merger (Kay, 1993; 155), indicating how the British business culture was much more at home in smaller enterprises than in the big firms which emerged after 1950. This conclusion ignores the success stories of ICI and GEC related in section 6.2, not to mention the multinational enterprises we shall examine later. However, it is a sad indictment of the strategies pursued over the post-war period, begging important questions about the ability of key decision makers to organise the firms they created.

The corporate shake-out and new trends

Negative impressions are inescapable when reviewing British business history up to the 1970s, and as Alford (1988; 66) argues: 'Major shortcomings in company organisation and management have been at the centre of Britain's unsatisfactory economic performance'. Indeed, the economic difficulties of the post-1973 period witnessed a major corporate shake-out of those firms which were simply incapable of coping with the chill winds of intensive domestic and international competition. Millward (1994; 124–32) describes how by the 1970s the economy in general was experiencing a process of deindustrialisation, as employment in the manufacturing sector declined, along with its contribution to total output and overseas earnings, and in this context we can see how weakly-managed firms disappeared in significant numbers. However, while by the 1980s the British industrial sector was smaller, those firms would prove to be much more capable of withstanding the new pressures, especially those which had developed a strong international dimension. Similarly, the services sector experienced a period of dramatic growth from the late-1970s, and we shall see later the City of London especially prospered. It was these multinational and service sector businesses which went on to provide the nucleus of a more dynamic corporate sector in the 1980s and 1990s, and when combined with the acceptance of new political attitudes associated with reasserting managerial prerogatives in the workplace and stimulating entrepreurship through tax incentives one can see clear evidence of rapid business development (Brittan, 1989; 4–7).

One of the key issues affecting British economic performance over the last hundred years has been a relatively poor productivity record, and especially after 1945 managers were accused of hiding behind the sellers' market of the post-war period and refusing to take the hard decisions necessary which would have overhauled production practices (Clutterbuck & Crainer, 1988; 11–3). The Donovan Commission which examined industrial relations in the late-1960s had concluded that, while trade unions were reluctant to relinquish traditional workshop practices, the main reason for sluggish productivity performance and the increasing number of short, unofficial 'wildcat' strikes was the failure of management to introduce the most recent innovations in labour and production control (Hawkins, 1976; 194–6). Industrial relations had been experiencing a major transformation over the post-war period, largely as a result of the full employment economy which persisted through to the early-1970s. This resulted in a system which favoured workplace bargaining, rather than the collective bargaining arrangements formerly conducted by employers' asssociations and trade union leaders, giving local union officials, especially the shop steward, much greater power over the workforce. Clearly, though, management failed to respond effectively to the new situation, and control of the shopfloor continued to remain in union hands as a result of this weakness. British Leyland was perhaps the most-quoted example of this anarchic situation, because the 400 separate bargaining units covering 170,000 employees worked with a payment system which had been in existence since the inter-war years, limiting the ability of management to implement new ideas (Lewchuk, 1987; 206–10).

The industrial relations situation was evidently a major problem up to the 1970s, but after the major corporate shake-out just described one can begin to discern a growing realisation among executives that new approaches could be tried, once a fundamental revision of attitudes and traditions had been effected. The reform of industrial relations legislation in 1980, 1982 and 1984 certainly undermined trade union influence and power, while the significant rise in unemployment to over three million by 1983 also created considerable uncertainty within the workforce (Roberts, 1989; 65–74). This allowed management the opportunity to reassert its position in the workplace, and with the substantial decline in strike activity by the mid-1980s there had been a dramatic improvement in productivity (Pollard, 1992; 398). Some of this improvement can be attributed to the loss of employment in the manufacturing sector, from 7.1 million in June 1979 to 5.1 million in June 1987, a trend partly caused by the closure of many of the least efficient firms. On the other hand, Richardson (1992; 441) emphasises how the 'combination of job redesign, scrapping of custom and practice, new manning levels, increased flexibility, reduced demarcation, and increased effort' provided further signs of a much-changed environment. The defeat of the National Union of Mineworkers (NUM) in a lengthy dispute in 1984–1985 perhaps epitomised the new situation, particularly as this union had twice humiliated previous Conservative governments (in 1972 and 1974). This indicates how the pendulum had by then swung decisively in favour of management, although one might also add that an American, Ian MacGregor, had been recruited as chairman of the National Coal Board, revealing the high profile given to foreign businessmen in the 1980s.

British Leyland and Michael Edwardes

An excellent example of how management was beginning to change its approach can be found in British Leyland. This firm had been one of the most unsuccessful mergers of the late-1960s (see section 6.3), principally because its chief executive, Donald Stokes, had failed to integrate the activities of its main constituents and impose an effective M-form structure in 1970. After British Leyland's collapse in 1975 and its nationalisation, the enterprise was passed to the new Labour government's agent for industrial intervention, the National Enterprise Board (NEB), and while substantial government aid was provided much of this money simply went into subsidising losses (and jobs). In fact, it was not until the appointment in 1977 of Sir Michael Edwardes as chief executive that fundamental changes were made to the organisation (Edwardes, 1983; 36–59). As head of Chloride, the main battery supplier to British Leyland, and a member of the NEB, Edwardes was well placed to observe the problems which had dogged the car firm's progress since 1968, and while his strategy was no doubt heavily dependent upon continued state aid he was also able to reinvigorate the management. Not only did he boldly confront the trade unions and terminate many of the old workshop practices, he also restructured the business, splitting the car division (BL) from the trucks and buses. More importantly, Edwardes wanted to change the management culture within the firm, insisting on a smaller board of just six, compared to Stokes' fourteen, and delegating responsibility to managers who were hand-picked after extensive pyschological assessments. There has been criticism of BL's 'market-led failure', and the new cars introduced in 1981 ('metro') and 1983 ('maestro') were initially produced in insufficient numbers either to cover total charges or boost market share (Church, 1994; 105). Similarly, output per employee was only just beginning to reach the levels achieved in 1968, of 5.6 cars per employee per annum, because the introduction of a new payments system (measured day work) to replace the old incentive scheme had created severe staffing problems (Lewchuk, 1987; 214–20). On the other hand, in organisational and industrial relations terms, the business had experienced a period of fundamental change which was symptomatic of the general changes affecting many sectors over this period, indicating how fresh management was beginning to adopt new approaches to what had been up to the 1970s major obstacles to improved performance.

Another vital point to make about BL's revitalisation after its sad demise in 1975, as well as the defeat of the NUM in 1985, was the use of foreign expertise. In this context, one must emphasise that as a South African Sir Micheal Edwardes was not shackled by the traditions of what we noted earlier was a highly conservative British business culture. Similarly, his successor, Graham Day, was a Canadian who had previously been recruited by the Conservative government to reorganise the loss-making nationalised enterprise, British Shipbuilders. It was under Day's management that BL was split up and sold off in parts, the car division (now renamed Rover) going in 1988 to British Aerospace for what was regarded as a paltry sum, £150 million (Church, 1994; 106–7). The most notable development of the Edwardes/Day era, however, was the collaborative deal signed with the Japanese car giant Honda in 1979, and much of the technological and commercial success achieved by Rover since the early-1980s has been a direct consequence of this relationship. This was a further reflection of the most important trend affecting business across the world by the 1970s, the internationalisation of production, and the British car industry provides a classic illustration of how global co-operation was becoming the hallmark of market exploitation.

British multinationals and internationalisation trends

Of course, ever since its creation in 1967, Ford of Europe had developed a co-operative strategy based on collaboration between its operations in Britain and West Germany, and by 1979 General Motors (operating through its British subsidiary, Vauxhall) had also rationalised along similar lines (Church, 1994; 107–11). This new trend was known either as 'sourcing' or 'networking', by which different parts of the final product are manufactured in various countries, and brought together for final assembly in another country. By the 1980s, all major car producers had built global systems based on this classic example of the internationalisation of production (Walshe, 1992; 374–9). Indeed, between 1950 and 1962, 364 foreign subsidiaries were implanted in the UK, over 300 of which were American, indicating how the high-growth sectors like automobiles, office machinery and electrical goods were already taking on an international flavour (Bostock & Jones, 1994; 110–7). This trend has also shown no signs of abating, and more recently Japanese firms have assisted substantially in rejuvenating the electronics and automobile industries (Trevor, 1987; 13–26). For example, in the 1980s two major Japanese car manufaturers (Nissan and Honda) established plants in the UK, contributing significantly to the recent dramatic renaissance experienced by this industry. It is also interesting to note that after BMW purchased Rover Cars from British Aerospace in 1993, the entire British industry had passed into foreign ownership. Likewise, many vital industries like electronics and petro-chemicals were by the 1980s dominated by multinational companies which owed no particular allegiance to a single country (Bostock & Jones, 1994; 89). Nevertheless, it was vital that British firms should participate in this global race for supremacy, given what Cantwell (1989; 18–23) describes as the emergence after 1945 of 'global capitalism', or 'the rapid growth of international economic interdependence'. At the same time, as long as these subsidiaries continued to provide both employment and a major contribution to Britain's balance of payments the situation need not cause too much concern, but clearly the 'Britishness' in British industry was declining dramatically by the 1980s.

Another crucial point to make with regard to the internationalisation of British business was the historical tendency of many large-scale British firms to develop into multinationals (Stopford, 1974; 303), and in the post-war period this has shown no sign of abating. Indeed, there is a tremendous increase in British foreign direct investment (fdi), but it is important to note that significant changes occurred in both the geographical distribution of this activity and, crucially, the management structures developed by the leading firms. Up to 1939, of course, British fdi had exceeded any other economy (see section 5.2), but many have been critical of both the poor returns reaped by parent companies and the ineffective organisations used to control far-flung subsidiaries located mostly in 'safe' Empire markets (Jones, 1986; 13–20). It is also important to note that up to the 1960s British multinational activity retained these characteristics, and Stopford & Turner (1985; 68) have likened them to outmoded 'battleships [which] were in the wrong industries and wrong countries'. Furthermore, while the world's total fdi reached over $94,000 million by 1967, the American share (50.4 per cent) far exceeded that of the UK (14.1 per cent), even though the latter was actually the second largest (Bostock & Jones, 1994; p.2).

This weakening position was yet another manifestation of the problems facing British business up to the 1970s, but it is vitally important to note that crucial changes to both geographical and product directions of multinational strategy had already started to appear during the 1960s. In the first place, much more attention was paid to the expanding European markets in the 1960s and 1970s, while Hamill (1988; 2–17) has revealed how the acquisition of American firms, especially by conglomerate holding companies (see below), has been the dominant tendency over the last fifteen years. Similarly, manufacturing also replaced services and primary production as the major contributor to British fdi (Stopford & Turner, 1985; 8–10, 69 *passim*). Furthermore, much greater co-ordination between parent and subsidiaries has become evident, leading to the elaboration of truly multinational organisations capable of overcoming the many barriers to improved profitability (Jones, 1986; 15). More recently, the service sector has once again reasserted its old position as the major contributor to British fdi, because banks and other financial institutions, along with hotels and advertising agencies, have been building up global empires. Nevertheless, British multinationals like BP and Shell in petrochemicals, RTZ and Consolidated Gold in extractive activity, Glaxo and SmithKline Beecham in drugs and toiletries, and ICI and Unilever in chemicals and food, have realised that 'global survival calls for strategies which combine geographical, technological and marketing factors' (Stopford & Turner, 1985; 264). This helps to explain why British fdi has contined to increase over the last twenty years, and by 1990 it accounted for no less than 25.1 per cent of the UK economy's gross domestic output, compared to 7.9 per cent in the USA and 6.8 per cent in Japan. Of course, the American and Japanese economies are much larger than the UK's, but such a rate of investment is indicative of the strengthened belief in overseas activity as a key to competitiveness.

A good example of how British multinationals were beginning to improve their management structure was ICI. Indeed, since its creation in 1926 ICI has consistently been regarded as perhaps the most important flagship of British business, providing a model for other businesses to follow. Very early on, under the direction of Sir Harry McGowan and Sir Alfred Mond (later Lord Melchett), ICI had succeeded in creating a single entity out of its four major constituents (see section 5.2), and in the 1930s became the first British M-form (Reader, 1975). Admittedly, the M-form was only a crude imitation of its American counterparts like Du Pont, and its chairman up to 1950, Lord McGowan, was regarded as an autocratic leader who was reluctant to delegate much responsibility to divisional managers (Channon, 1973; 142–4). One should also note how ICI tended to be dominated by scientists, but the appointment as chairman in 1960 of Paul Chambers, a former civil servant, brought a new approach to management. Chambers had been finance director at ICI since 1948, and he was committed to breaking down the old allegiance to technology-led strategies, emphasising how the management culture would change dramatically from the 1960s. As Chambers said at the time of ICI's unsuccesful bid for Courtaulds in 1962 (see section 6.3): 'We must see . . . that our whole organisation is sensitive to growth and sensitive to change. We have changed from a narrow technical approach to a broad commercial approach'. However, even though in 1962 the American consultants McKinsey & Co. were called in to advise on a substantial reform, 'the style and mode of operation of the main board and the broad corporate culture of ICI were remarkably resistant to change throughout the 1960s and 1970s' (Pettigrew, 1985; 72). Nevertheless, Chambers was able to initiate a process of greater decentralisation which was substantially augmented after 1973 when John Harvey-Jones became an executive director in charge of organisation and services, substantially improving ICI's organisational effectiveness (Pettigrew, 1985; 395–425). Harvey-Jones was particularly successful in introducing organisational development (OD) into ICI, indicating how some of the more successful firms were utilising highly advanced management techniques in coping with international competition.

Of course, not all British multinationals were as successful as ICI, and one must remember the case of Dunlop, a firm which had been one of the earliest to venture abroad. By 1985, however, becasue of its failure 'to build a sustainable global business', Dunlop had been acquired by the same Japanese firm it had helped to establish a rubber-manufacturing plant as long ago as 1909, Sumitomo (Stopford & Turner, 1985; 5). Nevertheless, the realisation evident in the strategies pursued by many British multinationals has over the last twenty years provided the British economy with a stronger corporate sector capable of meeting foreign competition head on in world markets, and to some extent this has helped to banish the old attitudes which had been such an obstacle to improved performance. One might refer in this context to firms like Glaxo, which, while originally being a New Zealand manufacturer of milk powder, evolved into a British pharmaceutical multinational during the 1920s, establishing subsidiaries in both Empire and other economies (Davenport-Hines, 1986b; 137–61). By 1993 Glaxo featured among the top ten European companies, according to a measure based on company performance (*Management Today*, 1993; 66), and in 1992 its total sales of health-care goods ($7,209,000 million) ranked seventh in the world (*Med-Ad-News*, 1993; 10). Even larger than Glaxo in this field was SmithKline Beecham, at third (with sales of $9,133,000 million), a company which was only created in 1989 after Bob Baumann merged the British firm of Beechams (already a major multinational) with the American counterpart SmithKline. Along with other successful British multinationals like Reuters, Cable & Wireless, Wellcome and Rothmans, these firms were among the most successful in Europe, providing a solid base for future development.

This evidence of aggressive expansion by multinationals is a crucial manifestation of the changes affecting British business over the last thirty years. Of course, one might argue that the reduction in national ownership of major industries and firms had gone much further in this country, especially in eliminating the 'Britishness' of even the largest and most successful businesses. This was not only the case among the multinationals, but increasing concern could be expressed at other leading firms losing their national identity. For example, not only was Rover linked with Honda, and later BMW, by the mid-1980s GEC was also heavily involved in a host of ventures with the French firm, Thomson, and ICL had established links with the Japanese computer giant Fujitsu (Ferry, 1993; 234–44); while since the late-1960s British Aerospace has collaborated in several military and civil European projects (Gardner, 1981; 140–8, 217–22, 252–8). Nevertheless, in the new global marketplace, made smaller by the introduction of highly sophisticated satellite communication systems, such partnerships are crucial to survival, and British management is very much involved in the internationalisation process. It is a movement which bucks the trends described in previous chapters, and indeed those outlined in the analysis of post-war merger strategy, marking the beginning of a new era for British business which is characterised by stronger management and improved organisation. In this context, one should also mention the successful branded and packaged goods manufacturers, because we have seen consistent evidence of good performance in this sector since the late-nineteenth century (see section 4.3). By 1993, five UK companies (Grand Metropolitan, RHM, Cadbury Schweppes, Allied Lyons, and Associated British Foods) were among the ten most profitable food producers in Europe (*Grocer*, 1993; 15), while other successful firms like Guiness and Argyll have kept pace with new moves in what is a fast-moving sector.

Mergers and the conglomerate

The internationalisation of British business in the last twenty years has clearly been one of the most important developments in the history of this sector, and there seems little doubt that it has improved the performance of many firms, in spite of the more difficult trading circumstances of the last twenty years. However, it is important to place this in context, because other trends were apparent at exactly the same time which qualify to some extent any optimistic interpretation of recent British business evolution. Indeed, going hand in hand with the process of internationalisation was another increasingly dominant characteristic of British business by the 1980s, the rise of the conglomerate. To a significant extent, as we saw in section 6.4, large-scale companies had been diversifying and integrating since the 1960s, and Channon (1973; 67) indicates how the number of firms with Related and Unrelated product ranges increased significantly between 1950 and 1970 (see Table 6.3). By the 1980s, however, Utton (1982; 24–5) reveals that such had been the extent of diversification that the largest 200 firms operated equally in at least three or four industries, while many of these firms had plants in every one of the 120 different industry categories. Walshe (1991; 350) has also illustrated how from the early-1970s conglomerate style mergers consistently accounted for at least twenty per cent of acquisitions, while in certain years (1972, 1985 and 1988) this proportion rose to fifty per cent. This makes it increasingly difficult to classify individual companies, as Wardley (1991; 280–8) has noted, but by 1985 there were seven conglomerates among the top fifty British companies, including Hanson Trust (with a market value of £2,522.3 million) and Trafalgar House (£1,130.2 million). Most mergers since the 1950s had been associated with horizontal concentration, but clearly the scope of business activity had changed fundamentally by the 1980s.

It is also important to emphasise how, as Table 6.4 reveals, expenditure on mergers increased substantially after 1984, rising to yet another all-time record of £24,592 million in 1988 (at 1987 prices). Even at the height of the late-1960s and early-1970s mergers, this figure had never exceeded £14,000 million, but between 1986 and 1989 annual expenditure averaged almost £21,000 million, while in 1984 and 1985 it was higher than in any other year except 1968 and 1972. Firms were clearly engaged in a huge 'merger mania', committing between 1986 and 1989 on average fifty-four per cent of all gross domestic capital formation to acquisitions, compared to the previous peak of forty-three per cent over the period 1967–1973 (George, Joll & Lynk, 1991; 84–7). This in itself is interesting, but the surge was also noticable for another reason, because it was associated with the absorption of very large firms by equally big predators. Previously it had been felt that large, diversified firms were immune to takeover pressures, because of the managerial problems associated with absorbing such unwieldy acquisitions. This is similar to the sentiments expressed during the inter-war period, when contemporaries complained about the shortage of managers capable of controlling large firms. However, by the mid-1980s British businessmen were clearly much more confident of their ability, after having learnt much more from American firms and consultants about the available techniques (Guterl, 1989; 63–6), and consequently household names like Imperial Tobacco, Coats Patons, Distillers, and Debenhams were absorbed into other giants.

It is important to note, though, that in charting the rise of the British conglomerates this form of business has often been associated with a form of speculation in which entrepreneurs pursue a ruthless strategy of asset-stripping as a means of transferring wealth from one group of shareholders to another. Hanson Trust demonstrates this trend extremely well, because its senior executives, James Hanson and George White, have systematically acquired low technology businesses with large market shares (bricks, coal, cement, cigarettes and batteries) and sold off lucrative subsidiaries or set tough targets for their managers. This naturally ensures a steady flow of profits into the central fund, which in turn is used to buy more firms. As one televison programme noted: 'The money pouring in for Hanson shareholders comes from numerous sources, but *not* the growth of the industries in his care' (Hampden-Turner & Trompenaars, 1993; 318). This programme was entitled 'The Lords of Decline', and perhaps it encapsulated the point made by Sampson (1992; 122), that British conglomerates 'are too pre-occupied with short-term profits to think much about wider responsibilities to culture and communities'. It was an approach which contrasted sharply with the methods employed in Japanese *keiretsu*, because as we saw in section 5.1 these organisations were based on co-operation and integration as a means of improving a firm's competitiveness.

The 'Big Bang' and merger activity

In attempting to explain the renewed interest in mergers after 1983, it is important to refer to global trends, because British business was being affected by 'merger mania' after 1984 in much the same way as the USA, and especially by the desire to create greater markets for corporate control (Chandler, 1992; 26–9). More importantly, the major reorganisation of Britain's financial markets at the end of 1986, or what has passed into the language as the 'Big Bang' (Thomas, 1986; 1–9), must be regarded as the major stimulus. This confirms our earlier point that merger activity was primarily based on the need to sustain the growing market for corporate control which arose out of the divorce between control and ownership. George, Joll and Lynk (1991; 85–6) have also argued that the state of financial markets is a key influence on merger activity, and certainly after 1986 the City of London was ready to embark on an orgy of financial speculation. The most obvious change was the introduction of computerised dealing, and the old floor of the Stock Exchange was abandoned for serried banks of screens connected to a master machine which would provide as much information as the market-makers required (Thomas, 1986; 162–3). Crucially, though, the 'Big Bang' was associated with the abolition of long outmoded regulations which, as we noted in section 6.1, had been constraining the Stock Exchange's operations. In particular, minimum commission rates were outlawed and the distinction between brokers and jobbers terminated (Kay, 1988; 144–7). Another important reform allowed Stock Exchange firms to be run by organisations which were not members of that institution, providing banks, insurance companies and foreign investment houses (including the world's largest, Nomura from Japan and Merrill Lynch from the USA) with direct access to the market. Kay (1988; 146) exaggerates when he claims that the 'old school tie has been shredded and the "Old Pals Act" repealed in the post-Big Bang era', because senior positions in the major financial institutions are still populated by the same people who have traditionally held such posts. On the other hand, many City practices were revolutionised by the 'Big Bang', and up to 1991 the City witnessed a period of rapid expansion.

Another significant aspect of the 'Big Bang' was its impact on institutional investors, because computerisation has significantly enhanced the fund manager's ability to rate funds accurately, providing the opportunity to pursue profit maximisation even more intensely than they had in the past. By 1983, of the total capital marketed on the London Stock Exchange, institutional investors held sixty-five per cent of the loan capital and fifty-five per cent of the ordinary shares (Thomas, 1986; 16–9), creating a situation in which firms were obliged to protect themselves against takeover threats by pursuing short-term strategies aimed at encouraging shareholder loyalty. As Nigel Lawson noted in 1986, when he was Conservative chancellor of the exchequer, 'the big institutional investors react to short-term pressure on investment performance' (Clutterbuck & Crainer, 1988; 313). Kay (1988; 146) has also argued that after the 'Big Bang' an even greater emphasis on this approach was necessary because of the greater accuracy of asset valuation. This might even suggest that the divorce between control and ownership, which had been evident since the 1940s, was beginning to reverse by the 1970s, such was the increased influence of institutional investors over management. It was this pressure which was making even successful and highly diversified firms vulnerable to takeover bids, and when this activity is aimed simply at speculative gain one can seriously question its economic viability.

Another feature of City practices which must be examined was the continued presence of questionable practices like insider trading and artificial share dealing prior to a takeover bid, practices which have badly tarnished the City's reputation (Fallon and Sroder, 1987; 269–82). One might remember that the City has always operated as a kind of 'gentlemen's club', and that information is freely transmitted through the usual avenues of lunch and drinks meetings. On the other hand, insider trading has since 1980 been illegal, but Hilton (1987; 84–7) has demonstrated how share prices still have a tendency to rise significantly during what ought to be secret takeover bid negotiations. The most dramatic instance of such dubious practices came in 1986, when an estimated £300 million was used to inflate the price of Guiness shares in order to ease its acquisition of the Scotch whisky group Distillers. Furthermore, just as in our earlier analysis of company performance after mergers, one can find little evidence that the mid-1980s surge benefitted the firms concerned in the short-term, undermining further attempts by management to compete in the global marketplace (Fallon & Sroder, 1987; 282).

The role of government: mergers and privatisation

Disregarding the internationalisation process described earlier, the increased intensity of merger activity after 1984 was one of the most obvious signs of change affecting British business in the last decade. Once again, though, it is evident that, just as in the 1950s and 1960s, competition policy proved to be largely benign. In 1973 a further attempt to tighten up on trading abuses was made, when the Fair Trading Act was passed, extending the criterion for reference by the Minister to what was now known as the Monopolies and

Mergers Commission (MMC) from one-third to one-quarter of the market, and creating a Director General of Fair Trading who was responsible for restrictive practices at the new Office of Fair Trading (Swann et al, 1974; 215–23). The service sector was also brought within the ambit of this legislation in 1976, under the Restrictive Trade Practices (Services) Order, while a Competition Act in 1980 provided the MMC with authority to investigate nationalised industries. This reveals how the continued fight against restrictive practices had featured prominently in successive governments' attempts to encourage greater competition, but as Walshe (1992; 350–70) illustrates very little was done to prevent the huge number of mergers which led to much greater levels of horizontal combination. In fact, over the period 1973–88 4,167 mergers qualified for reference to the MMC, the vast majority of which were horizontal in nature, but only three per cent were actually investigated, and even then in two cases out of five no action was taken. We noted in section 6.4 how concentration levels had stabilised during the 1970s, and although evidence for the 1980s has so far not been calculated it seems unlikely that it would have increased further, especially given the increase in import penetration from 16.6 per cent of domestic demand in 1970 to 35.2 per cent by 1987 (Crafts & Woodward, 1992; 16). However, management had been allowed to build up either oligopolistic or even monopolistic market positions without too much interference from statutory bodies like the MMC. This provided what Walshe (1992; 379) tentatively describes as 'a cushion for managerial incompetence and induced managerial sloth, leading to general losses in industrial efficiency'.

This conclusion might well stand as an indictment of post-war competition policy in general, and it is striking that successive governments have been willing to undermine trade association activity, while at the same time implicitly encourage horizontal combination which has substantially increased industrial concentration levels. However, after the election in 1979 of a Conservative government committed to reducing substantially the size of Britain's public sector – by 1979 nationalised industries employed over two million people and accounted for ten per cent of total output – one can discern some decisive attempts at encouraging greater competition in certain parts of the economy by 'privatising' government-owned industries and firms. Dunkerley and Hare (1991; 409–16) have demonstrated how nationalisation had to a large extent been employed as a solution to pressing problems in ailing industries, but the Conservatives were convinced that the 'feather-bedding' of management, by preventing the possibility of bankruptcy, was stifling enterprise. This government had also promised substantial income tax reductions, and between 1979 and 1990 total asset sales worth almost £28,500 million were made or planned for this purpose, providing the Treasury with an opportunity to balance the books. On the other hand, given what many people regarded as the low price at which share prices were set, one might argue that much more money could have been raised from the privatisation programme, but such a discussion inevitably moves us into the realm of political decision-making, and this must not distract us from our main theme.

In fact, the privatisation programme started very hesitantly, and by the 1983 general election only 6.2 per cent of the £28,500 million had been raised, but thereafter share issues continued apace. One of the largest privatisations was British Telecom in 1984, and Wardley (1991; 280) has calculated that by 1985 this firm was Britain's largest in terms of market value, at £12,780 million. British Petroleum was the second largest (at £9,496 million), after the government had sold its majority shareholding in three tranches between 1979 and 1984. Further down this list of top fifty companies comes Cable & Wireless at fourteenth (£2,340 million), after similar share issues in 1981, 1983 and 1985, while from 1985 other giants like British Gas (1986), the Rover Group (formerly British Leyland cars) (1988), and the electricity supply industry (1991) all found themselves back in the private sector. It was a massive programme aimed principally at reinvigorating the respective managements, and government established a series of regulatory bodies – for example the Office of Gas Supply (OFGAS) and the Office of Telecommunications (OFTEL) – to ensure that those large businesses which possessed a virtual monopoly over their markets would not exploit their customers. However, while some of the firms which were transferred back to private ownership, for example Ferranti, Amersham International and the Rover Group, performed effectively in the 1980s, there is little evidence that former nationalised industries were more productive after privatisation (George, Joll & Lynk, 1991; 353–61).

The City's influence

It is perhaps too soon to analyse the performance of this privatisation programme, particularly as many of the new firms are still coming to terms with the managerial and organisational consequences of their metamorphosis. In one sense, though, there is general disquiet, because the salaries of many executives in the newly-privatised sector leapt considerably, as did salaries in most boardrooms. These increases were justified by arguing that British business needed to recruit good managers if it was to compete in the global marketplace, but few believed this, and Sampson (1992; 109–15) regards the trend as a further manifestation of the 'high-handedness' so typical of British senior executives. One might well bear in mind, though, what we have been discussing in earlier sections, that as private companies they were now vulnerable to exactly the same financial pressures as their counterparts, and in particular the need to maintain shareholder loyalty. This reveals how privatisation was simply another feature of the post-war period's most important business trend, namely, the growing influence of the City over British business. Indeed, the major merchant banks participated extensively in the privatisation share issues, earning substantial commissions from what were the largest flotations of the era. Their task was made easy by the generous prices at which shares were set, not to mention the extensive advertising campaigns, but this partnership was indicative of the role played by financial institutions in directing much of what happens in British business. By the late-1980s, considerable concern was being expressed in particular about the role played by institutional investors and their influence on business strategy, especially in relation to investment and research. A Confederation of British Industry (CBI) task-force actually concluded in 1987 that these bodies were not responsible for business taking a short-termist approach towards investment and research. On the other hand, this would appear to contradict much of the evidence compiled by Clutterbuck & Crainer (1988; 311–27), who emphasise poor communication between the City and its clients as a major problem. This was a point reinforced by the Wilson Committee (examining the role of financial institutions in the late-1970s), because it concluded that the main problem would appear to have been the widely held preconceptions about the City, rather than any actual practices perpetrated by leading financial institutions.

Conclusion

It is easy, of course, to point an accusing finger at an elitist group of allegedly greedy speculators whose wealth is accumulated at the expense of other sectors in the economy, and as we saw in section 2.4 this exercise has been going on since the 1760s and 1770s when 'stockjobbers' were accused of disrupting the economy (Bowen, 1992; 38–53). On the other hand, one must not regard businessmen as passive agents in this relationship, because as the CBI task-force also concluded: 'Many British companies have given insufficient weight to long-term development [due to] underlying economic and political factors, including inadequate profitability' (Clutterbuck & Crainer, 1988; 322). In other words, the quality of British management must be a central issue in this debate, and as we have argued consistently throughout this study one can question the extent to which both the key decision makers and their subordinates were capable of matching many of their foreign counterparts. There could well have been rational reasons why up to the 1940s business organisation in Britain was very different to the conventions adopted in, for example, the USA, Germany and Japan. For example, the heavy transaction costs involved in internalising many functions which were carried on efficiently by a host of intermediaries and the weak commercial pressures to use mass-production methods played a significant role in the determination of business methods. However, the substantial increase in operational scale and the pursuit of vertical integration or diversification after 1950 brought new organisational challenges, but this chapter has revealed how many firms proved incapable of adapting structure to strategy. The exceptions to this rule would appear to have been powerful multinationals like BP, Shell, RTZ and Glaxo, as well as those companies forging international partnerships with foreign firms.

There is no doubt that, in dealing with the severe problems arising from stagnating international trade, by the 1980s Britain's business culture had changed dramatically, and the firms developing a strong international dimension had clearly led the way in breaking the old mould. It was companies like this which were using the business schools more extensively for both post-experience training of their existing managers, and to recruit new managers with the increasingly-respectable Master of Business Administration degree (MBA). Qualified people were, indeed, beginning to find their way into senior positions by the mid-1980s (Wilson, 1992; 59, 133–7). Sampson (1992; 113) reveals how the 'old boy' network still exists in 1990s boardrooms, but at the same time he also explains how businessmen took on a ruthles streak, priding themselves on how their firms had become 'leaner and fitter'. Other observers are also positive about the signs of a greater awakening to the competitive challenges of the 1980s and 1990s (Clutterbuck & Crainer, 1988; 350–3: Ferry, 1993; xi), and the revival in fortunes of the Rover Group (foremerly British Leyland's car operations) can be used as an example of this surge forward. Of course, one might point out that even though the performance of this particular company was undoubtedly better by the late-1980s (under the management of a Canadian, Graham Day), it only held thirteen per cent of the British car market by 1988, compared to British Leyland's fifty per cent share in 1968. Similarly, import penetration has only fallen over the last decade because Japanese manufacturers like Nissan and Honda have started producing cars in this country.

There is clearly no single conclusion one can draw from this brief study of British business in the 1990s, because while on the one hand there are striking examples of world leaders among the multinationals (Stopford & Turner, 1985; 264–5), conversely many problems remain in terms of attitudes at the most senior levels (Sampson, 1992; 114–5). One might also mention in this context the dominance achieved by overseas interests in key industries like automobiles, electronics and office machinery, emphasising how the 'Britishness' of many firms has been marginalised. Of course, as we noted earlier, the internationalisation of production so evident over the last thirty years was forcing British firms to participate in this process, and ties with foreign firms, for example between ICL and Fujitsu (Campbell-Kelly, 1989; 340–2), has substantially improved competitiveness. On the other hand, such alliances have often been forced on industries by inherent weaknesses in both their strategies and structures, and in this context the continuity evident in the British business culture and its impact on managerial attitudes undoubtedly played a major role in undermining performance. Notwithstanding these points, developing an international dimension, whether by forging alliances or establishing overseas operations, would appear to be the key to survival and financial strength. Of course, the demise of Dunlop quoted earlier indicates how this strategy did not always provide a cast-iron guarantee of success, but this case also emphasises the crucial importance of matching structure to strategy, and many British firms were beginning to realise this from the 1980s. Referring specifically to Ferry's (1993; ix-xv) claim that there has been a recent dramatic 'renaissance' in British business, we can consequently end this history on a positive note, albeit a note tinged with sadness that such an awakening did not take place fifty years earlier.

Guide to further reading

General works

The only studies of the whole period are provided in P. L. Payne 'Industrial entrepreneurship and management in Great Britain', in P. Mathias & M. M. Postan (eds), *The Cambridge Economic History* of Europe, VII, Part I (1978), and in the pamphlet by C. J. Schmitz, *The Growth of Big Business in the United States and Western Europe*, 1850–1939 (1993). S. Pollard, *The Genesis of Modern Management* (1965) covers the early years leading up to 1840, and the twentieth century is examined by L. Hannah, *The Rise of the Corporate Economy* (1983). A source for the period 1880–1950 is A. D. Chandler, *Scale and Scope* (1990), but as we have noted in section 1.2 care must be taken with the perspective adopted by this American scholar. Other useful sources for the twentieth century are L. Hannah (ed) *Management Strategy and Business Development. An Historical and Comparative Study* (1976), D. F. Channon, *The Strategy and Structure of British Enterprise* (1973), and J. Ferry, *The British Renaissance. How to Survive and Thrive despite any Recession* (1993). For a statistical overview of big business since 1905, see P. Wardley, 'The anatomy of big business: aspects of corporate development in the twentieth century', *Bus Hist*, XXXIII (1991).

Business culture

This subject has recently been examined in much greater detail, especially by M. C. Casson, 'Entrepreneurship and business culture', and T Corley, 'The entrepreneur: the central issue in business history?', both in J. Brown & M. B. Rose (eds), *Entrepreneurship, Networks and Modern Business* (1983). W. D. Rubinstein, *Capitalism, Culture, and Decline in Britain, 1750–1990* (1993) also examines the broader debate relating to British socio-cultural characteristics, while an international comparison has been attempted in C.

Hampden-Turner & F. Trompenaars, *The Seven Cultures of Capitalism: Value Systems for Creating Wealth in the United States, Britain, Japan, Germany, France, Sweden, and the Netherlands* (1993).

Managerial recruitment and training

This subject is rarely examined in the literature covering the pre-1914 era, although S. Pollard, *The Genesis of Modern Management* (1965) has some useful material on early-nineteenth century industry, while the utility sector is covered by T Gourvish, 'A British business elite: the chief executive managers of the railway industry, 1850–1922', *Business History Review*, XLVII (1973), and by J. F. Wilson, *Lighting the Town* (1991). For the twentieth century, see S. Keeble, *The Ability to Manage* (1992), as well as R. Locke, *Management and Higher Education since* 1940 (1984), and J. F. Wilson, *'The Manchester Experiment': A History of Manchester Business School, 1965–1990* (1992).

Business finance

Here again, there are no general studies for the whole period, but P. Cottrell, *Industrial Finance, 1830–1914* (1980) and W. A. Thomas, *The Finance of British Industry, 1918–1976* (1978) cover many of the most important issues. Similarly, the two-volume study of British Imperialism (1993) by P. Cain & A. G. Hopkins provides useful insights into City practices. For the early period, one should also read F. Creuzet (ed), *Capital Formation in the Industrial Revolution* (1972). The banking sector is well covered in the booklet by M. Collins, *Banks and Industrial Finance in Britain, 1800–1939* (1991), as well as by F. Capie & M. Collins, *Have the Banks Failed British Industry?* (1992), while for merchant banking S. D. Chapman, *The Rise of Merchant Banking* (1984) is the standard source. For more recent developments in the City, see W. A. Thomas, *The Big Bang* (1986), as well as W. Kay, 'Big Bang and after', in R. Heller (ed), *The Complete Guide to Modern Management* (1988).

Multinationals

The most useful work on this crucial subject is J. M. Stopford & L. Turner, *Britain and the Multinationals* (1985), while for the period up to 1939 see J. M. Stopford, 'The origins of British-based multinational manufacturing enterprises', *Business History Review*, XLVIII (1974), and G. Jones 'Origins, management and performance', in G. Jones (ed), *British Multinationals:*

Origins, Management and Performance (1986). Some of the views expressed in these sources are also analysed by S. Nicholas, 'The expansion of British multinational companies: testing for managerial failure', in J. Foreman-Peck (ed), *New perspectives on the Late Victorian Economy. Essays in Quantitative Economic History, 1860–1914* (1991). Statistics on the levels of foreign direct investment can be found in J. Dunning, 'Changes in the level and structure of international production: the last 100 years', in M. Casson (ed), *The Growth of International Business* (1983). See also F. Bostock & G. Jones, 'Foreign multinationals in British manufacturing, 1850–1962', *Bus Hist*, XXXVI (1994) for a study of this activity.

Business abroad

The three countries examined in this study each have an enormous literature, but space limits us to only the most obvious sources. A. D. Chandler, *The Visible Hand* (1977) is the most significant for the USA, while his *Scale and Scope* (1990) exends this analysis to Germany and Britain. The German scene, however, is better revealed in two articles by J. Kocka, 'Entrepreneurs and managers in German industrialisation', in P. Mathias & M. M Postan (eds), *The Cambridge Economic History of Europe*, VII,Part I (1978), and 'The rise of the modern industrial enterprise in Germany', in A. D. Chandler & H. Daems (eds), *Managerial Hierarchies: Comparative Perspectives on the Rise of the Modern Industrial Enterprise* (1980). On Japan, a good introduction is K. Yamamura, 'The industrialisation of Japan: entrepreneurship, ownership and management', in Mathias, P. & Postan, M. M (eds), *The Cambridge Economic History of Europe*, Vol VII, Part II (1978), while more detail on later developments is provided by Y. Suzuki, *Japanese Management Structures, 1920–80* (1991). For a distinctly American view of this economy, see M. W. Fruin, *The Japanese Enterprise System* (1992), to be contrasted with T Yui, ''The enterprise system in Japan: preliminary considerations on internal and external relations', *Japanese Yearbook on Business History*, 8 (1991).

Labour management

The most important source covering workshop management in the period up to 1939 is C. Littler, *The Development of the Labour Process in Capitalist Societies* (1982). Other works of note are E. Hobsbawm, 'The labour aristocracy in nineteenth century Britain', in E. Hobsbawm (ed), *Labouring Men: Studies in the History of Labour* (1964), J. Melling, 'Non-commissioned officers', *Social History* (1980), and H. F. Gospel & C. Littler (eds), *Managerial Strategies and Industrial Relations* (1983). On wider issues, see

R. Fitzgerald, *British Labour Management and Industrial Welfare, 1846–1939* (1988).

Business and the State

L Hannah, *The Rise of the Corporate Economy* (1983) has covered many aspects of this subject for the period 1880–1975, while other useful studies are J. Turner (ed), *Businessmen and Politics. Studies of Business Activity in British Politics, 1900–1945* (1984), and M. A. Utton, *The Political Economy of Big Business* (1982).

Economic theory and business history

Much of this literature will be too theoretical for many readers, but some of the problems are tackled in the two articles by C. Lee (1990), 'Corporate behaviour in theory and history: I. The evolution of theory', *Bus Hist*, XXXII (1990), and 'Corporate behaviour in theory and history: II. The historian's perspective', *Bus Hist*, XXXII (1990). More detailed analyses of the key issues can be found in K. D. George, C. Joll & E. L. Lynk, *Industrial Organisation. Competition, Growth and Structural Change* (1991), or in P. J. Devine *et al* (eds), *An Introduction to Industrial Economics* (1976). One article which is essential reading is R. H. Coase, 'The nature of the firm', *Economica*, IV (1937), raising issues which are further examined in O. E. Williamson, *The Economics of Discretionary Behaviour: Managerial Objectives in a Theory of the Firm* (1964).

Case-studies

The number of business histories has expanded considerably over the last thirty years, but because of space limitations readers are referred to F. Goodall, *A Bibliography of British Business History* (1987) for a cross-referenced (yet incomplete) listing of works on companies and entrepreneurs. Potted biographies are also available in D. J. Jeremy (ed), *The Dictionary of Business Biography*, Vols I-VI (1984–6), and A. Slaven (ed), *Dictionary of Scottish Business Biography*, Vols (1990). Other useful collections can be found in L. Hannah (ed), *Management Strategy and Business Development: An Historical and Comparative Study* (1976), B. Supple (ed), *Essays in British Business History* (1977), and B. Supple (ed), *The Growth of Big Business* (1992).

Bibliography

Where just the name of a town is given, this indicates a university press.

Abbreviations: *Bus Hist – Business History*
      Ec H R – Economic History Review

Aaronson, S. (1992), 'Serving America's business? Graduate business schools and American business, 1945–60', *Bus Hist*, XXXIV, No 1.

Acton Society Trust (1956), *Management Succession: the Recruitment, Selection and promotion of Managers*, Acton Society Trust.

Aldcroft, D. (1964), 'The entrepreneur and the British economy, 1870–1914', *Ec H R*, XII.

Alford, B. W. E. (1973), *W. D. & H. O. Wills and the Development of the UK Tobacco Industry, 1786–1965*, Methuen.

Alford, B. W. E. (1976), 'The Chandler thesis – some general observations', in Hannah, L. (ed), *Management Strategy and Business Development*, Macmillan.

Alford, B. W. E. (1977), 'Entrepreneurship, business performance and industrial development', *Bus Hist*, XIX.

Alford, B. W. E. (1988), *British Economic Performance, 1945–1975*, Macmillan.

Allen, L. A. (1958), *Management and Organisation*, Chapman Hall.

Anderson, B. L. (1969), 'The attorney and the early capital markets in Lancashire', in Harris, J. R. (ed), *Liverpool and Merseyside: Essays in the Economic and Social History of the Port and its Hinterland*, Frank Cass & Co.

Anderson, B. L. (1972), 'The attorneys and the early capital market', in F. Creuzet (ed), *Capital Formation in the Industrial Revolution*, Methuen, 1972.

Anderson, M. L. (1971), *Family Structure in Nineteenth Century Lancashire*, Cambridge.

Armstrong, J. (1990), 'The rise and fall of the company promoter and the financing of British industry', in Van-Helten, J. J. & Cassis, Y. (eds), *Capitalism in a Mature Economy: Financial Institutions, Capital Export and British Industry, 1870–1939*, Edward Elgar.

Ashton, T. S. (1955), *An Economic History of England: the Eighteenth Century*, Manchester.

Ashton, T. S. (1959), 'Business history', *Bus Hist*, I, No 1.

Bamberg, J. H. (1994), *The History of the British Petroleum Co*, Vol II, *The Anglo-Iranian Years, 1928–1954*, Cambridge.

Barley, L. J. (1932), *The Riddle of Rationalisation*, George Allen & Unwin.

Barnes, W. (1989), *Managerial Catalyst: the Story of London Business School, 1964–1989*, Paul Chapman Publishing.

Barnett, C. (1986), *The Audit of War: the Illusion and Reality of Britain as a Great Power*, Macmillan.

Bendix, R. (1956), *Work, Authority and Industry: Ideologies of Management in the Course of Industrialisation*, Wiley, Chapman & Hall.

Berg, M. (1994), 'Factories, workshops and industrial organisation', in Floud, R. & McCloskey, D. (eds), *The Economic History of Britain since 1700*, Vol I, Cambridge.

Berle, A. A. & Means, C. C. (1932), *The Modern Corporation and Private Property*, Macmillan.

Born, K. E. (1983), *International Banking in the Nineteenth and Twentieth Centuries*, Berg Publishers.

Bostock, F. & Jones, G. (1993), 'Foreign multinational investment in the United Kingdom, 1850–1962', mimeo.

Bostock, F. & Jones, G. (1994), 'Foreign multinationals in British manufacturing, 1850–1962', *Bus Hist*, XXXVI, No 1.

Bowden, S. & Collins, M. (1992), 'The Bank of England, industrial regeneration, and hire purchase between the wars', *Ec H R*, XLV.

Bowen, H. V. (1992), '"The Pests of Human Society"; stockbrokers, jobbers and speculators in mid-eighteenth century Britain', *History*, LXXVIII, No 252.

Bowie, J. A. (1930), *Education for Business Management*, Manchester.

Boyce, G. (1992), 'Corporate strategy and accounting systems: a comparison of developments at two British steel firms, 1898–1914', in Harvey, C. & Jones, G. (eds), 'Organisational Capability and Competitive Advantage', Special Issue of *Bus Hist*, XXXIV.

Boyson, R. (1970), *The Ashworth Cotton Enterprise: The Rise and Fall of a Family Firm, 1818–1880*, Oxford.

Braverman, H. (1977), *Labour and Monopoly Capitalism*, Macmillan.

Brittan, S. (1989), 'The Thatcher government's economic policy', in Kavanagh, D. & Seldon, A. (eds), *The Thatcher Effect*, Oxford.

Broadberry, S. N. & Crafts, N. F. R. (1992), 'Britain's productivity gap in the 1930s: some neglected factors', *Journal of Economic History*, 52, No 3.

Brown, J. (1993), 'Success and adversity: entrepreneurship in agricultural engineering, 1800–1939', in Brown, J. & Rose, M. B. (eds), *Entrepreneurship, Networks and Modern Business*, Manchester.

Brown, J. & Rose, M. B. (1993), 'Introduction' to *Entrepreneurship, Networks and Modern Business*, Manchester.

Buchinsky, M. & Polak, B. (1993), 'The emergence of a national capital market in England, 1710–1880', *Journal of Economic History*, 53, March.

Burgess, K. (1975), *The Origins of British Industrial Relations: the Nineteenth Century Experience*, Croom Helm.

Byatt, I. C. R. (1979), *The British Electrical Industry, 1875–1914*, Oxford.

Cain, P. J. & Hopkins, A. G. (1993), *British Imperialism: Innovation and Expansion, 1688–1914*, Longman.

Cain, P. J. & Hopkins, A. G. (1993a), *British Imperialism: Crisis and Deconstruction, 1914–1990*, Longman.

Cairncross, A. K. & Hunter, J. B. K. (1987), 'The early growth of Messrs J. & P. Coats, 1830–1883', *Bus Hist*, Vol 29, No 2.

Calder, K. E. (1993), *Strategic Capitalism: Private Business and Public Purpose in Japanese Industrial Finance*, Princeton.

Campbell, R. H. (1961), *Carron Company*, Edinburgh.

Campbell-Kelly, M. (1989), *ICL: A Business and Technical History*, Oxford.

Cantwell, J. (1989), 'The changing form of multinational expansion in the twentieth century', in Teichova, A, Levy-Leboyer, M. & Nussbaum, H. (eds), *Historical Studies in International Corporate Business*, Cambridge.

Capie, F. & Rodrik-Bali, G. (1982), 'Concentration in British banking, 1870–1920', *Bus Hist*, XXIV.

Capie, F. & Collins, M. (1992), *Have the Banks Failed British Industry?*, Institute of Economic Affairs.

Carswell, J. (1960), *The South Sea Bubble*, Alan Sutton.

Carter, D. (1988), 'The buy-out formula', in Heller, R. (ed), *The Complete Guide to Modern Management*, Harrap.

Carter, G. R. (1913), *The Tendency towards Industrial Combination*, Constable.

Cassis, Y. (1985a), 'Management and strategy in the English joint stock bank, 1890–1914', *Bus Hist*, XXVII.

Cassis, Y. (1985), 'Bankers in English society in the late nineteenth century', *Ec H R*, XXXVIII.

Casson, M. C. (1987), *The Firm and the Market: Studies of Multinational Enterprise and the Scope of the Firm*, Oxford.

Casson, M. C. (1993), 'Entrepreneurship and business culture', in Brown, J. & Rose, M. B. (eds), *Entrepreneurship, Networks and Modern Business*, Manchester.

Central Policy Review Staff [CPRS] (1975), *The Future of the British Car Industry*, HMSO.

Chaloner, W. (1963), *People and Industries*, Frank Cass.

Chandler, A. D. (1962), *Strategy and Structure: Chapters in the History of the Industrial Enterprise*, Cambridge, Mass.

Chandler, A. D. & Daems, H. (1974), 'Introduction – The rise of managerial capitalism and its impact on investment strategy in the Western world and Japan', in Daems, H. & Van der Wee, H. (eds), *The Rise of Managerial Capitalism*, Leuven.

Chandler, A. D. & Daems, H. (1974a), 'Structure and investment decisions in the United States', in Daems, H. & Van der Wee, H. (eds), *The Rise of Managerial Capitalism*, Leuven.

Chandler, A. D. (1976), 'The development of modern management structure in the US and UK', in Hannah, L. (ed), *Management Strategy and Business Development*, Macmillan.

Chandler, A. D. (1977), *The Visible Hand: the Managerial Revolution in American Business*, Cambridge, Mass.

Chandler, A. D. (1980), 'The United States: seedbed of managerial capitalism', in Chandler, A. D. & Daems, H. (eds), *Managerial Hierarchies: Comparative Perspectives on the Rise of the Modern Industrial Enterprise*, Harvard.

Chandler, A. D. (1990), *Scale and Scope: the Dynamics of Industrial Capitalism*, Cambridge, Mass.

Chandler, A. D. (1992), 'Managerial enterprise and competitive capabilities', in Harvey, C. & Jones, G. (eds), 'Organisational Capability and Competitive Advantage', Special Issue of *Bus Hist*, XXXIV.

Channon, D. F. (1973), *The Strategy and Structure of British Enterprise*, Harvard.

Chapman, S. D. (1967), *The Early Factory Masters*, David & Charles.

Chapman, S. D. (1969), 'The Peels in the early English cotton industry', *Bus Hist*, XI.

Chapman, S. D. (1972), *The Cotton Industry in the Industrial Revolution*, Macmillan.

Chapman, S. D. (1974), 'The textile factory before Arkwright: a typology of factory development', *Business History Review*, 48.

Chapman, S. D. (1979), 'Financial restraints on the growth of firms in the cotton industry, 1790–1850', *Ec H R*, XXXII.

Chapman, S. D. (1984), *The Rise of Merchant Banking*, George Allen & Unwin.

Chapman, S. D. (1992), *Merchant Enterprise in Britain: From the Industrial Revolution to World War I*, Cambridge.

Chatfield, M. (1972), *A History of Accounting Thought*, Krieger.

Chatfield, M. (1977), *A History of Accounting Thought*, R. F. Krieger, New York.

Child, J. (1969), *British Management Thought: A Critical Analysis*, George Allen & Unwin.

Church, R. (1993), 'The family firm in industrial capitalism: international perspectives on hypotheses and history', *Bus Hist*, XXXV, No 4.

Church, R. (1994), *The Rise and Decline of the British Motor Industry*, Macmillan.

Clapham, J. (1926), *An Economic History of Modern Britain*, I, Cambridge.

Clapham, J. (1951), *An Economic History of Modern Britain*, III, Cambridge.

Clements, R. V. (1958), *Managers: a Study of their Careers in Industry*, George Allen & Unwin.

Clutterbuck, D. & Crainer, S. (1988), *The Decline and Rise of British Industry*, Mercury Books

Coase, R. H. (1937), 'The nature of the firm', *Economica*, IV.

Coleman, D. C. (1969), *Courtaulds – an Economic and Social History*, Vol I, Oxford.

Coleman, D. C. (1973), 'Gentlemen and Players', *Ec H R*, XXVI.

Coleman, D. C. (1980), *Courtaulds: an Economic and Social History*, Vol II, Oxford.

Coleman, D. C. (1987), 'The uses and abuses of business history', *Bus Hist*, XXIX.

Coleman, D. C. (1987a), 'Failings and achievements: some British businesses, 1910–1980', *Bus Hist*, XXIX, No 4.

Collins, M. (1990), 'English bank lending and the financial crisis of the 1870s', *Bus Hist*, XXXII, No 2.

Collins, M. (1991), *Banks and Industrial Finance in Britain, 1800–1939*, Macmillan.

Constable, T. & McCormick, R. (1987), *The Making of British Managers*, British Institute of Management.

Cook, P. L. (1958), 'The calico printing industry', in Cook, P. L. (ed), *Effects of Mergers: Six Studies*, George Allen & Unwin.

Cooke, T. E. (1986), *Mergers and Acquisitions*, Basil Blackwell.

Cooper, J. (1984), *The Management and Regulation of Banks*, Macmillan.

Copeman, G. (1955), *Leaders of British Industry: a Study of their Careers*, Gee.

Corley, T. A. B. (1989), 'The nature of multinationals, 1870–1939', in Teichova, A, Levy-Leboyer, M. & Nussbaum, H. (eds), *Historical Studies in International Corporate Business*, Cambridge.

Corley, T. A. B. (1993), 'The entrepreneur: the central issue in business history?', in Brown, J. & Rose, M. B. (eds), *Entrepreneurship, Networks and Modern Business*, Manchester.

Corley, T. A. B. (1994), 'Britain's overseas investments in 1914 revisited', *Bus Hist*, XXXVI, No 1.

Cottrell, P. L. (1980), *Industrial Finance, 1830–1914*, Methuen.

Cowling, K. (1980), *Mergers and Economic Performance*, Cambridge.

Crafts, N. F. R. & Woodward, N. W. C. (1992), 'The British economy since 1945: introduction and overview', in Crafts, N. F. R. & Woodward, N. W. C. (eds), *The British Economy since 1945*, Oxford.

Crouzet, F. (1972), 'Introduction' to *Capital Formation in the Industrial Revolution*, Methuen.

Crouzet, F. (1972a), 'Capital Formation in Great Britain during the Industrial Revolution', in *ibid*.

Crouzet, F. (1985), *The First Industrialists*, Cambridge.

Cyert, R. M. & March (1963), *A Behavioural Theory of the Firm*, Prentice-Hall.

Davenport-Hines, R. P. T. (1984), *Dudley Docker: The Life and Times of a Trade Warrior*, Cambridge.

Davenport-Hines, R. P. T. (1986), 'Introduction' to Davenport-Hines, R. P. T. (ed), *Markets and Bagmen: Studies in the History of Marketing and British Industrial Performance, 1830–1939*, Frank Cass.

Davenport-Hines, R. P. T. (1986a), 'Tait, Andrew Wilson', in Jeremy, D. J. (ed), *Dictionary of Business Biography*, Vol V, Butterworth.

Davenport-Hines, R. P. T. (1986b), 'Glaxo as a multinational before 1963', in Jones, G. (ed), *British Multinationals: Origins, Management and Performance*, Gower.

Davenport-Hines, R. P. T. (1989), 'Vickers and Schneider: a comparison of new British and French multinational strategies 1916–26', in Teichova, A., Levy-Leboyer, M. & Nussbaum, H. (eds), *Historical Studies in International Corporate Business*, Cambridge.

Davenport-Hines, R. P. T. (1992), *Glaxo: a History to 1962*, Cambridge.

Davis, L. (1966), 'The capital markets and industrial concentration: the US and the UK, a comparative study', *Ec H R*, XIX.

Davis, L. & Huttenback, R. A. (1987), *Mammon and the Pursuit of Power: The Political Economy of British Imperialism, 1860–1912*, Cambridge.

Davis, W. (1970), *Merger Mania*, Constable.

Devine, P. J. (1976), 'The firm', 'Corporate growth' and 'State intervention in the private sector' in Devine, P. J., Jones, R. M., Lee, N. & Tyson, W. J. (eds), *An Introduction to Industrial Economics*, George Allen & Unwin.

Diaper, S. (1986), 'Merchant banking in the inter-war period: the case of Kleinwort, Sons & Co', *Bus Hist*, XXVIII, No 4.

Dickson, P. G. M. (1967), *The Financial Revolution in England: A Study in the Development of Public Credit, 1688–1756*, Macmillan.

Downie, J. (1958), *The Competitive Process*, Duckworth.

Drummond, D. (1989), '"Specifically designed"? Employers' labour strategies and worker responses in British railway workshops, 1838–1914', *Bus Hist*, XXXI, No 2.

Du Bois, A. B. (1938), *The English Business Company after the Bubble Act, 1720–1800*, Oxford.

Dunkerley, I. & Hare, G. (1991), 'The nationalised industries', in Crafts, N. F. R. & Woodward, N. (eds), *The British Economy since 1945,* Oxford.

Dunning, J. (1983), 'Changes in the level and structure of international production: the last 100 years', in Casson, M. (ed), *The Growth of International Business,* George Allen & Unwin.

Dunning, J. (1988), *Explaining International Production,* George Allen & Unwin.

Dupree, M. (1984), 'Broadhurst, Sir Edward Tootal', in Jeremy, D. J. (ed), *Dictionary of Business Biography,* Vol V, Butterworth.

Dyas, G. P. & Thanheiser, H. T. (1976), *The Emerging European Enterprise,* Macmillan.

Edelstein, M. (1982), *Overseas Investment in the Age of High Imperialism: The United Kingdom, 1850–1914,* Methuen.

Edey, H. C. (1979), 'Company accounting in the nineteenth and twentieth centuries', in Lee, T. A. (ed), *The Evolution of Corporate Financial Reporting,* Thomas Nelson.

Edwardes, M. (1983), *Back from the Brink: An Apocalyptic Experience,* Pan.

Edwards, J. R. (1989), 'Industrial cost accounting developments in Britain to 1830: a review article', *Accounting and Business Research,* XIX.

Edwards, J. R. & Newell, E. (1991), 'The development of industrial cost and management accounting before 1850: a survey of the evidence', *Bus Hist,* XXXIII, No 1.

Edwards, M. M (1967), *The British Cotton Trade, 1780–1815,* Manchester.

Elbaum, B. & Lazonick, W. (1986), 'An institutional perspective on British decline', in Elbaum, B. & Lazonick, W. (eds), *The Decline of the British Economy,* Oxford.

Erickson, C. (1959), *British Industrialists: Steel and Hosiery, 1850–1950,* Cambridge.

Evans, G. H. (1936), *British Corporation Finance, 1775–1850,* Johns Hopkins Press.

Fallon, I. & Sroder, J. (1987), *Takeovers,* Hamish Hamilton.

Farnie, D. A. (1979), *The English Cotton Industry and the World Market, 1815–1896,* Oxford.

Farnie, D. & Yonekawa, S. (1988), 'The emergence of the largest firm in the cotton spinning industries of the world, 1883–1938', *Textile History,* 19, No 2.

Farnie, D. A. (1992), 'The calico printing industry and the world market, 1890–1940: the survival of independent printing firms in co-existence with the Calico Printers' Association', mimeo.

Farnie, D. A. (1993), 'The marketing strategies of Platt Bros & Co. Ltd of Oldham, 1906–1940', *Textile History,* 24, No 2.

Feinstein, C. (1994), 'Success and failure: British economic growth since 1948', in Floud, R. & McCloskey, D. (eds), *The Economic History of Britain since 1700,* Vol III, Cambridge.

Ferry, J. (1993), *The British Renaissance: How to Survive and Thrive despite any Recession,* Heinemann.

Firth, M. (1976), *Share Prices and Mergers,* Gower.

Fitton, R. S. (1989), *The Arkwrights: Spinners of Fortune,* Manchester.

Fitzgerald, P. (1927), *Industrial Combination in England,* George Allen & Unwin.

Fitzgerald, R. (1988), *British Labour Management and Industrial Welfare, 1846–1939,* Croom Helm.

Fitzgerald, R. (1989), 'Employers' labour strategies, industrial welfare, and the response to New Unionism at Bryant & May, 1888–1930', *Bus Hist*, XXXI, No 2.

Fleischman, R. K. & Parker, L. D. (1990), 'Management accounting early in the British Industrial Revolution: the Carron Company, a case study', *Accounting and Business Research*, XX.

Fleischman, R. K. & Parker, L. D. (1992), 'The cost-accounting environment in the British Industrial Revolution iron industry', *Accounting, Business and Financial History*, II.

Fleischman, R. K. & Tyson, T. N. (1993), 'Cost accounting during the industrial revolution: the present state of historical knowledge', *Ec H R*, XLVI, No 3.

Flinn, M. W. (1962), *Men of Iron: the Crowleys in the Early Iron Industry*, Edinburgh.

Florence, P. S. (1961), *Ownership, Control and Success of Large Companies*, Sweet and Maxwell.

Foreman-Peck, J. (1994), 'Industry and industrial organisation in the inter-war years', in Floud, R. & McCloskey, D. (eds), *The Economic History of Britain since 1700*, Vol III, Cambridge.

Foreman-Peck, J. & Millward, R. (1994), *Public and Private Ownership of British Industry, 1820–1990*, Oxford.

Francis, A. (1980), 'Families, firms and finance capital: the development of UK industrial firms with particular reference to their ownership and control', *Sociology*, 14.

Fraser, W. H. (1981), *The Coming of the Mass Market, 1850–1914*, Macmillan.

Fruin, M. W. (1992), *The Japanese Enterprise System*, Oxford.

Gardner, C. (1981), *British Aircraft Corporation: A History*, Batsford.

Garner, S. P. (1954), *The Evolution of Cost Accounting to 1925*, Alabama.

Gatrell, V. A. C. (1977), 'Labour, power and the size of firms in Lancashire cotton in the second quarter of the nineteenth century', *Ec H R*, XXX.

George, K. D, Joll, C. & Lynk, E. L. (1991), *Industrial Organisation. Competition, Growth and Structural Change*, Routledge.

Gerschenkron, A. (1966), *Economic Backwardness in Historical Perspective*, Cambridge, Mass.

Gospel, H. F. (1983), 'Managerial structures and strategies: an introduction', in Gospel, H. F. & Littler, C. R. (eds), *Managerial Strategies and Industrial Relations*, Heinemann.

Gourvish, T. R. (1972), *Mark Huish and the London & North Western Railway*, Leicester.

Gourvish, T. R. (1973), 'A British business elite: the chief executive managers of the railway industry, 1850–1922', *Business History Review*, XLVII, Autumn.

Gourvish, T. R. (1980), 'Railway enterprise', in Church, R. (ed), *The Dynamics of Victorian Business: Problems and Perspectives to the 1870s*, George Allen & Unwin.

Gourvish, T. R. (1987), 'British business and the transition to a corporate economy: entrepreneurship and management structures', *Bus Hist*, XXIX, No 4.

Grieves, K. (1989), *Sir Eric Geddes*, Manchester.

Grocer (1993), 'British manufacturers at the top', April 17.

Guenault, P. H. & Jackson, J. M. (1974), *The Control of Monopoly in the UK*, Longman.

Guterl, F. V. (1989), 'Europe's secret weapon', *Business Month*, 134, October.

Habakkuk, H. J. (1962), *American and British Technology in the Nineteenth Century*, Cambridge.

Habakkuk, H. J. (1968), *Industrial Organisation since the Industrial Revolution*, Southampton.

Hague, D. C. (1983), *The IRC: an Experiment in Industrial Intervention*, George Allen & Unwin.

Hamill, J. (1988), 'British acquisitions in the United States', *National Westminster Bank Quarterly Review*, August.

Hampden-Turner, C. & Trompenaars, F. (1993), *The Seven Cultures of Capitalism: Value Systems for Creating Wealth in the United States, Britain, Japan, Germany, France, Sweden, and the Netherlands*, Doubleday.

Handy, C. (1988), *Making Managers*, Pitman.

Hannah, L. (1974), 'Mergers in British manufacturing industry, 1880–1918', *Oxford Economic Papers*, XXVI.

Hannah, L. (1974a), 'Takeover bids in Britain before 1950: an exercise in business "prehistory"', *Bus Hist*, XVI, No 1.

Hannah, L. (1976), 'Strategy and structure in the manufacturing sector', in Hannah, L. (ed), *Management Strategy and Business Development. An Historical and Comparative Study*, Methuen.

Hannah, L. & Kay, J. (1977), *Concentration in Modern Industry. Theory, Measurement and the UK Experience*, Methuen.

Hannah, L. (1980), 'Visible and invisible hands in Great Britain', in Chandler, A. D. & Daems, H. (eds), *Managerial Hierarchies: Comparative Perspectives on the Rise of the Modern Industrial Enterprise*, Harvard.

Hannah, L. (1983), *The Rise of the Corporate Economy*, Second Edition, Methuen.

Hannah, L. (1983a), 'New issues in British business history', *Business History Review*, 57.

Hannah, L. (1991), 'Scale and scope: towards a European visible hand', *Bus Hist*, XXXIII.

Hannah, L. (1994), 'The economic consequences of the state ownership of industry, 1945–1990', in Floud, R. & McCloskey, D. (eds), *The Economic History of Britain since 1700*, Vol III, Cambridge.

Harrison, A. E. (1981), 'Joint stock company flotation in the cycle, motor-vehicle and related industries, 1882–1914', *Bus Hist*, XXIII.

Hart, P. (1979), 'On bias and concentration', *Journal of Industrial Economics*, XXVII, No 3

Hasson, C. J. (1932), 'The South Sea Bubble and Mr Snell', *Journal of Accountancy*, 54.

Hawke, G. R. (1970), *Railways and Economic Growth in England and Wales, 1840–1870*, Oxford.

Hawkins, K. (1976), *British Industrial Relations 1945–1975*, Barrie & Jenkins.

Hayward, K. (1989), *The British Aircraft Industry*, Manchester.

Hertner, P. & Jones, G. (1986), 'Multinationals: theory and history', in Hertner, P. & Jones, G. (eds), *Multinationals: Theory and History*, Gower.

Hilton, A. (1987), *City within a State. A Portrait of Britain's Financial World*, I. B. Taurus.

Hirschmeier, J. & Yui, T. (1975), *The Development of Japanese Business, 1600–1973*, George Allen & Unwin.

Hobsbawm, E. J. (1964), 'The labour aristocracy in nineteenth century Britain', in Hobsbawm, E. J. (ed), *Labouring Men: Studies in the History of Labour*, Weidenfeld & Nicolson.

Holden, R. (1992), 'The architect in the Lancashire cotton industry, 1850–1914: the example of Stott & Sons', *Textile History*, 23, No 2.

Holmes, A. R. & Green, E. (1987), *Midland. 150 Years of Banking History*, Oxford.

Honeyman, K. (1982), *Origins of Enterprise: Business Leadership in the Industrial Revolution*, Manchester.

Hoppit, J. (1987), *Risk and Failure in English Business, 1700–1800*, Cambridge.

Howe, A. C. (1984), *Cotton Masters, 1830–1860*, Oxford.

Howe, A. C. (1984a), 'Dixon, Sir Alfred Herbert', in Jeremy, D. J. (ed), *Dictionary of Business Biography*, Vol II, Butterworth

Hudson, P. (1986), *The Genesis of Industrial Capital. A Study of the West Riding Wool Textile Industry, c.1750–1850*, Cambridge.

Hudson, P. (1992), *The Industrial Revolution*, Edward Arnold.

Hunt, B. C. (1936), *The Development of the Business Corporation in England, 1800–1867*, Russell & Russell.

Hutchinson, D. & Nicholas, S. (1993), 'Modelling the growth strategies of British firms', *Bus Hist*, XXIX, No 4.

Hyde, F. E. (1962), 'Economic theory and business history', *Bus Hist*, V, No 1.

Hyde, F. E. (1977), 'Economic theory and business history: a comment on the theory of profit maximisation', in Tucker K. A. (ed), *Business History: selected readings*, Macmillan.

Ingham, G. (1984), *Capitalism Divided? The City and Industry in British Social Development*, Macmillan.

Irving, R. J. (1975), 'New industries for old? Some investment decisions of Sir W. G. Armstrong, Whitworth & Co Ltd, 1900–1914', *Bus Hist*, XVII.

James, H. (1990), 'The German experience and the myth of British cultural exceptionalism', in Collins, B. & Robbins, K. (eds), *British Culture and Economic Decline*, Weidenfeld & Nicolson.

Jefferys, J. B. (1938), *Trends in Business Organisation in Great Britain since 1856*, mimeo of Ph D, London.

Jefferys, J. B. (1954), *Retail Trading in Britain, 1850–1950*, Cambridge.

Jenkins, D. T. (1984), 'Douglas, George', in Jeremy, D. J. (ed), *Dictionary of Business Biography*, Vol II, Butterworth.

Jeremy, D. (1991), 'The enlightened paternalist in action: William Hesketh Lever at Port Sunlight before 1914', *Bus Hist*, XXXIII, No 1.

Jeremy, D. J. (1990), *Capitalists and Christians: Business Leaders and the Churches in Britain, 1900–1960*, Oxford.

Jeremy, D. J. (1993), 'Survival strategies in Lancashire textiles: Bleachers' Association Ltd to Whitecroft plc, 1900–1980s', *Textile History*, 24 (2).

John, A. H. (1950), *The Industrial Development of South Wales, 1750–1850*, University of Wales Press.

Johnman, L. (1986), 'The large manufacturing companies of 1935', *Bus Hist*, XXVI, II, No 2.

Johnston, C. (1982), *MITI and the Japanese Miracle*, Stanford.

Jones, E. (1978), *A History of GKN*, Vol I, *Innovation and Enterprise, 1759–1918*, Macmillan.

Jones, G. (1984), 'The 'Old Aunts': governments, politicians and the oil business', in Turner, J. (ed), *Businessmen and Politics. Studies of Business Activity in British Politics, 1900–1945*, Heinemann.

Jones, G. (1984a), 'The expansion of British multinational manufacturing 1890–1939', in Okochi, A. & Inoue, T. (eds), *Overseas Business Activities*, Tokyo.

Jones, G. (1986), 'Origins, management and performance', in Jones, G. (ed), *British Multinationals: Origins, Management and Performance*, Gower.

Jones, G. (1986a), 'The performance of British multinational enterprise, 1890–1945', in Hertner, P. & Jones, G. (eds), *Multinationals: Theory and History*, Gower.

Jones, G. & Rose, M. (1993), 'Family Capitalism', *Bus Hist*, XXXV, No 4.

Jones, H. (1983), 'Employers' welfare schemes and industrial relations in inter-war Britain', *Bus Hist*, XXV, No 1.

Jones, R. & Marriott, O. (1970), *The Anatomy of a Merger*, Pan.

Jones, S. (1978), 'The cotton industry and joint-sock banking in Manchester, 1825–1850', *Bus Hist*,

Jones, S. (1988), 'Cotton employers and industrial welfare between the wars', in Jowitt, J. A. & McIvor, A. J. (eds), *Employers and Labour in the English Textile Industries, 1850–1939*, Routledge.

Joyce, P. (1980), *Work, Society and Politics: The Culture of the factory in Later Victorian England*, Harvester Press.

Kay, J. (1993), *Foundations of Corporate Success: How Business Strategies Add Value*, Oxford.

Kay, W. (1988), 'Big Bang and after', in Heller, R. (ed), *The Complete Guide to Modern Management*, Harrap.

Keeble, S. (1992), *The Ability to Manage*, Manchester.

Kennedy, W. P. (1974), 'Foreign investment, trade and growth in the UK, 1870–1913', *Explorations in Economic History*, XI.

Kennedy, W. P. (1976), 'Institutional response to economic growth: capital markets in Britain to 1914', in Hannah, L, *Management Strategy and Business Development. An Historical and Comparative Study*, Methuen.

Kennedy, W. P. (1987), *Industrial Structure, Capital Markets and the Origins of British Economic Decline*, Cambridge.

Killick, J. R. & Thomas, W. A. (1970), 'The provincial stock exchanges', *Ec H R*, XXIII.

Kirby, M. W. (1973), 'Government intervention in industrial organisation: coal-mining in the 1930s', *Bus Hist*, XV.

Kirby, M. W. (1974), 'The Lancashire cotton industry in the inter-war years: a study in organisation change', *Bus Hist*, XVI.

Kirby, M. W. (1988), 'Product proliferation in the British locomotive building industry, 1850–1914: an engineer's paradise?', *Bus Hist*, XXX, No.3.

Kirby, M. W. (1992), 'Institutional rigidities and economic decline: reflections on the British experience', *Ec H R*, XLV.

Kirzner, I. M. (1976), *The Economic Point of View: an Essay in the History of Economic Thought*, Sheed & Ward.

Kocka, J. (1971), 'Family and bureaucracy in German industrial management', *Business History Review*, 45.

Kocka, J. (1978), 'Entrepreneurs and managers in German industrialisation', in

Mathias, P. & Postan, M. M (eds), *The Cambridge Economic History of Europe*, VII,Part I, Cambridge.

Kocka, J. (1980), 'The rise of the modern industrial enterprise in Germany', in Chandler, A. D. & Daems, H. (eds), *Managerial Hierarchies: Comparative Perspectives on the Rise of the Modern Industrial Enterprise*, Harvard.

Kono, T. (1984), *Strategy and Structure of Japanese Enterprises*, Macmillan.

Kuehn, D. (1975), *Takeovers and the Theory of the Firm*, Macmillan.

Lamoreaux, N. (1985), *The Great Merger Movement in American Business, 1895–1904*, Cambridge.

Landes, D. S. (1969), *The Unbound Prometheus: Technological Change and Industrial Development in Western Europe from 1750 to the Present*, Cambridge.

Lavington, F. (1921), *The English Captial Markets*, Methuen.

Lazonick, W. (1983), 'Industrial organisation and technological change: the decline of the British cotton industry', *Business History Review*, CVII.

Lazonick, W. (1991), *Business Organisation and the Myth of the Market Economy*, Cambridge.

Lee, C. H. (1972), *A Cotton Enterprise, 1795–1840: A History of McConnel & Kennedy, Fine Cotton Spinners*, Manchester.

Lee, C. (1990), 'Corporate behaviour in theory and history: I. The evolution of theory', *Bus Hist*, XXXII.

Lee, C. (1990a), 'Corporate behaviour in theory and history: II. The historian's perspective', *Bus Hist*, XXXII.

Lee, N. (1976), 'Performance and government intervention in the industrial sector', in Devine, P. J., Jones, R. M., Lee, N. & Tyson, W. J. (eds), *An Introduction to Industrial Economics*, George Allen & Unwin.

Levy, H. (1911), *Monopoly and Competition: A Study in English Industrial Organisation*, Macmillan.

Lewchuk, W. (1983), 'Fordism and British motor car employers, 1896–1932', in Gospel, H. F. & Littler, C. R. (eds), *Managerial Strategies and Industrial Relations*, Heinemann.

Lewchuk, W. (1987), *American Technology and the British Vehicle Industry*, Cambridge.

Littler, C. (1982), *The Development of the Labour Process in Capitalist Societies: a Comparative Study*, Heinemann.

Littler, C. (1983), 'A comparative analysis of managerial structures and strategies', in Gospel, H. F. & Littler, C. R. (eds), *Managerial Strategies and Industrial Relations*, Heinemann.

Lloyd-Jones, R. & Le Roux, A. A. (1980), 'The size of firms in the cotton industry: Manchester 1815–1841', *Ec H R*, XXXIII.

Locke, R. R. (1984), *Management and Higher Education since 1940*, Cambridge.

Locke, R. R. (1993), 'Education and entrepreneurship: an historian's view', in Brown, J. & Rose, M. B. (eds), *Entrepreneurship, Networks and Modern Business*, Manchester.

London Clearing Banks (1978), *Evidence by the Committee of the London Clearing Banks to the Committee to Review the Functioning of Financial Institutions*.

Lorenz, E. & Wilkinson, F. (1986), 'The shipbuilding industry', in Elbaum, B. & Lazonick, W. (eds), *The Decline of the British Economy*, Oxford.

Lovell, J. (1992), 'Employers and craft unionism: a programme of action for British shipbuilding, 1902–1905', *Bus Hist*, XXXIV, No 4.

Lowenfeld, H. (1909), *All About Investment*, Financial Review of Reviews.

Luffman, G. A. & Reed, R. (1984), *The Strategy and Performance of British Industry, 1970–1980*, Macmillan.

MacGregor, D. H. (1906), *Industrial Combination*, George Bell & Sons, Cambridge.

McKendrick, N. (1960), 'Josiah Wedgwood: an eighteenth century entrepreneur in salesmanship and marketing techniques', *Ec H R*, XII.

McKendrick, N. (1961), 'Josiah Wedgwood and factory discipline', *Historical Journal*, IV.

McKendrick, N. (1970), 'Josiah Wedgwood and cost accounting in the industrial revolution', *Ec H R*, XXIII.

McKinlay, A. & Zeitlin, J. (1989), 'The meanings of managerial prerogative: industrial relations and the organisation of work in British engineering, 1880–1939', *Bus Hist*, XXXI, No 2.

Macleod, C. (1992), 'Strategies for innovation: the diffusion of new technology in nineteenth century British industry', *Ec H R*, XLV, No 2.

Macrosty, H. W. (1907), *The Trust Movement in British Industry: a Study of Business Organisation*, Longman.

Management Today (1993), 'Dark days at the top', December.

Mantoux, P. (1928), *The Industrial Revolution in the Eighteenth Century*, Jonathan Cape.

Marris, R. (1964), *The Economic Theory of 'Managerial Capitalism'*, Macmillan.

Marrison, A. J. (1995), *British Business and Protection, 1903–1932*, Oxford, forthcoming.

Marshall, A. (1919), *Industry and Trade*, Macmillan.

Martin, R. & Moores, B. (1985), *Management Structures and Techniques*, Philip Allan.

Mathias, P. (1979), 'Capital, credit and enterprise in the industrial revolution', in Mathias, P. (ed), *The Transformation of England. Essays in the Economic and Social History of England in the Eighteenth Century*, Methuen.

Matthews, D. (1988), 'Profit-sharing in the gas industry, 1889–1914', *Bus Hist*, XXX, No 4.

Med-Ad-News (1992), 'The top 50 companies by health care sales', September.

Meeks, A. (1977), *Disappointing Marriage: A Study of the Gains from Mergers*, Cambridge.

Melling, J. (1980), 'Non-commissioned officers', *Social History*, 6.

Melling, J. (1983), 'Employers, industrial welfare, and the struggle for work-place control in British industry, 1880–1920', in Gospel, H. F. & Littler, C. R. (eds), *Managerial Strategies and Industrial Relations*, 1983, Heinemann.

Mennell, W. (1962), *Takeover. The Growth of Monopoly in Britain, 1951–1961*, Lawrence & Wishart.

Michie, R. (1986), 'The stock exchange and the British economy, 1870–1939', in Van-Helten, J. J. & Cassis, Y. (eds), *Capitalism in a Mature Economy: Financial Institutions, Capital Export and British Industry, 1870–1939*, Edward Elgar

Middlemass, K. (1979), *Politics in Industrial Society. The Experience of the British System since 1911*, Andre Deutsch.

Millward, R. (1991), 'The causes of the 1940s nationalisations: a survey', Working Papers in Economic and Social History, University of Manchester, No 10.

Millward, R. (1994), 'Industrial and commercial performance', in Floud, R. & McCloskey, D. (eds), *The Economic History of Britain since 1700*, Vol III, Cambridge.

Miyamoto, M. (1986), 'Emergence of national market and commercial activities in Tokugawa Japan, with special reference to the development of the rice market', *Osaka Economic Papers*, 36, No. 1–2.

Mond, A. (1927), *Industry and Politics*, Macmillan.

Morgan, E. V. & Thomas, W. A. (1962), *The Stock Exchange: Its History and Functions*, Elek Books.

Morikawa, H. (1975), 'Management structure and control devices for diversified *zaibatsu* business', in Nakagawa, K. (ed), *The Strategy and Structure of Big Business*, Tokyo.

Morikawa, H. (1992), *Zaibatsu*, Tokyo.

Moyle, J. (1971), *The Pattern of Ordinary Share Ownership*, Cambridge.

Musson, A. E. (1959), 'The Great Depression in Britain, 1873–1896: a reappraisal', *Journal of Economic History*, XIX.

Musson, A. E. (1978), *The Growth of British Industry*, Batsford.

Nakaoka, T. (1992), 'A giant home electronics company in a declining textile region: postwar strategy of Matsushita Denki', paper delivered at Hagley Museum, Wilmington, mimeo.

Nakagawa, K. (1974), 'The structures and motives of investment by private enterprise in Japan before the Second World War', in Daems, H. & Van der Wee, H. (eds), *The Rise of Managerial Capitalism*, 1974, Leuven.

Nakagawa, K. (1975), 'Strategy and structure in Japanese business', in Nakagawa, K. (ed), *The Strategy and Structure of Big Business*, Tokyo.

Neal, L. (1994), 'The finance of business during the industrial revolution', in Floud, R. & McCloskey, D. (eds), *The Economic History of Britain since 1700*, Vol I, Cambridge.

Nelson, D. (1975), *Managers and Workers*, Madison.

Nelson, R. L. (1959), *Merger Movements in American Industry, 1895–1956*, Princeton.

Newbould, G. D. (1970), *Management and Merger Activity*, Guthstead.

Newbould, G. D. & Jackson, A. S. (1972), *The Receding Ideal*, Guthstead.

Nicholas, S. (1983), 'Agency contracts, institutional modes and the transition to foreign direct investment by British manufacturing multinationals before 1939', *Journal of Economic History*, XLII.

Nicholas, S. (1984), 'The overseas marketing performance of British industry, 1870–1914', *Ec H R*, XXXVII, No 4.

Nicholas, S. (1991), 'The expansion of British multinational companies: testing for managerial failure', in Foreman-Peck, J. (ed), *New perspectives on the Late Victorian Economy. Essays in Quantitative Economic History, 1860–1914*, Cambridge.

Nishimura, S. (1971), *The Decline of Inland Bills of Exchange in the London Money Market, 1855–1913*, Cambridge.

Nishizawa, T. (1994), 'Higher education and training in post-war Japan', paper presented to the Fourth Anglo-Japanese Conference, mimeo.

Nockolds, H. (1976), *Lucas: the First Hundred Years*, Vol I & II, Macmillan.

Olson, M. (1982), *The Rise and Decline of Nations: Economic Growth, Stagflation and Social Rigidities*, New Haven.

Parker, R. H. (1969), *Management Accounting: An Historical Perspective*, Augustus Kelley.

Parker, W. (1973), 'Through growth and beyond: three decades in economic and business history', in Cain, P. J. & Uselding, P. J. (eds), *Business Enterprise and Economic Change*, Kent State.

Pascale, R. T. & Athos, A. (1982), *The Art of Japanese Management*, Penguin.

Payne, P. L. (1967), 'The emergence of the large-scale company in Great Britain', *Ec H R*, XX.

Payne, P. L. (1978), 'Industrial entrepreneurship and management in Great Britain', in Mathias, P. & Postan, M. M (eds), *The Cambridge Economic History of Europe*, VII, Part I, Cambridge.

Payne, P. L. (1984), 'Family business in Britain: an historical and analytical survey', in Okochi, A. & Yasuoka, S. (eds), *Family Business in the Era of Industrial Growth*, Tokyo.

Payne, P. L. (1988), *British Entrepreneurship in the Nineteenth Century*, Macmillan.

Payne, P. L. (1990), 'Entrepreneurship and British economic decline', in Collins, B. & Robbins, K. (eds), *British Culture and Economic Decline*, Wiedenfeld & Nicolson.

Penrose, E. T. (1959), *The Theory of the Growth of the Firm*, Oxford.

Perkin, H. (1989), *The Rise of Professional Society: England since 1880*, Routledge.

Pettigrew, A. (1985), *The Awakening Giant. Continuity and Change in ICI*, Basil Blackwell.

Platt, D. C. M. (1986), *Britain's Investments Overseas on the Eve of the First World War*, Macmillan.

Political and Economic Planning [PEP] (1957), *Industrial Trade Associations: Activities and Organisation*, George Allen & Unwin.

Pollard, S. (1965), *The Genesis of Modern Management*, Cambridge, Mass.

Pollard, S. (1972), 'Fixed capital in the industrial revolution in Britain', in Creuzet, F. (ed), *Capital Formation in the Industrial Revolution*, Methuen.

Pollard, S. (1978), 'Labour in Great Britain', in Mathias, P. & Postan, M. M (eds), *The Cambridge Economic History of Europe*, Vol VII, Part I, Cambridge.

Pollard, S. (1989), *Britain's Prime and Britain's Decline: The British Economy, 1870–1914*, Edward Arnold.

Pollard, S. (1992), *The Development of the British Economy, 1914–1990*, Edward Arnold.

Pollard, S. (1994), 'Entrepreneurship, 1870–1914', in Floud, R. & McCloskey, D. (eds), *The Economic History of Britain since 1700*, Vol III, Cambridge.

Porter, J. H. (1974), 'The commercial banks and the financial problems of the English cotton industry', *Revue Internationale d'Histoire de la Banque*, IX.

Porter, M. E. (1980), *Competitive Strategy: Techniques for Analyzing Industries and Competitors*, Free Press, New York.

Porter, M. E. (1990), *The Competitive Advantage of Nations*, Macmillan.

Prais, S. J. (1976), *The Evolution of Giant Firms: A Study of the Growth of Concentration in Manufacturing Industry in Britain*, Cambridge.

Pressnell, L. S. (1956), *Country Banking in the Industrial Revolution*, Oxford.

Prior, A. & Kirby, M. (1993), 'The Society of Friends and the family firm, 1700–1830', Discussion Paper EC11/93, Lancaster University Management School.

Pumphrey, A. (1959), 'The introduction of industrialists into the British peerage: a study in adaptation of a social institution', *American Historical Review*, 65.

Reader, W. J. (1959), 'The United Kingdom Soap Manufacturers' Association and the English soap trade', *Bus Hist*, I, No 2.

Reader, W. J. (1970), *Imperial Chemical Industries*, Vol I, *The Forerunners 1870–1926*, Oxford.

Reader W. J. (1975), *Imperial Chemical Industries: A History*, Vol II, Oxford.

Reader, W. J. (1976), 'ICI and the State', in Hannah, L. (ed), *Management Strategy and Business Development: An Historical and Comparative Study*, Methuen.

Reader, W. J. (1977), 'Imperial Chemical Industries and the state, 1926–1945', in Supple, B. (ed), *Essays in British Business History*, Oxford.

Reader, W. J. (1979), *A House in the City. A Study of the City and of the Stock Exchange based on the Records of Foster & Braithwaite, 1825–1975*, Batsford.

Redford, A. (1964), *Labour Migration*, Manchester.

Reed, M. C. (1969), 'Railways and the growth of the capital market', in Reed, M. C. (ed), *Railways in the Victorian Economy: Studies in Finance and Economic Growth*, David & Charles.

Richardson, R. (1992), 'Trade unions and industrial relations', in Crafts, N. F. R. & Woodward, N. W. C. (eds), *The British Economy since 1945*, Oxford.

Ricketts, M. (1987), *The Economics of Business Enterprise,* Wheatsheaf.

Rimmer, W. G. (1960), *Marshalls of Leeds, Flax Spinners, 1788–1886*, Cambridge.

Robbins, K. (1990), 'British culture versus British industry', in Collins, B. & Robbins, K. (eds), *British Culture and Economic Decline*, Weidefeld & Nicolson.

Roberts, B. C. (1989), 'Trade unions', in Kavanagh, D. & Seldon, A. (eds), *The Thatcher Effect*, Oxford.

Roberts, D. (1979), *Paternalism in Early Victorian England*, Croom Helm.

Roberts, R. (1984), 'The administrative origins of industrial diplomacy: an aspect of government-industry relations, 1929–1935', in Turner, J. (ed), *Businessmen and Politics. Studies of Business Activity in British Politics, 1900–1945*, Heinemann.

Roberts, R. (1992), 'Regulatory responses to the rise of the market for corporate control in Britain in the 1950s', *Bus Hist*, XXXIV, No 1.

Roberts, R. (1993), 'What's in a name? Merchants, merchant bankers, accepting houses, issuing houses, industrial bankers and investment bankers', *Bus Hist*, XXXV, No 3.

Rodgers, T. (1986), 'Sir Allan Smith, the Industrial Group and the politics of unemployment, 1919–1924', *Bus Hist*, XXVIII, No 1.

Roll, E. (1930), *An Early Experiment in Industrial Organisation*, Longman.

Rose, M. B. (1977), 'The role of family in the provision of capital in Samuel Greg and Co. 1784–1840', *Bus Hist*, XIX.

Rose, M. B. (1993), 'Beyond Buddenbrooks: the family firm and the management of succession in nineteenth-century Britain', in Brown, J. & Rose, M. B. (eds), *Entrepreneurship, Networks and Modern Business*, Manchester.

Ross, D. (1990), 'The clearing banks and industry – new perspectives on the inter-war years', in Van-Helten, J. J. & Cassis, Y. (eds), *Capitalism in a Mature Economy: Financial Institutions, Capital Export and British Industry, 1870–1939*, Edward Elgar.

Rowlinson, M. (1988), 'The early application of scientific management by Cadbury', *Bus Hist*, XXX, No 4.

Rubinstein, W. D. (1981), *Men of Property: The Very Wealthy in Britain since the Industrial Revolution*, Croom Helm.

Rubinstein, W. D. (1990), 'Cultural explanations for Britain's economic decline: how true?', in Collins, B. & Robbins, K. (eds), *British Culture and Economic Decline*, Wiedenfeld & Nicolson.

Rubinstein, W. D. (1993), *Capitalism, Culture, and Decline in Britain, 1750–1990*, Routledge.

Rule, J. (1986), *The Labouring Classes in Early Industrial England, 1750–1850*, Longman.

Sampson, A. (1992), *The Essential Anatomy of Britain: Democracy in Crisis*, Hodder & Stoughton.

Sanderson, M. (1972), *The Universities and British Industry, 1850–1970*, Routledge.

Sanderson, M. (1988), 'The English civic universities and the "Industrial Spirit", 1870–1914', *Historical Research*, 61, No 144.

Saul, S. B. (1962), 'The motor industry to 1914', *Bus Hist*, V, No 1.

Saul, S. B. (1968), 'The machine tool industry in Britain to 1914', *Bus Hist*, X, No 1.

Saul, S. B. (1970), 'Introduction' to Saul, S. B. (ed), *Technological Change: the United States and Britain in the Nineteenth Century*, Methuen.

Saul, S. B. (1970a), 'The market and the development of the mechanical engineering industries in Britain, 1860–1914', in Saul, S. B. (ed), *Technological Change: the United States and Britain in the Nineteenth Century*, Methuen.

Saul, S. B. (1973), *The Myth of the Great Depression, 1873–1896*, Macmillan.

Schmitz, C. J. (1993), *The Growth of Big Business in the United States and Western Europe, 1850–1939*, Macmillan.

Schumpeter, J. A. (1934), *The Theory of Economic Development: An Inquiry into Profits, Capital and Credit*, Harvard.

Scott, J. (1984), *The Directors of Industry. The British Corporate Network, 1904–76*, Polity Press.

Scott, J. (1987), 'Intercorporate structure in Britain, the United States and Japan', *Shoken Keizai*, 160, June.

Scott, J. D. (1962), *Vickers: a History*, Weidenfeld & Nicolson.

Scranton, P. (1983), *Proprietary Capitalism*, Cambridge.

Scranton, P. (1991), 'A review of *Scale and Scope*', *Technology and Culture*, 32, No 4.

Shaw, C. (1983), 'The large manufacturing employers of 1907', *Bus Hist*, XXV, No 1.

Singleton, J. (1991), *Lancashire on the Scrapheap: The Cotton Industry, 1945–1970*, Oxford.

Singh, A. (1971), *Takeovers: Their Relevance to the Stock Market and the Theory of the Firm*, Cambridge.

Slaven, A. (1977), 'A shipyard in depression: John Browns of Clydebank, 1991–1938', *Bus Hist*, XIX, No 2.

Smiles, S. (1859), *Self-Help*, reprinted by Sidgwick & Jackson, with an introduction by Sir Keith Joseph, 1986.

Smith, A. (1776), *The Wealth of Nations*, Vols I & II.

Stanworth, P. & Giddens, A. (1974), 'An economic elite: company chairmen', in Stanworth, P. & Giddens, A. (eds), *Elites and Power in British Society*, Cambridge.

Stanworth, P. & Giddens, A. (1975), 'The modern corporate economy: interlocking directorships in Britain, 1906–1970', *Sociological Review*, 23, No 1.

Stopford, J. (1974), 'The origins of British-based multinational manufacturing enterprises', *Business History Review*, XLVIII.

Stopford, J. M. & Turner, L. (1985), *Britain and the Multinationals*, John Wiley & Sons.

Supple, B. (1962), 'The uses of business history', *Bus Hist*, IV, No 2.

Supple, B. (1977), 'A framework for British business history', in Supple, B. (ed), *Essays in British Business History*, Oxford.

Supple, B. (1991), 'Scale and scope: Alfred Chandler and the dynamics of industrial capitalism', *Ec H R*, XLIV.

Suzuki, Y. (1991), *Japanese Management Structures, 1920–1980*, Macmillan.

Swann, D, O'Brien, D. P, Maunder, W. P. J, Howe, W. S. (1974), *Competition in British Industry: Restrictive Practices Legislation in Theory and Practice*, George Allen & Unwin.

Tann, J. (1970), *The Development of the Factory*, Cornmarket Press.

Tann, J. & Aitken, J. (1992), 'The diffusion of the stationary steam engine from Britain to India, 1790–1830', *Indian Economic & Social History Review*, I, No 1.

Thomas, A. B. (1978), 'The British business elite: the case of the retail sector', *Sociological Review*, Vol 26, No 2.

Thomas, S. E. (1931), *British Banks and the Finance of Industry*, P. S. King & Son.

Thomas, W. A. (1973), *The Provincial Stock Exchanges*, Frank Cass & Co.

Thomas, W. A. (1978), *The Finance of British Industry, 1918–1976*, Methuen.

Thomas, W. A. (1986), *The Big Bang*, Philip Allan.

Thompson, E. P. (1967), 'Time, work-discipline, and industrial capitalism', *Past & Present*, XXXVIII.

Tilly, R. (1974), 'The growth of large-scale enterprise in Germany since the middle of the nineteenth century', in Daems, H. & Van Der Wee, H. (eds), *The Rise of Managerial Capitalism*, Leuven.

Tolliday, S. (1987), *Business, Banking and Politics: The Case of Steel, 1918–1936*, Cambridge, Mass.

Trevor, M. (1985), 'Japanese Companies in the UK', in Trevor, M. (ed), *The Internationalisation of Japanese Business: European and Japanese Perspectives*, Westview Press, Colorado

Turner, G. (1969), *Business in Britain*, Eyre & Spottiswoode.

Turner, G. (1971), *The Leyland Papers*, Eyre & Spottiswoode.

Turner, J. (1984), 'The politics of business', in Turner, J. (ed), *Businessmen and Politics. Studies of Business Activity in British Politics, 1900–1945*, Heinemann.

Turner, J. (1988), 'Servants of two masters: British trade associations in the first half of the twentieth century', in Yamazaki, H. & Miyamoto, M. (eds), *Trade Associations in Business History*, Tokyo.

Tweedale, G. (1995), *Steel City: Entrepreneurship, Strategy and Technology in Sheffield, 1743–1993*, Oxford, forthcoming.

Ueda, Y. (1986), 'Intercorporate networks in Japan: a study of interlocking directorates in modern large corporations', *Shoken Keizai*, 157, September.

Urwick, L. (1929), *The Meaning of Rationalisation*, Nisbet.

Urwick, L. (1938), 'The development of scientific management in Great Britain', *British Management Review*, III.

Urwick, L. (1960) (ed.), *Problems of Growth in Industrial Undertakings*, Pitman.

Utton, M. A. (1972), 'Some features of the early British merger movements in British manufacturing industry', *Bus Hist*, XIV, No 1.

Utton, M. A. (1974), 'On measuring the effects of industrial mergers', *Scottish Journal of Political Economy*, February.

Utton, M. A. (1982), *The Political Economy of Big Business*, Martin Robertson.

Wada, K. (1991), 'The development of tiered-inter-firm relationships in the automobile industry: a case study of Toyota Motor Corporation', *Japanese Yearbook on Business History*, VIII.

Walshe, J. G. (1991), 'Industrial organisation and competition policy', in Crafts, N. F. R. & Woodward, N. W. C. (eds), *The British Economy since 1945*, Oxford.

Ward, J. R., *The Finance of Canal Building in Eighteenth Century England*, Oxford.

Wardley, P. (1991), 'The anatomy of big business: aspects of corporate development in the twentieth century', *Bus Hist*, XXXIII, No 2.

Westall, O. (1992), *The Provincial Insurance Co, 1903–1938: Family, Markets and Competitive Growth*, Manchester.

Wheatcroft, M. (1970), *The Revolution in British Management Education*, Pitman.

Whitley, R. (1973), 'Commonalities and connections among directors of large financial institutions', *Sociological Review*, 21, No 4.

Whitley, R. (1981), *Masters of Business*, Tavistock.

Whittle, P. (1837), *A History of the Borough of Preston*, Vol II, Whittle, Preston.

Wiener, M. J. (1981), *English Culture and the Decline of the Industrial Spirit, 1850–1980*, Cambridge.

Wilkins, M. (1986), 'Japanese multinational enterprise before 1914', *Business History Review*, 60.

Wilkins, M. (1986a), 'The history of European multinationals: a new look', *Journal of European Economic History*, 15.

Wilkins, M. (1988), 'European and North American multinationals, 1870–1914: comparisons and contrasts', *Bus Hist*, XXX, No 1.

Wilkins, M. (1991) (ed), *The Growth of Multinationals*, Edward Elgar.

Williamson, O. E. (1964), *The Economics of Discretionary Behaviour: Managerial Objectives in a Theory of the Firm*, Englewood Cliffs, New York.

Williamson, O. E. (1975), *Markets and Hierarchies: Analysis and Antitrust Implications*, Free Press, New York.

Williamson, O. E. (1985), *The Economic Institutions of Capitalism: Firms, Markets, Relational Contracting*, Free Press, New York.

Williamson, O. E. (1986), *Economic Organisation: Firms, Markets and Policy Control*, Wheatsheaf.

Wilson, C. (1954), *The History of Unilever: A Study in Economic Growth and Social Change*, Vol II, Cassell.

Wilson, C. (1957), 'The entrepreneur in the industrial revolution', *History*, XLII.

Wilson, C. (1965), 'Economy and society in Late Victorian Britain', *Ec H R*, XXXII.

Wilson, C. (1968), *Unilever, 1945–1965: Challenge and Response in the Post-War Industrial Revolution*, Cassell.

Wilson, J. F. (1985), 'A strategy of expansion and combination: Dick, Kerr & Co., 1897–1914', *Bus Hist*, XXXVII, No 1.

Wilson, J. F. (1988), *Ferranti and the British Electrical Industry, 1864–1930*, Manchester.

Wilson, J. F. (1991), *Lighting the Town: A Study of Management in the North West Gas Industry, 1805–1880*, Paul Chapman.

Wilson, J. F. (1992), *The 'Manchester Experiment': a History of Manchester Business School, 1965–1990*, Paul Chapman.

Wilson, J. F. (1995), 'Modern management education in Britain: how to deal with business culture', in Amdam, R. P. (ed), *Management Education and Business Performance*, Routledge.

Wilson, J. F. (1996), *Ferranti: a Family Company*, forthcoming.

Wright, J. F. (1962), 'The capital market and the finance of industry', in Worswick, G. D. N. & Ady, P. H. (eds), *The British Economy in the 1950s*, Oxford.

Wurm, C. A. (1989), 'International industrial cartels, the state and politics: Great Britain between the wars', in Teichova, A, Levy-Leboyer, M. & Nussbaum, H. (eds), *Historical Studies in International Corporate Business*, Cambridge.

Yamamura, K. (1968), 'A reexamination of entrepreneurship in Meiji Japan (1868–1912)', *Ec H R*, XXI.

Yamamura, K. (1975), 'A compromise with culture: the historical evolution of the managerial structure of large Japanese firms', in Williamson, H. F. (ed), *The Evolution of International Management Structures*, Delaware.

Yamamura, K. (1978), 'The industrialisation of Japan: entrepreneurship, ownership and management', in Mathias, P. & Postan, M. M (eds), *The Cambridge Economic History of Europe*, Vol VII, Part II.

Yamazaki, H. (1989), 'Mitsui Bussan during the 1920s', in Teichova, A, Levy-Leboyer, M. & Nussbaum, H. (eds), *Historical Studies in International Corporate Business*, Cambridge.

Yasuoka, S. (1975), 'The tradition of family business in the strategic decision process and management structure of *zaibatsu* business: Mitsui, Sumitomo, and Mitsubishi', in Nakagawa, K. (ed), *The Strategy and Structure of Big Business*, Tokyo.

Young, A. K. (1979), *The Soga Shosha: Japan's Multinational Trading Companies*, Westview Press, Colorado.

Yui, T. (1988), 'Development, organisation, and business strategy of industrial enterprises in Japan (1915–1935)', *Japanese Yearbook on Business History*, 5.

Yui, T. (1991), 'The enterprise system in Japan: preliminary considerations on internal and external relations', *Japanese Yearbook on Business History*, 8.

Zeitlin, J. (1983), 'The labour strategies of British engineering employers, 1890–1922', in Gospel, H. F. & Littler, C. R. (eds), *Managerial Strategies and Industrial Relations*, 1983, Heinemann.

Zeitlin, M. (1974), 'Corporate ownership and control: the large corporation and the capitalist class', *American Journal of Sociology*, 79.

Index

Author index

Subject index

Subject index

Lazards, 184
Lee, G., 28
Lee, J., 146
Leontieff Paradox, 93
Lever Bros, 96–7, 101, 105, 110, 111, 150, 159, 164
Lipton's, 96
Lloyds bank, 125, 187
Lombe's mill, 23
London & North Eastern Railway Co., 40
London & North Western Railway Co., 38
London Business School, 220–1
London School of Economics (LSE), 40, 117, 146
Lowther's coalmines, 34

McConnel & Kennedy, 61
McGowan, Sir H., 150, 171, 173, 231
MacGregor, I., 228
McKenna, Sir R., 173
McKinsey & Co., 216, 232
management,
 challenge, 21–3, 32
 'cult of the amateur', 116–7, 119, 221–3
 education, 40, 75, 81, 117, 146, 153–4, 156, 214, 219–22, 240
 functional, 11–15, 26, 37, 60, 135–6
 'gentlemen & players', 31, 39, 42, 116–7, 118, 150–2, 153, 177, 218, 240
 literature, 29, 153, 156
 'movement', 146, 153, 156, 160
 operational, 11–15, 26, 32–7 passim, 61, 135–6, 227–8
 salaries, 27, 238–9
 strategic, 11–15, 21–2, 60, 135–6
 training, 26–7, 29, 31, 37, 40, 81, 153–4, 214, 218–22
management buy-out (MBO), 224, 226
managerial capitalism, 11, 13, 84, 133, 177–8, 180–1, 190–2, 204–5, 213–4, 223, 239–41
 American, 6–7, 63–70 passim, 177, 239
 German, 7, 70, 116, 178, 239
 Japanese, 80–1, 138, 239
managerial theories, 205–6
managing partners, 27–9, 32, 36
Manchester, 28

Business School, 220–1
College of Technology, 153
cotton industry, 52
stock exchange, 50, 128, 129
University of, 40, 117, 143, 146
market-cum-technological scene, 83–4, 87–98 passim, 102, 108, 112, 113, 118, 131–2, 178–9, 180–1, 197, 204
 American, 63–5, 69–70
 German, 75
 Japanese, 82
marketing, 55, 59–60, 84, 90–3, 96–7, 105
 American, 63–4
 German, 71
 Japanese, 79–80, 82
Marshalls Ltd., 114–5, 116
Marxist views, 36, 78, 137, 139, 161
mass production, 68–9, 93
Mather & Platt, 159
Matsushita, 138, 139, 140
mercantile capitalism, 23
merchant banks, 55–6, 58, 91, 123, 184–5, 188–9, 238–9
merchants, 23, 52–3, 58–60, 88
 commission agents, 59, 90–1
 commission merchants, 55, 56
 Japanese, 78, 81
mergers, 102–5, 109, 144–6, 160, 164–5, 175, 181, 194–7, 200–1, 208–14, 224–6, 233–5
 antagony, 208–9, 211
 aggressive, 102, 197
 American, 65–6, 102
 beneficiaries, 212–3
 conglomerates, 233–5
 corporate uncertainty, 213
 defensive, 102, 105, 155, 197, 223
 federal structures, 103–4, 106, 223, 233
 German, 71, 72–3
 government role, 197, 199–201
 integration, 106–8, 154–5
 Japanese, 79
 short-termism, 212–4
 subsidiary sales, 226
 synergy, 208, 209–11, 212, 223, 225
 utility, 205, 212–3, 223
Metropolitan Amalgamated Railway Carriage & Wagon Co., 109–10, 145, 168